Teach Yourself®
Microsoft®
PowerPoint® 2000

Teach Yourself®
Microsoft®
PowerPoint® 2000

Tom Badgett

IDG Books Worldwide, Inc.
An International Data Group Company

IDG
BOOKS
WORLDWIDE
Foster City, CA • Chicago, IL • Indianapolis, IN • New York, NY

Teach Yourself® Microsoft® PowerPoint® 2000

Published by
IDG Books Worldwide, Inc.
An International Data Group Company
919 E. Hillsdale Blvd., Suite 400
Foster City, CA 94404
`www.idgbooks.com` (IDG Books Worldwide Web site)

Screen shots reprinted with permission from Microsoft Corporation.

ISBN: 0-7645-3283-9

Printed in the United States of America

10 9 8 7 6 5 4 3 2 1

1P/SS/QU/ZZ/IN

Distributed in the United States by IDG Books Worldwide, Inc.

Distributed by CDG Books Canada Inc. for Canada; by Transworld Publishers Limited in the United Kingdom; by IDG Norge Books for Norway; by IDG Sweden Books for Sweden; by IDG Books Australia Publishing Corporation Pty. Ltd. for Australia and New Zealand; by TransQuest Publishers Pte Ltd. for Singapore, Malaysia, Thailand, Indonesia, and Hong Kong; by Gotop Information Inc. for Taiwan; by ICG Muse, Inc. for Japan; by Norma Comunicaciones S.A. for Colombia; by Intersoft for South Africa; by Le Monde en Tique for France; by International Thomson Publishing for Germany, Austria and Switzerland; by Distribuidora Cuspide for Argentina; by Livraria Cultura for Brazil; by Ediciones ZETA S.C.R. Ltda. for Peru; by WS Computer Publishing Corporation, Inc., for the Philippines; by Contemporanea de Ediciones for Venezuela; by Express Computer Distributors for the Caribbean and West Indies; by Micronesia Media Distributor, Inc. for Micronesia; by Grupo Editorial Norma S.A. for Guatemala; by Chips Computadoras S.A. de C.V. for Mexico; by Editorial Norma de Panama S.A. for Panama; by American Bookshops for Finland. Authorized Sales Agent: Anthony Rudkin Associates for the Middle East and North Africa.

For general information on IDG Books Worldwide's books in the U.S., please call our Consumer Customer Service department at 800-762-2974. For reseller information, including discounts and premium sales, please call our Reseller Customer Service department at 800-434-3422.

For information on where to purchase IDG Books Worldwide's books outside the U.S., please contact our International Sales department at 317-596-5530 or fax 317-596-5692.

For consumer information on foreign language translations, please contact our Customer Service department at 800-434-3422, fax 317-596-5692, or e-mail rights@idgbooks.com.

For information on licensing foreign or domestic rights, please phone +1-650-655-3109.

For sales inquiries and special prices for bulk quantities, please contact our Sales department at 650-655-3200 or write to the address above.

For information on using IDG Books Worldwide's books in the classroom or for ordering examination copies, please contact our Educational Sales department at 800-434-2086 or fax 317-596-5499.

For press review copies, author interviews, or other publicity information, please contact our Public Relations department at 650-655-3000 or fax 650-655-3299.

For authorization to photocopy items for corporate, personal, or educational use, please contact Copyright Clearance Center, 222 Rosewood Drive, Danvers, MA 01923, or fax 978-750-4470.

Library of Congress Cataloging-in-Publication Data

Badgett, Tom.
    Teach yourself Microsoft PowerPoint 2000 / Tom Badgett
        p.   cm.
    ISBN 0-7645-3283-9 (alk. paper)
    1. Computer graphics. 2. Microsoft PowerPoint (Computer file)
3. Business presentations--Graphic methods--Computer programs.
I. Titles.
T385.B265 2000
006.6'869--dc21   99-19965
                                                        CIP

ABOUT IDG BOOKS WORLDWIDE

Welcome to the world of IDG Books Worldwide.

IDG Books Worldwide, Inc., is a subsidiary of International Data Group, the world's largest publisher of computer-related information and the leading global provider of information services on information technology. IDG was founded more than 30 years ago by Patrick J. McGovern and now employs more than 9,000 people worldwide. IDG publishes more than 290 computer publications in over 75 countries. More than 90 million people read one or more IDG publications each month.

Launched in 1990, IDG Books Worldwide is today the #1 publisher of best-selling computer books in the United States. We are proud to have received eight awards from the Computer Press Association in recognition of editorial excellence and three from Computer Currents' First Annual Readers' Choice Awards. Our best-selling ...For Dummies® series has more than 50 million copies in print with translations in 31 languages. IDG Books Worldwide, through a joint venture with IDG's Hi-Tech Beijing, became the first U.S. publisher to publish a computer book in the People's Republic of China. In record time, IDG Books Worldwide has become the first choice for millions of readers around the world who want to learn how to better manage their businesses.

Our mission is simple: Every one of our books is designed to bring extra value and skill-building instructions to the reader. Our books are written by experts who understand and care about our readers. The knowledge base of our editorial staff comes from years of experience in publishing, education, and journalism — experience we use to produce books to carry us into the new millennium. In short, we care about books, so we attract the best people. We devote special attention to details such as audience, interior design, use of icons, and illustrations. And because we use an efficient process of authoring, editing, and desktop publishing our books electronically, we can spend more time ensuring superior content and less time on the technicalities of making books.

You can count on our commitment to deliver high-quality books at competitive prices on topics you want to read about. At IDG Books Worldwide, we continue in the IDG tradition of delivering quality for more than 30 years. You'll find no better book on a subject than one from IDG Books Worldwide.

John Kilcullen
Chairman and CEO
IDG Books Worldwide, Inc.

Steven Berkowitz
President and Publisher
IDG Books Worldwide, Inc.

*Eighth Annual
Computer Press
Awards ≥1992*

*Ninth Annual
Computer Press
Awards ≥1993*

*Tenth Annual
Computer Press
Awards ≥1994*

*Eleventh Annual
Computer Press
Awards ≥1995*

IDG is the world's leading IT media, research and exposition company. Founded in 1964, IDG had 1997 revenues of $2.05 billion and has more than 9,000 employees worldwide. IDG offers the widest range of media options that reach IT buyers in 75 countries representing 95% of worldwide IT spending. IDG's diverse product and services portfolio spans six key areas including print publishing, online publishing, expositions and conferences, market research, education and training, and global marketing services. More than 90 million people read one or more of IDG's 290 magazines and newspapers, including IDG's leading global brands — Computerworld, PC World, Network World, Macworld and the Channel World family of publications. IDG Books Worldwide is one of the fastest-growing computer book publishers in the world, with more than 700 titles in 36 languages. The "...For Dummies®" series alone has more than 50 million copies in print. IDG offers online users the largest network of technology-specific Web sites around the world through IDG.net (http://www.idg.net), which comprises more than 225 targeted Web sites in 55 countries worldwide. International Data Corporation (IDC) is the world's largest provider of information technology data, analysis and consulting, with research centers in over 41 countries and more than 400 research analysts worldwide. IDG World Expo is a leading producer of more than 168 globally branded conferences and expositions in 35 countries including E3 (Electronic Entertainment Expo), Macworld Expo, ComNet, Windows World Expo, ICE (Internet Commerce Expo), Agenda, DEMO, and Spotlight. IDG's training subsidiary, ExecuTrain, is the world's largest computer training company, with more than 230 locations worldwide and 785 training courses. IDG Marketing Services helps industry-leading IT companies build international brand recognition by developing global integrated marketing programs via IDG's print, online and exposition products worldwide. Further information about the company can be found at www.idg.com.
1/24/99

Acquisitions Editor
Andy Cummings

Development Editors
Ellen L. Dendy, Elizabeth Collins,
Ken Brown

Technical Editor
Bill Karow

Copy Editors
Corey Cohen, Nancy Rapoport,
Amanda Kaufmann, Ami Knox

Project Coordinators
Valery Bourke, Tom Missler

Book Designers
Daniel Ziegler Design, Cátálin Dulfu,
Kurt Krames

Graphics and Production Specialists
Linda Boyer, Angela F. Hunckler,
Brent Savage, Kathie Schutte,
Janet Seib, Michael Sullivan

Proofreaders
Kelli Botta, Nancy Price,
Rebecca Senninger,
York Graphics Services

Indexer
York Graphics Services

Tom Badgett is a prolific author and one of the
founders of U.S. Internet, Inc., a full-service Internet
provider. He has been a regular contributor to several
publications and has written numerous books on
productivity applications, games, networking, and
multimedia, including IDG Books Worldwide's *Teach
Yourself Office 97*. This is his fourth book dedicated
to PowerPoint, and he has produced a videotape
series about this program.

To Jordan, for all of her potential. I'm watching you, girl!

Welcome to
Teach Yourself

Welcome to Teach Yourself, a series read and trusted by millions for nearly a decade. Although you may have seen the Teach Yourself name on other books, ours is the original. In addition, no Teach Yourself series has ever delivered more on the promise of its name than this series. That's because IDG Books Worldwide recently transformed Teach Yourself into a new cutting-edge format that gives you all the information you need to learn quickly and easily.

Readers told us that they want to learn by doing and that they want to learn as much as they can in as short a time as possible. We listened to you and believe that our new task-by-task format and suite of learning tools deliver the book you need to successfully teach yourself any technology topic. Features such as our Personal Workbook, which lets you practice and reinforce the skills you've just learned, help ensure that you get full value out of the time you invest in your learning. Handy cross-references to related topics and online sites broaden your knowledge and give you control over the kind of information you want, when you want it.

More Answers . . .

In designing the latest incarnation of this series, we started with the premise that people like you, who are beginning to intermediate computer users, want to take control of their own learning. To do this, you need the proper tools to find answers to questions so you can solve problems now.

In designing a series of books that provide such tools, we created a unique and concise visual format. The added bonus: Teach Yourself books actually pack more information into their pages than other books written on the same subjects. Skill for skill, you typically get much more information in a Teach Yourself book. In fact, Teach Yourself books, on average, cover twice the skills covered by other computer books — as many as 125 skills per book — so they're more likely to address your specific needs.

WELCOME TO TEACH YOURSELF

...In Less Time

We know you don't want to spend twice the time to get all this great information, so we provide lots of time-saving features:

▶ A modular task-by-task organization of information: any task you want to perform is easy to find and includes simple-to-follow steps
▶ A larger size than standard makes the book easy to read and convenient to use at a computer workstation. The large format also enables us to include many more illustrations — 500 screen illustrations show you how to get everything done!
▶ A Personal Workbook at the end of each chapter reinforces learning with extra practice, real-world applications for your learning, and questions and answers to test your knowledge
▶ Cross-references appearing at the bottom of each task page refer you to related information, providing a path through the book for learning particular aspects of the software thoroughly

▶ A Find It Online feature offers valuable ideas on where to go on the Internet to get more information or to download useful files
▶ Take Note sidebars provide added-value information from our expert authors for more in-depth learning
▶ An attractive, consistent organization of information helps you quickly find and learn the skills you need

These Teach Yourself features are designed to help you learn the essential skills about a technology in the least amount of time, with the most benefit. We've placed these features consistently throughout the book, so you quickly learn where to go to find just the information you need — whether you work through the book from cover to cover or use it later to solve a new problem.

You will find a Teach Yourself book on almost any technology subject — from the Internet to Windows to Microsoft Office. Take control of your learning today, with IDG Books Worldwide's Teach Yourself series.

Teach Yourself
More Answers in Less Time

Go to this area if you want special tips, cautions, and notes that provide added insight into the current task.

Search through the task headings to find the topic you want right away. To learn a new skill, search the contents, chapter opener, or the extensive index to find what you need. Then find — at a glance — the clear task heading that matches it.

Opening a Blank Presentation

One of your options for developing a new slide show is to launch PowerPoint and open a blank presentation. From within this blank file, you can create new slides, choose a color scheme, and so on, to design a new presentation.

The upper-left figure on the next page shows the opening PowerPoint screen, in which you can choose a blank document. The New Office Document dialog box appears in the upper-right figure. Both of these starting points let you choose a blank document as a starting place for a new presentation.

When you open a blank presentation, the first thing you see is a New Slide dialog box. Here, you can choose a slide AutoLayout, which is the basic design of the first slide in the new presentation. Most of the time, you'll probably insert a title slide first, so accept the default presented here and click OK. The basic three-part PowerPoint window now opens, with the title slide on the right side of the display.

The title slide prompts you, "Click to add title." When you do that, PowerPoint opens a text-edit box so you can type a title. As you can see in the lower-left figure on the facing page, whatever you type in the title position also shows up to the left, in the Outline section of the window. You have the option of creating new slides in the right-hand slide section or of adding slides and text to the outline on the left.

A new, blank presentation contains only the one slide you chose from the opening screen. Continue building your presentation by adding new slides (press Ctrl-M). Every time you add a slide, you'll see the same New Slide with AutoLayout screen. Choose the type of slide you want to create, and you're on your way to designing your first presentation.

To add some color and design pizzazz to your slide show, you can use one of the built-in design templates. (Some of the available templates are listed in the lower-right figure on the facing page.)

Learn the concepts behind the task at hand and, more important, learn how the task is relevant in the real world. Time-saving suggestions and advice show you how to make the most of each skill.

TAKE NOTE

USING AUTOLAYOUT DESIGNS
PowerPoint includes 24 AutoLayout slide designs. Although you can manually add components, such as a picture box for a table, your design work will go faster and easier if you use the appropriate pre-built design for the slide show you are designing. Even if a particular AutoLayout contains items you don't want, it is easier to remove elements than to add them.

ADDING MORE EFFECTS TO YOUR SLIDES
Applying a design template isn't the only way to add color and interest to your slides. Choose Background or Slide Color Scheme from the Format menu to change other slide featur .

After you learn the task at hand, you may have more questions, or you may want to read about other tasks related to the topic. Use the cross-references to find different tasks to make your learning more efficient.

CROSS-REFERENCE
See Chapter 4 for an introduction to getting your show on the road. You'll find more design tips in Chapter 9.

32

SHORTCUT
Blank isn't always better. Try opening a presentation with a color scheme enabled by choosing templates from the New dialog box.

Use the Find It Online element to locate Internet resources that provide more background, take you on interesting side trips, and offer additional tools for mastering and using the skills you need. (Occasionally you'll find a handy shortcut here.)

The current chapter name and number always appear in the top right-hand corner of every task spread, so you always know exactly where you are in the book.

Who This Book Is For

This book is written for you, a beginning to intermediate PC user who isn't afraid to take charge of your own learning experience. You don't want a lot of technical jargon; you *do* want to learn as much about PC technology as you can in a limited amount of time. You need a book that is straightforward, easy to follow, and logically organized, so you can find answers to your questions easily. And, you appreciate simple-to-use tools such as handy cross-references and visual step-by-step procedures that help you make the most of your learning. We have created the unique Teach Yourself format specifically to meet your needs.

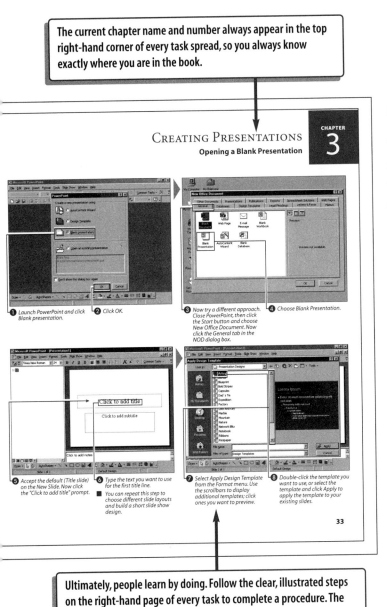

CREATING PRESENTATIONS
Opening a Blank Presentation

CHAPTER
3

❶ Launch PowerPoint and click Blank presentation.

❷ Click OK.

❸ Now try a different approach. Close PowerPoint, then click the Start button and choose New Office Document. Now click the General tab in the NOD dialog box.

❹ Choose Blank Presentation.

❺ Accept the default (Title slide) on the New Slide. Now click the "Click to add title" prompt.

❻ Type the text you want to use for the first title line.

■ You can repeat this step to choose different slide layouts and build a short slide show design.

❼ Select Apply Design Template from the Format menu. Use the scrollbars to display additional templates; click ones you want to preview.

❽ Double-click the template you want to use, or select the template and click Apply to apply the template to your existing slides.

33

Ultimately, people learn by doing. Follow the clear, illustrated steps on the right-hand page of every task to complete a procedure. The detailed callouts for each step show you exactly where to go and what to do to complete the task.

Personal Workbook

It's a well-known fact that much of what we learn is lost soon after we learn it if we don't reinforce our newly acquired skills with practice and repetition. That's why each Teach Yourself chapter ends with your own Personal Workbook. Here's where you can get extra practice, test your knowledge, and discover ideas for using what you've learned in the real world. There's even a Visual Quiz to help you remember your way around the topic's software environment.

Feedback

Please let us know what you think about this book, and whether you have any suggestions for improvements. You can send questions and comments to the Teach Yourself editors on the IDG Books Worldwide Web site at **www.idgbooks.com.**

Personal Workbook

Q&A

❶ You can start a new PowerPoint presentation in four basic ways. What are they?

❷ How do you change text on an existing text slide?

❸ Describe the difference between a *design template* and a *presentation design*.

❹ What is the *AutoContent Wizard*? How do you start it?

❺ PowerPoint supports presentation types in addition to a conventional slide show with a stand-up presenter. What are they?

❻ The AutoLayout section of the New Slide dialog box lets you choose how individual slides appear. How do you open this dialog box?

❼ How can you edit the font characteristics of existing text on a PowerPoint slide?

❽ When might you want to create a PowerPoint presentation with only one slide?

ANSWERS: PAGE 302

40

After working through the tasks in each chapter, you can test your progress and reinforce your learning by answering the questions in the Q&A section. Then check your answers in the Personal Workbook Answers appendix at the back of the book.

WELCOME TO TEACH YOURSELF

Another practical way to reinforce your skills is to do additional exercises on the same skills you just learned without the benefit of the chapter's visual steps. If you struggle with any of these exercises, it's a good idea to refer to the chapter's tasks to be sure you've mastered them.

CREATING PRESENTATIONS
Personal Workbook

CHAPTER
3

Read the list of Real-World Applications to get ideas on how you can use the skills you've just learned in your everyday life. Understanding a process can be simple; knowing how to use that process to make you more productive is the key to successful learning.

EXTRA PRACTICE

1. Launch PowerPoint and open a new, blank presentation.

2. Demonstrate two ways to access the New Presentation dialog box.

3. Open a new PowerPoint presentation with a presentation design to create a single-slide certificate.

4. Launch PowerPoint and start the AutoContent Wizard.

5. Open an existing or new PowerPoint presentation and select a slide. Then open the New Slide dialog box and select an AutoLayout to change the appearance of the current slide.

6. Open an existing or new PowerPoint presentation and apply a different presentation design.

REAL-WORLD APPLICATIONS

✔ You've been asked to introduce a nationally recognized guest speaker at your professional group's next meeting. You're intimidated by the thought of speaking in front of all those people. Not to worry. Launch PowerPoint and start the AutoContent Wizard. Choose Carnegie Coach from the second wizard screen and click Introducing a Speaker. When you complete the Wizard, you will have a PowerPoint presentation that will train you in presenting a speaker.

✔ You are learning PowerPoint on the fly as you produce presentations, and you'd like some ongoing help. Click the Office Assistant and choose Options. At the lower-right corner of the Options tab of the Office Assistant dialog box, click Show the Tip of the Day at startup to turn on automatic tips that appear each time you launch PowerPoint.

Visual Quiz

Describe how to open the dialog box shown here.

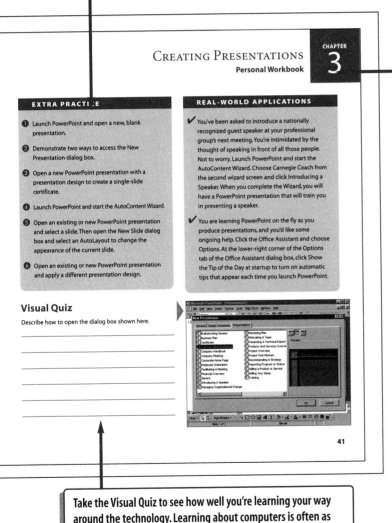

41

Take the Visual Quiz to see how well you're learning your way around the technology. Learning about computers is often as much about how to find a button or menu as it is about memorizing definitions. Our Visual Quiz helps you find your way.

xiii

Acknowledgments

What you're reading is more than just a book. It represents the hard work and creativity of many, many people.

Teach Yourself PowerPoint 2000 features a brand-new concept and design. As you use it, keep in mind the hard work from IDG Books Worldwide's Andy Cummings and the team who created this new Teach Yourself package. Know that development editors Ellen Dendy, Elizabeth Collins, and Ken Brown worked long hours to ensure that what you receive is timely, accurate, and useful. I'd also like to thank Bill Karow for his keen-eyed technical edit, and copy editors Corey Cohen, Nancy Rapoport, Amanda Kaufmann, and Ami Knox and production coordinators Valery Bourke and Tom Missler for the time they put into this book.

This title, like all others, is a team effort. We hope you find it useful, and maybe even interesting. Your comments are welcome at *tbadgett@usit.net*.

Contents

Welcome to Teach Yourself viii

Acknowledgments xv

Part I: Basic Skills 2

Chapter 1: Understanding PowerPoint Basics 4

Opening the Program 6

Using the Menus 8

Using Shortcut Menus 10

Using the Toolbars 12

Using the Dialog Boxes 14

Controlling the View 16

Chapter 2: Getting Help 20

Using the Office Assistant 22

Using the PowerPoint Help System 24

Using Detect and Repair 26

Chapter 3: Creating Presentations 30

Opening a Blank Presentation 32

Using the AutoContent Wizard 34

Using Design Templates 36

Using Presentation Designs 38

Chapter 4: Showing Your Work 42

Setting Up the Show 44

Viewing the Show 46

Projecting the Show 48

Take It with You — Pack and Go 50

Chapter 5: Using Other Presentation and Design Aids **54**

Using Notes Pages 56

Using Handouts 58

Adding Headers and Footers 60

Using the Spell Checker 62

Using Find and Replace 64

Using Undo 66

Configuring AutoCorrect 68

Chapter 6: Printing Your Work **72**

Installing a Printer 74

Using Page Setup 76

Selecting a Printer and Properties 78

Choosing What to Print 80

Printing to a File 82

Part II: Advanced Design Skills **86**

Chapter 7: Editing the Masters **88**

Changing Master Colors 89

Changing Master Text 92

Changing the Slide Background 96

Modifying Footer Data 97

Editing the Notes and Handout Masters 99

Chapter 8: Using Animation **104**

Adding Animation 106

Adding Slide Transitions and Sounds 110

Using Action Buttons 112

CONTENTS

Chapter 9: Changing Layout and Design **116**

Changing Slide Layout 118

Setting the Color Scheme 120

Changing the Slide Background 122

Using Design Templates and Fonts 126

Formatting Bullets and Numbers 128

Chapter 10: Using Pictures, Sound, and Movies **132**

Adding Pictures to Your Slides 134

Adding Images to the ClipArt Gallery 138

Recording Sound for PowerPoint 142

Adding Sounds to Your Slides 144

Capturing Movies for PowerPoint 146

Adding Movies to Your Slides 148

Chapter 11: PowerPoint and Microsoft Office **152**

PowerPoint and Microsoft Word 154

PowerPoint and Microsoft Access 158

PowerPoint and Microsoft Excel 160

PowerPoint and Microsoft Outlook 162

Chapter 12: Using Other Objects on Your Slides **168**

Using Rulers and Guides 170

Adding Comments 172

Inserting Slides from Other Presentations 174

Using Text Boxes 176

Using WordArt 178

Using Charts 180

Using Tables 182

Inserting Objects from Other Applications 184

CONTENTS

Part III: Advanced Presentation Skills 188

Chapter 13: Preparing for the Show 190

Rehearsing the Show 192

Recording Show Narration 194

Creating Summary (Agenda) Slides 196

Using Special Presentation Objects 198

Chapter 14: Presenting the Show 202

Using Meeting Minder 204

Navigating Through Your Show 206

Using Online Collaboration 208

Using the Web in Discussions 212

Broadcasting the Show 216

Using the Send To Feature 220

Chapter 15: PowerPoint and the World Wide Web 224

Using Hyperlinks 226

Saving a Slide Show as a Web Page 230

Moving PowerPoint Web Pages to a Server 232

Accessing PowerPoint Shows on the Web 236

Part IV: Programming and Customization 240

Chapter 16: Customizing PowerPoint 242

Using Customize Features 244

Reviewing and Setting Options 248

Using the Common Tasks Toolbar 250

Creating Custom Toolbars 252

Chapter 17: Using Macros 256

Recording New Macros 258

Playing and Editing Macros 260

Setting Macro Security Options 262

Contents

Chapter 18: Compatibility Issues **266**

Saving a Slide Show to Another Format 268

Saving Files Online 270

Opening Other File Formats 272

Saving PowerPoint Slides as Graphics 274

Chapter 19: PowerPoint Design Tips **278**

Design Effective Slides 280

Design for Proper Mood or Effect 282

Design for Random Control 284

Use Brainstorming 286

Use Outlining 288

Use a Storyboard 290

Write a Script 292

Use Text Effectively 294

Use Photographs 296

Appendix A: Personal Workbook Answers **300**

Appendix B: Designing Slides **318**

Index: **321**

Teach Yourself®
Microsoft®
PowerPoint® 2000

PART

I

CHAPTER **1** **Understanding PowerPoint Basics**

2 **Getting Help**

3 **Creating Presentations**

4 **Showing Your Work**

5 **Using Other Presentation and Design Aids**

6 **Printing Your Work**

Basic Skills

Basics. A good foundation. You need these for any new endeavor, including learning your way around PowerPoint 2000. In this section, I show you the main features of the program, discuss getting help beyond what I can provide in this book, and describe in some detail how to create basic presentations, show your presentations to other people, and print the slides you create.

Even if you've used previous versions of PowerPoint, I suggest you review the material in Part I. PowerPoint 2000 builds on previous releases, to be sure, but it also takes advantage of features and conventions that are new with Windows 98, so some familiar things have changed, mostly for the better. Once you have this basic level of understanding, you'll be ready to tackle the more advanced tasks covered in later sections of this book.

CHAPTER 1

MASTER THESE SKILLS

▶ Opening the Program

▶ Using the Menus

▶ Using Context Menus

▶ Using the Toolbars

▶ Using the Dialog Boxes

▶ Controlling the View

Understanding PowerPoint Basics

PowerPoint 2000 is a Microsoft Windows program. If you are already familiar with Windows and Windows-compliant programs, you will have no problem launching the program and using its features. This version of PowerPoint is designed for Windows 98, however, which is somewhat different from previous versions of Windows, even Windows 95. In this chapter, I'll help you get started with this program, whether or not you have previous experience with Microsoft Office products.

As Microsoft's software development teams mature, they get better at upgrades. This upgrade of PowerPoint provides some powerful new features, but they won't startle you if you have experience with previous versions. For example, you won't see much difference in how PowerPoint 2000 launches. You will, however, notice an immediate difference in how the menus and toolbars operate. PowerPoint tracks what you do with the program and tries to present you with the features you really use. Review the sections on using menus and toolbars in this chapter for more details.

Instead of a full-screen display that shows only the current slide you are editing, as was common in previous versions of PowerPoint, you'll see a composite view that lets you manipulate and manage an outline and notes sections in addition to the slide itself. See the "Controlling the View" task in this chapter for more information on this feature.

Other differences and enhancements will become obvious as you use the program, so try to keep an open mind. You can discover new features and new techniques by reading online help, by trying the procedures I point out, and by watching someone else work with the program.

Have you ever noticed how you subconsciously want to move the mouse or operate the keyboard when you see someone else stepping through a program's features? That's because no two of us approach the same software problem or operation in the same way. You should watch what the other person is doing and try to learn a better, more efficient, or simply different way of performing a task. For now, here are the basics.

Opening the Program

There are a few ways to open PowerPoint: (1) Choose Open Office Document or New Office Document from the Start menu or the Office Shortcut bar; (2) Choose PowerPoint from Programs on the Start menu, from the Office Shortcut bar, or from My Computer; (3) Choose a PowerPoint file from any folder.

How you launch PowerPoint depends on what you're doing at the time. For example, if you receive a PowerPoint file via e-mail, you'll launch the program by double-clicking the file icon inside your e-mail message.

Drag a filename from Windows Explorer to the Desktop and you can launch PowerPoint at any time by double-clicking it. Or launch PowerPoint from inside Windows Explorer by navigating to a folder and choosing a file.

The top-left figure on the facing page shows the New Office Document dialog box from the Start menu. This display assumes you are running PowerPoint with a full install of Office 2000. PowerPoint alone or Office with fewer components will show fewer options here. You can start a presentation design from the Presentations tab template or from a Design Templates tab background.

Although these are the methods Microsoft pushes, I find them cumbersome. I launch PowerPoint first and choose New Presentation from the opening screen.

Launch PowerPoint from the Programs list on the Start menu, or from the Office Shortcut bar, to present the screen on the upper right of the facing page. The Office Assistant may look different depending on how many times you've launched PowerPoint and whether you have changed any settings.

The AutoContent Wizard helps you choose a pre-programmed template and other presentation features, whereas a design template helps you choose a color scheme and graphics to augment your own designs. Choose a blank presentation to see the screen at the lower right of the facing page.

TAKE NOTE

▶ CHOOSING OBJECTS

In Windows, you normally select an object by double-clicking it, but Windows 98 configured as a Web page requires a single click. Remember this difference as you follow instructions in this and other chapters.

▶ CREATING TASK-BAR SHORTCUTS

With Windows 98 (or Windows 95 with Internet Explorer 4.0), you can put a PowerPoint shortcut on the task bar. Click Start, choose Programs, point to PowerPoint, hold down the right mouse button while dragging the PowerPoint program entry to the task bar, and choose Create Shortcut from the shortcut menu.

CROSS-REFERENCE

See Chapter 3 for information on what to do once you've opened PowerPoint.

FIND IT ONLINE

Choose Office on the Web from the PowerPoint Help menu, or point your browser to **www.microsoft. com/powerpoint** for more PowerPoint information.

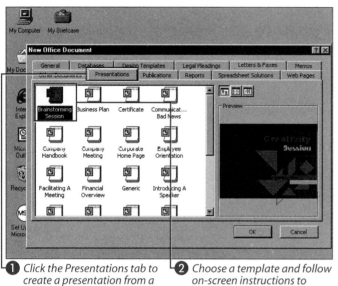

1 *Click the Presentations tab to create a presentation from a preprogrammed template, which is a PowerPoint file with certain features already enabled for you.*

2 *Choose a template and follow on-screen instructions to create a presentation.*

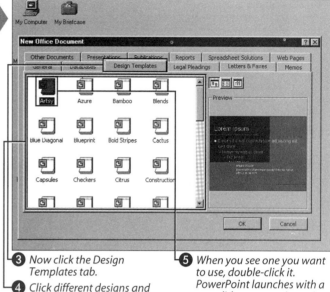

3 *Now click the Design Templates tab.*

4 *Click different designs and look at the preview of each one displayed at the right.*

5 *When you see one you want to use, double-click it. PowerPoint launches with a one-slide presentation using the design you selected.*

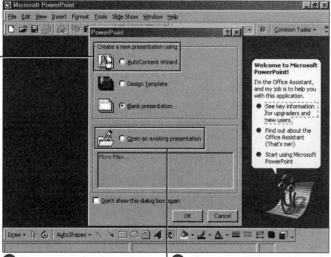

6 *Now try opening PowerPoint in a different way. Click Start, choose Programs, and choose Microsoft PowerPoint. Use the AutoContent Wizard to create a new presentation.*

7 *Close PowerPoint and launch it again. This time, open an existing presentation.*

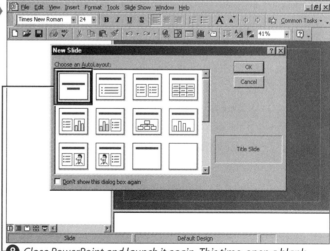

8 *Close PowerPoint and launch it again. This time, open a blank presentation and choose an AutoLayout design for the first slide.*

Using the Menus

The menu bar is the second bar on the screen, just below the title bar that shows the program name and the current file-name. As you can see by looking at the figures to the right, most of the menu items, such as File, are the same as those you see in virtually any other Windows application. There's one, however, that is unique to PowerPoint — Slide Show.

If you pause your mouse pointer over a menu item, the appearance of the menu item changes, to show you have selected it. You will see a raised button outline around the menu item.

If you click one of the menu items — for example, Edit — you get a pull-down menu of Edit commands. This is not the full list of menu commands. If you click on the downward-facing arrows at the bottom of a pull-down menu, a list of additional commands appears. Once you use one of these additional commands, PowerPoint anticipates your habits, and adds it to the primary list. As you can see in the upper-right figure on the facing page, PowerPoint will display the Paste as Hyperlink command as one of the primary Edit menu commands once you start using it.

At times, a menu command on a pull-down menu is not available, and is thus displayed in gray text. This simply means that conditions required to use that command haven't been met. For example, if there is nothing selected on a slide, outline, or other screen area, you can't use the Cut and Copy commands.

You can select a command without viewing a pull-down menu. You'll see small icons to the left of some of the menu commands: These are the icons for the commands on the toolbar. You can click a toolbar icon rather than selecting a command from the menu. Likewise, you can use a keyboard shortcut, such as Ctrl-A for Select All.

If a menu command has an ellipsis after it, clicking the command opens a dialog box. If a menu command has an arrow icon after it, there is a submenu of additional choices for that command. Move your mouse pointer down to the command, then slide it to the right into the submenu and make your selection.

TAKE NOTE

▶ DISPLAYING PULL-DOWN MENUS

If you want to open another pull-down menu, move the cursor off the current menu and select a different menu.

▶ CHANGING MENU DISPLAY

From the Tools menu, choose Customize and click the Options tab. Set menu animations to change the way menus appear.

CROSS-REFERENCE

Read the next two tasks for additional navigation instructions and tips on using shortcut menus and toolbars.

FIND IT ONLINE

See a slide show PowerPoint Basics tutorial at **www. orst.edu/instruction/ed596/ppoint/pphome.htm**.

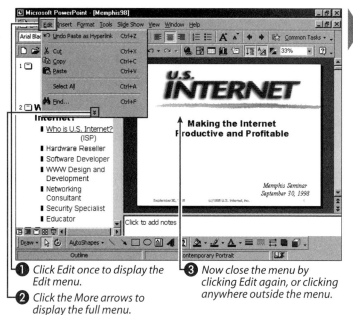

1 Click Edit once to display the Edit menu.

2 Click the More arrows to display the full menu.

3 Now close the menu by clicking Edit again, or clicking anywhere outside the menu.

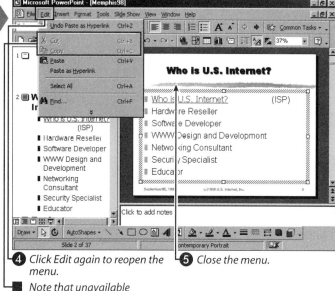

4 Click Edit again to reopen the menu.

■ Note that unavailable commands appear grayed-out.

5 Close the menu.

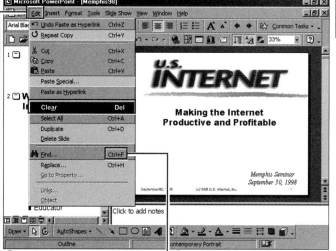

6 Open the Edit menu again and select one of the less-used commands, such as Clear. Reopen the menu by clicking Edit once, and note that this command now appears.

7 Choose a command to perform and use its keyboard shortcut instead of selecting the command from the menu.

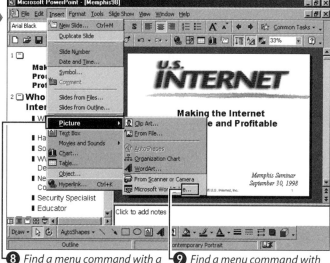

8 Find a menu command with a right-pointing arrow and open the submenu.

9 Find a menu command with an ellipsis and open the associated dialog box.

Using Shortcut Menus

Besides the main menu bar, PowerPoint supplies a wide range of shortcut menus, which are menus of commands that pop up when you right-click an object. As you can see in the first figure on the facing page, a shortcut menu appears when you right-click the Office Assistant.

Shortcut menus contain some of the same menu commands that you can select from the main menu bar. In addition, they often contain commands that you won't find anywhere else. This shortcut menu for the Office Assistant gives you four options, two of which open dialog boxes with additional choices.

If you right-click inside the slide window of a PowerPoint presentation, you'll see a much larger shortcut menu, like that shown in the upper-right figure on the facing page. You can cut, copy, or paste from this menu or from the Edit menu on the main menu bar. Except for Exit Edit Text, the other commands on this shortcut menu are also available from the main menu. Shortcut menus provide access to menu commands within the context you're likely to use them. That is why they are sometimes called *context menus*.

Want to see what toolbars are displayed and which ones are not? Right-click any visible toolbar to open the shortcut menu shown at the lower left of the facing page. Later in this chapter, you'll see how to use this shortcut menu to display a variety of toolbars.

Many shortcut menus are similar. Most of them contain cut, copy, paste, and hyperlink commands. The choices in the middle of the popup menu change with the type of object. For example, click on a clip-art image within a slide, and you'll see the shortcut menu shown at the lower right of the facing page.

Again, you can see why these are sometimes called context menus. This menu shows an awareness of the object type: Edit Picture, Hide Picture, Grouping, Order, and so on. Using shortcut menus saves time because you don't have to move the mouse up to the main PowerPoint menu, and you frequently get a narrower range of choices that reflect what you can do with the selected object.

TAKE NOTE

▶ UNDERSTANDING MENUS

Not all objects have shortcut menus. You can pop up a shortcut menu for a toolbar, for example, but individual objects on that toolbar don't have menus. You'll also see different menus depending on whether you select an object before you right-click it.

▶ USING SHORTCUTS DURING A SHOW

When you right-click a slide during a slide show, you see a shortcut menu that helps you navigate through the show. You can move forward and back in the show, jump to a specific slide, and choose other options that help you make the most of your PowerPoint slide show.

CROSS-REFERENCE

See Chapter 4 for more information on slide show shortcut menus.

FIND IT ONLINE

Visit Media Service's PowerPoint Tutorial page at www.eiu.edu/~mediasrv/PPtut.html.

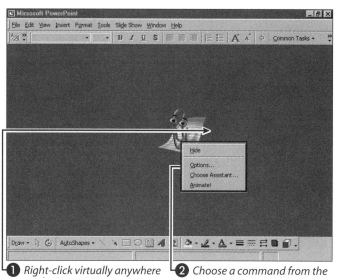

1 Right-click virtually anywhere on the PowerPoint screen (including the Office Assistant) to display a shortcut menu.

2 Choose a command from the menu as you would from the main menu.

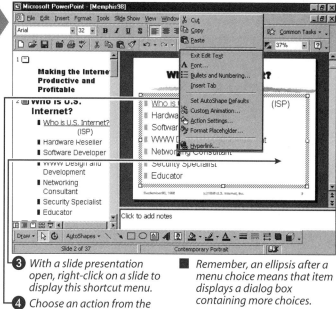

3 With a slide presentation open, right-click on a slide to display this shortcut menu.

4 Choose an action from the menu as you would from the main menu.

■ Remember, an ellipsis after a menu choice means that item displays a dialog box containing more choices.

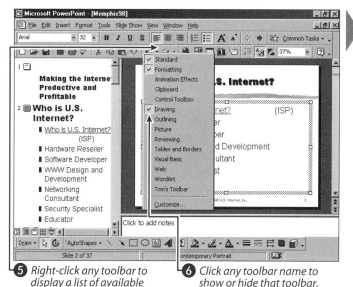

5 Right-click any toolbar to display a list of available toolbars.

■ A checkmark means that the toolbar is already displayed on the screen.

6 Click any toolbar name to show or hide that toolbar.

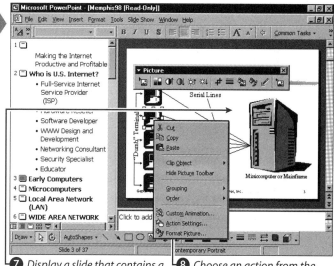

7 Display a slide that contains a graphic. Right-click the graphic to open a shortcut menu for that object.

8 Choose an action from the menu as you would from the main menu.

Using the Toolbars

Windows is a graphical environment, and PowerPoint 2000 is full of graphical toolbars to access the program's features. Toolbars are floating objects (bars, rectangles, or squares) that include small pictures (icons) representing PowerPoint commands. Instead of choosing a command from a menu, you can choose that command by clicking on its toolbar icon.

When the program runs, PowerPoint displays the standard toolbar just below the menu bar. (See the upper-left figure on the following page.) You can select up to 12 additional toolbars by choosing them from a list. You can also change the items that appear by default on the toolbars.

PowerPoint is relatively intelligent about the way it handles toolbars, similar to the way it handles menus (see the previous sections). You can display additional commands by clicking on the Common Tasks label on the standard toolbar. This displays another toolbar as an ancillary menu attached to the standard toolbar. Grab the title bar of the Common Tasks toolbar with your mouse to position it anywhere on the PowerPoint screen as a standalone toolbar.

You have yet another option for expanding the standard toolbar. Notice the double arrows to the right of Common Tasks. Click them to display another 15 or so toolbar buttons (upper-right figure, facing page). When you click one of these icons, PowerPoint assumes you may want to reuse that command and adds it to the standard toolbar.

You can change which toolbar buttons appear on this drop-down toolbar. To do so, click Add or Remove Buttons at the bottom of the toolbar. A list of toolbar buttons appears (lower-left figure, facing page). Those with a checkmark beside them are displayed on the toolbar, while those without a checkmark can be added. Check or uncheck the entries you see here, or click the down arrow at the bottom of this display to reveal yet more choices.

PowerPoint also displays the drawing toolbar by default. The drawing toolbar is positioned at the bottom of the PowerPoint screen (lower-right figure, next page).

TAKE NOTE

DISPLAYING OTHER TOOLBARS

PowerPoint has about 15 built-in toolbars. The standard and drawing toolbars display by default. Right-click any displayed toolbar to reveal a list of available toolbars. Click any entries in the list to display or remove toolbars.

MOVING TOOLBARS

PowerPoint decides where to place selected toolbars. However, you can move a toolbar anywhere on the PowerPoint screen by grabbing the bar with the mouse and dragging it to a new location. Pull a toolbar into the center of the display and it sprouts a title bar. Dock it to a side of the screen and it behaves more like the standard toolbar.

CROSS-REFERENCE

See Chapter 16 for additional details on adding items to toolbars and other toolbar-customizing functions.

FIND IT ONLINE

For a diagram of toolbar, text enhancement, and view button functions, see **www.wcupa.edu/_SERVICES/ vpis.act/ppoint4**.

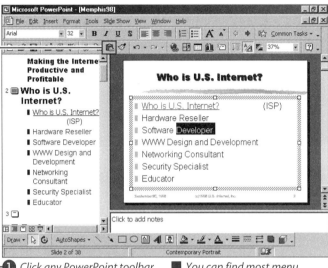

1 *Click any PowerPoint toolbar icon to carry out a specific command.*

■ *You can find most menu commands on a toolbar. Clicking a toolbar icon is usually faster than selecting a menu command.*

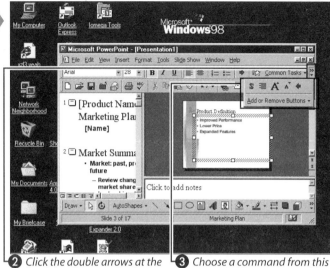

2 *Click the double arrows at the far right of the standard toolbar to display additional toolbar icons (which vary based on what you've done so far).*

3 *Choose a command from this expanded list as you would from any toolbar display.*

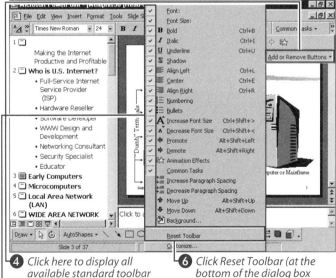

4 *Click here to display all available standard toolbar commands.*

5 *Check or uncheck items to add them or remove them from the toolbar.*

6 *Click Reset Toolbar (at the bottom of the dialog box beyond the view of this figure) to restore defaults, or click Customize to make more changes.*

7 *Display the drawing toolbar and pause over an icon to pop up a Tool Tip. Click a menu item to see additional menus.*

8 *Choose an action, such as drawing a rectangle.*

9 *Move the mouse onto the slide and drag the chosen shape to the size you want.*

13

Using the Dialog Boxes

If you've used any Windows program, you are probably familiar with dialog boxes. These interactive objects contain choices about the task you are currently performing. After you make your selection and click OK, the program uses that information to carry out the selected task.

Dialog boxes frequently appear when you choose menu items. For example, when you select File ⇨ Open, a dialog box opens (see the upper-left figure on the facing page). Most Windows programs use an Open dialog box similar to this one. There are differences, however. This is a rich dialog box that demonstrates many of the differences in the PowerPoint 2000 user interface.

The icon bar at the left looks like the one in many of Microsoft's new programs. Select a file and see a preview of that file to the right rather than a simple filename. Notice the supplemental toolbar that includes a Search the Web icon and a shortcut menu. PowerPoint 2000, remember, is a Web-centric product that supports loading and saving files across the Internet, if you have the proper access and permissions.

Other dialog boxes are simpler than the Open dialog box. The upper-right figure on the next page, for example, shows the New Slide dialog box, used to add a slide to a presentation or to open a new, blank presentation. In some dialog boxes, such as the Open dialog box, you are prompted to enter data from the keyboard or choose from drop-down menus. In the New Slide dialog box, on the other hand, you make

selections by clicking. First, you click a slide type and then you click OK.

You may also encounter tabbed dialog boxes, such as the Customize dialog box shown at the lower left of the facing page. These dialog boxes contain a great deal of information divided into tabs that look like the tabs on a file folder. Click a tab to see its contents. Often you will make selections from more than one tab before you are finished with that dialog box.

Finally, you'll find that PowerPoint 2000 is full of wizards — simple programs or interactive instructions that launch automatically when you choose certain tasks. Consider the wizard dialog box in the figure at the lower right of the following page. This is the Projector Wizard, which you can launch from the Set Up Show dialog box, available on the Slide Show menu. Most wizards present multipurpose dialog boxes that let you enter data, choose something from a list, and click on navigation buttons to move through the wizard steps.

TAKE NOTE

DISPLAYING DIALOG BOXES

Remember that menu items ending with an ellipse usually open dialog boxes. In a few cases, an Office Assistant tip or instruction for carrying out the selected task appears instead. Just click OK and follow the instructions.

CROSS-REFERENCE

See Chapter 3 for more information on using PowerPoint wizards.

FIND IT ONLINE

For more tips on understanding the PowerPoint interface, visit **www.commerce.ubc.ca/MBAcore/ tutorials/powerpoint/ppt2.html**.

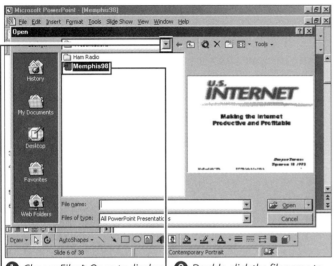

① *Choose File ➪ Open to display the Open dialog box. Navigate to the folder that contains the file you want to load.*

② *Double-click the filename to open the PowerPoint presentation you selected.*

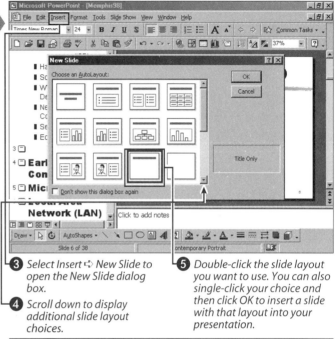

③ *Select Insert ➪ New Slide to open the New Slide dialog box.*

④ *Scroll down to display additional slide layout choices.*

⑤ *Double-click the slide layout you want to use. You can also single-click your choice and then click OK to insert a slide with that layout into your presentation.*

⑥ *Click any tab in a tabbed dialog box to bring the contents of that tab to the front of the display.*

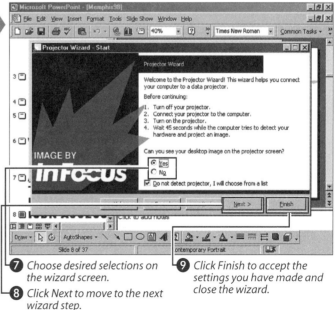

⑦ *Choose desired selections on the wizard screen.*

⑧ *Click Next to move to the next wizard step.*

⑨ *Click Finish to accept the settings you have made and close the wizard.*

Controlling the View

All versions of PowerPoint offer several ways to view your slide show. There is the slide view, which you use to create slides. You can also use an outline view, a notes view, a slide sorter view, and a slide show view. In the past, you selected one view at a time. PowerPoint 2000 combines three of these views — slide, outline, and notes — to give you a quick reference and overview of your presentation on one screen (see the upper-left figure on the next page).

The outline and slide portions of this screen are shown at about one-third actual size, but you can change this default easily. (See the top-right figure on the following page, which shows the slide window at 75 percent.) Notice that PowerPoint automatically inserts a miniature image so you can see the whole slide as well.

The slide sorter view is useful while you are working on a presentation. Choose this view to present a display such as that in the lower-left figure on the next page. In this view, it's easy to rearrange slides, hide slides, or cut slides.

Suppose you want to see more of your slides and less of the PowerPoint menus and toolbars and such. Uncheck the toolbars you want to hide and move the remaining ones around, if you wish. Now you will have more room on the screen for your slides (lower-right figure, next page).

You can always choose the slide show view to look at any slide full-screen, of course. If you want to restore the toolbars you've removed, right-click on any remaining toolbar or on the menu bar and check the toolbars you want to restore. Drag the menu bar back to its top-of-screen position, if you have moved it. You can also Customize the dialog box. Click the Toolbars tab of this dialog box and enable the toolbars you want to use.

TAKE NOTE

▶ REMOVING COLOR FROM SLIDES

If you're printing your show on a monochrome printer, you may want to remove color first: This lets you preview the effect of losing color before you waste paper on combinations that don't work well. From the View menu, choose Black and White to display the show in black and white. You can also right-click any slide and choose Black and White from the shortcut menu.

▶ DISPLAYING MINIATURES

You can display miniature versions of your slides at any time. From the View menu, choose Slide Miniature.

CROSS-REFERENCE
See Chapter 16 for more information on changing toolbars and making other custom changes to the way the program operates.

FIND IT ONLINE
For a visual breakdown of each of the view options, check out **www.nmc.vt.edu/workshops/Powerpoint/views.html**.

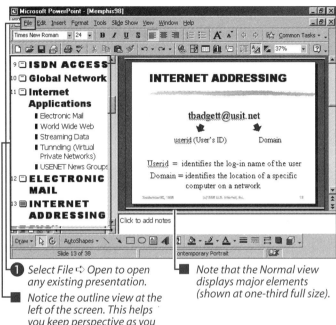

① *Select File ➪ Open to open any existing presentation.*

■ *Notice the outline view at the left of the screen. This helps you keep perspective as you work on show design.*

■ *Note that the Normal view displays major elements (shown at one-third full size).*

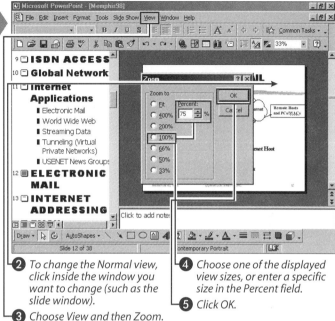

② *To change the Normal view, click inside the window you want to change (such as the slide window).*

③ *Choose View and then Zoom.*

④ *Choose one of the displayed view sizes, or enter a specific size in the Percent field.*

⑤ *Click OK.*

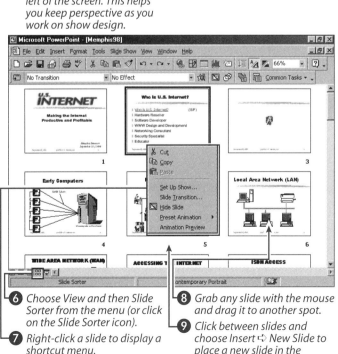

⑥ *Choose View and then Slide Sorter from the menu (or click on the Slide Sorter icon).*

⑦ *Right-click a slide to display a shortcut menu.*

⑧ *Grab any slide with the mouse and drag it to another spot.*

⑨ *Click between slides and choose Insert ➪ New Slide to place a new slide in the selected position.*

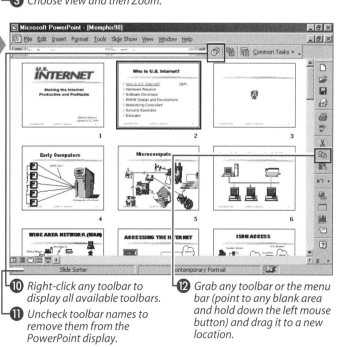

⑩ *Right-click any toolbar to display all available toolbars.*

⑪ *Uncheck toolbar names to remove them from the PowerPoint display.*

⑫ *Grab any toolbar or the menu bar (point to any blank area and hold down the left mouse button) and drag it to a new location.*

17

Personal Workbook

Q&A

1 What are three ways to open the PowerPoint 2000 program?

_____

_____

_____

2 How do you discover the keyboard shortcuts for menu items?

_____

_____

_____

3 Describe two ways to make PowerPoint display all available choices under a specific menu.

_____

_____

_____

4 Describe how to change which toolbars are shown on the PowerPoint screen.

_____

_____

5 The Normal PowerPoint view shows three program elements. What are they?

_____

_____

_____

6 How can you tell which PowerPoint menu items open a dialog box?

_____

_____

_____

7 What is the procedure for displaying a shortcut menu?

_____

_____

_____

8 How can you exit a shortcut menu without choosing any of the menu choices?

_____

_____

ANSWERS: PAGE 301

EXTRA PRACTICE

1 Launch the Office Shortcut bar, if it is not already displayed on your screen.

2 Remove the standard toolbar and move the main menu to the right side of the PowerPoint screen.

3 Display the New Office Document dialog box and choose a Blank Presentation.

4 Turn on menu animation to change the way PowerPoint menus are displayed.

5 Turn on Slide Show view and display the Show Shortcut menu.

6 Display a presentation in Normal view, then zoom the slide display to 50 percent of full size.

REAL-WORLD APPLICATIONS

✔ We all use software applications differently. The ability to add and remove toolbars and even to move the position of the menu bar helps you get the most out of this program. You can remove all toolbars and reposition the menu bar to one side of the screen, for example, opening up the PowerPoint screen to give you more flexibility in presentation design.

✔ If you're working with a relatively low-resolution screen (e.g., 640 by 480 pixels), you may find it difficult to see all parts of the slide you're designing. Zoom the slide to a larger display (up to 400 percent of normal) and then turn on miniatures so you can see how changes to the current slide affect the overall design.

Visual Quiz

Describe how to display the opening wizard screen shown here.

_____

_____

_____

_____

_____

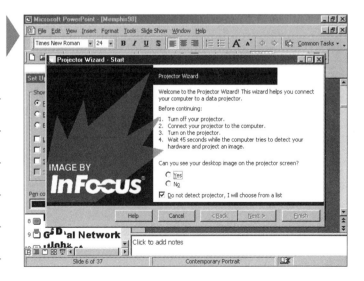

CHAPTER 2

MASTER
THESE
SKILLS

▶ Using the Office Assistant

▶ Using the PowerPoint Help System

▶ Using Detect and Repair

Getting Help

PowerPoint is easy to use. Its Windows-compliant interface and fairly intuitive design, coupled with this book, enable you to go from zero to advanced beginner pretty darn quick. On the other hand, there are times when you will need an answer for something you are trying to do right now and the solution isn't obvious.

At such times, you can call on PowerPoint's built-in help facility. You have three basic options: (1) typical Windows help topics that you can search, read, and print as you would in any other application; (2) the Office Assistant; and (3) Web-based help from Microsoft's site on the Internet.

I haven't always been too complimentary toward Microsoft's application help. Indeed, for Office 97, I hardly had a kind word to say. The company could still do better, but I believe you'll like Office 2000 help a lot better than that for previous versions. The help topics seem more extensive, the index and search features work better, and I like the new user interface.

Microsoft is also working hard to make online help truly online. The entire Office 2000 suite is based on a Web-centric design that makes your desktop work more like the World Wide Web, making access to Web-based help, support files, templates, drawings and art, and other useful material a whole lot easier. If you're not using the Web now, or if you are using it minimally, this might be a good time to consider turning up the heat. If you're using PowerPoint in a corporate, networked environment, the online features will come into play there as well, particularly if your company has a direct, high-speed connection to the Internet.

You'll have to find out for yourself whether this version of Microsoft application help is better than before, and see what you think of the new system. In this chapter, I give you the basics of the new PowerPoint help system and assist you in getting more than you thought out of this useful online tool.

Using the Office Assistant

The Office 2000 Assistant is an enhanced Office 97 Assistant. The default assistant is still an animated paper clip (Clipit), but with a modern, open design. And with PowerPoint 2000 you have some new assistants you can choose, including Rocky, a happy yellow dog. The Assistant — whether Clipit, Rocky, a cat, or one of the others — can be on top of everything you do. You can modify some of his habits, ask him questions, or send him into hiding until further notice.

Clipit, good ol' Rocky, or another assistant will pop up at odd moments to offer suggestions (a light bulb appears when the Assistant has a tip) or to answer questions. Press F1 or choose Microsoft PowerPoint Help from the Help menu to display the Assistant at will. Click him any time he's on-screen to ask him a question.

Look at the top-left figure on the next page. This is the default assistant's basic query dialog box, though it may look different the first time you see it.

Try typing New User under the *What would you like to do?* prompt. Notice how this winsome wirehead writes on a notepad and turns the pages while you enter your query. This is typical Assistant behavior. He'll scratch his head or make noise to get your attention, and wiggle his eyebrows while he waits for you. When you click Search, Clipit lists a number of items that may interest you as a new user (upper-right figure, next page).

If you select one of these items — say, *Create a Template* — a help topic on that item appears to the right, as you can see in the lower-left figure on the next page. This is the standard text Help system familiar to Windows users, but it has a new look you'll probably like. The Assistant stays on the screen for more help if you need it.

Want to change the way the Assistant works? You can do that with the Office Assistant dialog box (lower-right figure, next page). Use the Options tab in this box to set some of the Assistant's behaviors. Choose another Assistant using the Gallery tab.

TAKE NOTE

USING WHAT'S THIS? HELP

You can get help by choosing What's This? from the Help menu. What's This? is a Help utility that pops up short descriptions of on-screen objects when you click them. Once you enable this feature, you can click PowerPoint objects to display the description box associated with them. Press Esc to cancel the What's This? question-mark cursor.

CROSS-REFERENCE
See Chapter 8 for more information on using the new version of the Windows hyperlink Help system.

FIND IT ONLINE
Updated information about PowerPoint and other Office products is available at **www.microsoft.com/office**.

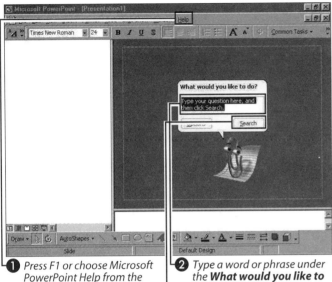

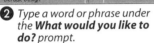

1 *Press F1 or choose Microsoft PowerPoint Help from the Help menu to display the Office Assistant, then click the Assistant to ask a question.*

2 *Type a word or phrase under the **What would you like to do?** prompt.*

3 *Click Search to see a list of Help topics.*

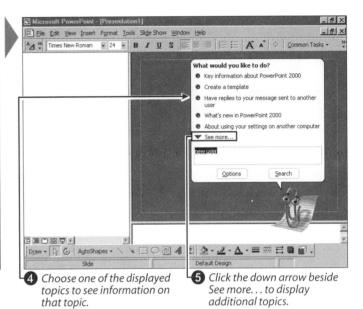

4 *Choose one of the displayed topics to see information on that topic.*

5 *Click the down arrow beside See more... to display additional topics.*

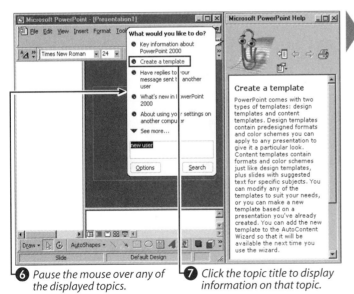

6 *Pause the mouse over any of the displayed topics.*

■ *The bullet beside the topic lights up and the cursor changes to a hyperlink hand.*

7 *Click the topic title to display information on that topic.*

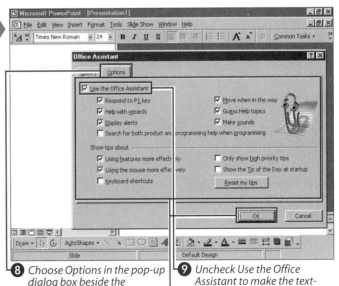

8 *Choose Options in the pop-up dialog box beside the Assistant to access this Options tab.*

9 *Uncheck Use the Office Assistant to make the text-based Help system the default.*

10 *Enable or disable any other options. Click OK.*

Using the PowerPoint Help System

The PowerPoint 2000 Help system is similar to its earlier versions, but you'll notice some user interface changes as you begin using this part of the program.

You can use the Options button to display an option to turn off the Office Assistant. (The Assistant is on by default.) When you press F1 or choose Microsoft PowerPoint Help from the Help menu, the text-based Help system displays. As you can see in the upper-left figure on the next page, the Help system window has three tabs on the left and Help text on the right. By default, the Help system opens to the Answer Wizard tab. The Answer Wizard works a lot like the Assistant: Ask questions in one window and the answers appear in another.

If you've used Microsoft Windows applications before, you will be familiar with the other two tabs in the Help window: Contents and Index. The Contents tab displays a tree of topics on the left. When you select a topic, it appears on the right, as shown in the upper-right figure on the next page.

The Index tab offers another window into the information stored in the Help file. When you type the first letter of a search keyword, the search engine jumps immediately to the first entry in the keyword list that begins with that letter. Type a second letter to limit the displayed list to words that start with the first two letters you have typed, and so on.

For example, I started typing the word autocorrect. After I typed auto, the keyword list moved down the alphabet to display autocorrect and the keywords around it. I selected autocorrect from the list and double-clicked it to display a list of topics associated with this keyword at the bottom of the screen. The first topic was automatically selected and its text was displayed in the box to the right (lower-left figure, next page). If you type enough of the keyword to bring it to the top of the list, you can press Enter to display the text of that selected Help topic.

Notice the navigation buttons at the top of the lower-left figure. You can hide the tabbed part of the dialog box and also step through the help topics you've displayed with the Back and Forward buttons, just as if you were moving through Web pages in a browser. By closing the tabbed dialog box side of the Help window, you can work with your presentation and view the help text right next to it.

TAKE NOTE

► NAVIGATING THE HELP SYSTEM

Much of PowerPoint's Help system is based on hyperlinked text. When you click on a word that's a different color or underlined, additional information about that topic is displayed. Hyperlinks are a convenient way to follow a series of steps to learn about a topic.

CROSS-REFERENCE

See Chapters 3 and 5 for help on using the finer features of PowerPoint.

FIND IT ONLINE

Choose Office on the Web from the Help menu to find information about Office products in general and PowerPoint in particular.

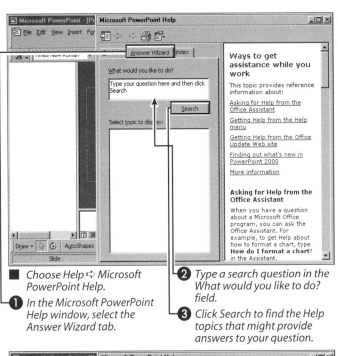

■ Choose Help ➪ Microsoft PowerPoint Help.

1 In the Microsoft PowerPoint Help window, select the Answer Wizard tab.

2 Type a search question in the What would you like to do? field.

3 Click Search to find the Help topics that might provide answers to your question.

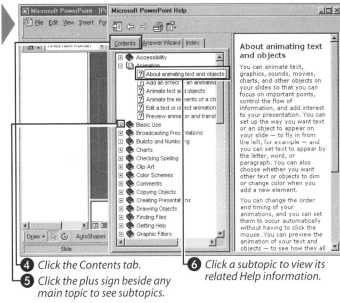

4 Click the Contents tab.

5 Click the plus sign beside any main topic to see subtopics.

6 Click a subtopic to view its related Help information.

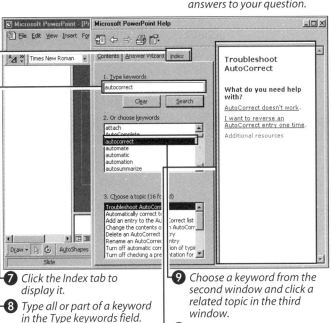

7 Click the Index tab to display it.

8 Type all or part of a keyword in the Type keywords field.

9 Choose a keyword from the second window and click a related topic in the third window.

10 Read the text about that topic in the box to the right.

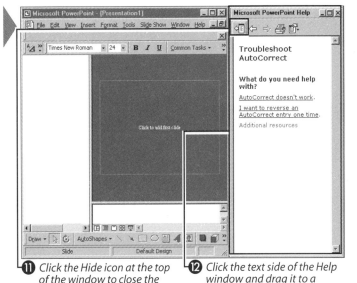

11 Click the Hide icon at the top of the window to close the tabbed side of the window.

■ The Hide icon changes to Show.

12 Click the text side of the Help window and drag it to a convenient location on the PowerPoint screen.

Using Detect and Repair

It shouldn't happen, but it does. For no apparent reason, PowerPoint (or another of your Office applications) gets flaky and doesn't run right any more. If this happens, you can try the new Detect and Repair facility built into Office. Choose Detect and Repair from the Help menu to open the dialog box shown in the upper right of the facing page.

This utility repairs errors in the registry, reinstalls missing or damaged files, and generally shores up a flagging PowerPoint. If Detect and Repair can't find the operating system on your hard drive and the Windows CD-ROM isn't in a drive, you'll see the dialog box displayed in the lower-left corner of the following page.

You'll see several informational displays as the process completes, telling you what this wizard is doing as it works. As the program runs, a counter tells you how much longer the process will take. If your Office installation is severely damaged, it could take 30 minutes or more. Figure on 15 minutes at the very least, even if everything is mostly okay. You shouldn't pay too much attention to the progress indicator. It will jump forward and backward in time as various tasks are loaded and the program tries to evaluate how much work is left to do. Just figure it will take 30 minutes or so for Office to load and you won't be disappointed.

Although under Windows 98, it is theoretically possible to keep working on something else while such a process runs (you can run the Windows disk-defragmenting utility in the background, for example, but it will take a whole lot longer), doing so isn't a good idea. If you access a file that Detect and Repair needs, Detect and Repair repeats at least part of the process, perhaps several times. This process is basically a reinstall of Office, with the installer looking for changed, missing, or damaged files. Let it do its work unhindered and your results will be better and the process faster.

When Detect and Repair is complete, you will be notified that you must restart your computer. You can restart immediately by choosing Yes from this dialog box, or delay the restart until later by choosing No.

When you do restart the machine after running Detect and Repair, you'll see the dialog box shown in the bottom-right figure on the facing page. This box indicates that the final reconfigure step is about to be completed. When this wizard is through, you can relaunch PowerPoint and continue your work.

TAKE NOTE

▶ LAUNCHING POWERPOINT AFTER DETECT AND REPAIR

The first time you run PowerPoint or another of your Office 2000 applications after running Detect and Repair, you may be asked some questions you've already answered before, such as your name and your initials. This is normal, because many of the Office files may have been updated or replaced. Also, you may notice some subtle differences in some dialog boxes. This is okay.

CROSS-REFERENCE

See Chapter 5 for more help on using PowerPoint 2000.

FIND IT ONLINE

www.microsoft.com/office is an ongoing resource for Office 2000 updates, news, hints, FAQs, and more. Visit it frequently for the latest information.

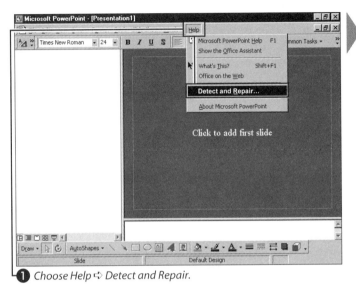

❶ *Choose Help ⇨ Detect and Repair.*

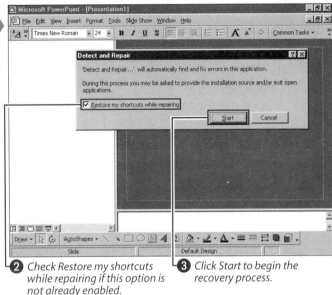

❷ *Check Restore my shortcuts while repairing if this option is not already enabled.*

❸ *Click Start to begin the recovery process.*

❹ *Insert your Office 2000 installation CD-ROM when you are prompted.*

❺ *Click OK to continue the Detect and Repair process. Click Yes to reboot when prompted.*

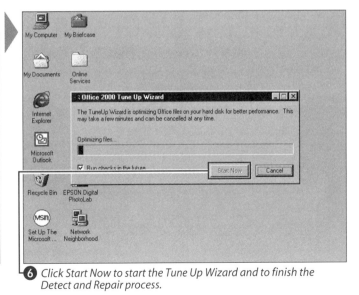

❻ *Click Start Now to start the Tune Up Wizard and to finish the Detect and Repair process.*

Personal Workbook

Q&A

1 Describe the three basic types of online help available in PowerPoint 2000.

_____

_____

_____

2 How do you activate the What's This? cursor?

_____

_____

_____

3 What single keystroke can you use to display the Office Assistant character?

_____

_____

_____

4 How can you turn off the Office Assistant to use standard text-based help?

_____

_____

_____

5 Which menu sequence displays information about your version of PowerPoint and shows you technical data about your computer system?

_____

_____

_____

6 What would you do to add a new personality to your Office Assistant?

_____

_____

_____

7 When you see the What would you like to do? prompt, which PowerPoint help object is on the screen?

_____

_____

_____

8 When would you use the PowerPoint Detect and Repair facility?

_____

_____

ANSWERS: PAGE 301

EXTRA PRACTICE

1 Use the mouse to hide the Office Assistant.

2 Ask the Office Assistant to display topics that relate to New User.

3 Turn on What's This? and use it to display information about the Office Assistant.

4 Use your mouse to have the Office Assistant conduct one of its animation actions.

5 Display the Contents tab of the Help window and expand the Clip Art topic to show the available subtopics.

6 Display PowerPoint Help, hide the tabbed side of the dialog box, and move the resulting display to another part of the screen.

REAL-WORLD APPLICATIONS

✔ Sometimes it is inconvenient to switch between Help and an application. With PowerPoint 2000, you can have Help instructions on the screen at the same time you work on a presentation design. Simply display online Help, hide the tabbed side of the dialog box, and move the text part of the display to a convenient part of the screen. It'll stay there while you work and you can ask it for additional Help.

✔ The default Office Assistant, Rocky, is friendly and likeable, but some users I've talked with don't like his insistence. If you don't want to be interrupted for awhile, click on the Assistant, choose Options and uncheck Use the Office Assistant on the Options tab of this dialog box. You can make other changes in this box, such as turning off sounds.

Visual Quiz

Describe how to display the opening wizard screen shown here.

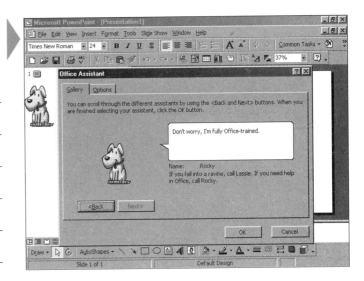

CHAPTER 3

**MASTER
THESE
SKILLS**

▶ Opening a Blank Presentation

▶ Using the AutoContent Wizard

▶ Using Design Templates

▶ Using Presentation Designs

Creating Presentations

PowerPoint's user-oriented design really shines. I like the fact that you can use basic, mostly automated, features to help you build simple presentations. As you learn more and as your presentation needs evolve, you can move up to more sophisticated features and capabilities. This chapter covers beginning and intermediate features and lays the groundwork for more advanced work, covered later in the book.

There are four basic ways to start a presentation design in PowerPoint 2000: (1) open a blank presentation and add features and slides as you go; (2) use the AutoContent Wizard for step-by-step help in choosing pre-programmed templates and color schemes; (3) choose a design template as a starting point; or (4) choose a presentation design as a starting point.

The four tasks in this chapter show you how to use each of these approaches to starting a presentation. First, though, I want to expand the description of the PowerPoint program itself.

What is a presentation program, anyway? Basically, it is a software application that helps you organize ideas and present them with visual aids such as text charts, drawings, animation, graphs, sound, and motion video. These visual aids are placed on successive computer screens arranged in the form of a slide show. Each slide can contain multiple visual elements that are presented all at once or sequentially, and each presentation typically contains one slide for every one to five minutes of material.

You can deliver a presentation to a small audience directly on the computer display screen. This is useful for one-on-one sales presentations, for example, or for kiosk applications at a trade show, when one or two people may stop at a booth to learn about a company or product. For larger audiences, presenters typically use projectors that connect to a computer's video card to display very large images (up to several feet wide). The latest versions of PowerPoint let you use the Internet to broadcast information to a very large audience that is widely dispersed.

Let's get started. This chapter shows you how to use many PowerPoint features to build your own company or personal presentations. Later chapters build on the basics to expand your understanding of the software's functionality.

Opening a Blank Presentation

One of your options for developing a new slide show is to launch PowerPoint and open a blank presentation. From within this blank file, you can create new slides, choose a color scheme, and so on, to design a new presentation.

The upper-left figure on the next page shows the opening PowerPoint screen, in which you can choose a blank document. The New Office Document dialog box appears in the upper-right figure. Both of these starting points let you choose a blank document as a starting place for a new presentation.

When you open a blank presentation, the first thing you see is a New Slide dialog box. Here, you can choose a slide AutoLayout, which is the basic design of the first slide in the new presentation. Most of the time, you'll probably insert a title slide first, so accept the default presented here and click OK. The basic three-part PowerPoint window now opens, with the title slide on the right side of the display.

The title slide prompts you, "Click to add title." When you do that, PowerPoint opens a text-edit box so you can type a title. As you can see in the lower-left figure on the facing page, whatever you type in the title position also shows up to the left, in the Outline section of the window. You have the option of creating new slides in the right-hand slide section or of adding slides and text to the outline on the left.

A new, blank presentation contains only the one slide you chose from the opening screen. Continue building your presentation by adding new slides (press Ctrl-M). Every time you add a slide, you'll see the same New Slide with AutoLayout screen. Choose the type of slide you want to create, and you're on your way to designing your first presentation.

To add some color and design pizzazz to your slide show, you can use one of the built-in design templates. (Some of the available templates are listed in the lower-right figure on the facing page.)

TAKE NOTE

▶ USING AUTOLAYOUT DESIGNS

PowerPoint includes 24 AutoLayout slide designs. Although you can manually add components, such as a picture box for a table, your design work will go faster and easier if you use the appropriate pre-built design for the slide show you are designing. Even if a particular AutoLayout contains items you don't want, it is easier to remove elements than to add them.

▶ ADDING MORE EFFECTS TO YOUR SLIDES

Applying a design template isn't the only way to add color and interest to your slides. Choose Background or Slide Color Scheme from the Format menu to change other slide features.

CROSS-REFERENCE

See Chapter 4 for an introduction to getting your show on the road. You'll find more design tips in Chapter 9.

SHORTCUT

Blank isn't always better. Try opening a presentation with a color scheme enabled by choosing templates from the New dialog box.

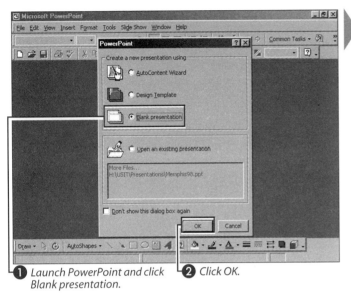

1 *Launch PowerPoint and click Blank presentation.*

2 *Click OK.*

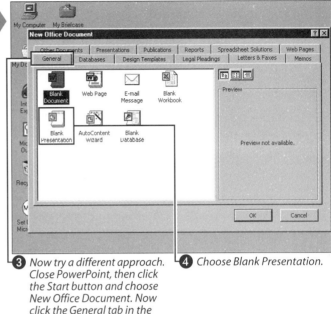

3 *Now try a different approach. Close PowerPoint, then click the Start button and choose New Office Document. Now click the General tab in the NOD dialog box.*

4 *Choose Blank Presentation.*

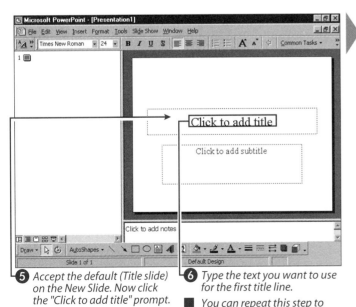

5 *Accept the default (Title slide) on the New Slide. Now click the "Click to add title" prompt.*

6 *Type the text you want to use for the first title line.*

■ *You can repeat this step to choose different slide layouts and build a short slide show design.*

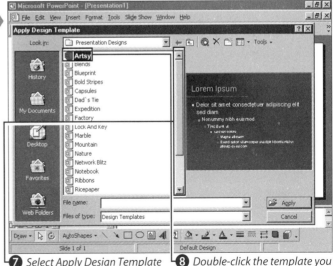

7 *Select Apply Design Template from the Format menu. Use the scrollbars to display additional templates; click ones you want to preview.*

8 *Double-click the template you want to use, or select the template and click Apply to apply the template to your existing slides.*

Using the AutoContent Wizard

If you'd like a little more help with your presentation design than you get by starting with a blank presentation, consider using the AutoContent Wizard. Choose this wizard from the General tab of the New Presentation dialog box to display the opening wizard screen, shown at the upper left on the facing page.

This is a relatively simple wizard that steps you through the process of creating a new presentation. The first step is to select a presentation type (see the upper-right figure on the facing page). These types are preprogrammed presentations with dummy data that you can replace with your own information. Presentation types include Recommending a Strategy, Employee Orientation, Project Overview, and Selling a Product or Service. You'll see a different list when you click different presentation category buttons in the middle of this dialog box. These presentations include color schemes, graphics, and sample text on a series of slides so you can simply enter your own data to produce a core presentation.

Ask design professionals and they'll invariably say these designs are awful and that you should really do your own. I don't agree. They are not unique (everyone with PowerPoint 2000 has them), and they are don't always match my sense of professional business design, but they do offer a starting point. As you learn your way around PowerPoint 2000, use these designs and learn from them. You can modify them and create your own later.

The wizard will also help you choose a presentation style (see the lower-left figure on the following page). The choices are On-screen, Web, overhead foils, and 35mm slides. Choosing the appropriate presentation style is actually more important than it may seem. The slides you create are formatted differently for each style, including different aspect ratios for the different styles. You can change the presentation style at any time, but you may also have to adjust fonts, move graphics, or change text to make everything fit.

The final wizard screen, shown at the lower right of the facing page, lets you add a custom title to the presentation and set the footer text.

When you've finished using the wizard, you can modify the appearance of the slides with the Slide Layout and Design Template choices from the Format menu, if you wish.

TAKE NOTE

CHOOSING PRESENTATION TYPES

PowerPoint has a number of preprogrammed presentations that are good starting points for your designs. You can also add templates of your own to this display. From the Presentation Type Wizard dialog box, click Add and navigate to a previously created PowerPoint presentation. When you choose this file, it is inserted as a Presentation Type template.

CHANGING PRESENTATION STYLE

Even if you've used the AutoContent Wizard to start a new presentation design, you can change the presentation style. From the Slide Show menu, choose Set Up Show and select the style from the Set Up Show dialog box.

CROSS-REFERENCE

Check out Chapter 10 for some ideas on adding creative and attention-getting elements to your PowerPoint presentations.

SHORTCUT

To learn what Microsoft did to create the autocontent you're using, select View↓ Slide Master and click various elements of the design.

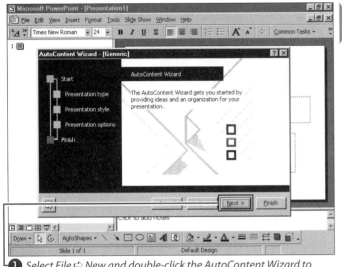

❶ Select File ➪ New and double-click the AutoContent Wizard to open it. Then click Next to open the Presentation Type Wizard screen.

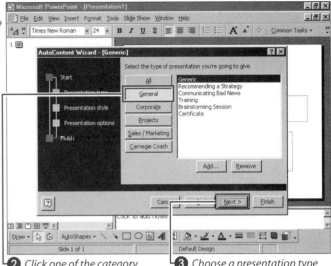

❷ Click one of the category buttons to display a list of available presentation types.

❸ Choose a presentation type and click Next to move to the next wizard screen.

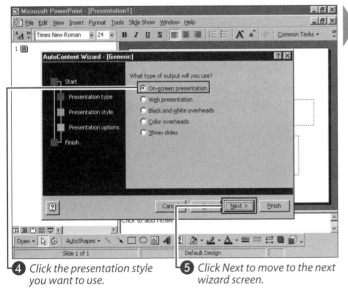

❹ Click the presentation style you want to use.

❺ Click Next to move to the next wizard screen.

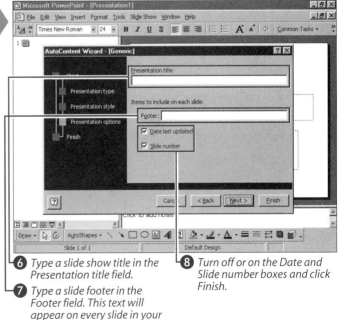

❻ Type a slide show title in the Presentation title field.

❼ Type a slide footer in the Footer field. This text will appear on every slide in your presentation.

❽ Turn off or on the Date and Slide number boxes and click Finish.

Using Design Templates

A slide template is a design for a PowerPoint presentation that has some color and graphics already in place. The color scheme and graphics automatically appear on every slide in the presentation. PowerPoint's predesigned templates each include a coordinated color scheme and background graphics such as a border or a graphic bar under the title text. These templates have descriptive names such as *Artsy*, *Blueprint*, *Nature*, and *Strategic*.

You can select a design template from the New Office Document dialog box or the opening PowerPoint screen, or by choosing the template from the Format menu inside PowerPoint.

The upper-left figure on the facing page shows the design templates displayed in the New Office Document dialog box. Click one of these templates (Artsy, Azure, and so on) to see a preview at the right. Sample text is included but it is "greeked," so the text is gobbledygook. Study these templates carefully. There's probably one that sets the right mood for your current presentation. Also, you'll learn something about PowerPoint slide design.

As you can see from the figure at the upper-right of the facing page, you can work from a similar list of templates after you open PowerPoint. This dialog box, however, shows only options for PowerPoint and not for Word, Excel and Access documents. Depending on the method you use to display the templates list, you may see slightly different choices, as you can see in the lower-left figure.

Once you've chosen a design template, PowerPoint either opens the New Slide dialog box — where you choose an AutoLayout (for new presentations) — or simply applies the chosen design template to an existing presentation. If you're applying the template to an existing presentation, all the slides will be converted to the new design.

If you are applying the template to a new presentation, you'll have a show with one slide (see the lower-right figure on the facing page). Now you can type text in the existing slide, add new slides, change the header and footer, and so on to complete the presentation.

TAKE NOTE

▶ INSTALLING TEMPLATES

When you are selecting a template, you may see a message that tells you a particular template has not yet been installed. If you have the Office 2000 or PowerPoint 2000 install diskettes or CD-ROM, you can click OK to install the template.

▶ ADDING SLIDES

Once you have selected a design template for a new PowerPoint presentation, choose New Slide from the Insert menu to add more slides. Choose an AutoLayout, add your text, and repeat as necessary.

CROSS-REFERENCE

See Chapter 9 for more information on enhancing your presentations with layout and design changes.

FIND IT ONLINE

Try **www.microsoft.com/office/enhpowerpoint.asp** for downloadable PowerPoint enhancements and add-ins, including new templates.

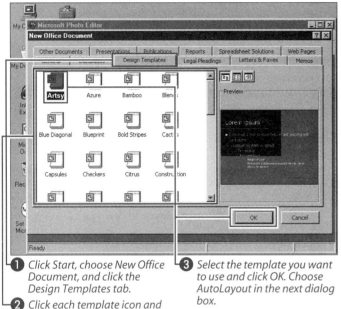

1 Click Start, choose New Office Document, and click the Design Templates tab.

2 Click each template icon and look at the preview at the right of the display.

3 Select the template you want to use and click OK. Choose AutoLayout in the next dialog box.

4 Relaunch PowerPoint, choose Design Templates on the opening dialog box, then click one or more design templates to preview the designs.

5 Select a design, click OK, or double-click the design name. Choose AutoLayout for the first slide. Create additional slides as desired.

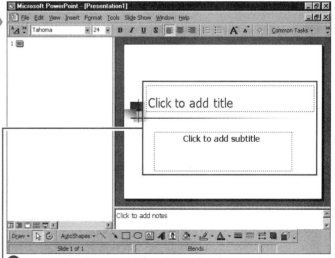

6 Now change the template by choosing Apply Design Template from the Format menu. Double-click a different design to apply it to the presentation you have open.

7 Type required text on the first slide and add new slides as necessary.

Using Presentation Designs

Presentation designs are similar to design templates, except they include slides that contain colors, graphics, AutoLayout designs, and sample text. These designs help you with the structure and mood that fit the topic of a new presentation.

To select a presentation design, you can click the Presentation Designs tab in the New Office Document dialog box. Alternatively, from within PowerPoint, you can click the Presentations tab in the New Presentation dialog box.

In either case, you can click a presentation design to see a preview of that design. (See the upper-left figure on the facing page.) After you choose the design you want, PowerPoint creates a sample presentation with a unified theme.

With most presentation designs, the first slide you see is for the title. The design makes room for a presentation title and perhaps a subtitle. Step through the slides (use Page Down or the scrollbars) to edit the information that is automatically included. Switch to the Slide Sorter view for an overview of the entire presentation (see the upper-right figure on the facing page). Alternately, you can use the outline on the left side of the slide screen, if you wish, to add or remove slides or edit slide text.

Double-click any slide in the Slide Sorter view to edit it. Click any existing text and PowerPoint opens the associated text box for editing, as shown in the lower-left figure on the next page. I've shown this slide at 66 percent with the outline and notes windows shrunk. Grab the bars between the slide and other objects and drag to view more of a particular window while keeping the other windows readily available.

PowerPoint chooses a text style that matches the presentation design. To change fonts, open the Font dialog box (see the lower-right figure on the next page). Remember that the presentation designs are just starting points. You should step through each sample slide, try to relate it to the presentation you are designing, and consider ways to make each slide — and the entire presentation — uniquely yours.

Different presentation designs use different fonts and different font sizes. When you open a new blank document, the default font is Times New Roman, with slide titles in 44-point text and bulleted lists and other text in 32-point. Change these defaults as required. Consider the size of your audience and how you will present the material (computer screen, projector, printout, and so on). You can also adjust color and other font characteristics from this dialog box.

> **TAKE NOTE**
>
> **CREATING CERTIFICATES**
>
> PowerPoint is designed to help you build slide shows. However, the drawing and design tools it contains also are useful for creating certificates, booklet covers, signs, and announcements. Choose Certificate from the Presentations tab of the New Presentation dialog box to get an idea. Use this as a starting point for making your own one-slide presentation to sell something or to make an announcement.

CROSS-REFERENCE

There's more information on creating PowerPoint presentations in Chapter 12.

FIND IT ONLINE

Try www.microsoft.com/ork to browse the Office Resource Kit for additional information on PowerPoint design concepts.

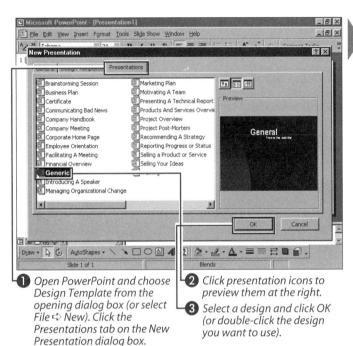

1 *Open PowerPoint and choose Design Template from the opening dialog box (or select File ➪ New). Click the Presentations tab on the New Presentation dialog box.*

2 *Click presentation icons to preview them at the right.*

3 *Select a design and click OK (or double-click the design you want to use).*

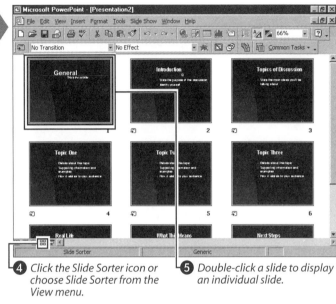

4 *Click the Slide Sorter icon or choose Slide Sorter from the View menu.*

5 *Double-click a slide to display an individual slide.*

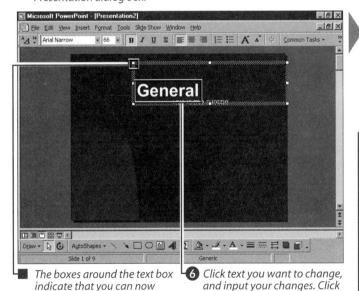

■ *The boxes around the text box indicate that you can now edit the text.*

6 *Click text you want to change, and input your changes. Click outside the text box to accept the text.*

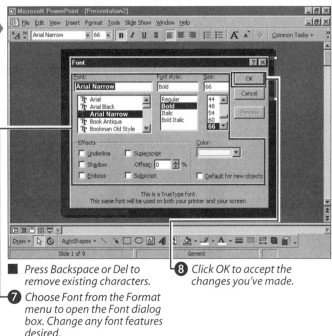

■ *Press Backspace or Del to remove existing characters.*

7 *Choose Font from the Format menu to open the Font dialog box. Change any font features desired.*

8 *Click OK to accept the changes you've made.*

39

Personal Workbook

Q&A

1 You can start a new PowerPoint presentation in four basic ways. What are they?

_____

_____

_____

_____

2 How do you change text on an existing text slide?

_____

_____

_____

3 Describe the difference between a *design template* and a *presentation design*.

_____

_____

_____

4 What is the *AutoContent Wizard*? How do you start it?

_____

_____

_____

5 PowerPoint supports presentation types in addition to a conventional slide show with a stand-up presenter. What are they?

_____

_____

_____

6 The AutoLayout section of the New Slide dialog box lets you choose how individual slides appear. How do you open this dialog box?

_____

_____

_____

7 How can you edit the font characteristics of existing text on a PowerPoint slide?

_____

_____

8 When might you want to create a PowerPoint presentation with only one slide?

_____

_____

ANSWERS: PAGE 302

EXTRA PRACTICE

1 Launch PowerPoint and open a new, blank presentation.

2 Demonstrate two ways to access the New Presentation dialog box.

3 Open a new PowerPoint presentation with a presentation design to create a single-slide certificate.

4 Launch PowerPoint and start the AutoContent Wizard.

5 Open an existing or new PowerPoint presentation and select a slide. Then open the New Slide dialog box and select an AutoLayout to change the appearance of the current slide.

6 Open an existing or new PowerPoint presentation and apply a different presentation design.

REAL-WORLD APPLICATIONS

✔ You've been asked to introduce a nationally recognized guest speaker at your professional group's next meeting. You're intimidated by the thought of speaking in front of all those people. Not to worry. Launch PowerPoint and start the AutoContent Wizard. Choose Carnegie Coach from the second wizard screen and click Introducing a Speaker. When you complete the Wizard, you will have a PowerPoint presentation that will train you in presenting a speaker.

✔ You are learning PowerPoint on the fly as you produce presentations, and you'd like some ongoing help. Click the Office Assistant and choose Options. At the lower-right corner of the Options tab of the Office Assistant dialog box, click Show the Tip of the Day at startup to turn on automatic tips that appear each time you launch PowerPoint.

Visual Quiz

Describe how to open the dialog box shown here.

_____

_____

_____

_____

_____

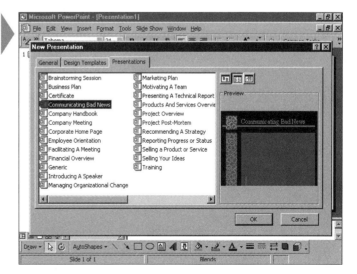

CHAPTER 4

MASTER THESE SKILLS

▶ Setting Up the Show

▶ Viewing the Show

▶ Projecting the Show

▶ Take It with You — Pack and Go

Showing Your Work

I have a saying I share with many new computer users: "Remember that no matter what you put into your computer, the ultimate goal is to get something out of it." You may be typing a letter using a word-processing program. The purpose of that letter is to have a printed document that you can send to someone. A spreadsheet? The goal is to create a document that tells you something about your business or personal finances.

The same is true of PowerPoint 2000. You may spend agonizing hours preparing a presentation, but the ultimate goal is a relatively brief performance in which you show the audience your work. Guidelines vary on how long it takes to prepare a presentation. I've heard people say they spend an hour of preparation for every minute of the slide show.

Assuming you know something about the topic you want to discuss and you are reasonably familiar with PowerPoint, you can do a lot better than that. I usually plan about a 3:1 ratio. If I'm asked to do a 20-minute presentation about a topic I know, I can put together a credible, though basic, PowerPoint slide show to support the presentation in about an hour.

Notice I said "basic" presentation. If I'm trying to really impress the audience and I want to use animation, custom graphics, sounds, maybe even motion video, or if I have to conduct more basic research, that ratio can climb dramatically. In this case, a 20-minute show can take me more than five or six hours.

Thankfully, there are ways to reduce this ratio. For one thing, don't think of any presentation as an isolated event. Think of it as a building block to help you with other presentations. Think in modules. As you create graphics or animation for a new show, think about previous work you've done. Perhaps you can use one or more slides from previous efforts. And, if you're frequently called upon to make presentations in your field, create generic slides — sales figures, trends, markets, competition — that will fit in multiple shows.

In this chapter, I show you how to use the basic presentations you learned to create in previous chapters.

Setting Up the Show

Among PowerPoint's strengths is the ability to start with a basic presentation and customize it for different audiences. You can also set parameters that control how the program functions in Slide Show view.

The top-left figure on the facing page shows a presentation setup screen. The settings in the Show type group tell PowerPoint how this show will be presented. The most common choice is Presented by a speaker (full screen). I use this setting 99 percent of the time.

If you're using PowerPoint as a training or promotional aid for individual users, you can choose between the full screen and a window. You can also set the show to run continuously so observers can watch as much or as little as they want. The final two choices let you turn off narration or animation. You might want to do this if you are presenting the show on a computer without a sound card, for example, or if you're using a slow machine.

The Set Up Show dialog box also lets you choose a range of slides instead of the full set, select a custom show (more on that later), and bypass preset timings. And you can change the color of the pen you use to draw on slides during a presentation via the pull-down window in the lower-left corner of this box.

Suppose you want to customize a slide show. First set up one or more custom shows. Look at the figure at the upper right of the following page. This is the Custom Shows dialog box, which is empty until you create a custom show. To do so, open the Define Custom Show dialog box (lower-left figure, following page). You can arrange the existing slides in any order and even use the same slide more than once. This means you can build a show with all your basic material, and then rearrange the slides for specific audiences.

Check out the lower-right figure on the next page. This is the Custom Shows dialog box from the top-right figure, only this time it contains some custom shows, which are designed from the slides and other objects in the current slide show. To use one of these custom shows, display the Set Up Show dialog box (from the Slide Show menu) and choose the version you want to use from the list.

TAKE NOTE

TIMING A SHOW

After you have created a custom show, you may need to find out how long it will take you to cover the edited material. From the Slide Show menu, choose Rehearse Timings. PowerPoint will display the first custom show slide and a timer. Start talking and move through the slides as if you were in front of your audience. PowerPoint will keep an accurate record of how long each slide's material required.

CROSS-REFERENCE

See Chapter 13 for additional information on steps you can take to prepare a PowerPoint presentation for a public audience.

FIND IT ONLINE

www.presentations.com is a multi-purpose site that offers hints on improving meeting and presentation skills, as well as hardware and design tips.

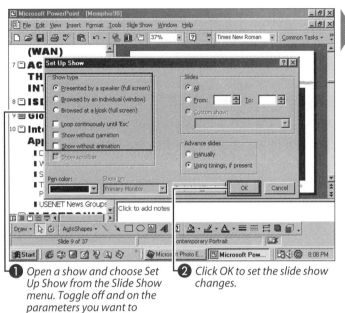

① Open a show and choose Set Up Show from the Slide Show menu. Toggle off and on the parameters you want to change.

② Click OK to set the slide show changes.

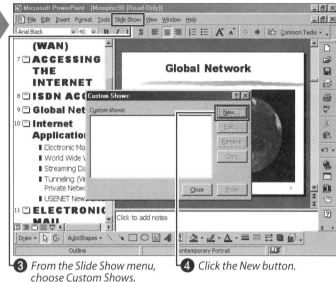

③ From the Slide Show menu, choose Custom Shows.

④ Click the New button.

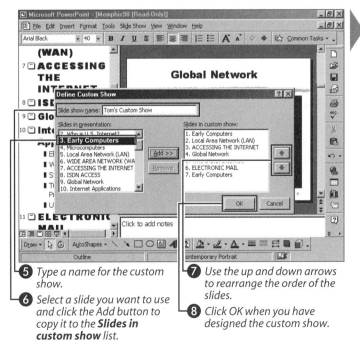

⑤ Type a name for the custom show.

⑥ Select a slide you want to use and click the Add button to copy it to the **Slides in custom show** list.

⑦ Use the up and down arrows to rearrange the order of the slides.

⑧ Click OK when you have designed the custom show.

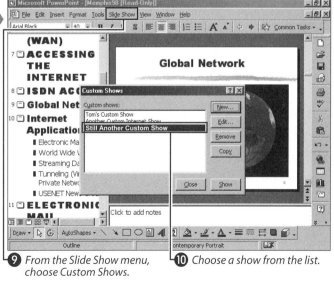

⑨ From the Slide Show menu, choose Custom Shows.

⑩ Choose a show from the list.

Viewing the Show

To view your presentation, you can use the Slide Show option from the View menu. In Slide Show view, you can hide the outline and notes sections as well as all program menus and toolbars to present the current slide in full-screen view (see the top-left figure on the following page). Use this view for on-screen or projected shows.

Once in Slide Show view, you can advance to the next slide with one of these keys: Spacebar, Enter, N, down arrow, Page Down, or right arrow. To back up one slide, hold down the Ctrl key and press the left mouse button, or press one of the following keys: left arrow, P, up arrow, Page Up, or Backspace.

PowerPoint supports a number of other navigation keys. I can never seem to remember all the possibilities, but you can always display a list of available command keys, such as the one shown at the upper right of the following page. You have several such tools at your disposal while you are presenting a PowerPoint slide show.

Other PowerPoint utilities can be useful during a live presentation. You can access them from a shortcut menu (lower-left figure, facing page). In addition to slide navigation choices, this menu lets you access some presentation utilities, including the Meeting Minder and the Slide Meter. You can also use this shortcut menu to choose different pointer devices. Arrow is the default. If you choose Pen, you can use your mouse to draw on the screen (lower-right figure, next page), guiding the viewer's attention to a particular area of the slide. Note that anything you draw with the pen isn't permanent. Any marks you make disappear when you move to another slide or close the Slide Show view.

TAKE NOTE

▶ EXITING A SLIDE SHOW PRESENTATION

Press Esc at any time during a presentation to return to the screen that you were viewing prior to starting the slide show. If you were viewing the slides in Slide Sorter view before starting the slide show, you will be returned to the Slide Sorter if you press Esc during a show. You can also use the Slide Show shortcut menu. Just choose End Show after right-clicking on any slide.

▶ SKIPPING SLIDES IN A PRESENTATION

If you decide to skip one or more slides in a presentation, don't delete them. Instead, select the slide you don't want to use, and then choose Hide Slide from the Slide Show menu. The hidden slide will not be displayed during a show, but it will appear in the Slide, Slide Sorter, and Outline views.

CROSS-REFERENCE

See Chapter 14 for more information on using the presentation utilities described in this chapter.

FIND IT ONLINE

Try **http://www.computertips.com/Microsoft office/MsPowerPoint/aheader.htm** for ongoing PowerPoint tips.

❶ *With a presentation open, click the Slide Show icon (or select View ⇨ Slide Show) to display a show in full-screen mode.*

■ *Use the Slide Show navigation keys to move forward and backward in the presentation.*

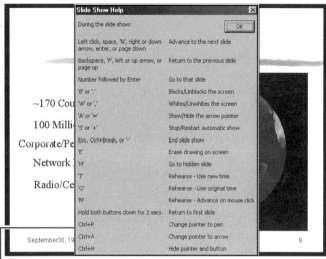

❷ *Press F1 to display the Slide Show Help screen.*

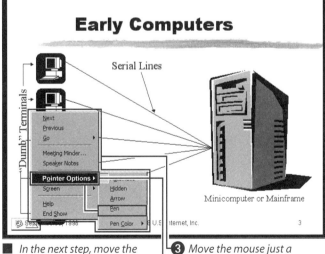

■ *In the next step, move the mouse just enough so that PowerPoint senses it has been moved.*

❸ *Move the mouse just a fraction to display the slide command button. Click this icon to display the shortcut menu.*

❹ *Select Pointer Options ⇨ Pen.*

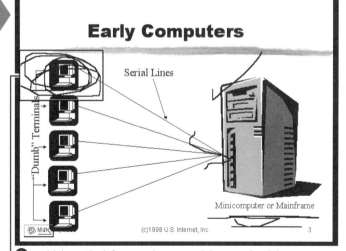

❺ *Hold down the left mouse button and draw on the slide.*

Projecting the Show

PowerPoint is an excellent tool for one-on-one training or for augmenting your sales presentation to a small group. The computer screen is too small for larger audiences, however. That's when you need a projector.

There are two common technologies: large-screen (projection) television and direct computer projection. The upper-left figure on the facing page shows a typical computer-to-projector hardware connection. If you are using a projector that connects directly to your computer, you won't need the interface box shown in this drawing.

Two popular computer-projector technologies exist today: self-contained projectors with a wire that connects directly to your computer's monitor port, and LCD screens that connect to your computer and use an overhead projector. If you're using the LCD/overhead combination, you'll need a projector with plenty of power. Standard overhead projectors use 400- or 600-watt bulbs. These are marginal for use with PowerPoint. A 900-watt or larger bulb is a better — if more expensive — choice.

PowerPoint 2000 includes a projector-setup wizard. The opening wizard screen is shown in the upper-right figure on the following page. As you move through the wizard screens, you can choose which computer you are using and review instructions for turning on projector output.

As you step through this wizard, you'll have a chance to choose the projector you are using from a list — or to have PowerPoint try to detect it — and you can test sound output as well. The projector-selection screen is shown in the lower-left figure on the following page.

When the wizard is finished, it sets the screen display for optimum display with the projector you have specified. This includes changing the screen resolution to match the capabilities of the projector. Next, the Set Up Show dialog box reopens.

TAKE NOTE

CHOOSING A PROJECTOR

Check the resolution supported by the projector you choose. The standard computer screen displays 640 pixels by 480 pixels. If you use your machine with a higher resolution — 800-by-600 or 1,024-by-768 — then the presentations you design depend on this resolution. A projector that can display only the standard resolution won't do a good job with your high-resolution PowerPoint presentations.

PROJECTING THE IMAGE

Projection hardware may include a standard computer interface and connecting cables. If you're using a desktop machine, remove the cable that goes to your monitor and plug in the cable from the projector. If you're using a laptop machine, you may have to choose external display from a setup menu or you may have to press a special key combination to turn on the external monitor port. Use the Projector Wizard to help you.

CROSS-REFERENCE

See Chapter 16 for more information on preparing the show and making PowerPoint work your way.

FIND IT ONLINE

www.presentersuniversity.com/ offers tips, instruction, graphics, and other presentation resources.

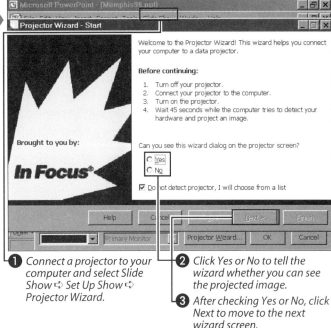

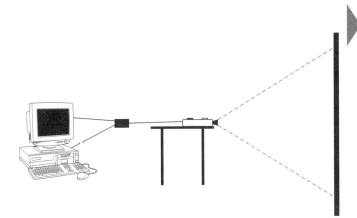

■ *You can connect your computer directly to a VGA or RGB projector, or use a VGA-to-NTSC converter to send the computer output to a standard television or projection television.*

① *Connect a projector to your computer and select Slide Show ➪ Set Up Show ➪ Projector Wizard.*

② *Click Yes or No to tell the wizard whether you can see the projected image.*

③ *After checking Yes or No, click Next to move to the next wizard screen.*

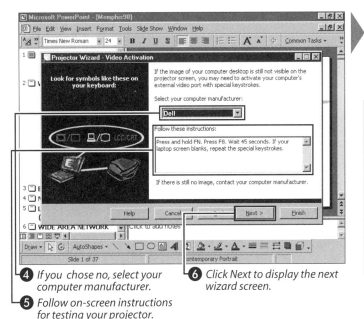

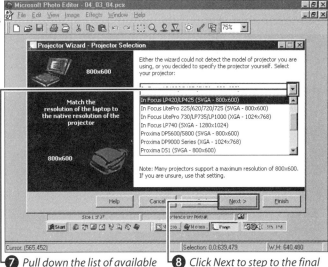

④ *If you chose no, select your computer manufacturer.*

⑤ *Follow on-screen instructions for testing your projector.*

⑥ *Click Next to display the next wizard screen.*

⑦ *Pull down the list of available projectors if you told PowerPoint you would choose from a list. Otherwise, the wizard will try to detect your projector hardware for you.*

⑧ *Click Next to step to the final wizard screen.*

Take It with You — Pack and Go

owerPoint 2000 is relatively efficient at storing presentations, but if you use screen captures, scanned art, sound files, and other multimedia elements, a PowerPoint file can still be large. That's where the Pack and Go Wizard comes in. Use this wizard to copy a presentation and the PowerPoint viewer onto a floppy-disk set or other storage device.

The opening screen for the Pack and Go Wizard is shown in the upper-left figure on the next page. Here you let PowerPoint know which presentation you want to pack, whether to include the viewer, and so on.

You can include just the current presentation or multiple presentations. Browse your disk to choose any additional presentations you want to include in the pack-and-go package.

You'll want to make sure that all the fonts you use will be available at the other end, so you can preserve your presentation in the exact format you carefully chose when creating it. PowerPoint comes equipped with an Embed TrueType fonts option (upper-right figure, next page) that takes care of this for you if you select it (at the Links screen).

After you answer all the questions, the wizard provides a summary of what it will do next (lower-left figure, following page), and then starts its work. You'll have to insert disks as required until the entire presentation is stored to disk.

Although this wizard is designed primarily to help you transfer a large presentation file to another computer via floppy disks, it is also an excellent tool for sending files to someone over the Internet.

Some Internet e-mail servers limit the size of the files you can send and some e-mail readers can't handle large files. Use Pack and Go to compress the presentation and copy it to floppy disks. This generates a series of files, each less than 1.2MB. Most e-mail programs will handle files of this size.

You can also send your files to someone else via e-mail, create one e-mail message for each floppy in the set using PowerPoint's Insert ⇨ File (or the proper command sequence in your e-mail program for attaching a file to an e-mail message), and specify the file on each floppy. Note that the first floppy in a Pack and Go set includes two files: one that will unpack the presentation (pngsetup.exe) and the first piece of the presentation (pres0.ppz). Each of the other disks contains one file, which is a slice of the total presentation file.

TAKE NOTE

GETTING PACK AND GO HELP

On the first screen of the Pack and Go Wizard is a question-mark icon. Click this icon to display the Office Assistant, which will walk you through completing the information the wizard needs to pack your presentation.

CROSS-REFERENCE

See Chapter 18 for more information on transferring a PowerPoint presentation to another computer.

FIND IT ONLINE

For a look at what someone else has done with Pack and Go, try **http://www.osha-slc.gov/NewInit/ BBIM/dwnloads/.html**.

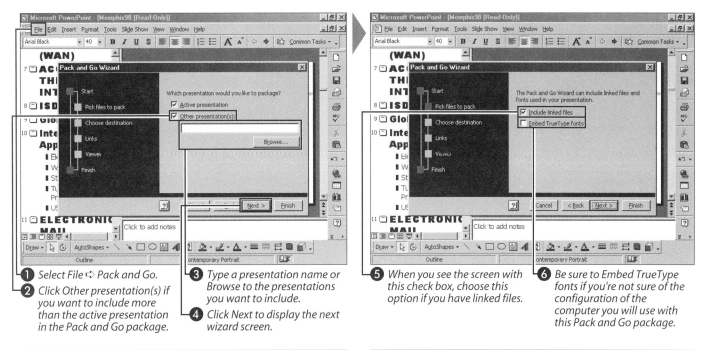

❶ Select File ➪ Pack and Go.

❷ Click Other presentation(s) if you want to include more than the active presentation in the Pack and Go package.

❸ Type a presentation name or Browse to the presentations you want to include.

❹ Click Next to display the next wizard screen.

❺ When you see the screen with this check box, choose this option if you have linked files.

❻ Be sure to Embed TrueType fonts if you're not sure of the configuration of the computer you will use with this Pack and Go package.

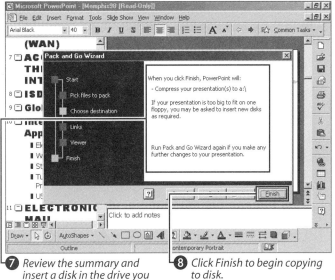

❼ Review the summary and insert a disk in the drive you specified earlier.

❽ Click Finish to begin copying to disk.

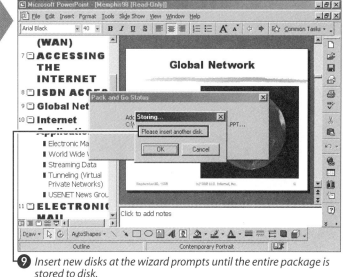

❾ Insert new disks at the wizard prompts until the entire package is stored to disk.

Personal Workbook

Q&A

1 How much time can you expect to spend preparing a 20-minute PowerPoint presentation?

_____

_____

_____

_____

2 What dialog box do you use to specify how your PowerPoint presentation will be displayed?

_____

_____

_____

_____

3 Describe how to create a show that uses only a specified range of slides from a PowerPoint presentation.

_____

_____

_____

4 How can you turn off animation and narration in a PowerPoint slide show that has these features incorporated into its design?

_____

_____

_____

_____

5 What is the purpose of the Projector Wizard?

_____

_____

_____

_____

6 What two general types of projector technology are commonly used with PowerPoint presentations?

_____

_____

_____

_____

ANSWERS: PAGE 303

EXTRA PRACTICE

1. Open the dialog box required to change the color of the pen you use to draw on a slide during a slide show.

2. Launch the Projector Wizard and specify a particular brand and model of projector instead of letting the wizard choose the projector for you.

3. Create a Pack and Go floppy-disk set that includes the PowerPoint Viewer.

4. Open the dialog box required to help you time a custom PowerPoint presentation.

5. Open the dialog box required to create a custom show from an existing PowerPoint presentation.

6. Display a list of available custom shows, select one, and display the Slide Show view.

REAL-WORLD APPLICATIONS

✔ You can use the Pack and Go Wizard to store one or more PowerPoint presentations, along with the PowerPoint Viewer, so you can carry a set of floppy disks or high-capacity disks to another computer in a distant city. Even if you are carrying a laptop with your presentation on it, it is a good idea to create a pack-and-go package to give you a backup in case you have a problem with your laptop.

✔ PowerPoint can help you build a suite of presentations to cover a wide range of needs. You can create different shows for each presentation, or you can design a generic show that includes all of the slides you are likely to need and create custom shows from this generic slide list using the Custom Shows dialog box from the Slide Show menu.

Visual Quiz

Describe how to display the dialog box shown here.

_____

_____

_____

_____

_____

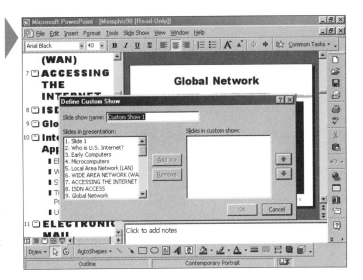

CHAPTER **5**

MASTER
THESE
SKILLS

▶ **Using Notes Pages**

▶ **Using Handouts**

▶ **Adding Headers and Footers**

▶ **Using the Spell Checker**

▶ **Using Find and Replace**

▶ **Using Undo**

▶ **Configuring AutoCorrect**

Using Other Presentation and Design Aids

I've said it before and it's worth repeating: PowerPoint is flexible enough to let you use as much or as little of its power as you know, understand, or need at the moment. With the information I've covered so far in this book, you can design and build basic PowerPoint presentations and present a show. You can use only this level of PowerPoint functionality and still get a lot out of the program.

The good news, however, is that PowerPoint offers a wide range of other useful features, utilities, and tools to help you enhance your presentation design and your effectiveness as a presenter. You may not use them every time you do a show, but you'll use some of them some of the time as you gain expertise with the program.

In this chapter, I show you how to use such basic presentation aids as slide headers and footers, the multilevel Undo, AutoCorrect, and speaker's notes and handouts. You'll learn how to use these features as part of your presentation design and as aids to enhance the presentation itself.

In later chapters I cover even more of PowerPoint's features, so you can use this book as you would the software — take or leave as much of the information and the capabilities as you need right now and pick up more later. At the same time, don't forget to push yourself a little as you learn more about PowerPoint and the presentation process in general.

I remember a job interview I had many years ago. I arrogantly informed my prospective employer that I had ten years of experience in the field. I'll never forget his response: "What we have to find out is whether you have ten years of experience or one year of experience ten times." Don't get stuck doing the same thing in the same way. Vary your presentations. You'll have more fun and your audience will be grateful.

Using Notes Pages

If you think of PowerPoint as simply an electronic slide-show program, you will get some functionality out of it, but you'll miss some of its power. I use this program to present text charts, drawings, and pictures to an audience of 2 to 200 people. But PowerPoint can do more. Consider the Notes Pages feature, for example.

The Notes section is used to document or annotate individual slides to serve as speaker notes or as audience handouts. Like a Word document header or footer, space for notes is always there whether you use it or not.

In the Normal PowerPoint view, you can see the beginnings of the notes for the current slide in the window just below the slide.

Check out the upper-left figure on the following page. It shows the Notes view on a page by itself, separate from other elements such as the outline and slide. Have you ever received copies of a PowerPoint presentation after it's over? If the speaker has designed the slides properly, they are fairly sparse, have little detail, and may be difficult to follow a day after the speech. Notes pages as handouts are more useful.

When your slide show is complete, you can print the Notes pages. The slide image will be at the top of the page and the note at the bottom. All slides will print, even those without notes. Adding notes to your slides doesn't mean that you will see notes during a presentation: you see them only when you turn on Notes Pages view.

You may also want to use the Notes pages as illustrations in a longer document. To do this, send the Notes pages to a Microsoft Word document using the dialog box shown in the lower-left position on the following page. A sample slide show in Word is shown in the lower-right figure on the facing page. A large slide show or one with photographs and other graphic elements can take awhile to export.

Include the notes with the slide images for use as captions. Alternately, choose the Blank lines next to slides option in the Write-Up dialog box and write new captions.

TAKE NOTE

► CHANGING NOTES DISPLAY SIZE

PowerPoint notes are displayed at 33 percent of full size. That's too small to read on most screens. Use the size field (the small window that says 33%) on the toolbar to display notes at 50 percent or larger so it's easier to read and type new ones. If you make the Notes display quite large, you can still tell how much of the available area you are using by referring to the thumbnail that is automatically displayed with the Notes page.

► FRAMING SLIDES

Click the Frame Slides button in the Print dialog box to outline each slide on the Notes pages.

CROSS-REFERENCE

See the next section, "Using Handouts," for information on another useful presentation view that you will find helpful.

FIND IT ONLINE

Visit the University of Georgia's Frequently Asked Questions and Answers page at **http://www.uga.edu/~ucns/helpdesk/information/howto/Windows/**.

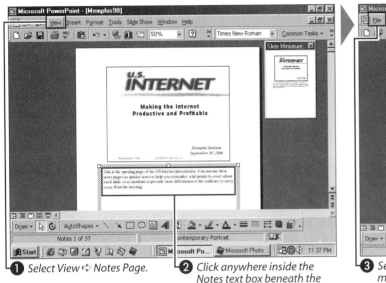

1 Select View ➪ Notes Page.

2 Click anywhere inside the Notes text box beneath the current slide and type notes to accompany this slide.

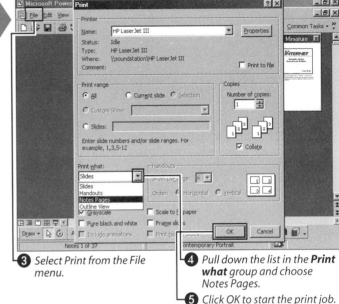

3 Select Print from the File menu.

4 Pull down the list in the **Print what** group and choose Notes Pages.

5 Click OK to start the print job.

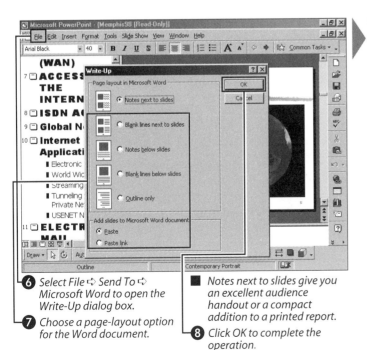

6 Select File ➪ Send To ➪ Microsoft Word to open the Write-Up dialog box.

7 Choose a page-layout option for the Word document.

■ Notes next to slides give you an excellent audience handout or a compact addition to a printed report.

8 Click OK to complete the operation.

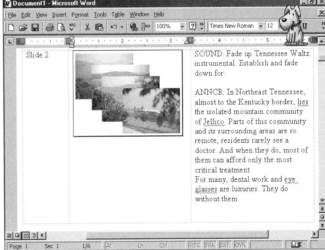

■ Wait! This could be a lengthy process if you use a lot of slides or numerous graphic images in your presentation.

■ This figure shows a slide with notes inserted into Microsoft Word.

Using Handouts

As noted earlier, you can use Notes pages as audience handouts. Another PowerPoint utility, Handouts, is also useful for giving the audience something to carry away from your presentation.

When you print slides, PowerPoint uses landscape formatting (i.e., with the page on its side) and prints one slide to a full piece of 8.5 × 11 paper. Notes pages, remember, print the slide image at the top of a portrait-formatted page, with the notes in the lower half. Handouts print two, four, or six slide images on a single piece of paper. You can see a typical Notes page at the upper left of the next page and a Print dialog box for printing four slides on a single-page handout at the upper right.

You can't display handouts on the screen: you can only print them. Use handouts when a text description of each slide is less important than just providing a complete set of slides for the audience. With up to six slides per page, Handouts can also save a lot of paper versus printing each slide on a single piece of paper.

You have some other choices for formatting handouts in the Print dialog box. For example, you can tell PowerPoint to frame the slides, meaning it'll draw a line around each slide on the handout page to separate it from the background and from other slides. This option is particularly useful when you put six images on a page — it helps readers distinguish them from each other.

The lower left figure on the facing page shows PowerPoint handouts in a "four-up" format — four slides to a page. At the lower right you can see a handout with six slides per page. Which format you choose depends on the material you're covering, the audience, and what tools you need to leave with them.

One of the problems with handout pages is they print with only the images you specify and no additional text. At the very least, you'll want to put a page number and perhaps the title of the presentation on each handout page. This is easy to do using a footer (see the next task for more information on this procedure).

TAKE NOTE

▶ PRINTING SELECT HANDOUT SLIDES

You don't have to print all the slides in your presentation on the handout pages. Click the button next to the Slides label in the Print dialog box, and then enter the range of slides you want to print. You can use a contiguous range of slides, individual slides, or a combination: 1, 5, 8-12, 16, 22.

▶ CHANGING ORDER OF HANDOUT SLIDES

By default, the slides on a handout sheet print in horizontal order, with slide one at the top left, slide two at the top right, slide three under slide one, and so on. You can change the order by clicking the buttons beside the Horizontal and Vertical labels in the Handouts group in the Print dialog box.

CROSS-REFERENCE

See the next task, "Adding Headers and Footers," for more information on formatting slides with recurring information at the top and bottom.

FIND IT ONLINE

For tips on how and when to use handouts, see http://www.uwf.edu/~coe/tutorials/technolo/power pnt/powerpnt.htm#6.

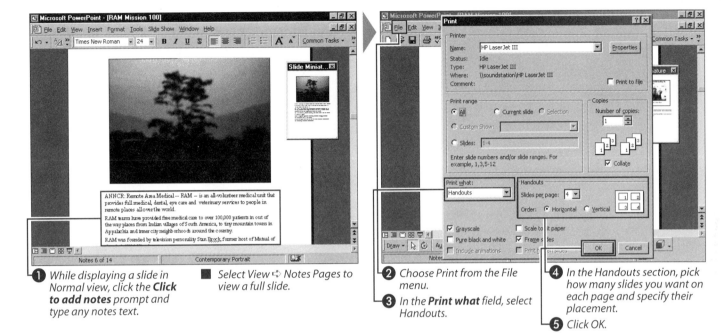

1 While displaying a slide in Normal view, click the **Click to add notes** prompt and type any notes text.

■ Select View ➪ Notes Pages to view a full slide.

2 Choose Print from the File menu.

3 In the **Print what** field, select Handouts.

4 In the Handouts section, pick how many slides you want on each page and specify their placement.

5 Click OK.

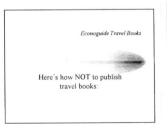

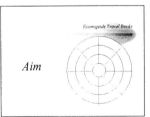

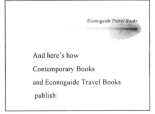

■ You can't display handouts on the screen — you have to print them to see them. Here's a four-slide handout.

■ Here's a portion of a six-slide handout. I like this format better than having only four slides per page.

Adding Headers and Footers

Headers and footers let you add recurring information to each slide or handout. You might include the show title, the date it was designed or presented, slide numbers, and perhaps a copyright notice.

Adding a footer to one or more slides in a PowerPoint presentation is easy using the tabbed dialog box shown at the upper left on the facing page. The Notes and Handouts tab is on top by default, so you have to click the Slide tab to see the options in this figure.

By default, a Date and time field is available in the slide footer, and there's space for you to type your own footer. Placing a fixed date in the footer is a simple matter of typing it in the blank field below the Fixed radio button. To change the date to match your computer's internal clock, click the radio button next to Update automatically and choose the date format from the pull-down list. (See the upper-right figure on the facing page.)

The Slide tab has two more check boxes that can help you customize the slide footer: Slide number and Don't show on title slide. If you click Slide number, PowerPoint places a number in the lower right of the current slide or all slides (depending on whether you click Apply or Apply to All when you exit this dialog box). The footer appears in the bottom middle and the date in the bottom left.

Click Don't show on title slide to make the title slide special. Typically, you don't want the footer text on the title slide simply because you are displaying all of the information you would put in the footer on the title slide anyway.

As you can see, the Notes and Handouts tab contains a different set of options (lower-left figure, facing page). Notes and handouts are intended to be printed on paper, so you can give them a header as well as a footer. Notice particularly the Preview window on this tab. It shows you the placement of the four elements in the header and footer: the header text, the date, the page number, and the footer text. Check and uncheck these page elements to see where each appears.

TAKE NOTE

ADDING SLIDE HEADERS

Can't do it. Although this dialog box is titled Header and Footer, adding a header is possible only on the Notes and Handouts tab. On the Slide tab, all you can do is place footers. There's a good reason for this. Normally, you will use at least one title line for each slide. Having header on each slide would be redundant in most cases.

CHANGING HEADER AND FOOTER PLACEMENT

You can change the placement and appearance of the header and footer material from either the slide or the Notes and handout pages master screens (accessed by selecting View ➪ Master).

CROSS-REFERENCE

See Chapter 7 for more information on how to control the placement and appearance of headers and footers on your slides or Notes and handout pages.

FIND IT ONLINE

The six lessons at **http://www.iupui.edu/~jpcramer/ r547/SAC/ppt.htm** will help you improve your PowerPoint skills.

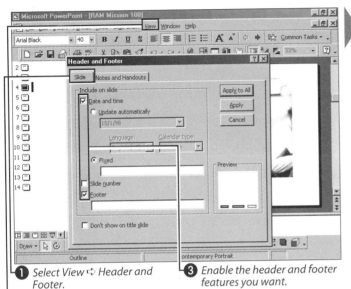

1 Select View ⇨ Header and Footer.

2 In the Header and Footer dialog box, click the Slide tab if it is not already on top.

3 Enable the header and footer features you want.

4 Click the button beside Update automatically.

5 Pull down the list of available formats in the Date field and select one.

6 Click on the Notes and Handouts tab.

7 Choose the elements you want to appear in the header and footer for notes and handouts.

■ Remember, you set slide headers and footers separately from those for notes and handouts.

8 Click Apply or Apply to All to make the changes.

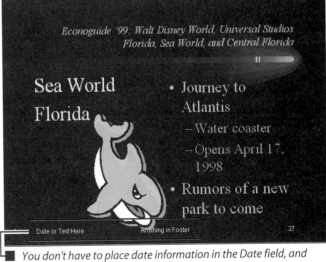

■ You don't have to place date information in the Date field, and nearly anything goes for a slide footer.

Using the Spell Checker

Many years ago in a college English class, a professor yelled my name, shook her head at my raised hand and quizzical expression, and observed: "Badgett, thank god you don't plan to be a writer. You'd never make it 'cause you can't spell worth a damn."

Some 35 years and 45 books later, I owe whatever modicum of success I enjoy to the computer and its built-in spell checker. PowerPoint's spell checker isn't a complete cure for a spelling-challenged presenter, but it will keep you out of serious trouble.

The spell checker is an automatic part of PowerPoint, but there's at least one item to check to make sure the checker works correctly: the language setting (see the top-left figure on the following page). If you select *no proofing* in the Language dialog box, none of your presentation will be spell-checked and, if you're like me, you could easily be embarrassed when you stand up in front of a group.

When you do select a language in this box, PowerPoint uses a squiggly red line to mark any words that don't appear in its internal directory. As you can see from the upper-right figure on the facing page, the spell checker will suggest correct spellings when you right-click a flagged word. Double-click the correct spelling to insert it into your slide. If your word is spelled correctly, you can add it to your personal (custom) dictionary. Another option is to tell the spell checker to ignore the word.

You can browse more possibilities for the highlighted word by choosing Spelling from the pop-up menu (lower-left figure, next page). As you choose correct words, ignore words, or add new words to your dictionary, the spell checker moves from slide to slide. If you choose a word that is close to what you want and click Suggest, you'll see one or more additional words that may be spelled similarly to the flagged word.

PowerPoint's built-in AutoCorrect feature can fix typos for you on the fly. You can add a word to the AutoCorrect list from the Spelling dialog box.

TAKE NOTE

CROSS-APPLICATION SPELL CHECKING

The PowerPoint spell checker shares dictionaries with Microsoft Word and other Office 2000 applications. You can build a custom dictionary in any Office product and use it in any other.

CHECKING THE SPELL CHECKER

When using the spell checker, keep in mind that it won't detect certain mistakes such as homonym errors — e.g., saying Electronic Male when you really mean *Electronic Mail*. The best advice I can give is to proofread your presentation, then print it and proofread it again.

CROSS-REFERENCE

See Chapter 11 for more information on using cross-application tools and techniques with PowerPoint 2000.

FIND IT ONLINE

Instructions for using Word 97/2000 to create your own custom dictionary for use in PowerPoint are at **http://www.microsoft.com/word/assistance/wdspdic1.asp**.

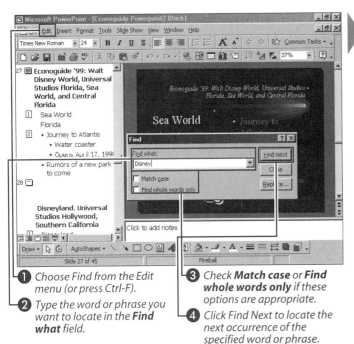

1. Choose Find from the Edit menu (or press Ctrl-F).

2. Type the word or phrase you want to locate in the **Find what** field.

3. Check **Match case** or **Find whole words only** if these options are appropriate.

4. Click Find Next to locate the next occurrence of the specified word or phrase.

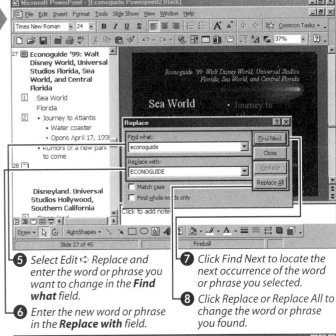

5. Select Edit ⇨ Replace and enter the word or phrase you want to change in the **Find what** field.

6. Enter the new word or phrase in the **Replace with** field.

7. Click Find Next to locate the next occurrence of the word or phrase you selected.

8. Click Replace or Replace All to change the word or phrase you found.

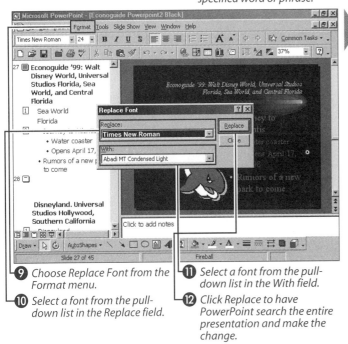

9. Choose Replace Font from the Format menu.

10. Select a font from the pull-down list in the Replace field.

11. Select a font from the pull-down list in the With field.

12. Click Replace to have PowerPoint search the entire presentation and make the change.

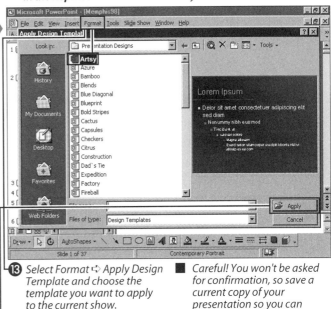

13. Select Format ⇨ Apply Design Template and choose the template you want to apply to the current show.

14. Click Apply to apply the template.

■ Careful! You won't be asked for confirmation, so save a current copy of your presentation so you can return to it if needed.

Using Find and Replace

What do you do when you've finished that last-minute, bet-your-job sales presentation and you learn that you've misspelled the client's name throughout? Easy: use Find and Replace, a valuable PowerPoint development tool.

Find and Replace is actually two utilities — one for find and another for replace. If you just want to locate a word or phrase somewhere in your current presentation, use Find (see the upper-left figure on the facing page). PowerPoint starts the search on the current slide, moves through the slides to the last one, and then starts over at the beginning each time you click Find Next.

Click the slide that contains the found word and make a change to the word or phrase. With the Find dialog box still on the screen, click Find Next to move to the next occurrence of the specified word or phrase. This process works well if you are making one or two changes; however, if you are changing many instances of a word or phrase, use Replace instead (see the upper-right figure on the following page). Notice that unless you check Match case in the Replace dialog box, the search routine won't care about the case of the search phrase. However, the Replace with field is case-sensitive, so you can replace one form of a word with another with this utility.

If you're using other Office 2000 applications — particularly Microsoft Word — you may be wondering how to use Find and Replace to locate special text features such as a specific font. In Word, you use an extra button in the Find or Replace dialog box. In PowerPoint, you must use the Replace Font utility (lower-left figure, next page). This is a semi-smart utility. If the new font causes a change in the way slide text fits the design, PowerPoint will automatically resize the text to make it fit. You'll see a message to this effect and have a chance to put things back the way they were. You can also turn off this automatic feature.

You can't change text attributes — bold, underline, and so on — in the same way as with Microsoft Word, but you can change information on the slide master (see Chapter 7) or apply the original or a new design template (lower-right figure, facing page).

TAKE NOTE

▶ FINDING PHRASES

If you're used to searching the Web, you may be tempted to enclose search phrases in quotation marks. Don't do this in PowerPoint. The quotes are treated as additional search characters and you won't find anything.

▶ REFINING FINDS

The PowerPoint Find routine locates any string of text you give it. Look for *re*, for example, and you'll find *treat*, *read*, and *reach*. Add a space after such search strings to narrow down the search.

CROSS-REFERENCE

See the section on AutoCorrect later in this chapter for tips on how to correct information as you type. Chapter 7 also covers this Find and Replace topic.

FIND IT ONLINE

http://www.microsoft.com/powerpointdev/tips/copsli.htm offers tips for using Copy and Paste to move objects and create slides.

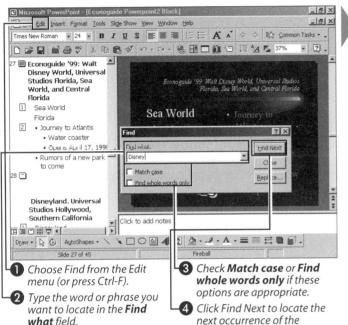

1 Choose Find from the Edit menu (or press Ctrl-F).

2 Type the word or phrase you want to locate in the **Find what** field.

3 Check **Match case** or **Find whole words only** if these options are appropriate.

4 Click Find Next to locate the next occurrence of the specified word or phrase.

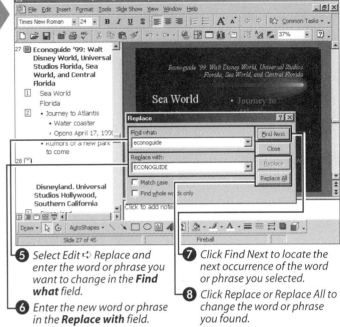

5 Select Edit ⇨ Replace and enter the word or phrase you want to change in the **Find what** field.

6 Enter the new word or phrase in the **Replace with** field.

7 Click Find Next to locate the next occurrence of the word or phrase you selected.

8 Click Replace or Replace All to change the word or phrase you found.

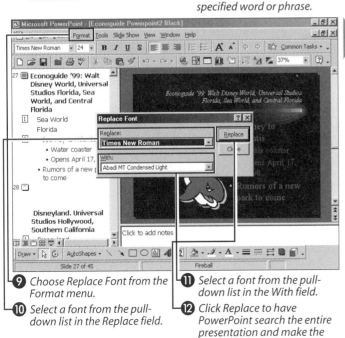

9 Choose Replace Font from the Format menu.

10 Select a font from the pull-down list in the Replace field.

11 Select a font from the pull-down list in the With field.

12 Click Replace to have PowerPoint search the entire presentation and make the change.

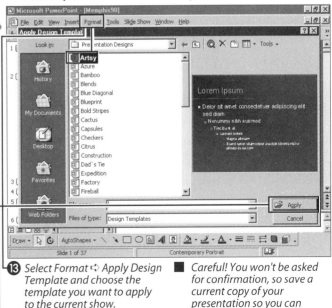

13 Select Format ⇨ Apply Design Template and choose the template you want to apply to the current show.

14 Click Apply to apply the template.

■ Careful! You won't be asked for confirmation, so save a current copy of your presentation so you can return to it if needed.

Using Undo

Did you ever wish you could push the words you just said back in your mouth, or pick yourself up from the bottom of the steps and try that descent again? That's what Undo does for your presentation design.

But wait! There's more. Undo stacks up all of your most recent actions — typing, Find and Replace, color settings — and lets you undo one or a series of them.

You can apply Undo in several ways. The most common method is to click the Undo icon (the square box with the left-facing arc and arrow) on the standard toolbar. One click cancels the last (most recent) action, a second click cancels the penultimate action, and so on. An action includes typing a single character as well as more global activities such as a search and replace. You can also choose Undo from the Edit menu or press Ctrl-Z.

Look at the upper-left figure on the following page. Do you see the list of recent actions that Undo can cancel? Unfortunately, Undo lists some tasks, such as typing, in a way that makes it hard to tell exactly what will be undone. The most recent tasks are at the top of the list. Undo one task by selecting the topmost action in the list, undo two actions by selecting the second entry in the list, and so on. When you choose an action, Undo selects all actions that follow it.

I sometimes undo an action, and then wish I had left well enough alone. PowerPoint covers this eventuality with a utility called Redo. Redo repeats actions you have previously cancelled with Undo. Like Undo, the Redo list is in inverse order, with the most recent

action on the top. Look at the upper-right figure on the next page. That list really is a top-down list. Think about it. On the Undo list, Replace Fonts was at the top with Typing on the bottom. I selected the second Typing entry from the Undo list, which included the Replace Fonts action above it. Now, the most recent action on the Redo list is the last one on the Undo list.

Normally, the Redo icon is hidden behind the More Buttons icon on the Standard toolbar. But you also can access the Undo/Redo command pair from the Edit menu (lower-left figure, next page).

TAKE NOTE

▶ CORRECTING TEXT ENTRY

Be careful as you undo text entries. Each character you type is a separate action, so to delete the word "two" from a slide, you need to use Undo three times. If you find and replace 20 occurrences of a particular word or phrase, on the other hand, the entire operation — all 20 replacements — is one action that you can undo with a single selection.

▶ CORRECTING GRAPHICS ENTRIES

Undo corrects graphics images and virtually anything else you can insert onto a PowerPoint presentation. Be aware, however, that undoing a graphics image can have profound effects on your PowerPoint slides. Backing out of undesired text entry may have minimal effects, but if you remove a graphics image, the slide's formatting is changed dramatically.

CROSS-REFERENCE

See the section earlier in this chapter on using Find and Replace, which is another way of changing previous actions.

FIND IT ONLINE

You'll find more about Undo and other PowerPoint features at **http://www.cant.ac.uk/title/PowerPoint/Part2/ppnt2.htm**.

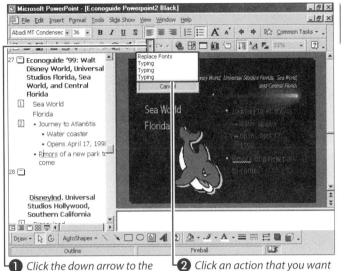

1 Click the down arrow to the right of the Undo icon on the standard toolbar.

2 Click an action that you want to undo.

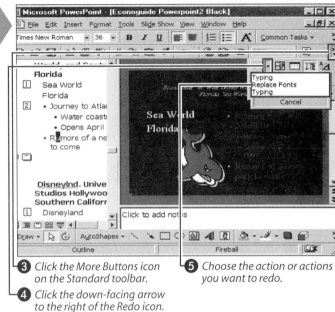

3 Click the More Buttons icon on the Standard toolbar.

4 Click the down-facing arrow to the right of the Redo icon.

5 Choose the action or actions you want to redo.

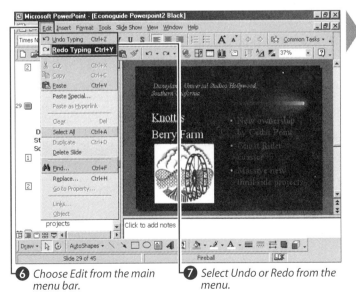

6 Choose Edit from the main menu bar.

7 Select Undo or Redo from the menu.

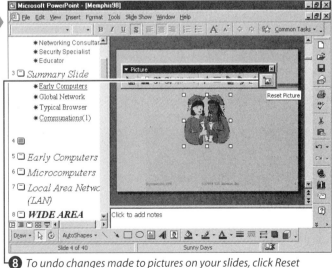

8 To undo changes made to pictures on your slides, click Reset Picture on the Picture toolbar.

Configuring AutoCorrect

If you've done any work at all in PowerPoint, you've probably already seen AutoCorrect. You can try it out by inserting a new slide in PowerPoint and typing a common text mistake, *adn*, in any text field. When you press the Space bar, AutoCorrect automatically enters the word *and*. Previous versions of AutoCorrect contained a small collection of commonly mistyped words and other errors to correct automatically. With PowerPoint 2000, the list has grown to include most of the common typing mistakes many of us make.

In addition, AutoCorrect will change straight quotes to smart quotes (nicely formed curly quotes instead of typewriter-style straight lines). These are great features that help us enter cleaner text and create more consistent documents.

You can enable and disable selected actions with the AutoCorrect dialog box shown at the upper left of the following page. Scroll through the list at the bottom of this box to get an idea of what AutoCorrect is doing for you. For one thing, this utility will convert standard typewriter symbols to graphics symbols. If you enter (c), for example, AutoCorrect replaces it with the copyright symbol, ©. Type two dashes and AutoCorrect changes them into an em dash (—), a long dash used to separate items in your text.

If you routinely type character combinations that AutoCorrect wants to turn into something else, you can change its behavior with the Exceptions dialog box (upper-right corner, next page).

You can also add your own typing changes to the AutoCorrect list. You can see from the lower-left figure on the facing page that I have added my own last name to the list. For some strange reason, I tend to leave off the last letter of my name when I'm typing things in a hurry. This AutoCorrect entry fixes that problem, and a number of other bad habits I have developed over the years. You can also use the Spelling dialog box (lower-right figure, facing page) to add new word pairs to AutoCorrect.

TAKE NOTE

CHANGING AUTOCORRECT CORRECTIONS

The best way to change an existing AutoCorrect entry is to select it in the list in the AutoCorrect dialog box, and then type your changes. When you click Replace, you will write the changes back to the existing location instead of creating a new entry.

OVERRIDING AUTOCORRECT

If AutoCorrect makes a change you don't want to accept, and you don't want to change this behavior permanently, simply backspace over the new entry. AutoCorrect will reverse the change, inserting your original text.

ADDING WORDS TO AUTOCORRECT

Use the spell checker to add word sequences to AutoCorrect. In the Spelling dialog box, click AutoCorrect after you have chosen the correct version of a misspelled word. The next time you misspell the word the same way, AutoCorrect will fix it for you.

CROSS-REFERENCE

Review the sections earlier in this chapter on spell checking and Find and Replace for other ways to correct text in your presentations.

FIND IT ONLINE

To read more about the AutoCorrect feature, visit http://www.uic.edu/depts/adn/seminars/wp-intro/autocorrect.html.

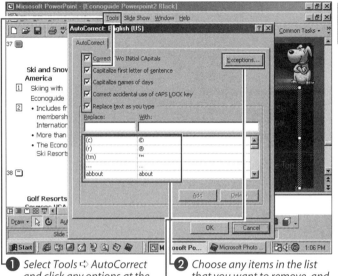

1 Select Tools ➪ AutoCorrect and click any options at the top of this dialog box that you want to disable.

2 Choose any items in the list that you want to remove, and delete them.

3 Click the Exceptions button.

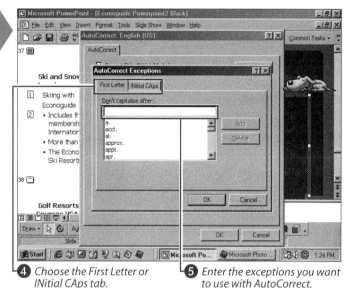

4 Choose the First Letter or INitial CAps tab.

5 Enter the exceptions you want to use with AutoCorrect.

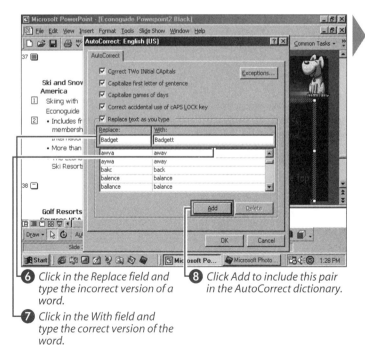

6 Click in the Replace field and type the incorrect version of a word.

7 Click in the With field and type the correct version of the word.

8 Click Add to include this pair in the AutoCorrect dictionary.

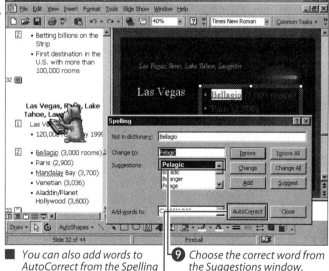

■ You can also add words to AutoCorrect from the Spelling dialog box, which appears when PowerPoint detects a word not in its dictionary.

9 Choose the correct word from the Suggestions window.

10 Click AutoCorrect to have PowerPoint add this incorrect/correct pair to the AutoCorrect function.

Personal Workbook

Q&A

1 Can you think of two different applications for PowerPoint's Notes pages?

_____

_____

_____

_____

2 What PowerPoint utility corrects common typing mistakes as you make them?

_____

_____

_____

_____

3 What PowerPoint feature lets you place recurring text at the bottom of each slide?

_____

_____

_____

_____

4 What PowerPoint facility would you use to change the location of header and footer information on slides, handouts, and Notes pages?

_____

_____

_____

_____

5 What menu sequence would you use to find a word or phrase somewhere within the current slide show?

_____

_____

_____

_____

6 How can you add custom words to the spell-checker dictionary?

_____

_____

_____

_____

ANSWERS: PAGE 303

EXTRA PRACTICE

① Disable the AutoCorrect feature that makes corrections as you type.

② Change the Normal view to one that shows just a slide with notes.

③ Open a slide show and print the first six slides as an audience handout on a single piece of paper.

④ Open an existing slide show and create a footer that displays the current date. This footer should change as the date changes.

⑤ Conduct several PowerPoint operations, Undo them, and then display the Redo list.

⑥ Configure AutoCorrect so that when you type your initials your full name is entered instead.

REAL-WORLD APPLICATIONS

✔ Designing PowerPoint presentations is a creative activity. Rarely will you start at the beginning, create the design, add the information, and quit. Experimenting with slide designs and trying different color schemes is part of the design process. As you follow this creative path, remember two things: save your work before making any global changes, and use Undo and Redo to test changes. You can easily correct a typing mistake or the text in a bulleted list, but if you change a font throughout your show or apply a new design template, backing out is a major process.

✔ If you make regular presentations about a topic, develop one or more PowerPoint presentations that you use repeatedly. Take the time to add a custom footer to the show each time you present it so it appears fresh.

Visual Quiz

Describe how to display the screen shown here.

_____

_____

_____

_____

_____

_____

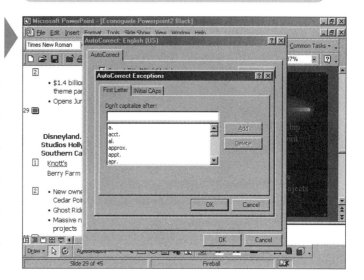

CHAPTER 6

MASTER THESE SKILLS

- ▶ **Installing a Printer**
- ▶ **Using Page Setup**
- ▶ **Selecting a Printer and Properties**
- ▶ **Choosing What to Print**
- ▶ **Printing to a File**

Printing Your Work

The ultimate object of any computer application is to retrieve the data you put into it in a meaningful way. You may ask the computer to manipulate that information, as in a database or spreadsheet application, or you may simply want to store data in a certain format and print it out when you're ready, as with a word processor.

This same goal applies to PowerPoint presentations, except that you usually want to retrieve PowerPoint data by displaying it on the computer screen or by projecting it so a large audience can see it.

However, you'll also want to print some or all of your PowerPoint data. You can use hardcopy from a PowerPoint presentation in a number of ways. Printouts of your slides are an excellent proofing tool, for example. I don't fully understand it (nor do the dozens of publishing and presentation professionals to whom I have put the question), but for some reason you are much more likely to spot errors in a manuscript, report,

or presentation from a printed page than you are on the computer screen. I suspect this phenomenon has to do with the years we have spent reading printed material. The eye-brain interface somehow makes assumptions — leaps of understanding — when we view material in this way.

You'll also want to print all or part of your presentations to use as a presentation aid to help you stay on track and remember what to say. Presentation printouts make excellent additions to a seminar syllabus, preshow promotion or documentation, and lectures and speeches where your audience can benefit from having hardcopy that reinforces the material you are covering.

In this chapter, I'll discuss the physical aspects of selecting and using a printer with PowerPoint, and I'll show you some of the ways to use PowerPoint hardcopy to enhance your programs.

Installing a Printer

When it comes to a program such as PowerPoint, I find one printer is rarely enough. I use laser printers for most of my office work and usually have at least a couple of these attached to my local-area network.

When I print PowerPoint information, however, I frequently want to print color pages or overhead-projector foils. For this purpose, you need a color printer. The good news is that very high-quality color printers are available for $200 to $500.

If you're not already familiar with what printers you have installed, check out the Printers dialog box from the Control Panel (upper-right corner, facing page). This sample shows three printers and an icon labeled Add Printer. Your display will differ because you will have more, fewer, or no printers installed.

Notice the check mark beside the HP LaserJet III icon, indicating that it is set as the default printer. If you click the Print icon on the Standard Toolbar or choose Print from the File menu without specifying a printer, the default printer will be used.

You can find out more about any of the installed printers with the Printer Properties dialog box, shown in the lower-left figure on the facing page. You can display additional information about the printer by clicking one or more of the tabs in this dialog box.

If you have no printer installed, or if you want to add one, open the wizard from the Printers dialog box. You will be prompted with a number of questions, but installation of the new printer is virtually automatic. Choose whether you are using a local or a networked printer, and then select the manufacturer and model (lower-right figure, next page). As the installation routine continues, you probably will be asked to insert the operating system CD-ROM. When you are done, a new printer icon appears in the Printers dialog box.

TAKE NOTE

USING PLUG AND PLAY

With Windows 95 or 98, you can probably install a new printer simply by plugging it in to your computer's parallel port and rebooting the machine. During operating system initialization, the port is scanned, the new hardware is detected, and the wizard launches automatically.

PRINTING TO A NON-EXISTENT PRINTER

You can install the software for a new printer whether or not you have that printer. Plug and Play won't work, but you can install and configure the printer, then print your PowerPoint presentation to a disk file. Copy this file to a diskette or e-mail it to someone else who does have this printer, and they can print your presentation.

CROSS-REFERENCE
See "Printing to a File" later in this chapter for more information on using a remote printer.

FIND IT ONLINE
You may want newer software for your printer. Point your browser to the manufacturer's site and look for drivers or download pages.

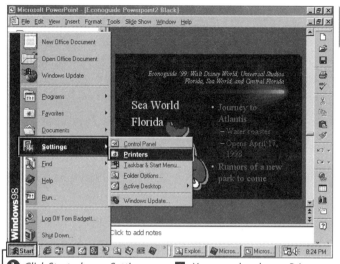

❶ Click Start, choose Settings, and then choose Printers to display the Printers dialog box.

■ You can also choose Printers from the Control Panel.

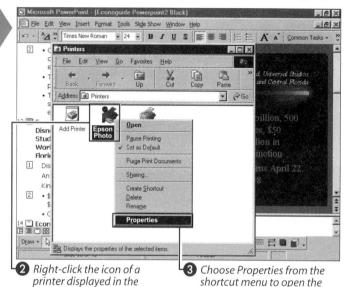

❷ Right-click the icon of a printer displayed in the Printers dialog box.

❸ Choose Properties from the shortcut menu to open the Printer Properties dialog box.

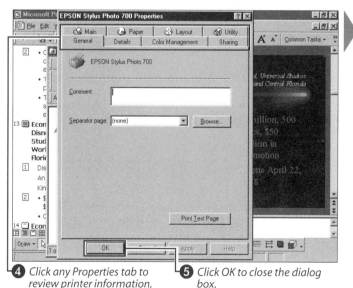

❹ Click any Properties tab to review printer information, and make changes or additions as required.

❺ Click OK to close the dialog box.

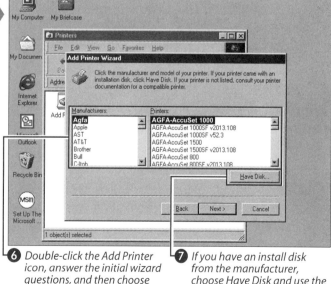

❻ Double-click the Add Printer icon, answer the initial wizard questions, and then choose the manufacturer and model from this screen.

❼ If you have an install disk from the manufacturer, choose Have Disk and use the manufacturer's driver instead of the one supplied with Windows.

Using Page Setup

The Page Setup utility in PowerPoint 2000 has two purposes: to set up the slide layout for the type of show you are designing, and to set some of the options for printing the show. The Page Setup utility uses separate settings for the slides and for Notes & Handouts.

You access the Page Setup options through the Page Setup command, shown in the upper-left figure on the facing page. The Page Setup dialog box (upper-right figure, next page) opens when you select this command. Notice the Orientation group at the right of this dialog box. It contains two sections, one for slides and another for notes, handouts, and outline. Landscape is the default layout for slides — they print along the wide side of the paper. Portrait layout is the default for everything else. You can change these settings, but your printouts probably won't look right.

At the left of the dialog box are settings for slide layout (Slides sized for), the width and height of the slides, and the slide numbering scheme. In general, you should accept the settings for width and height as well as orientation. You can change the slide numbering if you are printing just part of a show or if you want this printout to merge with printed slides from another show.

To use a slide show for something other than an on-screen presentation, you can make your selection from the *Slides sized for* drop-down list. By the way,

on-screen presentation includes projecting images from your computer. If you are designing a presentation for 35mm slides, for example, choose this option from the drop-down list (lower-left figure, next page).

If you change the slide layout, the width and height of the slides may change. When you choose 35mm slides, for example, the aspect ratio (ratio of width to height) changes to more closely match the layout of a slide. You will see 11.25 inches in the Width field and 7.5 inches in the Height field.

You can use PowerPoint to design banners, too. If you choose a Banner layout from the drop-down list, the width of the slides becomes 8 inches and the height is reduced to 1 inch. Clearly, this setting requires a different sort of slide design.

It's much better to make changes in this dialog box before you start designing slides. Once you have text and graphics in place, they can become distorted if you change the layout.

TAKE NOTE

USING CUSTOM SETTINGS

You can choose just about any slide size you want with the Custom setting in the Page Setup dialog box. Remember that all slides must have the same size settings, and you should test one or two slides with any Custom setting before you commit yourself to building a complete presentation with it.

CROSS-REFERENCE
Having trouble printing? Check out Chapter 2 for information on how to use PowerPoint's Help features.

FIND IT ONLINE
Learn more about printing your presentation at the Computer Services tutorial site: **http://www.rockhurst. edu/Computer_Services/Powerpoint/Page5.html**.

Using Custom Settings

Notice that as you change the setting in the *Slides sized for* field of this dialog box, the width and height information below this field may also change. You can change width and height data directly if you wish. You might want to do this to handle unusual slide content. Choose Custom from the *Slides sized for* field before setting your own width and height. Special settings — especially larger ones — likely won't be visible for standard, on-screen shows. After all, there's only so much screen real estate available. However, new color printers will print unusual sizes, so you may find Custom settings useful.

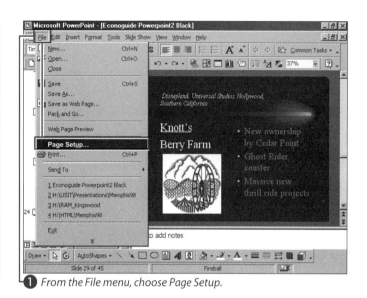

❶ From the File menu, choose Page Setup.

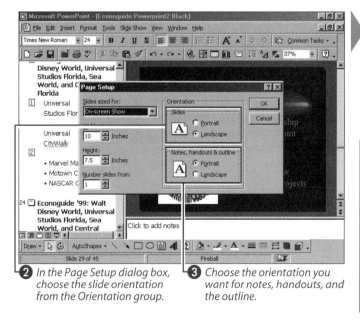

❷ In the Page Setup dialog box, choose the slide orientation from the Orientation group.

❸ Choose the orientation you want for notes, handouts, and the outline.

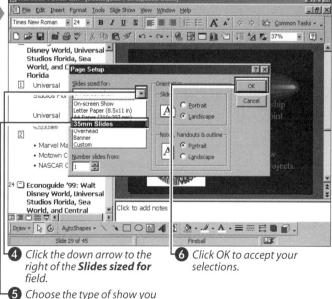

❹ Click the down arrow to the right of the **Slides sized for** field.

❺ Choose the type of show you are designing from the list.

❻ Click OK to accept your selections.

Selecting a Printer and Properties

With PowerPoint, it is easy to print your slide show or support documents such as handouts, outlines, or notes pages. You simply choose which printer you want to use—if you have more than one printer installed—and then set any special properties for this printer or your slide show before sending the file to the printer.

The options you have available will differ depending on what printer you are using. With some printers you have a wide range of options that you can select to control how your document will print. The Properties dialog box for the Canon BJC-620 is shown at the upper right of the facing page. With most printers, you can choose print quality and the type of paper you want. Most laser printers are very forgiving of paper stock, but ink jet printers perform a lot better if you specify the kind of paper you are using. This is particularly true if you are using coated paper (slick, high-quality paper) or transparencies (for overhead projection).

Most printers have a tabbed dialog box similar to the Canon BJC's. Each tab controls a different range of settings, including paper type, print quality, number of copies to print, and how the file will be printed. For example, the Copies & Methods tab for

the BJC-620 (lower-left figure on the next page) enables you to choose how many copies of the current document to print, whether to collate multiple printouts (print one whole presentation in sequence, then print another copy), and whether to use portrait or landscape orientation.

For contrast, look at the lower-right figure on the facing page. This is the Properties dialog box for a Hewlett-Packard 5MP PostScript printer. Not only does it have different tabs, but the information is also presented differently. This is a factor of the printer model and of the drivers provided by the printer's manufacturer.

TAKE NOTE

PRINTER SELECTION AND FILE FORMATTING

When you choose a printer, PowerPoint scans your presentation to confirm there are no conflicts in fonts or graphics in your slides. Different printers reproduce text and graphics differently, so changing a printer can cause slight variations in your show. For this reason, it is best to choose the printer you will use before you design the show. If you must change printers later, scan your presentation for any problems before you print it.

CROSS-REFERENCE
See "Choosing What to Print" and "Printing to a File" later in this chapter for more printer configuration information.

FIND IT ONLINE
Find a description of each type of print setting at **http://garfield.ir.ucf.edu/manual/lan/ppoint**.

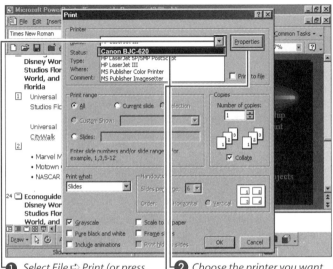

➊ Select File ➪ Print (or press Ctrl-P) to display the main Print dialog box, and click the down arrow next to the Name field.

➋ Choose the printer you want to use from this list.

➌ Click the Properties button to display a dialog box with available options for this printer.

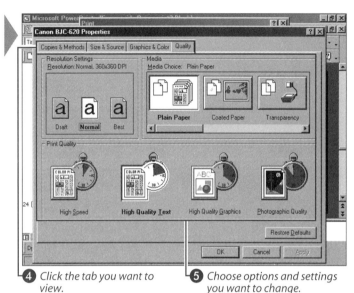

➍ Click the tab you want to view.

➎ Choose options and settings you want to change.

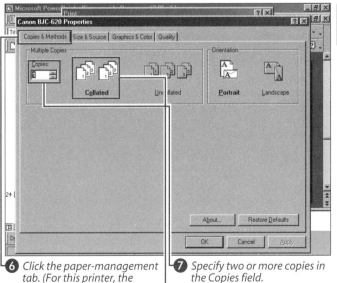

➏ Click the paper-management tab. (For this printer, the paper-management tab is titled Copies & Methods, but the tab name varies for different printers.)

➐ Specify two or more copies in the Copies field.

➑ Choose collated output if you want an entire document to print before subsequent copies are printed.

➒ If you have a second printer, specify it as the printer you want to use, and review the tabs.

■ If you don't have another printer, use this figure as a comparison to your own.

Choosing What to Print

You've already seen that any PowerPoint presentation includes several components: outline, Notes pages, audience handouts, and the slide show itself. You can print some or all of these by selecting one or more components associated with the current show in the Print dialog box.

The figure in the upper left of the facing page illustrates how to start a print routine. Consider the upper-right figure on the facing page. You'll see this dialog box whenever you print a PowerPoint presentation unless you bypass it by clicking the Print icon on the standard toolbar.

If you intend to print the entire slide show — not the outline or other components — in a standard format, you do not need to make any changes. Send the print job to your printer and the default settings shown in this figure will be used.

If you want to print only a part of the show, or a component other than the slides, you need to make some adjustments in the Print dialog box. You can choose which slides (or pages) to print, the number of copies, whether you want collated output, and whether you want to print the slide show or another element, such as the Notes pages.

The upper-right figure on the next page shows a list of print options in the Print what group, and I've made some additional changes to the default settings here. If you're printing handouts, for example, you'll want the slides framed. This option tells PowerPoint to place a black border around each slide, setting it off from the notes and the surrounding white space on the page.

If you're printing to a black-and-white printer, choose Grayscale for the best tonal range. When you print overhead transparencies or are using other special paper, however, print Pure black and white. This option turns all shades to either black or white, with minimal shading. Besides offering good contrast — giving some slides better visibility — this option uses toner more efficiently and may offer faster printing.

You can't view handouts onscreen: you can only print them. And, you'll print a different number of handouts on each page depending on your subject matter and your audience. Don't ignore the outline view, either: It's a useful way to make changes in a show, to add material, and to help you understand what material your show covers and what it needs. The outline is one of the best tools for designing a presentation or other document.

TAKE NOTE

▶ SETTING OTHER PRINT OPTIONS

Some of the options in the Print dialog box may not be available. If you don't have any animated sections on your slides, for example, you can't specify that animations be included in the printout. If no slides are hidden, you won't be able to check the Print hidden slides option in this dialog box.

CROSS-REFERENCE

See Chapter 14 for more information on using your presentation. Notice the Send To feature, which lets you transmit your presentation to another location.

FIND IT ONLINE

For more on printing your slide presentation, visit http://cma.cuslm.ca/estouest/office97.en/ powerpoint/lecon6/lec6_2.html./.

Deciding What to Print

Before you print an entire slide show, you should print one or two slides to make sure your printer settings are correct. From the Print dialog box you can click Current slide to print only the slide that is displayed in the PowerPoint editing window, for example. If you click the Slides button, a field opens up beside the entry so you can type a slide number or a range of slides. To type a single slide other than the one displayed, type the number. Print a range of slides by entering the first slide, a dash, and the last slide you want to print.

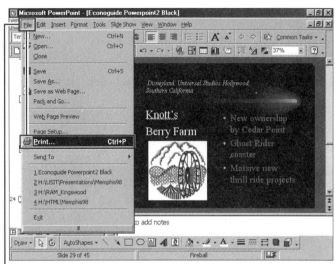

① Select File ⇨ Print to open the Print dialog box.

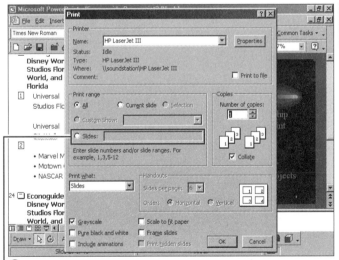

② Change the range of slides or pages to print.

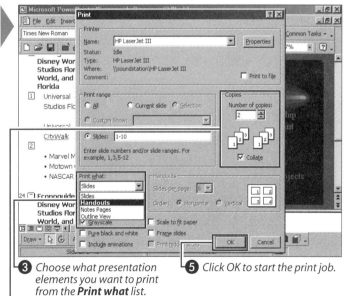

③ Choose what presentation elements you want to print from the **Print what** list.

④ Specify the number of copies and whether you want collated output.

⑤ Click OK to start the print job.

Printing to a File

Remember that during presentation design, PowerPoint formats the slides and other components according to the printer definition you are currently using. For the most part, differences among printers are slight, but some printers can cause significant variation in the way your show looks and prints.

You can install drivers for printers installed on other machines, and then print your presentations to a file. In addition, you may want to create file versions of printouts to enable you to create a slide show on one computer and print it on another, even if the machines don't use the same printer.

To send PowerPoint information to a file, specify the path and filename for the output in the dialog box shown at the upper left of the facing page. You can identify a printer file because it is stored with a .PRN extension.

The information this file contains depends on the type of printer you have selected. A PostScript printer places text printer commands in the file that can be interpreted by most other PostScript printers when you want to print the file. A Hewlett-Packard printer sends PCL (Printer Control Language) codes, text commands in a binary file. That means you can't read the file directly in a text editor or word-processing program.

The figure at the lower left of the facing page shows a portion of a PostScript file generated by a generic PostScript printer driver. PostScript printers generally create text files that you can read directly — and even edit — if you know your way around PostScript.

You can now copy a printer file to a floppy disk — if it will fit — or to another storage medium so you can carry it to a remote location and print it there. You can use a compression utility such as PKZIP to shrink the file so it will fit on a floppy or to make it easier to e-mail to another location.

To print the file, you must first uncompress it, if it is compressed, and then copy it to the printer as if the printer were another disk drive. You'll need to open a DOS window and issue the File Copy command, as shown in the lower-right figure on the facing page. Windows Explorer tries to be too smart: If you copy this PRN file from Explorer to your printer, you'll get an error message.

TAKE NOTE

PRINTING BINARY PRINTER FILES

Some printer output files are stored in non-text format. When you copy one of these files to a printer port, you may get an error message or the file may not print correctly. Try adding a **/b** after the Copy command to tell the printer it is receiving a non-text file.

CROSS-REFERENCE

See Chapter 17 for information on automating printing and other PowerPoint operations.

FIND IT ONLINE

Visit the Presentation Recommendations page for tips and advice: **http://www.cs.ucsb.edu/~matz/study/cs50/5-29/index.htm**.

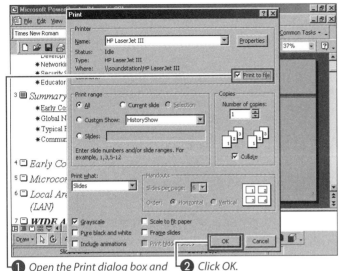

① Open the Print dialog box and choose **Print to file** in the upper-right corner.

② Click OK.

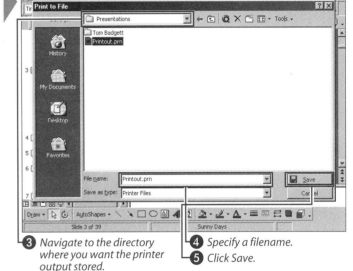

③ Navigate to the directory where you want the printer output stored.

④ Specify a filename.

⑤ Click Save.

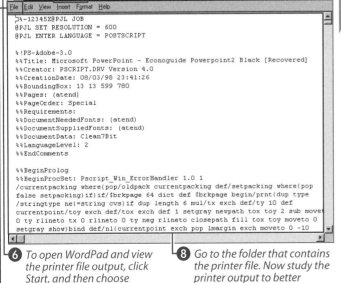

⑥ To open WordPad and view the printer file output, click Start, and then choose Accessories ➪ WordPad.

⑦ Choose Open from the WordPad File menu.

⑧ Go to the folder that contains the printer file. Now study the printer output to better understand how Print to File works.

⑨ Click Start, and then select Programs ➪ MS-DOS Prompt. Type **copy <path>\filename.prn lpt1:** and press Enter.

Personal Workbook

Q&A

1 What dialog box is used to install a new printer for use by PowerPoint?

_____

_____

_____

2 What file extension does PowerPoint automatically add to a printer output file?

_____

_____

_____

3 Describe how to change the default on-screen slide format to 35mm slides.

_____

_____

_____

4 How can you print the current slide show without using the Print dialog box?

_____

_____

_____

5 What keyboard shortcut opens the Print dialog box?

_____

_____

_____

6 Why would you want to install a printer definition and drivers for a printer you don't own?

_____

_____

_____

ANSWERS: PAGE 304

EXTRA PRACTICE

1 Display the Properties dialog box for your printer and choose a non-standard paper type, if that option is available for your printer.

2 How can you force Windows to launch the New Printer Wizard automatically?

3 Open the Print dialog box and tell PowerPoint to print an outline for the current show.

4 Open a PowerPoint presentation and print slides 1–5, 8, and 12 with a single operation.

5 Open a PowerPoint presentation and print the first 10 slides to a file instead of to the attached printer.

6 Install a new PostScript printer for use with PowerPoint, even if you don't own a PostScript printer.

REAL-WORLD APPLICATIONS

✔ Suppose you are asked to speak to a group in a distant city. The host has promised to have a computer and projector ready for you, but has also asked for audience handouts. You can send handouts to a print file and carry a floppy disk to make the final prints on the host's computer/printer after you arrive at your destination. Make sure to ask the precise model and manufacturer of the target printer before you create the printer file.

✔ PowerPoint can help you with presentations even if you don't have a projector and the group is too large to gather around your computer monitor. I create a PowerPoint presentation, then print slides four or six to a page and hand them out before the talk. The audience can follow along on the printed handouts while I'm talking.

Visual Quiz

Describe how to open the dialog box shown here.

_____

_____

_____

_____

_____

_____

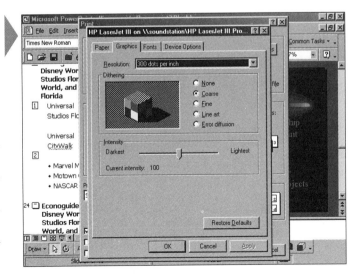

PART

II

CHAPTER **7**   **Editing the Masters**

8   **Using Animation**

9   **Changing Layout and Design**

10   **Using Pictures, Sound, and Movies**

11   **PowerPoint and Microsoft Office**

12   **Using Other Objects on Your Slides**

Contents of 'Desktop'

Name

My Computer

Network Neigh

Internet Explore

Microsoft Outloo

Recycle Bin

My Briefcase

3252-9

3259-6

3261-8

3262-6

3281-2

3286-3

DE Phone List

Device Manager

In

Iomega Tools

Advanced Design Skills

You're now ready to take PowerPoint 2000 to the next level of design. In Part I of this book, I covered the primary skills you need to create and use PowerPoint slide shows. If your presentation needs are modest and infrequent, you may rarely go beyond these basic capabilities. However, part of the appeal of using this versatile software package is taking it beyond the basics, learning how to make ordinary presentations stand out in a crowd.

In this part of the book, you'll learn how to take basic PowerPoint templates and modify them for a unique appearance. You'll discover how easy it is to use multimedia objects such as animation, sound, and even motion video within your presentations. And you'll see the value of the Microsoft suite approach to office applications.

Even if you consider yourself a beginner in presentation design, don't ignore these advanced skills. They aren't difficult to master, and they'll help make your PowerPoint presentations special.

CHAPTER 7

MASTER THESE SKILLS

▶ Changing Master Colors

▶ Changing Master Text

▶ Changing the Slide Background

▶ Modifying Footer Data

▶ Editing the Notes and Handout Masters

Editing the Masters

PowerPoint works like many multimedia and word-processing programs in that behind every new document you create is a set of master configuration settings that determine the format of your slides. This includes color scheme, placement of header and footer information, and fonts used, among other things.

This universal style definition is handled with master pages. A master page exists for each element of a presentation: one for the title slide, another for slides, another for handouts, and still another for Notes pages. You can view individual master pages and make changes as required to alter the appearance of the elements within your presentation.

The nice thing about the master concept is it enables you to enact global changes with ease. For example, make a change on a Slide Master, and all slides in the show controlled by that master immediately exhibit the same characteristic.

You can set different master settings for slides, Notes pages, and handouts. Or you can make no changes at all. PowerPoint predefines required settings. When you apply a slide layout, many settings, such as color and background objects, are chosen for you.

To have the utmost control over the appearance and content of your presentations, you must be able to control every aspect of the slide-show design. Knowing how to change the default settings on the master pages is key to this level of control. With this capability, you can, for example, change the location of footer information on your slides; change the bullet design and colors for bullet lists; adjust fonts for bullet lists, headings, and body text; and add or remove background graphics objects that appear on every slide.

Well, you get the idea. You can accept all the defaults the basic program and its associated templates and designs offer, or you can take things into your own hands and fine-tune your design to make it unique.

By the time you finish this chapter, you should be fairly comfortable changing background colors, adjusting text and slide layout, modifying the Notes pages and handouts backgrounds, and more.

Changing Master Colors

Color is an important part of any PowerPoint presentation. According to figures compiled from studies by the Wagner Institute for Color Research and the Tektronix printer manufacturing company, color can accelerate learning, retention, and recall by nearly 80 percent over a monochrome presentation. Color also increases willingness to read by up to 80 percent, and can improve selling efficiency by the same amount.

No presentation should contain more than about five colors, unless you are including full-color photographs. You can set the mood of the presentation by selecting different ranges of colors. Cyan and blue are cool colors, for example, whereas yellow and red are warm in mood. Magenta and green are transitional colors that can take on qualities of either warm or cool colors, though magenta is basically a warm color whereas green is a cool one.

Consider the figure at the upper left of the facing page. This slide uses the Blue Diagonal design template. Although this book is not in full color, you should be able to see the tones evident in this standard PowerPoint color scheme.

Now look at the upper-right figure. This is the Slide Master, which shows the background elements for all the slides in a particular show. You can modify many of the colors on this master to change the overall mood of the show.

The lower-left figure shows the Background dialog box along with a supplemental color dialog box. Use the Background dialog box to choose a different background color for the slides. You can change the color slightly to another tint of the original or to an entirely different color.

The lower-right figure shows the results of changing the background color from blue to black. By making the change on the master page, you have propagated this color change throughout the slide show.

TAKE NOTE

▶ DESIGNING FOR COLOR

Choose colors appropriate for your message. The Wagner Institute has shown how people react to color in interior design. Blue is a favorite color that elicits positive responses. Red is more emotional, and green is comfortable. Use yellow to get the attention of an audience quickly. Gray says "exclusive" or "quality," whereas white's message is sophistication or refinement. Black, however, isn't appealing to most people.

▶ BALANCING BACKGROUND AND TEXT COLORS

For slides, use dark backgrounds and lighter text and illustrations. Photographers and painters use color in this way to focus the viewer's attention. If you're designing for overhead foils, however, lighten the background, or you'll lose definition. Also be aware of your audience and the room where you'll make the presentation. If your background is dark and the projector underpowered, some slide objects may get buried in the dark background.

CROSS-REFERENCE

See "Changing Master Text" and "Changing the Slide Background" later in this chapter for more on modifying master images.

FIND IT ONLINE

If you want to know more about basic color theory, go to http//users.anderson.edu/~jfultz/color.html.

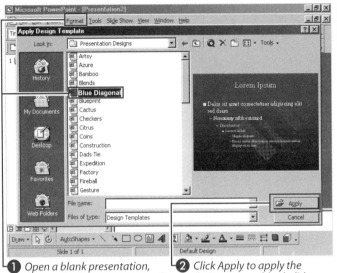

① Open a blank presentation, choose the Format menu, and select the Blue Diagonal design template.

② Click Apply to apply the design to your blank slide.

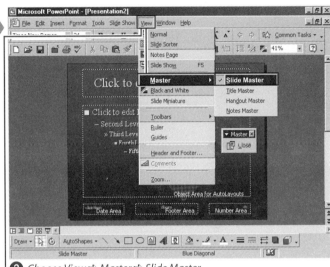

③ Choose View ➪ Master ➪ Slide Master.

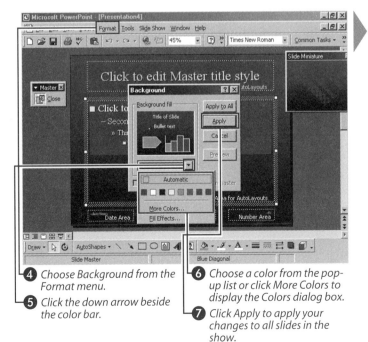

④ Choose Background from the Format menu.

⑤ Click the down arrow beside the color bar.

⑥ Choose a color from the pop-up list or click More Colors to display the Colors dialog box.

⑦ Click Apply to apply your changes to all slides in the show.

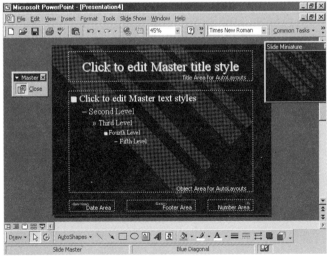

■ Because you are working in the Slide Master view, you don't need to choose Apply to All.

Changing Master Text

Text is another important part of your PowerPoint presentation, and not just because of the meaning it conveys. The text elements you place on your PowerPoint slides use a particular typeface. A typeface is a distinctive shape and design of type that makes a collection of letters recognizable. Typefaces are generally identified by name, such as Times Roman, Helvetica, Palatino, and Century Schoolbook. A font is a collection of all the characters available for a particular typeface and style.

When you open a new presentation, PowerPoint chooses fonts for the show. You can change these settings on individual slides — even individual lines on a slide. But when you change text elements on the Slide Master, those changes are propagated throughout the slide show.

To examine fonts, open a Slide Master, click in the title area or on a bullet, and check out the font and size in the format bar. As you can see in the upper-left figure on the next page, the title in the example presentation uses a 44-point Times New Roman font. Because this is the Slide Master, this font will be used for all the slide titles in this presentation. (If you don't see the format bar, right-click any toolbar and choose Format Bar from the shortcut menu.) Notice that PowerPoint places a selection box around the title when it is selected, so anything you do to any part of the title affects the whole title.

You can also change the size of the master title, as shown in the top-right figure on the following page.

After increasing the size of the master title and exiting the Slide Master view by clicking Close on the floating Master toolbar, all slides in the example show will feature a very large title.

You can use the Font dialog box, shown at the lower left of the facing page, to change other text attributes as well. Select any text you want to change before using this dialog box. The Title Master slide at the lower right of the facing page demonstrates another way to change font size using the format bar.

TAKE NOTE

► UNDERSTANDING FONT SIZE

Type size is measured in points. One point is equal to 1/72 of an inch, so 72-point type is about one inch tall. In most typefaces, 12-point type is standard for printed pages and is also a readable on-screen size. A 30- or 50-point size is appropriate for titles and headings or for bullet lists when the viewer will be farther than usual from the screen.

► USING SERIF AND SANS SERIF TYPE

Serif type (such as Times or Times Roman) includes upper and lower finishing strokes at the end of main strokes. Most typefaces use serifs, which are easier to read for lengthy text blocks. Sans serif type (such as Helvetica or Arial) is most often used in titles and headlines. In PowerPoint, you may want to choose sans serif type for bullet lists and other applications if the lines are short.

CROSS-REFERENCE
See Chapter 9 for more information on changing presentation text attributes.

FIND IT ONLINE
To learn about fonts and to pick up some free additional fonts for your PC, check out **http://www.onlinebusiness. com/shops/_computers/BEST_Fonts.shtml**.

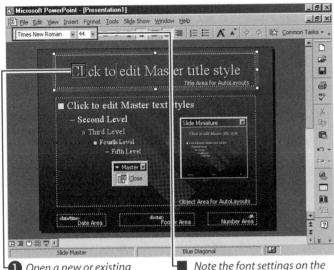

❶ Open a new or existing PowerPoint presentation and choose Format ⇨ Master ⇨ Slide Master. Click anywhere on the title text to select it.

■ Note the font settings on the format bar.

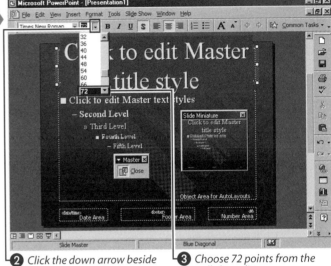

❷ Click the down arrow beside the font size on the format bar.

❸ Choose 72 points from the pull-down list.

■ The size of the title font immediately increases to about one inch.

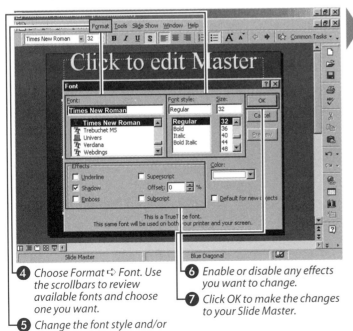

❹ Choose Format ⇨ Font. Use the scrollbars to review available fonts and choose one you want.

❺ Change the font style and/or size if you wish.

❻ Enable or disable any effects you want to change.

❼ Click OK to make the changes to your Slide Master.

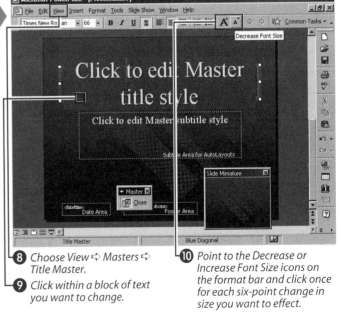

❽ Choose View ⇨ Masters ⇨ Title Master.

❾ Click within a block of text you want to change.

❿ Point to the Decrease or Increase Font Size icons on the format bar and click once for each six-point change in size you want to effect.

Changing the Slide Background

Many PowerPoint templates and presentation designs include interesting background designs, shapes, or graphics that appear behind your slide data. You may want to move elements of the slide background to make room for other objects or to replace some of them with other designs.

You can handle any changes to the background graphics using the Slide Master. Notice the upper-left figure on the next page. I've shown the Blue Diagonal design again, but this time I've grabbed the diagonal graphic and brought it down slightly to show how easy it is to move things around.

You can just as easily replace the diagonal graphic with something else. First you remove the default graphic, insert a new one, and then reformat the slide as required. Reformatting may be necessary, for example, if the new graphic is a different size or shape. The upper-right figure on the next page shows the beginning of this process. You can choose any of the clipart categories from this first screen. I've selected Borders and Frames for a basic background look.

Once you select a category, you then choose the specific clipart you want to appear on every slide. I've shown a half frame that is solid white outlined with black at the lower left of the next page. Notice the shortcut menu that appears when you choose one of the clipart images. This menu helps you manipulate the chosen image: Insert the clip, preview the clip, add the clip to your favorites or another category, and find similar clips.

Often the clipart you choose won't be sized for a full background and won't be positioned where you want them. You can grab an image to move it anywhere on the Slide Master and use the handles to resize it. You can see the start of this process in the lower-right figure on the next page.

Continued

TAKE NOTE

RESIZING IMAGES

When you select a graphic image or clipart object, small squares pop up at each corner and along the sides. These are called *handles*, and you can grab any handle to resize an image.

MANAGING POWERPOINT IMAGES

Office 2000 includes a shared image resource called the Clip Art Gallery — which is a misnomer, really, as it includes space for photographs, sounds, and motion video as well as clipart. The gallery is an organizational tool that enables you to group images into types and categories. Office 2000 provides many useable images, and you can add your own easily.

CHOOSING BACKGROUND GRAPHICS

Consider carefully the images you choose for slide backgrounds. The background shouldn't overpower the slide foreground. This happens if the background image is too busy, too large, or too bright. A background should contribute to the overall slide design, not detract from it.

CROSS-REFERENCE

See "Changing Master Colors" for ideas on how to change the appearance of your clipart background.

FIND IT ONLINE

For additional information about using graphics in PowerPoint, and to obtain some new images, visit **http://Plato.acadiau.ca/sandbox/ppt/graphic.htm**.

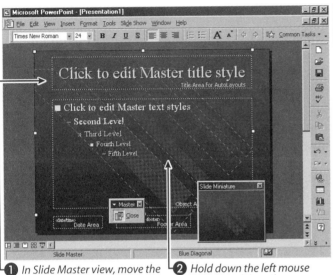

1 In Slide Master view, move the mouse pointer over the background until it changes to a double-ended pointer, and then click to select the background graphic.

2 Hold down the left mouse button and drag the background image to move it on the Slide Master.

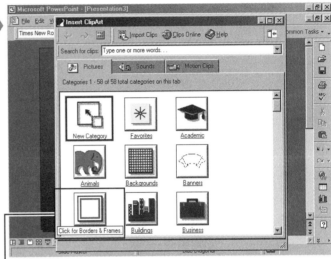

3 Remove the existing background graphic, choose Clip Art from the Insert menu, and then choose Borders and Frames.

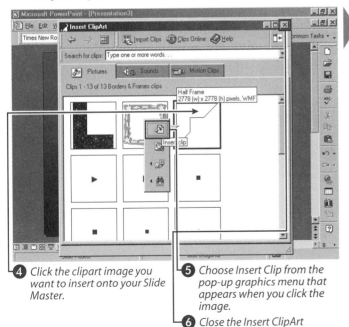

4 Click the clipart image you want to insert onto your Slide Master.

5 Choose Insert Clip from the pop-up graphics menu that appears when you click the image.

6 Close the Insert ClipArt dialog box.

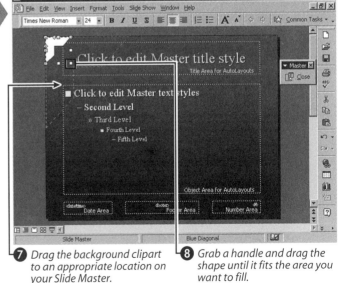

7 Drag the background clipart to an appropriate location on your Slide Master.

8 Grab a handle and drag the shape until it fits the area you want to fill.

Changing the Slide Background
Continued

Once you choose a background graphic, position it, and size it, you are ready to format the graphic and move any other slide elements as required to effect the final design.

The first thing you need to do is make the new graphic image truly a background image. This is a simple menu operation. With the image in the background, the foreground text appears.

What happens next depends on the slide design and the background graphic you have chosen. Most likely you'll want to change the color of the background object to match the slide color. You may also want to add or remove a border, and so on. You can handle these changes from the menu, too. In the Format AutoShape tabbed dialog box, you can set parameters for any slide object. Change the color of the object to match the slide colors, for example, and remove the border.

Again, depending on the design of your slides and the background graphic you have chosen, you may need to rearrange other slide elements. Each of the major slide objects is outlined with a dotted line. You can easily change the shape or position of the selected object.

When you have changed the size and placement of existing slide images to match the new background,

you're ready to return to Slide view and enter the text and other objects you want to use.

TAKE NOTE

CHANGING SLIDE BACKGROUNDS

Another way to change slide backgrounds is with the Background dialog box, which you open from the Format menu. This dialog box shows the current background fill colors and enables you to choose from a list of additional schemes. When you make a background choice from the list, you are shown how this change affects the other colors on the slide. You can also change fill effects, such as whether the background is a solid color or a shaded — light to dark — background. Click Apply to All to set the show theme.

FORMATTING INDIVIDUAL SLIDES

You can change the color scheme for part or all of specific slides without changing the design for the rest of the presentation. Display the slide you want to change, and select Slide Layout, Slide Background, or Slide Color Scheme from the Format menu. This is a useful technique for added emphasis or introducing a new section of the presentation. However, use individual slide color schemes carefully so as not to jar the audience.

CROSS-REFERENCE
See Chapter 15 for more on using the Web with PowerPoint (a good source for PowerPoint graphics).

FIND IT ONLINE
Search the Internet for "PowerPoint background" or start here: **www.vtc.edu.hk/tc/tytc/etu/powerpt/ppt.htm**.

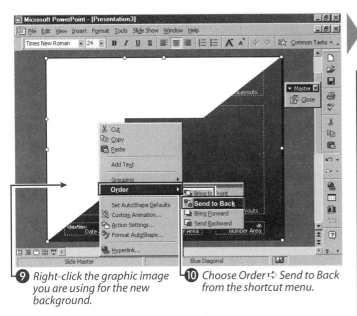

9 Right-click the graphic image you are using for the new background.

10 Choose Order ➪ Send to Back from the shortcut menu.

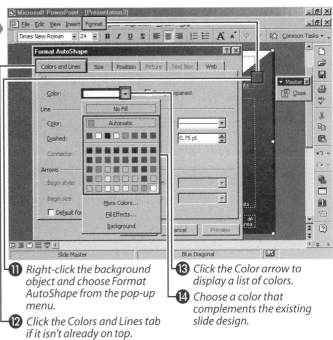

11 Right-click the background object and choose Format AutoShape from the pop-up menu.

12 Click the Colors and Lines tab if it isn't already on top.

13 Click the Color arrow to display a list of colors.

14 Choose a color that complements the existing slide design.

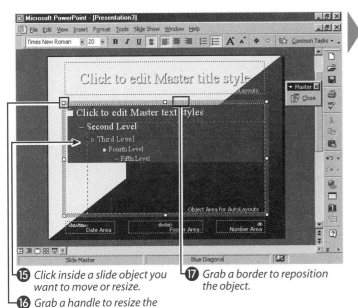

15 Click inside a slide object you want to move or resize.

16 Grab a handle to resize the object.

17 Grab a border to reposition the object.

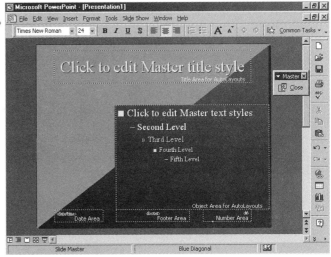

■ Remember, you are working on the Slide Master, so the final design you devise here will be propagated throughout your new or existing slide show.

■ Remember, too, that you can change these settings at any time, but you may have to change text size or color at the same time.

Modifying Footer Data

The basic PowerPoint slide layout designs are pretty good. Preformatted areas exist for slide titles, body objects, and footer information. In the footer, PowerPoint assumes you want the option of using date and time data at the left, some custom information in the middle, and a slide number on the right.

This layout works for most applications, and you'll probably accept these settings for most of your presentations. However, the nice thing about PowerPoint is that you don't have to live with its preset defaults. You can move these footer objects pretty much at will.

Suppose you want to reverse the text footer and the date footer. From the Slide Master you can easily rearrange these footer items by dragging and dropping them (see the upper-left figure on the following page).

Although PowerPoint places some default information in the Slide Master footer, you can add a graphic image, company logo, or other object to the footer area, for example, to give your presentation a decidedly custom look. Consider the upper-right figure on the facing page. This is the first step toward adding a custom company logo in the footer area of the Slide Master. You can create such images from existing corporate logo files, by scanning letterhead and editing it with Photoshop or another program. Experiment to get the correct size and shape for use as a slide footer.

The bottom two figures on the next page show you how to complete the task of adding a company logo or other custom image to the slide footer. Try to use colors complementary to your presentation design. Also remember that a slide footer should present secondary information — date, copyright, logo — and not primary presentation content.

TAKE NOTE

MOVING POWERPOINT OBJECTS

You can drag and drop almost any slide object with the mouse. However, it is sometimes difficult to place objects precisely where you want them with this method because PowerPoint assumes you want to snap these objects to an imaginary grid that specifies preset locations. To fine-tune object placement, click the object to select it, hold down the Ctrl key, and use the keyboard arrow keys to move the object in very small increments to wherever you wish.

USING CUSTOM FOOTERS

PowerPoint is a little stupid in handling custom footers. If you remove the Footer Area object and replace it with a custom graphic, you can't later add custom text footers to your slides. Even though you can still enter footer text in the Slide Footer dialog box, that text won't appear on your slides because there's no place for PowerPoint to put it.

CROSS-REFERENCE
See Chapter 5 for details on including headers and footers on your slides and other presentation elements.

FIND IT ONLINE
You can find a useful guide to designing a new Power-Point presentation at **http://www.wws.princeton.edu/documentation/PPMANUAL/index.htm.**

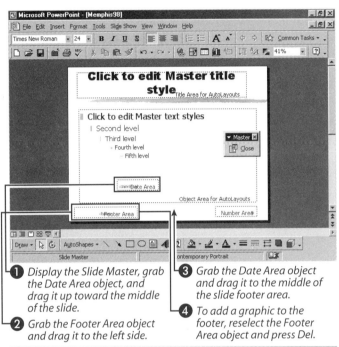

❶ Display the Slide Master, grab the Date Area object, and drag it up toward the middle of the slide.

❷ Grab the Footer Area object and drag it to the left side.

❸ Grab the Date Area object and drag it to the middle of the slide footer area.

❹ To add a graphic to the footer, reselect the Footer Area object and press Del.

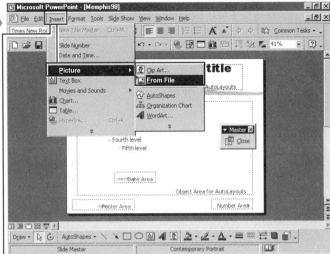

❺ Choose Insert ➪ Picture, and then choose either Clip Art or From File.

■ From File opens a dialog box that enables you to choose an image you've stored in a specific directory.

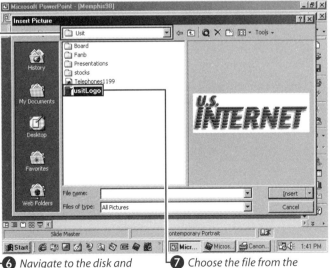

❻ Navigate to the disk and directory where the image you want to use in the slide footer is stored.

❼ Choose the file from the directory.

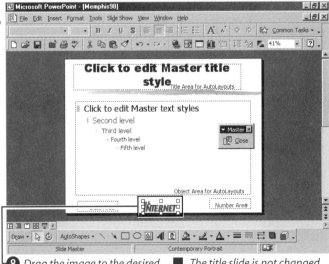

❽ Drag the image to the desired location on the Slide Master and size it appropriately.

■ Remember, changes to this master appear on all slides in your presentation.

■ The title slide is not changed unless you change the Title Master.

Editing the Notes and Handout Masters

Global changes aren't limited to the slides themselves. You can customize the Notes pages by making changes to a master page in much the same way as you change the Slide Master to customize the look of your slides.

Notes and handout pages are slightly different from slides in that these pages contain a header as well as a footer by default. You can add a header to a Slide Master, of course, but PowerPoint doesn't include one by default. In addition, two fixed objects appear on the Notes Master: a slide and the notes body area. Each of these objects occupies approximately half the available space on the Notes page. The Handout Master enables you to place two or more objects, plus the header and footer.

Among the things you can change on the Notes Master is the amount of space used by each of the objects therein, the placement of the objects, and the positioning and contents of the header and footer.

Suppose you want to reverse the position of the notes and the slide because the description you provide carries more weight than the slide itself. I show the first steps for such a procedure in the upper-left figure on the next page.

Similarly, you can add more emphasis to the slide image or the notes themselves by resizing these objects, as shown in the upper-right figure on the next page.

You have the same header and footer options on the Handout Master as you do on the Notes Master. In addition, a Handout Master toolbar, shown in the lower-left figure on the following page, enables you to choose how many slide images appear on each handout page.

For example, you can create a handout page with nine images instead of the default six, and you can align three slides on the left of the page, leaving room for notes on the right of the printed handout page (see the lower-right figure on the following page).

TAKE NOTE

MOVING MASTER PAGE AND SLIDE OBJECTS

You can use the desktop screen as a temporary storage area while you design slides or masters. Drag and drop an image off of the slide or master body onto the gray desktop. Make whatever changes you want on the slide or master body, and then drag and drop the stored image back on the slide.

RESIZING POWERPOINT OBJECTS

PowerPoint slide objects have a preset aspect ratio — the relationship between the width and height of the object. Images distort if you change this ratio drastically. To maintain the original aspect ratio, hold down the shift key as you resize an object with a corner handle.

CROSS-REFERENCE

See the previous section on modifying the Slide Master footer for information on how to change headers and footers on master pages.

FIND IT ONLINE

Visit **http://www.rdg.ac.uk/ITS/Topic/Graphics/ GrGlppt_01/ppt7.html#master** for more on creating a master.

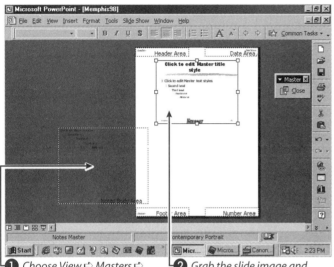

1️⃣ *Choose View ➪ Masters ➪ Notes Master to display the Notes Master, and then drag the Notes Body Area object off to one side.*

2️⃣ *Grab the slide image and drag it to the bottom of the slide.*

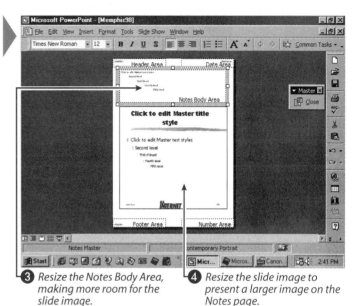

3️⃣ *Resize the Notes Body Area, making more room for the slide image.*

4️⃣ *Resize the slide image to present a larger image on the Notes page.*

5️⃣ *Display the Handout Master and choose a layout from the Handout Master toolbar.*

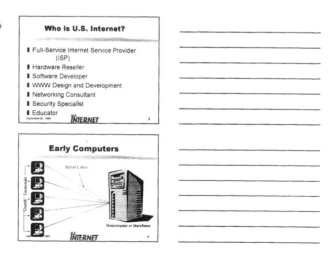

■ *When you choose three slides with side-by-side notes on the Handouts Master, the handouts print with lines for notes beside each slide. This lets your audience take notes relative to each point you present.*

Personal Workbook

Q&A

1 How does the use of color influence the effectiveness of your PowerPoint presentation?

_____

_____

2 With the exception of a full-color photograph or other image, what is the suggested maximum number of colors you should use in a PowerPoint presentation?

_____

_____

_____

3 What point size would you use to create a text block with characters approximately one inch tall?

_____

_____

4 A collection of all the characters available for a particular typeface and style is the definition of what PowerPoint screen object?

_____

_____

_____

5 What keyboard combination do you use to move a PowerPoint object by small increments?

_____

_____

6 What Office 2000 resource can you use in PowerPoint to store, view, and select clipart, sound, photographs, or video clips?

_____

_____

_____

7 What PowerPoint feature would you use to change the default number of slides on handout pages to nine?

_____

_____

8 Once you've removed a Slide Master object, such as a footer element, how would you replace it?

_____

_____

_____

ANSWERS: PAGE 305

EXTRA PRACTICE

1. Open an existing PowerPoint presentation and display the Slide Master.

2. Change the Slide Master title text from whatever default is set to 48-point Arial and make the font color black.

3. Open a blank PowerPoint presentation, select the Dad's Tie design template, and use the Slide Master display to remove the tie graphic from the left side of the slides.

4. Use the Slide Master to insert a custom graphic footer on all slides in a PowerPoint presentation.

5. Change the default handout pages to display three slides to a page, with room on the right for the audience to keep personal notes about each slide.

REAL-WORLD APPLICATIONS

✔ You want to distinguish your design from those of other speakers if you know those speakers will also be making presentations in PowerPoint. You can still use the preprogrammed designs, only spend some time customizing the design: add a company logo to the footer, change the background color and graphics, change the text color, and so on.

✔ Suppose you are using PowerPoint as the basis of a confidential report that you will print and share with a small audience, but which you do not want duplicated or shared indiscriminately. This is a good application for a custom background image. Use a company logo behind every slide to discourage duplication, for example, or create some text informing viewers that the report is proprietary and must not be copied.

Visual Quiz

Describe how to display the screen shown here.

_____

_____

_____

_____

_____

_____

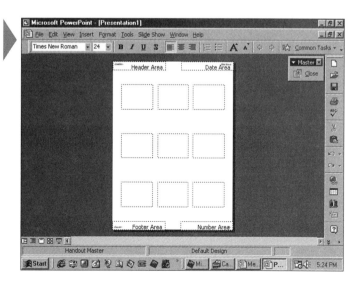

CHAPTER **8**

MASTER
THESE
SKILLS

▶ **Adding Animation**

▶ **Adding Slide Transitions and Sounds**

▶ **Using Action Buttons**

Using Animation

During the first 15 years or so that I used computers, everything was mostly text-based and some form of monochrome—IBM green screen, DEC black-on-white, or PC white-on-black. There were even a few innovative terminal manufacturers who tried white-on-amber. We expected—and needed—no more.

Today, of course, nearly everything we do with our computers involves color, sound, and even animation. Consider the Office Assistant, which by now is probably a familiar fixture on your PowerPoint screen. This creature has it all: color, sound, and animation. Doesn't he seem natural in his movements, expressions, and sounds?

Given this development platform, why should we be satisfied with flat, simplistic PowerPoint shows? We don't have to be. Built into this program are some fairly sophisticated animation features that you can use easily to augment the text and graphics message of your slide show. You can't easily access animation as sophisticated as the rascally Rocky, but there's a lot you can do to enhance your presentation.

In PowerPoint, animation refers to the movement of text and other slide objects, frequently coupled with sound. You can have a block of text "fly" onto the slide one line or one character at a time, for example. And you can add sound effects to accompany and emphasize this movement.

In addition, you can add transition effects between slides in much the same way that moviemakers sometimes add transitions between scenes. Transitions between PowerPoint slides can help you lead the audience to a different topic or concept, or simply add the feeling of motion to help keep your presentation alive.

Another form of action is really custom programming, of sorts, where you place an object on a slide and connect some action to that object. You can use this technique to launch another PowerPoint program, start a motion-video clip, play a sound, and so on.

This chapter discusses all of these animation techniques and shows how you can use motion—and the concept of motion—to add interest to your basic PowerPoint presentations.

Adding Animation

In my experience, few PowerPoint users apply animation and other features to their shows. Why? I suspect most users somehow believe these presentation enhancements are too hard to use. Not true!

Many of the presentation enhancements that make your show different are built into the program, and accessible with just a few mouse-clicks. To experiment, create a new presentation and choose a title slide from the New Slide AutoLayout screen. You'll have a single slide with two text areas, one for a title and one for a subtitle. Type something into each of these text areas.

Note the upper-left figure on the next page: this shows the first step in adding animation to the title part of this slide. You can make this text display in a number of ways, including Drop-In, Fly From Top, Dissolve, Wipe Right, and some interesting choices such as Drive-In, Laser Text, and Camera.

It would be difficult to adequately describe each of these effects, but you can try them out easily enough. Refer to the first figure again, and choose Typewriter from the Preset Animation menu. Nothing appears to happen, right? Now click the slide show icon at the bottom of the screen, or choose Slide Show from the View menu. There's your title slide, without the main title. Press the space bar or click the left mouse button.

You should see the title appear, one character at a time, and (assuming you have a sound card) you'll hear sounds like typewriter keys being pressed. This effect is popular with the "real-life" police shows when they show a subtitle or when they want to simulate the computer displaying information. (Since when has your computer clicked with each character as it displays information on the screen? Hollywood!)

A more dramatic version of the same effect is Laser Text. Try it.

You can also use some of these animation settings for graphics images. Check out the upper-right figure on the next page. PowerPoint knows the selected graphic is not a text image, so the text animation choices are not available from the Preset Animation menu.

These basic settings are pretty good, but PowerPoint lets you do a whole lot more, and custom animations aren't much harder than preset animations. The last two figures on the facing page show you custom slide show animation.

Continued

TAKE NOTE

LEARNING MORE ABOUT PRESET ANIMATION

Here's a quick way to see what else you can do with present animation features built into PowerPoint. Simply open a new presentation and choose the Brainstorming design template. This template includes a number of preset animation features you can study by clicking a slide object, then choosing Preset Animation from the Slide Show menu.

CROSS-REFERENCE

Refer to the "Adding Slide Transitions and Sounds" and "Using Action Buttons" sections of this chapter for more on customizing animation and presentations.

FIND IT ONLINE

To download Microsoft PowerPoint Animation Player, visit **http://plato.acadiau.ca/sandbox/ppt/inet.htm**.

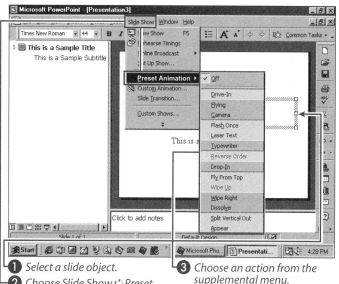

1 Select a slide object.
2 Choose Slide Show ➪ Preset Animation from the main menu.
3 Choose an action from the supplemental menu.

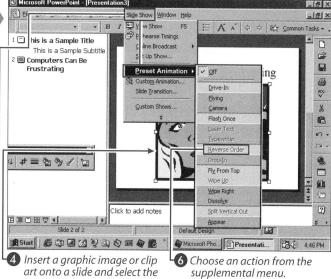

4 Insert a graphic image or clip art onto a slide and select the image.
5 Choose Slide Show ➪ Preset Animation.
6 Choose an action from the supplemental menu.

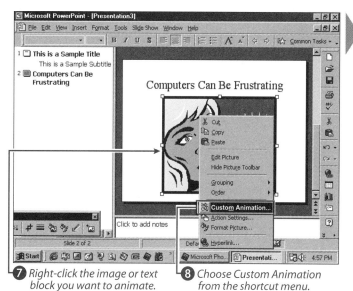

7 Right-click the image or text block you want to animate.
8 Choose Custom Animation from the shortcut menu.

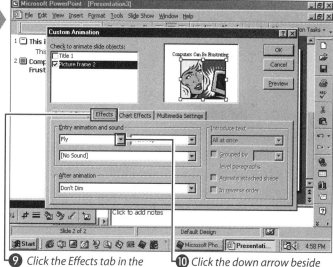

9 Click the Effects tab in the Custom Animation dialog box if it is not already displayed.
10 Click the down arrow beside the Entry animation and sound field to view a list of animation options.

Adding Animation

Continued

When preset animation doesn't give you the features you want, use the Custom Animation dialog box. The upper-left figure on the following page shows how you can choose unusual effects from Custom Animation's Effects tab.

At the top left of this dialog box is a list of objects on the current slide. Items with a check mark will be animated. The animation effect or action you select will apply to the highlighted item in this dialog box. In the upper-right figure on the following page, I've shown how to add sound to accompany the action selected in the first step. Sounds and animation together can enhance the presentation of an idea, but use these features carefully: If every object is animated and accompanied with sound, the effect can be detrimental.

Clicking the down arrow beside the After animation field (at the bottom of the Entry animation and sound group) tells PowerPoint what to do after an animated object is presented on the screen during a slide show (see the lower-left figure on the next page). You can have the image disappear after it animates, exit when you click your mouse next, or remain on the screen. In addition, you can have the object change colors when the next object displays. This option is useful when you want to show a progression of items on a single slide. You can animate one item in a bullet list, for example, talk about it, then bring in the next item. When the next item

displays, the previous item dims or changes color to indicate you have already covered that topic.

This isn't the only way to manage multiple objects on a single slide. Once you have set the animation and sound properties, you may also want to control what happens when. You do this with the Order & Timing tab of the Custom Animation dialog box, shown in the lower-right figure on the facing page.

These features provide powerful tools for controlling your slide presentation. I use them to display sequential screen shots or photographs on a single slide. I enjoy using a digital camera to document company or personal events, for example, and sometimes prepare computer-based slide shows of these pictures with PowerPoint. This multi-object animation feature lets you place several photographs on a single slide, in sequence, accompanied by sounds or music.

TAKE NOTE

USING CUSTOM SOUNDS WITH ANIMATION

At the bottom of the sound list on the Effects tab of the Custom Animation dialog box is an Other Sound choice. Click here to navigate to any sound file you have on your hard drive. You can record sounds of your own, use sounds supplied with other programs, and so on.

CROSS-REFERENCE

See Chapter 13 for more ideas on making your presentations unique and interesting.

FIND IT ONLINE

You can download sounds to accompany your slides at **http://www.hawkinzz.demon.co.uk/Downloads/Sounds/Sounds.htm.**

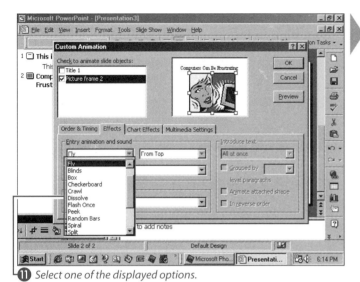

⓫ *Select one of the displayed options.*

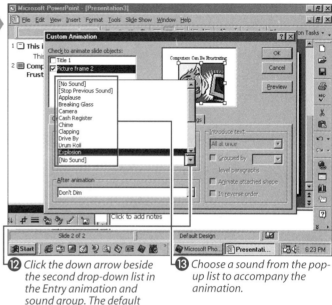

⓬ *Click the down arrow beside the second drop-down list in the Entry animation and sound group. The default choice is [No Sound].*

⓭ *Choose a sound from the pop-up list to accompany the animation.*

⓮ *Click the down arrow beside the After animation field (the default choice is Don't Dim).*

⓯ *Choose a color or action from the pop-up list.*

⓰ *Click More Colors to display a broader selection of possible colors to set after animation.*

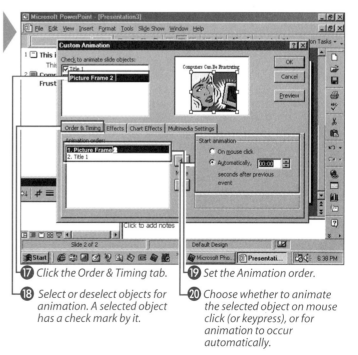

⓱ *Click the Order & Timing tab.*

⓲ *Select or deselect objects for animation. A selected object has a check mark by it.*

⓳ *Set the Animation order.*

⓴ *Choose whether to animate the selected object on mouse click (or keypress), or for animation to occur automatically.*

109

Adding Slide Transitions and Sounds

Slide transitions also add action to your slide shows by adding motion of some sort when you move from one slide to another. Movie and television-commercial designers use transitions between scenes. Popular transition techniques are wipes, dissolves, and fades.

A wipe sends an opaque bar or other object across the final image in a scene — from one side or from the top or bottom of the screen — erasing the scene as it goes and dragging the next scene onto the screen behind it. A fade gradually darkens the current scene and from the darkness brings up the next scene. A dissolve is a special kind of fade.

You can use these transitions and others to add interest to your slide show as you move from one slide to the next. As you can see from the upper-left figure on the next page, you set transitions from the Slide Show menu. The upper-right figure shows your choices for transition type. PowerPoint shows you a preview of any transition you choose in the dialog box; step through the available transitions to see how they work before you select one for a particular slide or for the whole show. As you can see, you have a wide range of choices, including blinds, boxes, and checkerboards.

Besides transition type, you can determine the timing (advance) of a transition. In other words, you can choose how to trigger the transition. At this point, PowerPoint becomes a little funny. When you set a transition effect, it is for the current slide, the one displayed on your screen, unless you click Apply to All when you close this dialog box. When you choose an Advance setting, it affects the closing of the current slide and the displaying of the next one. Suppose you set a Box Out transition and specify a 10-second advance for slide #2. With slide #1 on the screen, you can press the space bar on your keyboard and slide #2 appears with a Box Out transition. Ten seconds later, slide #3 appears.

The default Advance setting is On mouse click. Alternately, you can automate the transitions after a set number of seconds (see the lower-left figure on the following page) to create a self-running slide show that changes slides without you having to do anything.

Finally, you can set a sound to accompany the transition, as I've shown in the lower-right figure on the facing page.

TAKE NOTE

PLANNING TRANSITIONS

As with object animation, slide transitions can become tiresome if you use too many. Plan transitions to bridge subtopics within a presentation or to introduce a new concept. All rules can be broken, but generally you don't want a transition on every slide; and, if you use transitions, pick one or two and stick with them throughout the show. You can, however, use the Transitions dialog box to set automatic slide advance for every slide.

CROSS-REFERENCE
See Chapter 13 for hints on using narration with automated transitions to produce a self-running slide show.

FIND IT ONLINE
To sample Microsoft PowerPoint sounds, check out http://geocities.com/Hollywood/Boulevard/5901/sounds.html.

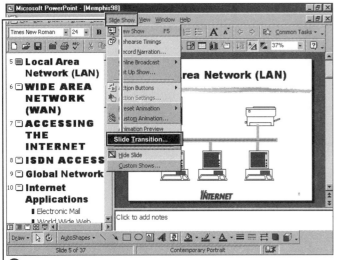

❶ Choose Slide Show ➪ Slide Transition from the main menu.

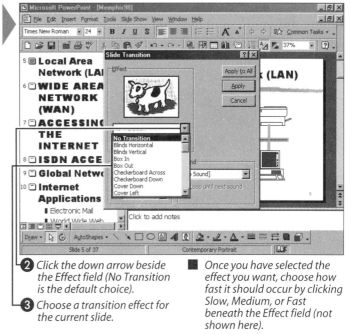

❷ Click the down arrow beside the Effect field (No Transition is the default choice).

❸ Choose a transition effect for the current slide.

■ Once you have selected the effect you want, choose how fast it should occur by clicking Slow, Medium, or Fast beneath the Effect field (not shown here).

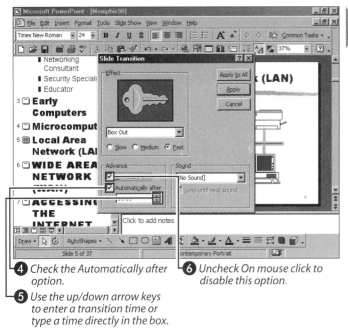

❹ Check the Automatically after option.

❺ Use the up/down arrow keys to enter a transition time or type a time directly in the box.

❻ Uncheck On mouse click to disable this option.

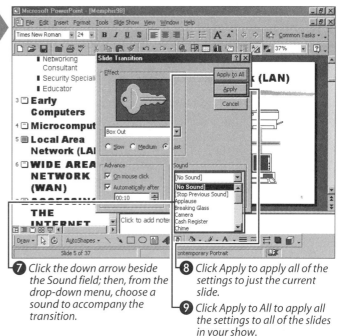

❼ Click the down arrow beside the Sound field; then, from the drop-down menu, choose a sound to accompany the transition.

❽ Click Apply to apply all of the settings to just the current slide.

❾ Click Apply to All to apply all the settings to all of the slides in your show.

Using Action Buttons

Action buttons are buttons you can add to your slides. When you click one of these buttons, PowerPoint conducts a specific action. For example, you could place a button on a slide at a transition point in your show to give you the option of skipping several of the next slides or launching another slide show, depending on your timing or audience preference. And you can enable these actions on mouse-click or mouse-over (when you just move your mouse over the object).

You add action buttons from the Slide Show. It's easy to select a button, click and drag it to position it on your slide, and to indicate its size. In the Action Settings dialog box, you can indicate what action you want to associate with the button. You can determine whether this action occurs when you pause the mouse over the button or when you click the button. The programming takes effect when you view the slide in Slide Show view.

Although you can choose from several program actions for action buttons, the most common one is hyperlink. This action works in a similar way to hyperlinks on the World Wide Web: You click the action button or pause over it, and PowerPoint jumps immediately to another slide in the show, opens a new show, opens a Web page or another file, and so on.

Two other options in the Action Settings dialog box help you format the action button. If you select Highlight click, PowerPoint changes the button's image when you click it so you can tell it is selected.

And you can associate a sound with the specified action — music, voices, sound effects, and so on. PowerPoint makes it easy to experiment with these settings until you achieve what you want.

TAKE NOTE

▶ USING ACTIONS WITHOUT BUTTONS

You can animate any graphic object on your slides by right-clicking the object and choosing Action Settings from the shortcut menu. When you use animation on pictures, clip art, or other objects and don't use obvious action buttons, you can hide a particular animation feature until you need it. The audience won't know it's there until you use it.

▶ CREATING AN ACTION-BUTTON TOOLBAR

Any PowerPoint menu with a visible bar at the top can be turned into a toolbar. Choose Action Buttons from the Slide Show menu, then grab the top of the button toolbar to drag it anywhere on the screen. It will stay there until you dismiss it.

▶ RETURNING FROM ACTION DESTINATIONS

Don't forget that you may want to return from wherever you go with an action setting. If one action jumps to another slide, for example, place another action on the destination slide to return to the last slide viewed. This same setting works even if you jump to another PowerPoint file.

CROSS-REFERENCE
See Chapter 17 to learn how you can create custom programs that can be accessed through action settings.

FIND IT ONLINE
The Hyperlink feature of the Action Settings dialog box enables you to link to any Web site during your show if you have Internet access.

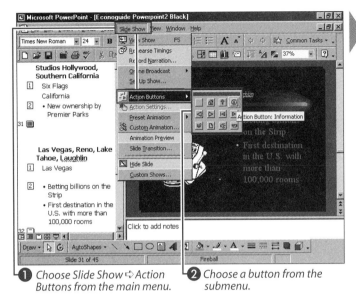

❶ Choose Slide Show ⟿ Action Buttons from the main menu.

❷ Choose a button from the submenu.

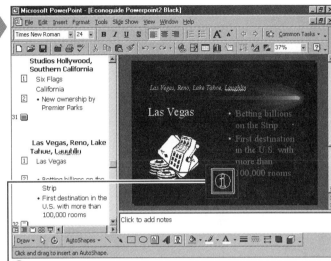

❸ Position the cross-hair mouse cursor where you want to place the action button, hold down the left mouse button, and drag the action-button shape to the desired size.

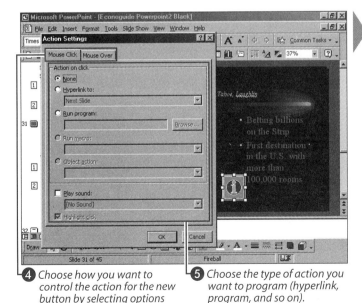

❹ Choose how you want to control the action for the new button by selecting options on the Mouse Click or Mouse Over tab.

❺ Choose the type of action you want to program (hyperlink, program, and so on).

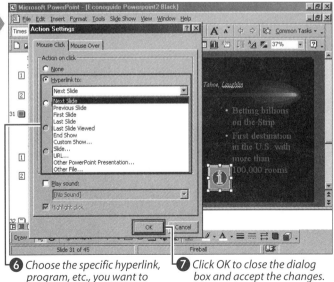

❻ Choose the specific hyperlink, program, etc., you want to access with this link.

❼ Click OK to close the dialog box and accept the changes.

113

Personal Workbook

Q&A

1 PowerPoint includes two types of slide animation. What are they?

_____

_____

_____

2 What is meant by _Laser Text animation_?

_____

_____

_____

3 How are slide animations and slide transitions similar? How are they different?

_____

_____

_____

4 Describe two ways to display the PowerPoint custom animation dialog box.

_____

_____

_____

5 What technical consideration might force you to change the color of an animated object in a PowerPoint slide show?

_____

_____

_____

6 What two methods can you use to advance slides with transitions?

_____

_____

_____

7 How do you display the Action Button submenu?

_____

_____

_____

8 What menu sequence do you use to animate slide objects that aren't action buttons?

_____

_____

_____

ANSWERS: PAGE 305

EXTRA PRACTICE

1. Open an existing PowerPoint presentation, choose an object, and add an action setting to it.

2. Open the Slide Transition dialog box and specify a slow dissolve transition for the current slide. Then make the appropriate settings to close this slide and move to the next one in 10 seconds.

3. Open the Custom Animation dialog box and apply these settings to a text object: Crawl from Bottom, applause sound, Red on next animation automatically after 12 seconds.

4. Create a custom toolbar from the Action Buttons menu.

5. Set random animation for all slides in your presentation with a single setting in the Transition dialog box.

REAL-WORLD APPLICATIONS

✔ Suppose you are asked to speak to a variety of audiences about a fairly technical topic. You can't always be sure what level of understanding your audience has. One solution is to create a show that includes action buttons that let you skip blocks of introductory material if you discover that your listeners already know it. You can even use action buttons to launch supplemental slide shows to provide additional detail on specific topics.

✔ You can use PowerPoint to help you document an event, a software program, or a company with photographs or screen shots. Use object animations to place multiple images on a single slide, positioning and sizing each one to overlay and augment previous ones. Add live sound, such as interviews with the subjects of your photos, and you have an effective, self-running slide show.

Visual Quiz

Describe how to display the screen shown here.

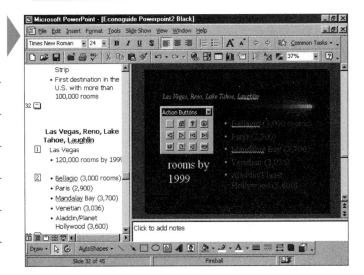

CHAPTER 9

MASTER
THESE
SKILLS

▶ Changing Slide Layout

▶ Setting the Color Scheme

▶ Changing the Slide Background

▶ Using Design Templates and Fonts

▶ Formatting Bullets and Numbers

Changing Layout and Design

I've already shown you the basics of PowerPoint layout and design. We've used the Slide Layout (AutoLayout) dialog box to choose the appearance of slides, and I've discussed using design templates to configure a slide show.

In this chapter, I want to go a little further in showing you how to control the appearance of a slide and the mood of your slide show.

You can use the slide designs supplied with PowerPoint or you can create your own. Compare your PowerPoint slide to a printed magazine or book page. Taken together, all of the elements in either medium create a layout. A layout is the arrangement of the elements that make up the page or screen. These elements might include text, graphics, photographs, boxes, and other static objects; white space and color space; motion video; and so on.

No single element of the layout is intended to stand on its own. Every slide element should relate in some way to every other element and, in some cases, to one or more elements on previous or following slides. If you change the typeface or typestyle used for a heading, for example, it may change how much information will fit on the page and it may require a change in the type used for the rest of the screen. Moreover, you should be careful about changing major elements (such as title typeface or style) in a single slide. Titles should have a unified look from slide to slide to tie the slides together and keep from jarring the audience.

As you design each screen, remember this general rule: visual material augments a presentation. It adds information to what the speaker is saying. Don't use graphics, motion video, animation, sound, or anything else just because you can. Use these elements because it's the proper thing to do in a given situation — because they augment some aspect of your presentation.

You can do anything you want with a PowerPoint slide, but a few minutes of extra thought can make a difference in the effectiveness of your presentation. And don't be afraid to refine a show after it is done. The really effective PowerPoint presentations are those you use more than once. Each time you reuse them is an opportunity to refine and fine-tune them.

Changing Slide Layout

PowerPoint includes 24 predefined slide layouts: bullet lists, graphics with bullet lists, text charts, spreadsheets, motion video, organization charts, and so on. The Slide Layout or AutoLayout dialog box — it changes names depending on how you access it — shows you designs you can modify or use as is.

You'll always see the AutoLayout dialog box when you open a new blank presentation or one that uses a design template. PowerPoint is simply asking you to choose the design of the first slide, most likely a title slide. You'll see AutoLayout again when you insert a new slide into an existing show while working with the design.

In addition, you can display the Slide Layout dialog box at any time to change the way an existing slide is formatted (see the upper-left figure on the facing page). Notice how PowerPoint presents these layout options. The first 12 options appear in the dialog box, with 12 more hidden until you scroll down to them. The first 12, which include a title slide and a blank slide, are the most common.

Once you have applied a layout design to a blank or existing slide, you will probably see one or more placeholders to help you insert new features onto your slide. The upper-right figure on the next page, for example, shows a blank slide with three layout placeholders: a title, a text block, and a graph or chart. These preformatted areas are designed to help you insert new information on your slides with minimal effort.

Click an item to select it; double-click to open it for data entry. For text entry — such as the title and the text box on the upper-right figure, next page — the insertion point is placed for new text entry right in the displayed object. With other items, such as the chart shown here, you may see a wizard or another application (lower-left figure, next page).

Finally, you can accept the size of these placeholders and their data or you can resize them, as shown in the final figure on the next page.

TAKE NOTE

▶ DISPLAYING THE COMMON TASKS TOOLBAR

If the Common Tasks toolbar isn't already visible, you can display it easily: Click Common Tasks on the Standard toolbar, and then drag the Common Tasks menu away from its docked position on the Standard toolbar and onto the PowerPoint desktop. Drag it anywhere on the screen, or remove it by clicking the close icon.

▶ CHANGING SLIDE OBJECTS

To edit existing data or add new information, double-click a slide object to open its associated program (such as the chart application shown on the facing page).

CROSS-REFERENCE
See Chapter 12 for ideas on creating layouts from scratch and using specific objects with your slides.

FIND IT ONLINE
PC World Today has a great article on the importance of creative presentation at **http://www.pcworld.com/ pcwtoday/article/0,1510,8042,00.html**.

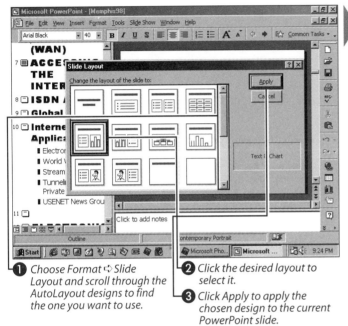

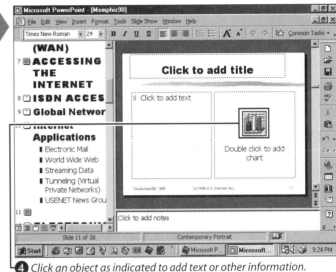

① Choose Format ⇨ Slide Layout and scroll through the AutoLayout designs to find the one you want to use.

② Click the desired layout to select it.

③ Click Apply to apply the chosen design to the current PowerPoint slide.

④ Click an object as indicated to add text or other information.

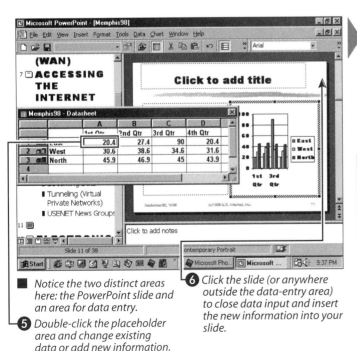

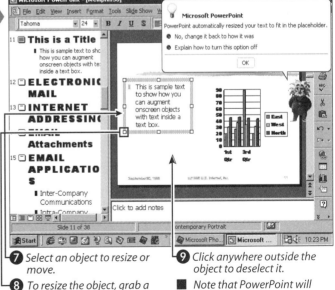

■ Notice the two distinct areas here: the PowerPoint slide and an area for data entry.

⑤ Double-click the placeholder area and change existing data or add new information.

⑥ Click the slide (or anywhere outside the data-entry area) to close data input and insert the new information into your slide.

⑦ Select an object to resize or move.

⑧ To resize the object, grab a handle and drag; move the object by grabbing it between the handles.

⑨ Click anywhere outside the object to deselect it.

■ Note that PowerPoint will help you by resizing text to fit the new object size. (You can reverse this formatting.)

119

Setting the Color Scheme

Chapter 7 introduced the concept of changing slide colors. You can also change a slide color scheme. A scheme defines background and associated colors for other items such as charts, bullet lists, and slide titles.

Color is an important part of presentation design. Different colors can elicit different responses from people. Red, for example, is an emotional color that can actually make a person's heart beat faster. The eye also takes longer to process red than any other color.

Dark blue projects a stable, trustworthy, and mature message. It can encourage fantasy, but it also has a calming effect, so don't use blue if you want the audience to be excited or upbeat. Light blue is generally considered youthful, masculine, and cool, while green's message is growth, positive, organic, or action. Green can help people feel comfortable in unfamiliar places, but choose green carefully: Many of us carry a prejudice against institutional green — the green of classrooms and chalkboards.

White is an important color. It is a pure color that denotes cleanliness, honesty, sophistication, refinement, or delicate things. In some slides, white also serves the important function of opening up the display; you can use white space to keep the slide from being cluttered. To set the slide color scheme, open the Slide Color Scheme dialog box (shown in the upper-left figure on the next page) from the Format menu. Then use the displayed schemes to make changes to the appearance of the main parts of your slides.

Six possible schemes are displayed. The one in the upper left is the current scheme; each of the remaining schemes changes one or more aspects of the design. The top-middle scheme changes the background. The upper-right scheme is black-and-white. The bottom three choices make more dramatic color-setting changes, but they maintain coordinated colors for the various parts of your slides — if the background changes, then text, bullets, and other features acquire compatible colors.

If you don't like the preset schemes PowerPoint suggests, you can display the Custom tab of this dialog box (lower-left figure, next page) and design your own color scheme. You can remove existing schemes from the list and, once you have created a custom look, add the custom design to the standard list.

Just as you can customize a scheme, you can build your own colors for slide objects via the Custom tab in the color dialog box (lower-right figure, next page). These Custom options let you make very subtle color changes for specific objects.

TAKE NOTE

APPLYING THE NEW SCHEME AFTER CUSTOMIZING

If you customize a PowerPoint color scheme, then later apply a new scheme to your entire slide show, the custom settings you made earlier will remain.

CROSS-REFERENCE

See Chapter 7 for tips on setting colors from the Slide Master.

FIND IT ONLINE

Visit **http://www.microsoft.com/office/ork/038/ 038.htm#top** for a good description of PowerPoint design and color schemes from Microsoft.

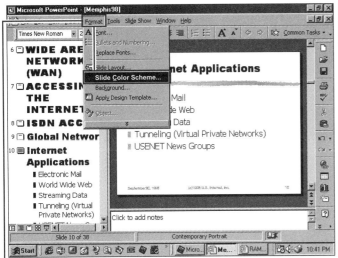

1 Select Format ⇨ Slide Color Scheme to open the Color Scheme dialog box.

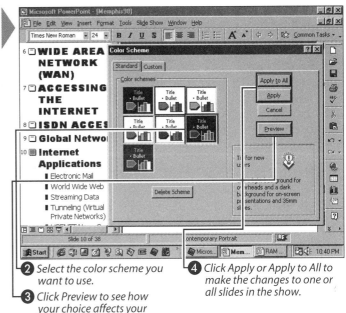

2 Select the color scheme you want to use.

3 Click Preview to see how your choice affects your presentation.

4 Click Apply or Apply to All to make the changes to one or all slides in the show.

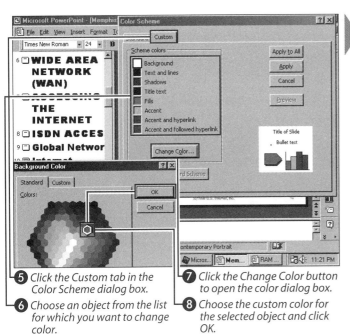

5 Click the Custom tab in the Color Scheme dialog box.

6 Choose an object from the list for which you want to change color.

7 Click the Change Color button to open the color dialog box.

8 Choose the custom color for the selected object and click OK.

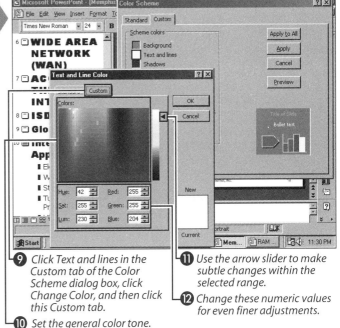

9 Click Text and lines in the Custom tab of the Color Scheme dialog box, click Change Color, and then click this Custom tab.

10 Set the general color tone.

11 Use the arrow slider to make subtle changes within the selected range.

12 Change these numeric values for even finer adjustments.

121

Changing the Slide Background

hapter 7 talked about changing slide background images; this section will expand that information a little, showing you how to adjust background colors. You can change background colors for every slide in your presentation by adjusting the background in your Slide Master, or choose to adjust the background color on only a single slide.

You change the basic background color for a slide or slides from a single dialog box accessible from the Format menu. Once you get the Background dialog box on the screen, you can view the current background and choose a variety of new colors for it.

Use the Preview button in this dialog box to view the current slide with the new settings before you actually make the change. If you don't like what you see, choose another color and click Preview again, and the current slide changes to reflect the new setting.

There are choices available to you that are not visible in the pop-up dialog box. If you want to use a color not displayed in this pop-up box, choose More Colors to show the Colors dialog box shown in the lower left of the facing page. Between the Standard and Custom tabs in the Colors box, you have a virtually unlimited range of colors and shades.

You can also use the Background dialog box to turn off graphics images placed in the background on the Slide Master. Again, use the Preview button to see how you like this change; simply uncheck Omit Background and choose Preview again to put things back the way they were.

When you select the background settings with this dialog box you have two choices: Apply or Apply to All. Use Apply to set a new background color for just the current slide and Apply to All to change the background for all slides in your show.

The Fill Effects dialog box, shown in the bottom right figure on the facing page, gives you a number of additional background choices. This option allows the kind of interesting color fades and changes you've probably seen in professional slides and on software background screens.

Continued

TAKE NOTE

CHANGING SINGLE SLIDE BACKGROUNDS

The ability to change the background on a single slide can help you match a particular slide to the information you want to put on it. In general, it is best to keep the color schemes the same for all slides. However, you can change individual slide colors for specific inserted objects, such as graphics or photographs.

PREVIEWING GRADIENT SETTINGS

To see how gradient settings affect your background design, open a slide show that uses the Azure, Blue Diagonal, or Mountain design templates, among others.

CROSS-REFERENCE

See Chapter 7 for more information about changing background colors through the Slide Master.

FIND IT ONLINE

To read more about how to change PowerPoint background colors, visit the Clemson University page at **http://cuweb.clemson.edu/ect_training/ppt/page9.htm**.

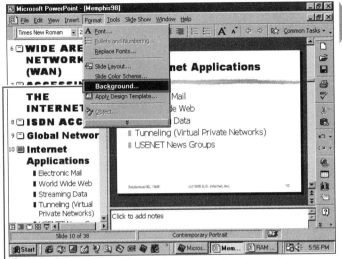

1 Choose Format ⇨ Background to open the Background dialog box.

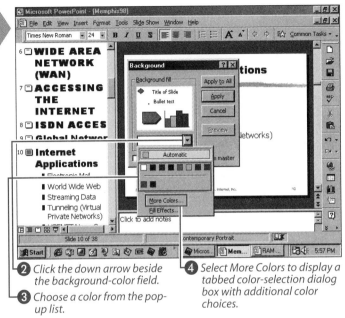

2 Click the down arrow beside the background-color field.

3 Choose a color from the pop-up list.

4 Select More Colors to display a tabbed color-selection dialog box with additional color choices.

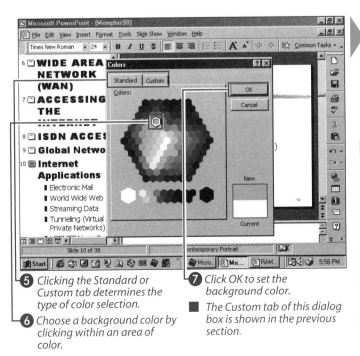

5 Clicking the Standard or Custom tab determines the type of color selection.

6 Choose a background color by clicking within an area of color.

7 Click OK to set the background color.

■ The Custom tab of this dialog box is shown in the previous section.

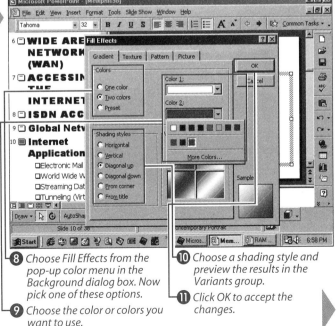

8 Choose Fill Effects from the pop-up color menu in the Background dialog box. Now pick one of these options.

9 Choose the color or colors you want to use.

10 Choose a shading style and preview the results in the Variants group.

11 Click OK to accept the changes.

Changing the Slide Background
Continued

Color and shading aren't the only tools you can use to determine how your slide backgrounds look. The Fill Effects dialog box (shown in the lower-right corner of the previous page) has three additional tabs with more background options: Texture, Pattern, and Picture.

The Texture tab offers a number of preset textures, from newsprint and white marble to parchment and purple mesh (see the upper-left figure on the facing page). Texture combines with color to help set the mood of your slides; however, use care in adding texture because the background image can distract from other images you plan to place on your slides. Textures generally work better for text charts or as borders for solid images such as photographs or screen shots.

Patterns are another slide addition (upper-right image, facing page). These are preformatted settings that combine foreground and background colors with patterns to create a unique background image. Like textures, patterns can add interest to your slides, but choose the look and color carefully so as not to detract from the presentation. You'll also want to use contrasting colors for any text and other images that overlay patterns and textures. Try setting boldface text attributes to further differentiate the text from the background.

You also can use pictures — photographs, drawings, graphics — as backgrounds. A photograph or meaningful drawing can help get your message across with less text or other graphics. Put the photograph in the background and use minimal text to make your point. You can use the same image on a range of slides to show the audience the main theme of the current discussion, or use a different image on each slide to carry individual messages.

After you choose settings from any of the Fill Effects tabs, you can preview the results in the Background dialog box.

TAKE NOTE

FINDING TEXTURE IMAGES

You can use a variety of graphics images as slide textures. Check the C:\Windows directory for an assortment of usable images. When you choose an image, it is added to the textures on the Texture tab.

USING TEXTURES AND PATTERNS

As a general rule, you should consider simplifying slide designs that use textures and patterns. Reduce the amount of text and avoid using graphics and other objects with textures and patterns.

FINDING PHOTOGRAPHS

You can use any photographs for PowerPoint presentations, but you need to digitize them. Options include scanning prints, negatives, or slides; having files stored to Kodak Photo CD (your local drugstore can probably have this done); and using a digital camera or video recorder to prepare photographs for PowerPoint.

CROSS-REFERENCE
For more information on using pictures and other graphics elements with your slides, see Chapter 10.

FIND IT ONLINE
Stock-photo agencies are good sources of photographs — though you'll pay for these images. Visit: **http://www.picturecube.com/** and **http://www.rightimage.com/**.

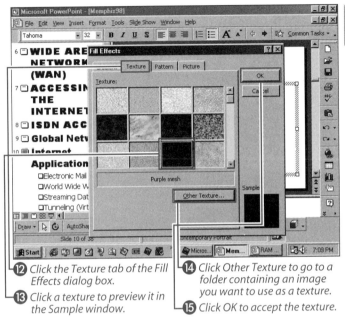

⓬ *Click the Texture tab of the Fill Effects dialog box.*

⓭ *Click a texture to preview it in the Sample window.*

⓮ *Click Other Texture to go to a folder containing an image you want to use as a texture.*

⓯ *Click OK to accept the texture.*

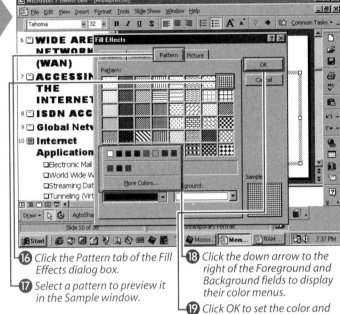

⓰ *Click the Pattern tab of the Fill Effects dialog box.*

⓱ *Select a pattern to preview it in the Sample window.*

⓲ *Click the down arrow to the right of the Foreground and Background fields to display their color menus.*

⓳ *Click OK to set the color and pattern.*

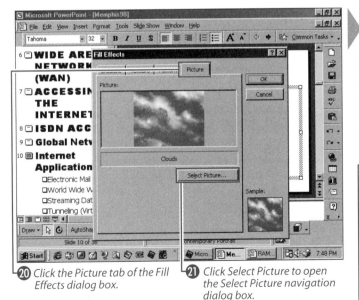

⓴ *Click the Picture tab of the Fill Effects dialog box.*

㉑ *Click Select Picture to open the Select Picture navigation dialog box.*

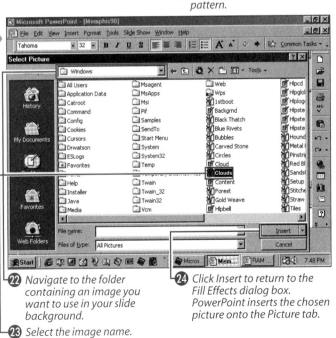

㉒ *Navigate to the folder containing an image you want to use in your slide background.*

㉓ *Select the image name.*

㉔ *Click Insert to return to the Fill Effects dialog box. PowerPoint inserts the chosen picture onto the Picture tab.*

Using Design Templates and Fonts

Selecting a design template is really another way of editing the Slide Master. A template is a collection of background designs, colors, and fonts, preformatted to make it easy for you to set a mood or color scheme for your entire presentation with a single setting. You can either accept the template's font settings or choose a new font of your own design.

As mentioned earlier, you can use design templates when you create a new presentation, but you can also choose a template for an existing show at any time. You can select different ones from a list of available designs and preview them on your screen.

You can change all the fonts in your show from the Slide Master (see Chapter 7), or you can use the Font dialog box (lower-left figure, facing page) to change or adjust font settings individually. The box shown is a fairly typical font and text attribute dialog box, and should be familiar to you if you've used any Microsoft product lately.

A couple of interesting choices — shadow and emboss — can help you differentiate titles and headings. The shadow attribute adds a shadow background to your text, giving it depth and character. The emboss attribute makes your text look like it has been pressed into the paper, giving it a 3D look. You can use more than one text attribute at a time, but study multiple settings carefully before you commit

to them in your show. Some attribute and font design combinations aren't all that attractive.

Of course, you can set the font and font size from the Format menu, as shown in the lower-right figure on the facing page. You are given a direct preview of the font choices, plus a pull-down list for selecting font size. And you can set font attributes such as underline, italics, and boldface from the Format bar without displaying the Font dialog box.

TAKE NOTE

USING TEMPLATES AND BACKGROUNDS

Custom backgrounds — including colors, textures, patterns and so on — take precedence over design-template settings. Suppose you use one template, change the background with custom settings, and then apply another template. The custom background settings remain, but the design template's graphics and text styles will be there, too.

CHANGING FONTS

You can change all of the text within a text box, the text for a single word, or individual characters. Click anywhere in a line of text and click the text-box border to change all the text. Double-click inside a word to select it and triple-click to select a whole line of text.

CROSS-REFERENCE

See Chapter 7 for more template and font information.

FIND IT ONLINE

For an archive of PowerPoint templates, go to **http://plato.acadiau.ca/sandbox/ppt/template/ template.htm**.

CHANGING LAYOUT AND DESIGN
Using Design Templates and Fonts

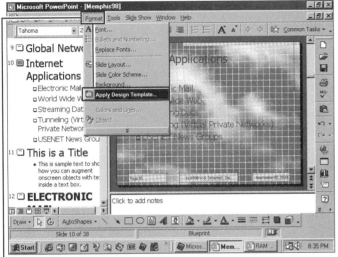

❶ *Choose Format ➭ Apply Design Template to open the Apply Design Template dialog box.*

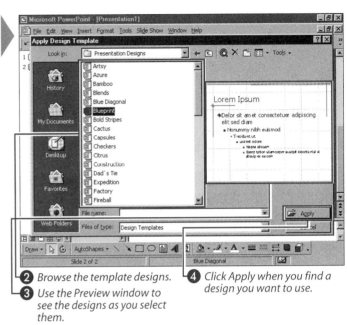

❷ *Browse the template designs.*

❸ *Use the Preview window to see the designs as you select them.*

❹ *Click Apply when you find a design you want to use.*

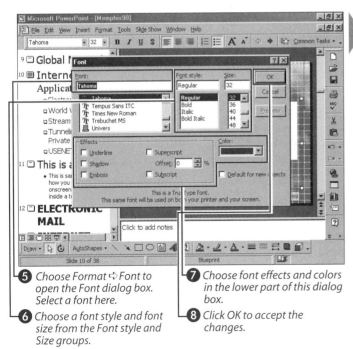

❺ *Choose Format ➭ Font to open the Font dialog box. Select a font here.*

❻ *Choose a font style and font size from the Font style and Size groups.*

❼ *Choose font effects and colors in the lower part of this dialog box.*

❽ *Click OK to accept the changes.*

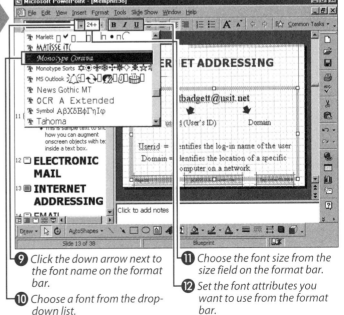

❾ *Click the down arrow next to the font name on the format bar.*

❿ *Choose a font from the drop-down list.*

⓫ *Choose the font size from the size field on the format bar.*

⓬ *Set the font attributes you want to use from the format bar.*

127

Formatting Bullets and Numbers

Bullet lists and numbered lists are a good way to summarize topics on your PowerPoint slides. When you choose an AutoLayout that includes a bullet or numbered list, PowerPoint chooses the bullet or number format based on the design template you are using. You can change the template defaults with the Bullets and Numbering dialog box, shown in the upper left of the facing page.

This is a fairly wide selection of preset bullets, including solid round, hollow round, square, 3D arrow, and so on. You can also choose a picture for the bullets in your list by opening the Picture Bullet dialog box (upper-right figure, next page). PowerPoint displays more than 60 picture bullet choices.

Although PowerPoint gives you plenty of choices for bullets, you don't have to use them. You can use any graphic image, ranging from a photograph to a drawing, as the bullets for your lists. For example, in the Symbol dialog box (accessed by clicking Character in the Bullets and Numbering dialog box), you can choose a special character such as a smiley face, a chevron, or a copyright symbol to be a bullet (lower-left figure, facing page).

You have similar choices for a numbered list, except you use the Numbered tab on the Bullets and Numbering dialog box (lower-right figure, next page). You choose the number style from this dialog box in much the same way you choose a bullet style for your bullet lists.

You can also select the starting number for the current list. PowerPoint automatically restarts the numbering with each new list, but you may want to continue the numbering from a previous list. Make this adjustment from the Numbered tab of the Bullets and Numbering dialog box.

TAKE NOTE

▶ CREATING BULLET AND NUMBERED LISTS

If you're not using a slide with a preformatted bullet- or numbered-list section, you can easily format lines of text for lists. Select the text and then click the bullet-list or numbered-list icon on the format toolbar. Remove bullets or numbers by selecting the text and clicking again on the bullet or number format bar icon.

▶ SELECTING BULLET TEXT

Click a line of text to work with a single line. The outline of the text box is cross-hatched. Click the cross-hatch outline to select all of the text within the text box.

▶ ADDING SPACE BETWEEN TEXT AND THE BULLET OR NUMBER

You can add a tab between the bullet and the first letter by first removing the bullet (click the bullet-list icon on the format bar). Press Tab and then Home to move the cursor to the beginning of the line. Then re-enable the bullet by clicking the format bar icon.

CROSS-REFERENCE

See Chapter 12 for tips on using other specialty objects with your PowerPoint presentation.

FIND IT ONLINE

Search for clip art of any subject at http://151.196.220.55/search/.

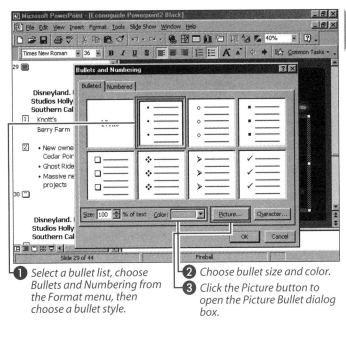

1 Select a bullet list, choose Bullets and Numbering from the Format menu, then choose a bullet style.

2 Choose bullet size and color.

3 Click the Picture button to open the Picture Bullet dialog box.

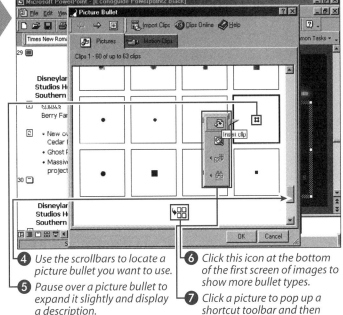

4 Use the scrollbars to locate a picture bullet you want to use.

5 Pause over a picture bullet to expand it slightly and display a description.

6 Click this icon at the bottom of the first screen of images to show more bullet types.

7 Click a picture to pop up a shortcut toolbar and then choose Insert Clip.

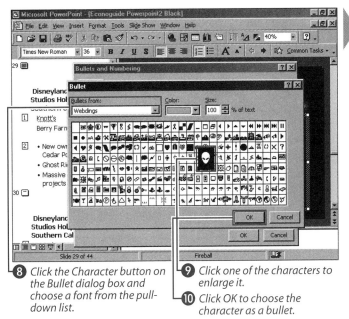

8 Click the Character button on the Bullet dialog box and choose a font from the pull-down list.

9 Click one of the characters to enlarge it.

10 Click OK to choose the character as a bullet.

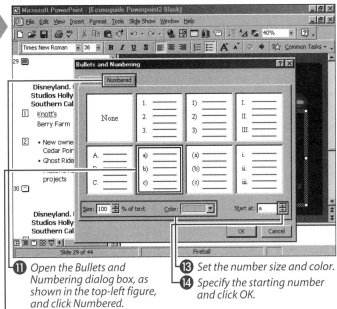

11 Open the Bullets and Numbering dialog box, as shown in the top-left figure, and click Numbered.

12 Click a numbering style to select it.

13 Set the number size and color.

14 Specify the starting number and click OK.

129

Personal Workbook

Q&A

1. When do you use the PowerPoint AutoLayout dialog box?

   _____

   _____

   _____

2. How do you display the Common Tasks toolbar?

   _____

   _____

   _____

3. What main menu entry would you use to place a company logo on a PowerPoint slide?

   _____

   _____

   _____

4. Describe two ways to change the font within a selected block of text.

   _____

   _____

   _____

5. Besides dragging the cursor, how can you select a single word? A sentence?

   _____

   _____

   _____

6. What PowerPoint dialog box would you use to add texture or patterns to a slide background?

   _____

   _____

   _____

7. Describe what happens to your custom slide background when you apply a different design template.

   _____

   _____

   _____

8. What color may denote excitement or danger to an audience?

   _____

   _____

ANSWERS: PAGE 306

Changing Layout and Design
Personal Workbook

EXTRA PRACTICE

1 Display the Common Tasks toolbar and drag it onto the PowerPoint screen. Dock it to the side of the display.

2 Open an existing PowerPoint presentation and apply a different design template.

3 Apply a texture to an existing PowerPoint presentation.

4 Apply a photograph or other graphic image as the slide background in an existing PowerPoint presentation.

5 Create a series of sentences in a plain text box, then create a bullet list by using clip art from the Clip Art Gallery.

REAL-WORLD APPLICATIONS

✔ It's easy to carry out a theme throughout your PowerPoint presentation. Suppose you are making a budget presentation to the management team at your company. You can use background photographs of key company locations and products as you discuss them. Moreover, you can format your bullet lists to use dollar signs, smiley faces, and so on during parts of your program.

✔ I mentioned earlier the importance of color in setting mood and helping to sell an idea in PowerPoint. There can be some subtle benefits to the colors you choose. For example, I try to research the organization or company to which I will be presenting a PowerPoint program. Then I use corporate colors, symbols, or themes as part of the presentation design. This type of presenter awareness can improve the impact of your message.

Visual Quiz

Describe how to display the screen shown here.

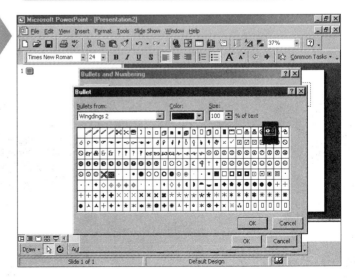

_____

_____

_____

_____

_____

CHAPTER 10

MASTER THESE SKILLS

▶ Adding Pictures to Your Slides

▶ Adding Images to the ClipArt Gallery

▶ Recording Sound for PowerPoint

▶ Adding Sounds to Your Slides

▶ Capturing Movies for PowerPoint

▶ Adding Movies to Your Slides

Using Pictures, Sound, and Movies

PowerPoint includes a wide-ranging collection of clipart and photographs accessible through the ClipArt Gallery. The Gallery even includes a few sounds and some video clips.

When I first started using computers, the screens were black or green. I wouldn't have considered using my computer to display full-color photographs, or to play sound or motion video. Today, as common as these features are, I find that relatively few users make serious use of them in presentations, and that's a mistake.

Consider a corporate presentation to employees in a remote office — people who may rarely have an opportunity to visit the "head shed" and meet with company owners and executives. Wouldn't it be informative to display photographs of key employees and play recorded statements in their own voices? Better yet, you can display a still image to serve as a placeholder or hold a text chart, and then click on an action button to play a motion video clip of one or more key management personnel.

You may think these concepts are difficult to implement, but they aren't. In my company,

U.S. Internet, we use PowerPoint and the World Wide Web for just this application. We have a reasonably inexpensive digital camera and an interested employee who takes pictures of events and people for use in our presentations.

We also use a digital video camera, and we have several employees who take 35mm slides and photographs regularly. We scan these photographs and use them in corporate documentation, Web pages, and presentations. With a little planning, you can develop some excellent, functional images that help you tell your story without hiring a professional photographer.

In this chapter, I show you how to use these built-in facilities and how to record sounds, pictures, and video of your own. This aspect of PowerPoint is one of the more exciting and interesting. You can use clipart and other objects in many Office 2000 applications, of course, but PowerPoint does a particularly good job of organizing the objects. It's easy to place these objects in presentations and to access them when it is time to show them off.

Adding Pictures to Your Slides

As trite as it sounds, a picture *can* be worth a thousand words. You could include text to tell a prospective customer that your new manufacturing facility is state-of-the-art, but a picture or two can prove it. You can *say* that the industrial site you are proposing for your international real estate client's new office complex is perfect for his needs, but a series of site photographs or drawings conveys that message more powerfully.

You can use pictures from the ClipArt Gallery or from files. PowerPoint accepts pictures in a variety of file formats, including PCX, TIFF, BMP, and GIF. These are formats commonly used with drawing programs, digital cameras, and scanners.

The ClipArt Gallery is the easiest source of all kinds of images for your PowerPoint slides. The figure at the upper left of the facing page illustrates the first step toward using the Gallery.

Once you have displayed the main Gallery screen, you can find a category (see the upper-right figure on the facing page) and a specific image you want to use fairly easily (lower-left figure, facing page). When you first install PowerPoint, it includes hundreds of clipart and photographic images and, of course, you can add your own from other programs or your own photo gallery.

Although the ClipArt Gallery is an easy way to group graphics files so you can find them easily, you don't have to use it. If you have your own images

stored elsewhere on your hard drive or network, you can load them directly, as shown in the lower-right figure on the facing page.

Continued

TAKE NOTE

▶ USING DIGITIZED IMAGES

Scanners and digital cameras are a good source for photographs and other graphics images. However, presentations with a lot of digital images can become quite large. Remember that PowerPoint uses only a 72-dot-per-inch (dpi) display. Using a 1,200-dpi, high-quality image is overkill and uses more disk space and loading time than you need. Images over 150 dpi won't give you any better quality; they just take more room and load more slowly.

▶ USING IMAGES FROM THE WEB

Thousands of images are available on the World Wide Web and you can capture them to your hard disk easily by right-clicking the image and choosing Save Picture As from the shortcut menu. In many cases, this is acceptable, but remember that the creative work of others is copyrighted. It may also be illegal to use images you find on the Web. I have had good luck in asking owners of online art for permission to use their images. If you give appropriate credit for the work and if you aren't using the pictures to make money directly from them, you can probably get permission.

CROSS-REFERENCE

See the following section on adding images to the ClipArt Gallery, plus Chapter 12 for more information on using images with your PowerPoint presentations.

FIND IT ONLINE

Click on Clips Online at the top of the ClipArt Gallery to download more clips for the Gallery.

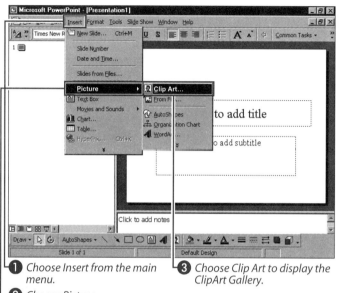

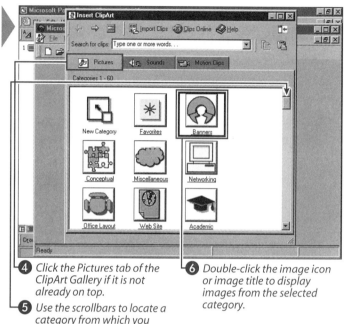

1 Choose Insert from the main menu.

2 Choose Picture.

3 Choose Clip Art to display the ClipArt Gallery.

4 Click the Pictures tab of the ClipArt Gallery if it is not already on top.

5 Use the scrollbars to locate a category from which you want to choose an image.

6 Double-click the image icon or image title to display images from the selected category.

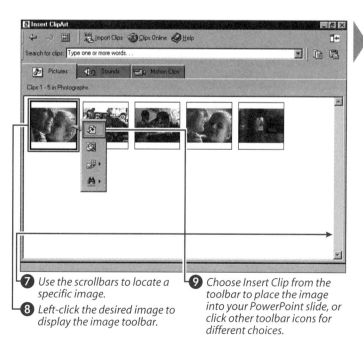

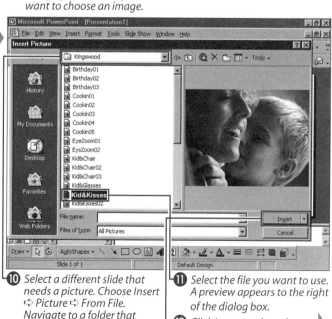

7 Use the scrollbars to locate a specific image.

8 Left-click the desired image to display the image toolbar.

9 Choose Insert Clip from the toolbar to place the image into your PowerPoint slide, or click other toolbar icons for different choices.

10 Select a different slide that needs a picture. Choose Insert ⇨ Picture ⇨ From File. Navigate to a folder that contains an image you want.

11 Select the file you want to use. A preview appears to the right of the dialog box.

12 Click Insert to place the chosen image onto your PowerPoint slide.

The ClipArt Gallery or graphics files you have saved to your hard drive are probably the most common sources for images you will use in PowerPoint presentations. However, depending on the type of presentations you produce, there may be other sources of useful images.

Many of my presentations involve Internet topics or training and information sessions about computer software. Many of the PowerPoint slides I prepare use screen shots, which are images captured directly from a computer display of the Web or computer software. You may find the same method useful.

You can easily add a screen shot to a new PowerPoint slide (see the upper-left figure on the following page). Once you have a new blank slide inserted, you'll need to open the application to display the screen you want to capture. The screen you want may be from a word processor, database program, drawing application, or a Web page.

This technique uses the Windows Clipboard to make a copy of the screen. Press Print Screen (or prtScn, or whatever the name of the key is on your keyboard) to capture a copy of the entire screen to the Clipboard, which is a special section of memory used to transfer data between applications. Use Alt–Print Screen to capture just the active window. Return to your PowerPoint slide and paste the captured image from the Clipboard onto the slide (upper-right figure, following page). The full-screen image is placed onto the current PowerPoint slide.

Grab the image and move it or resize it to fit the slide, as shown in the lower-left image. You can use Microsoft Photo Editor or another graphics program to crop the image.

With Office 2000, the Clipboard has been enhanced to enable you to copy up to 12 images into memory at one time (lower-right figure, next page). As long as you are copying an image directly from an Office 2000 application using Edit ⇨ Copy (this doesn't include screen shots), you can stack the images up and access them as you want. To use multiple objects from the Clipboard, place the cursor in a slide and click any Clipboard toolbar image. It will be copied from the Clipboard into your application.

TAKE NOTE

USING THE CLIPBOARD FOR OTHER DATA

This clipboard technique works well for other data such as Word text or Excel spreadsheet cells. Select information within another application and choose Edit ⇨ Copy to place the selected data onto the Clipboard. Open PowerPoint, display the slide you want to hold the copied data, and select Edit ⇨ Paste to move the data from the Clipboard to the slide.

FINDING CLIPART

Your Office installation CD-ROM includes hundreds of images. They don't all get copied to your hard drive during installation. Navigate to C:\program files\Microsoft Office\Clipart to find them.

CROSS-REFERENCE
See Chapter 11 for more information on using the Clipboard and other Office 2000 features to exchange data with PowerPoint.

SHORTCUT
With PowerPoint and another application both open, copy an image by clicking on the external app, copying data, switching to PowerPoint, and pasting data.

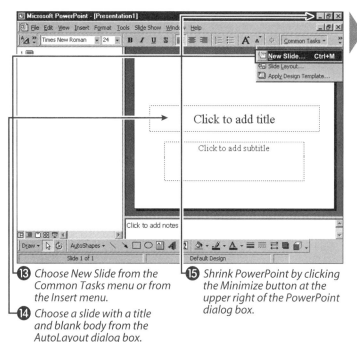

13 Choose New Slide from the Common Tasks menu or from the Insert menu.

14 Choose a slide with a title and blank body from the AutoLayout dialog box.

15 Shrink PowerPoint by clicking the Minimize button at the upper right of the PowerPoint dialog box.

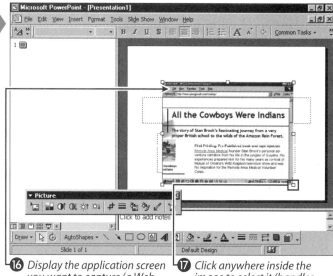

16 Display the application screen you want to capture (a Web page or other screen), press Print Screen, switch to PowerPoint, and choose Edit ⇨ Paste.

17 Click anywhere inside the image to select it (handles appear around the image).

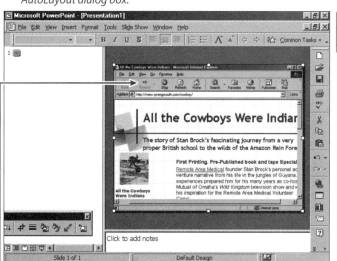

18 Drag the image where you want it on the PowerPoint slide and resize it if necessary.

■ Drag the image by a corner handle to maintain the proper aspect ratio.

■ You can cover the entire slide with the captured image, but you'll still want to include a title so the slide appears with a name in the presentation outline.

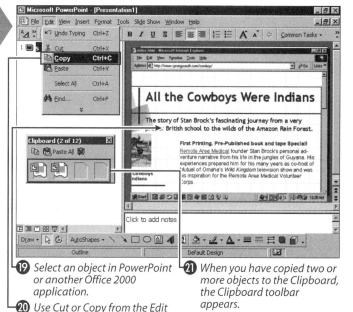

19 Select an object in PowerPoint or another Office 2000 application.

20 Use Cut or Copy from the Edit menu to place individual objects on the clipboard.

21 When you have copied two or more objects to the Clipboard, the Clipboard toolbar appears.

Adding Images to the ClipArt Gallery

The ClipArt Gallery in Office 2000 is different from the original. It makes room for sound and motion video, and it adds another level of image grouping. In this version, clipart, drawings, and photographs are all treated in a similar manner, so you can mix and match image types in a variety of ways to help you store and find the images you want to use with PowerPoint and other Office 2000 applications.

Although Office 2000 (and, by association, PowerPoint 2000) comes with hundreds of images you can use, you probably have images of your own that you'd like to organize through the Gallery. I'll show you how to do that in this section.

To add clipart, photographs, sounds, or motion video to the ClipArt Gallery, you use the Insert menu as if you were going to add something from the Gallery to a PowerPoint slide (see the upper-left figure on the next page).

With the ClipArt Gallery open (Insert ⇨ ClipArt dialog box), you have a number of options for working with its internal images and for importing other objects, all of which PowerPoint calls *clips* (upper-right figure, facing page). Note that the term *clip* in the Gallery can apply to a digitized photograph, a drawing, a sound file, or motion video.

The Gallery can hold a wide variety of images and other objects. When you're ready to add objects to the ClipArt Gallery, store those images on a hard drive that is accessible from your computer. Then choose the object or objects you want to import into the Gallery. Double-click a single filename; or single-click one filename, hold Ctrl, and click additional names to choose multiple images. Then click Import. The Clip Properties dialog box opens (lower-left figure, next page). This is a tabbed dialog box in which you enter a description and identify the category or categories to which the image belongs (bottom-right figure, next page).

Turn the page for more information on setting properties.

Continued

TAKE NOTE

ADDING IMAGES DIRECTLY INTO POWERPOINT

PowerPoint 2000 includes enhanced features for capturing images from a Twain-compliant scanner or digital camera. Choose Picture from the Insert menu, and then choose From Scanner or Camera to insert an image directly from an attached camera or scanner.

ADDING MULTIPLE IMAGES TO THE CLIPART GALLERY

If the folder display in the Add clip to Clip Gallery dialog box contains multiple images you want to import, you can select them in a group or individually. Click the first filename, press and hold the Shift key, and click another filename to select every image between those two files. Alternately, click the first name, and press and hold the Control key. Each subsequent file you click will be selected without selecting any of those between.

CROSS-REFERENCE

See the next task, "Recording Sound for PowerPoint," for more information on securing clips for the Gallery and for your PowerPoint slides.

FIND IT ONLINE

On the ClipArt Gallery main screen, click the Clips Online button to open a Web page with additional art for use in PowerPoint.

1 Choose Insert from the main menu.

2 Choose Picture.

3 Choose Clip Art to open the ClipArt Gallery.

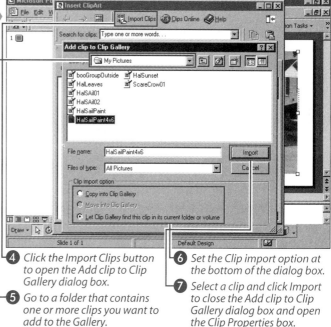

4 Click the Import Clips button to open the Add clip to Clip Gallery dialog box.

5 Go to a folder that contains one or more clips you want to add to the Gallery.

6 Set the Clip import option at the bottom of the dialog box.

7 Select a clip and click Import to close the Add clip to Clip Gallery dialog box and open the Clip Properties box.

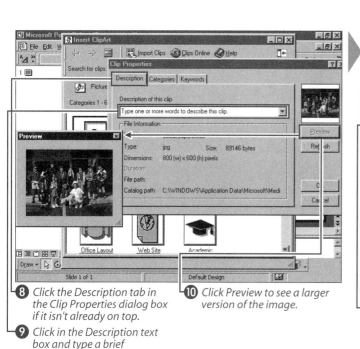

8 Click the Description tab in the Clip Properties dialog box if it isn't already on top.

9 Click in the Description text box and type a brief description of the clip.

10 Click Preview to see a larger version of the image.

11 Click the Categories tab.

12 Use the scrollbar to locate one or more categories you want to use for this image.

13 Click a category to select it.

14 Click New Category to create a new clip category for this image. The new category is automatically selected when you create it.

Adding Images to the ClipArt Gallery *Continued*

As you add images to the ClipArt Gallery, you may also want to type keywords in the Keywords tab of the Clip Properties dialog box (see the upper-left figure on the facing page). These keywords will help you find a specific image for a specific mood or topic, and they also give the Office Assistant something to look for as you create your slide shows. From time to time, the Assistant will pop up to say there is a clipart image you might want to use for a topic you have just entered in one of your slides. Your Assistant knows about such image properties through the keywords.

When you have set all the properties you want for the new image, you are ready to insert it into the category or categories you have specified for it. Note that the image can be stored once or twice, but it is not stored separately for each category into which you enter it. If you accepted the default on the Add clip to Clip Gallery dialog box — Copy into Clip Gallery — then the image is stored twice. It is stored once in its original location and once in the Clip Gallery. If you chose either of the other Clip Import options, the image is stored only once, in its original location on your hard drive or network.

What if you don't already have on disk the images you want to add to the ClipArt Gallery? You can use a scanner or a digital camera to capture images for use in your PowerPoint presentations. Assuming you have a scanner or camera attached to your computer, you can import images directly with PowerPoint's

built-in scanner and camera utility (see the upper-right figure on the next page).

Choose capture options from the dialog box shown at the lower left on the following page, and then click Insert or Custom Insert to display the image capture dialog box. The appearance of this dialog box varies with your capture hardware. I've shown a dialog box for a ScanPort color scanner in the figure at the lower right on the facing page. You will use the dialog associated with your capture hardware and software. Once you have one or more images captured in this way, you can import them into the ClipArt Gallery as described earlier in this section.

You can use conventional Copy and Paste procedures to copy the captured image from the capture software (my Twain scanner in this example) to the Gallery.

TAKE NOTE

ADDING IMAGES DIRECTLY FROM THE GALLERY

You can drag images from the Gallery directly onto a slide, bypassing the Insert menu. Click the Change to small window button at the upper right of the Gallery dialog box (or press Ctrl-Shift-<) to shrink the Gallery to one image wide so it takes up less room on the PowerPoint screen.

CROSS-REFERENCE

Later sections in this chapter show you how to capture audio and motion video for use in your PowerPoint presentations.

FIND IT ONLINE

Try this Microsoft site for a dynamic collection of images for PowerPoint and other Office applications: www.microsoft.com/clipgallerylive/default.asp.

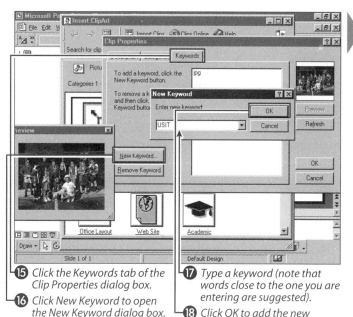

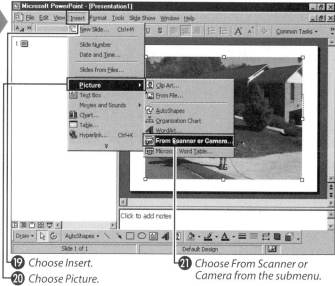

15 Click the Keywords tab of the Clip Properties dialog box.

16 Click New Keyword to open the New Keyword dialog box.

17 Type a keyword (note that words close to the one you are entering are suggested).

18 Click OK to add the new keyword to the list.

19 Choose Insert.

20 Choose Picture.

21 Choose From Scanner or Camera from the submenu.

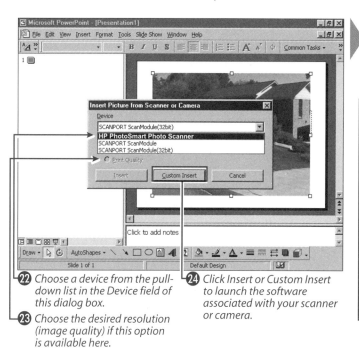

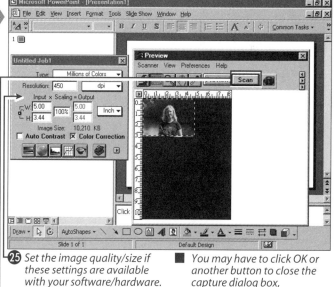

22 Choose a device from the pull-down list in the Device field of this dialog box.

23 Choose the desired resolution (image quality) if this option is available here.

24 Click Insert or Custom Insert to launch the software associated with your scanner or camera.

25 Set the image quality/size if these settings are available with your software/hardware.

26 Click Preview, Scan, or whatever button starts your device's capture routine.

■ You may have to click OK or another button to close the capture dialog box, depending on your image-capture hardware/software.

Recording Sound for PowerPoint

To use sound to make your PowerPoint slide shows stand out, you'll need a compatible sound card. You can find sound clips in files supplied with PowerPoint, with Windows, or on the Web. However, to make your presentations unique, you need unique sounds, which you can record yourself or, with the proper permissions, copy from other sources.

The next section of this chapter examines how to insert sound files into PowerPoint. This section focuses on how to record custom sounds using built-in utilities in Windows and Office 2000.

First, let's review connections to your computer through a sound card. Each sound card is a little different, but in general the options include those shown in the first figure on the next page. There are output connections for speakers, amplifiers, and headphones, and there are input connections for a CD player, tape deck, audio system preamp, or microphone.

When you have a microphone or other input device connected, you can use the Windows Sound recorder, available in the Entertainment menu of Windows 98 (upper-right figure, next page).

After you launch the Sound Recorder (lower-left figure, facing page), you can record, play back, and save sounds you capture via a microphone, CD player, tape deck, and so on. Just remember that commercial music is copyrighted, and there are stiff penalties for using someone else's creative work without permission.

As you record sounds with this utility, the green audio level line in the middle of the dialog box should fluctuate at least a little. You would expect this line to move like an oscilloscope with high-level audio input, but it probably won't. Just a little movement in the line as you record is sufficient. If the line is straight, on the other hand, you probably aren't recording anything.

By default, the Sound Recorder captures sound files at 22,050Hz (what Microsoft calls "radio quality") — about what you would expect from listening to a car radio. This is a good compromise format that gives reasonably good quality without requiring a new hard drive to store it. You can reduce storage requirements — and sound quality — by choosing a different format, as I have shown in the lower-right figure on the next page.

TAKE NOTE

CONNECTING A CD PLAYER TO YOUR SOUND CARD

If you don't have an internal connection between your CD-ROM drive and your sound card, or if the connection doesn't seem to work for recording, simply connect a cable from the headphone jack on the front of the CD drive to the microphone or line input on your sound card. Try both inputs to see which gives the best result. Also, make sure to use a stereo cable or mono cable and stereo-to-mono adapters at each end if you have a stereo sound card (most relatively new sound cards accept stereo inputs).

CROSS-REFERENCE

See Chapter 13 for more information on recording sound for PowerPoint presentations.

FIND IT ONLINE

For general technical information on sound cards, connecting them and using them, try Creative Labs' Sound Blaster page at **www.creativelabs.com**.

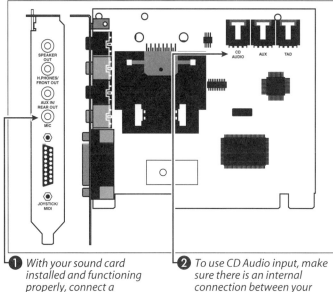

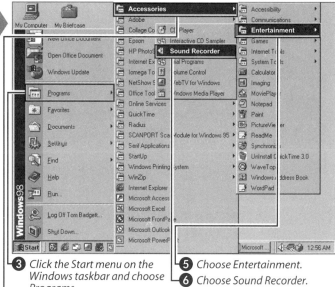

1 With your sound card installed and functioning properly, connect a microphone or other input device.

2 To use CD Audio input, make sure there is an internal connection between your CD-ROM drive and the sound card's audio input.

3 Click the Start menu on the Windows taskbar and choose Programs.

4 Choose Accessories.

5 Choose Entertainment.

6 Choose Sound Recorder.

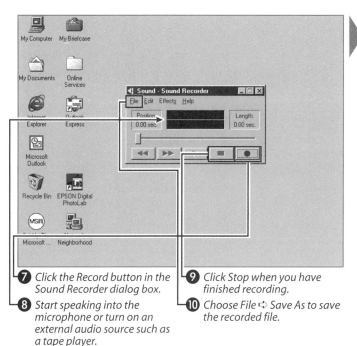

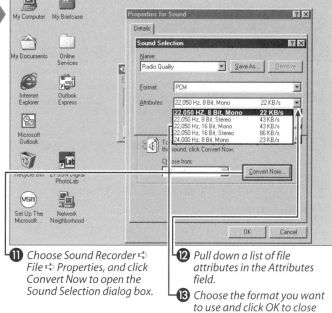

7 Click the Record button in the Sound Recorder dialog box.

8 Start speaking into the microphone or turn on an external audio source such as a tape player.

9 Click Stop when you have finished recording.

10 Choose File ⇨ Save As to save the recorded file.

11 Choose Sound Recorder ⇨ File ⇨ Properties, and click Convert Now to open the Sound Selection dialog box.

12 Pull down a list of file attributes in the Attributes field.

13 Choose the format you want to use and click OK to close the dialog box.

Adding Sounds to Your Slides

To PowerPoint and the ClipArt Gallery, a sound file is treated virtually the same as a clipart or other image file. You can add sound files to the ClipArt Gallery (details in the previous section of this chapter). Then you insert a sound object like you would any other Gallery object.

Launch the Gallery from the Insert menu (see the upper-left figure on the following page). When you launch the Gallery from the Sound insert menu, the sound tab is on top. As you can see from the upper-right figure on the next page, when you choose sound from the Insert menu, the Gallery hides the movie and clipart tabs.

Sound files in the Clip Gallery are shown as speakers with the names you specify when you import the sound (lower-left figure, next page). The description shown is not necessarily the same as the actual file-name as it is stored on disk.

When you insert the sound clip into a slide, you will see a relatively small speaker icon approximately in the center of your slide. You can leave it there, but you'll probably want to move it to a more convenient location. You may also want to resize it so it's more visible, as shown in the lower-right figure on the next page.

Remember that you can tell PowerPoint to play the sound automatically when the slide is displayed during a show, or you can have the sound play only when it is selected during a show. Your choice depends on what the sound contains and how you want to use it within your presentation. Obviously, if you are designing a stand-alone show — something the viewer controls — then you probably want to use automatic play.

TAKE NOTE

INSERTING SOUNDS FROM FILES

You don't have to use the Clip Gallery to insert sounds onto your slides. Select Insert ⇨ Movies and Sounds ⇨ Sound from File and then navigate to the folder containing the sound you want to use. You will select the sound directly from the file instead of from the Gallery.

SETTING PLAY OPTIONS

Right-click the sound icon on a PowerPoint slide and choose Edit Sound Object to open the Sound Options dialog box. You have a choice in this dialog box of looping the file until you stop it. By default, sounds play once and stop.

CHANGING SOUND ICON

To change the default sound icon, create an image you want to use (use the drawing toolbar to create simple objects) and place it on your slide. Right-click the image and choose Action Settings. Click Play Sound at the bottom of this dialog box and specify the sound file you want to use.

CROSS-REFERENCE
Chapter 13 includes more information about using sound in your slide shows.

SHORTCUT
You can preview a sound without opening Slide Show View. Right-click the sound object and choose Play Sound from the shortcut menu.

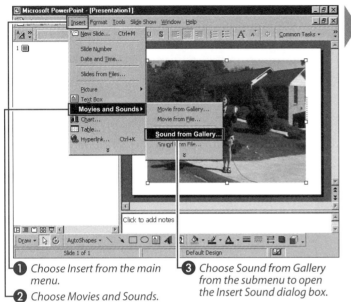

❶ *Choose Insert from the main menu.*

❷ *Choose Movies and Sounds.*

❸ *Choose Sound from Gallery from the submenu to open the Insert Sound dialog box.*

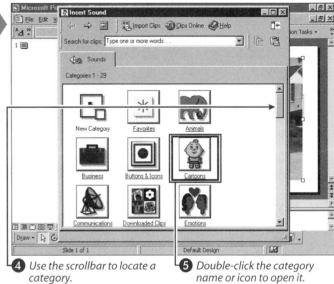

❹ *Use the scrollbar to locate a category.*

❺ *Double-click the category name or icon to open it.*

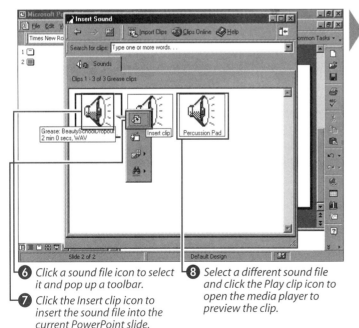

❻ *Click a sound file icon to select it and pop up a toolbar.*

❼ *Click the Insert clip icon to insert the sound file into the current PowerPoint slide.*

❽ *Select a different sound file and click the Play clip icon to open the media player to preview the clip.*

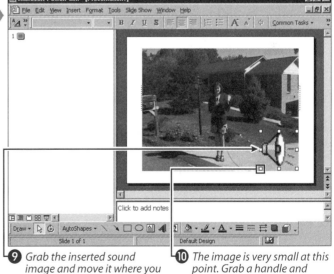

❾ *Grab the inserted sound image and move it where you want it on your slide.*

❿ *The image is very small at this point. Grab a handle and resize it if you want it to be more prominent.*

Capturing Movies for PowerPoint

Computer-based desktop video isn't for everyone. I predict, however, that with the influx of new technology at really attractive prices, it is now something for more people than before. In addition, products such as PowerPoint that make creative use of motion video on the computer will drive demand to new heights over the next few years.

You can use the ClipArt Gallery (or individual files) to insert motion video files into PowerPoint slides in much the same way you would a clipart picture, a photograph, or a sound file. As with these objects, however, motion video can be used in PowerPoint only after you've captured the clip and stored it on your hard drive.

The many facets of video capture are beyond the scope of this book, but I want to point out a couple of viable options that you are likely to come across as you research movies for PowerPoint. To capture a movie file from a camera or tape deck, you need an interface card and some cables. A couple of popular low-end devices are the Video Director 200 (Pinnacle Data Systems, Inc., **www.pinnacle.com**) and the buz (Iomega Corporation, **www.iomega.com/buz**). Many video adapter manufacturers also offer video capture cards. At the high end, IEEE 1394 high-speed serial interface cards are gaining popularity. Offerings are available from Radius, Inc. (**www.radius.com**), and many others.

Of course, the precise process of capturing video differs depending on the product you use, but basically you launch a capture software application that works with some specific hardware, give a filename, and spool a segment of video to disk. The top-left figure on the facing page illustrates how the Radius MotoDV product captures a digital video stream via IEEE 1394 (called Firewire, I-Link or something else, depending on the manufacturer).

If you're capturing just short clips, you may not need any editing. However, there are reasonably-priced editing options available, including Premier 5.0 from Adobe, which I have shown in the upper-right figure on the following page.

After you've captured and saved one or more clips to disk, you'll probably want to insert them into the ClipArt Gallery. Open the Gallery in Movie mode by choosing Insert ⇨ Movies and Sounds ⇨ Movie from Gallery. Now you can import your new clips and set clip properties to finish the import (shown in the bottom two figures on the next page).

TAKE NOTE

SETTING VIDEO FORMAT

Digital video (DV) editors frequently edit in Quicktime format and copy the finished clip out in native DV. To import a digital clip into PowerPoint, you need to save the clip as an .AVI file. Use the capture program or edit program to export to the proper format for PowerPoint compatibility.

CROSS-REFERENCE
See the earlier section in this chapter on capturing sound for similar interface concept discussions.

FIND IT ONLINE
There are many online resources for video information. Two you might begin with: **http:// www.videomaker. com/** and **http://www.dv.com**.

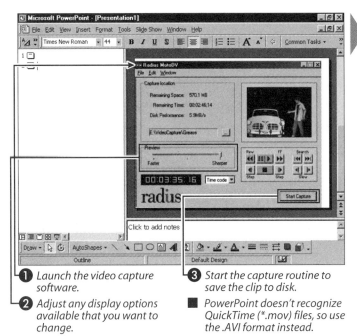

1 Launch the video capture software.

2 Adjust any display options available that you want to change.

3 Start the capture routine to save the clip to disk.

■ PowerPoint doesn't recognize QuickTime (*.mov) files, so use the .AVI format instead.

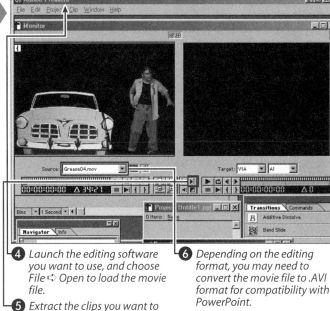

4 Launch the editing software you want to use, and choose File ➪ Open to load the movie file.

5 Extract the clips you want to use.

6 Depending on the editing format, you may need to convert the movie file to .AVI format for compatibility with PowerPoint.

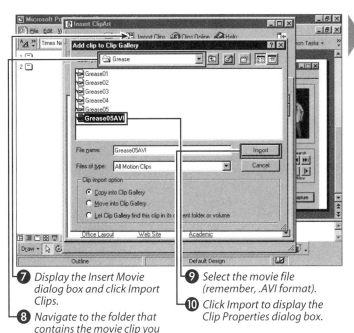

7 Display the Insert Movie dialog box and click Import Clips.

8 Navigate to the folder that contains the movie clip you want to import.

9 Select the movie file (remember, .AVI format).

10 Click Import to display the Clip Properties dialog box.

11 Set all of the clip properties you want, displaying each tab as required.

12 Click OK to store the clip in the Gallery.

Adding Movies to Your Slides

Once you have some motion video digitized and stored on your hard drive, the process of adding a movie clip to a PowerPoint slide should be as familiar and easy as adding a clipart image or sound file. You can use the ClipArt Gallery with its supplied motion clips, use clips you have put into the Gallery, or insert a movie clip directly from a disk file.

Start with the Insert menu, as shown in the upper-left figure on the facing page. If you want to insert a movie clip from a file, then choose Movie from File and navigate to the clip you want to use. You can also select a clip from the Gallery by choosing Movie from Gallery. As with other Gallery objects, you navigate through the available categories to find the one you want to use (see the next page, upper-right figure). Then you can review any clips available within the chosen category. You can also manage the Gallery and change clip properties from this view (lower-left figure, next page).

PowerPoint inserts the movie clip into a slide as it would a photograph or graphic image. The image is large enough for you to see the opening frame of the movie clearly, as illustrated by the final image on the following page. You can use the shortcut menu (right-click the movie image) to play the movie. When you choose Play Movie from the shortcut menu, PowerPoint uses an internal player to play the movie right on the slide wherever the opening frame is displayed.

You can format an inserted PowerPoint movie as a small icon (the original size, for example), or you can drag a handle to size the movie to cover the entire PowerPoint slide. As you make a movie image larger, you will lose some image quality, but the impact of a full-sized movie may well be worth the quality trade-off.

Remember, too, that many movies include sound, so you'll want to make sure you have a sound card installed and configured for use during your PowerPoint presentation.

TAKE NOTE

MOVIE PLAYBACK FORMATS

Full-motion video plays at approximately 30 video frames per second. The .AVI desktop video format plays at 15 frames per second. Many digital movie editors can maintain a full 30-frame format and export the clips back to tape without changing the frame rate. You may have to use an export function in your editor or video capture software to create an .AVI file compatible with PowerPoint.

TITLES FOR MOVIE SLIDES

Create a title for your movie slide so the title will show up in your outline and in any exported text you use.

CROSS-REFERENCE

See Chapter 14 for hints on navigating through a slide show with movies and other embedded objects.

FIND IT ONLINE

Many commercial sites (e.g., **http://www.kicksoda.com/ movies/movies.html**) include downloadable .AVI files. Get permission before using them in a presentation.

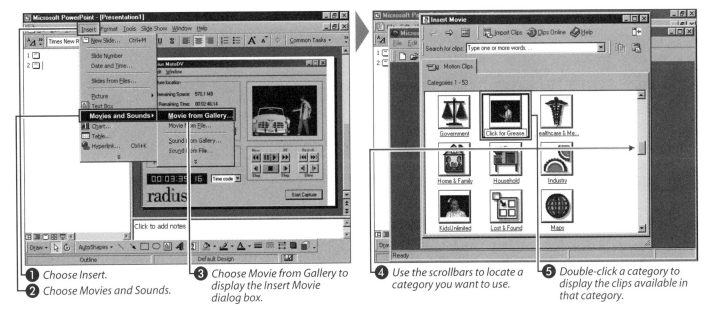

① *Choose Insert.*

② *Choose Movies and Sounds.*

③ *Choose Movie from Gallery to display the Insert Movie dialog box.*

④ *Use the scrollbars to locate a category you want to use.*

⑤ *Double-click a category to display the clips available in that category.*

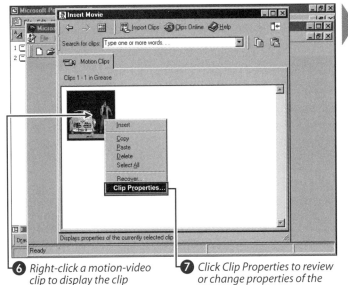

⑥ *Right-click a motion-video clip to display the clip shortcut.*

⑦ *Click Clip Properties to review or change properties of the selected clip.*

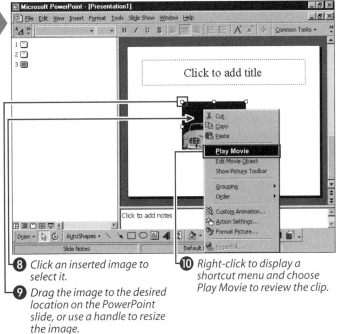

⑧ *Click an inserted image to select it.*

⑨ *Drag the image to the desired location on the PowerPoint slide, or use a handle to resize the image.*

⑩ *Right-click to display a shortcut menu and choose Play Movie to review the clip.*

149

Personal Workbook

Q&A

1 What is the main purpose of the ClipArt Gallery?

_____

_____

2 Describe how to add a new category to the ClipArt Gallery.

_____

_____

_____

3 What is the difference in displaying the Gallery for pictures and for sounds and movies?

_____

_____

_____

4 How can you play a sound file that you already have inserted into a PowerPoint slide?

_____

_____

5 How do you size a sound or movie clip to fit the current slide design?

_____

_____

6 If you cover the entire slide with a picture or other image, why is it important to include a slide title?

_____

_____

_____

7 What is the maximum image resolution you should use for PowerPoint images? Why?

_____

_____

8 What movie format is compatible with the Clip Gallery and PowerPoint slides?

_____

_____

ANSWERS: PAGE 307

150

EXTRA PRACTICE

1. Display a software application screen other than PowerPoint and capture the screen for inclusion in a PowerPoint slide.

2. Display the Gallery for sound objects, choose a category, and insert a sound into the current PowerPoint slide.

3. Insert a movie clip and play it from the slide view (without launching a PowerPoint slide show).

4. Insert a sound file into a PowerPoint slide, but don't use the default speaker sound icon.

5. Insert a movie or sound clip and set the clip to repeat until you stop it during a slide show.

6. Insert a sound file into a PowerPoint slide, and then change its property to 8,000Hz, 16-bit stereo.

REAL-WORLD APPLICATIONS

✔ Movies, pictures, and sound are important additions to PowerPoint shows that detail corporate procedures or new products, or introduce new employees. You can use a digital camera, digital video camera, or standard film camera to capture custom images, and then digitize them with video capture or by scanning prints. The Kodak Photo CD format is also an excellent source of digital images for your PowerPoint presentations. You can have any slide or negative converted to Photo CD format.

Visual Quiz

Describe how to display the screen shown here.

_____

_____

_____

_____

_____

_____

CHAPTER 11

MASTER THESE SKILLS

▶ **PowerPoint and Microsoft Word**

▶ **PowerPoint and Microsoft Access**

▶ **PowerPoint and Microsoft Excel**

▶ **PowerPoint and Microsoft Outlook**

PowerPoint and Microsoft Office

There are two camps when it comes to Microsoft software: love it and hate it. I won't fuel the fires of that argument here, but I will point out some of the strong points that Microsoft brings to the desktop when it comes to an integrated software bundle such as Office 2000.

Why do you think Microsoft markets a product such as Office 2000, with many software applications together? I can think of at least four good reasons: (1) to supply all the major applications likely needed at one time in an office environment; (2) to lock users into the products of a single vendor; (3) to ease the marketing of some products; and (4) to ease software integration so different applications can share functions and features.

Bundled software is a good idea from a user standpoint, too. Similarities among a suite's various applications mean that if you learn one successfully, it doesn't take much effort to learn the others. This is an important point in the case of PowerPoint 2000, a lesser-used application compared to Word or Excel. But it is there

on your Office 2000 CD-ROM when you need it. When you do, you already know the basics of how to use it from your experience with the suite's other applications.

Office 2000 includes Word for word processing; Excel for spreadsheet development; Outlook for e-mail, calendar, and contact management; Internet Explorer 5.0 and other Web support components; and other software, depending on which version you have. A popular additional application is Access for strong database management, but you might also have Publisher and other office-related tools.

As mentioned, Office 2000 is an integrated package, so the skills acquired from one part translate to the others. Perhaps more important, you can use many of the functions and features of one package inside another. Embedding an Excel spreadsheet inside a PowerPoint presentation is one example.

In this chapter I introduce some of the additional Office 2000 components as they relate to PowerPoint.

PowerPoint and Microsoft Word

Any office application, including Word, can be a window to your computer. You can load Word and access other applications from it anytime. Or load PowerPoint as your computer window. PowerPoint works nicely with these other programs. Here I show you some of the ways this PowerPoint-Word integration works.

You can insert PowerPoint objects directly into a Word document. Suppose you want to use some PowerPoint features to illustrate a point in Word. You can place a PowerPoint slide inside a Word document, as shown in the upper-left figure on the following page. Notice that PowerPoint chooses a title slide format by default, but you can easily change that with PowerPoint's Format menu (upper-right figure, following page).

When you insert a PowerPoint slide, Word's personality changes to use what Microsoft calls "in-place editing." In-place editing retains some features of Word but displays many features of PowerPoint. Notice the edge of the slide. It cuts the Word document about three-quarters of the way across. If you click in the Word document before typing anything in the slide, you lose the slide, PowerPoint closes, and you return to Word. You actually have PowerPoint menus and tools available inside Word!

With the Format menu, you can also change the slide's design template, color scheme, and so on.

Suppose you want to insert an entire presentation instead of just a single slide. You have two choices:

create a whole PowerPoint presentation in your Word document, starting with a single slide; or insert a presentation previously created in PowerPoint. You can see how to use the first method from the top-left figure on the facing page. Just choose PowerPoint Presentation instead of PowerPoint Slide.

Now look at the lower-left figure on the next page. When you choose the Create from File tab, you can insert any compatible object from your hard drive or network. After you choose a presentation, you return to the Object menu with the path and filename inserted. Click OK and the first slide of the selected presentation appears inside your Word document (lower-right figure, next page).

Continued

TAKE NOTE

► WORKING IN POWERPOINT FROM WORD

Choose Open from the slide shortcut menu to open the presentation in PowerPoint. After you edit the presentation in PowerPoint, select Update from the File menu and then choose Close & Return to Document to close PowerPoint and return to Word.

► INTERPRETING THE POWERPOINT-IN-WORD DISPLAY

Sometimes it's hard to tell whether you're looking at Word or PowerPoint-inside-Word. If the inserted slide has a wide border, then you're seeing the slide through a PowerPoint window. Notice, too, the choices on the Word menu bar. PowerPoint menus appear when the presentation is selected in PowerPoint view.

CROSS-REFERENCE

Refer to Chapter 12 to see how to insert other objects and data into PowerPoint presentations.

FIND IT ONLINE

Get a wealth of PowerPoint tips from WWW.Computer-Tips.com: **http://www.computertips.com/Microsoftoffice/MsPowerPoint/aheader.htm.**

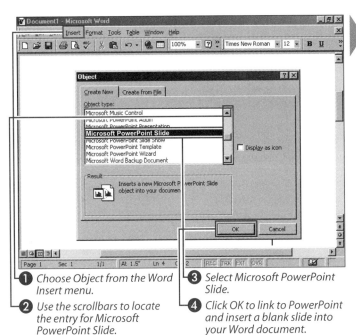

1 Choose Object from the Word Insert menu.

2 Use the scrollbars to locate the entry for Microsoft PowerPoint Slide.

3 Select Microsoft PowerPoint Slide.

4 Click OK to link to PowerPoint and insert a blank slide into your Word document.

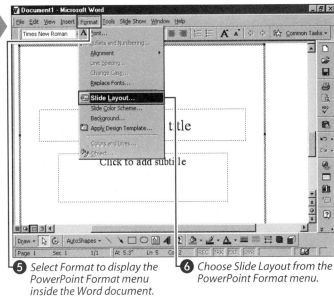

5 Select Format to display the PowerPoint Format menu inside the Word document.

6 Choose Slide Layout from the PowerPoint Format menu.

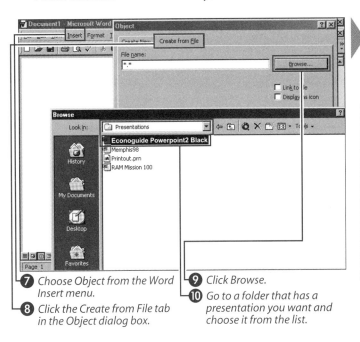

7 Choose Object from the Word Insert menu.

8 Click the Create from File tab in the Object dialog box.

9 Click Browse.

10 Go to a folder that has a presentation you want and choose it from the list.

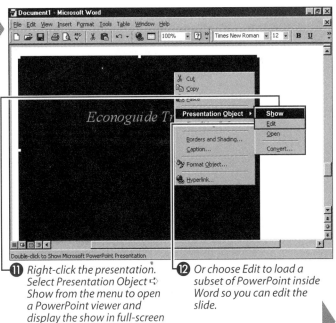

11 Right-click the presentation. Select Presentation Object ⇨ Show from the menu to open a PowerPoint viewer and display the show in full-screen mode.

12 Or choose Edit to load a subset of PowerPoint inside Word so you can edit the slide.

PowerPoint and Microsoft Word
Continued

The possibilities for interaction and cooperation between Word and PowerPoint are too rich and varied to cover here, but I want to suggest a few more ideas.

For one thing, you may want to convert an inserted presentation to a slide instead. You can do so in the Convert dialog box, which opens from the Presentation Object shortcut menu shown on the previous page. The upper-left figure on the next page shows the Convert dialog box. Converting a presentation to a slide changes the properties of your object.

If you double-click a presentation, for example, it opens in Slide Show view. Double-click a slide, on the other hand, and it opens in edit mode, with some PowerPoint menus displayed on the Word menu bar. A slide inserted in Word is more of a graphic object that enhances text but stands alone. A presentation is an interactive object tied to PowerPoint.

Here's another idea for Word. Behind every PowerPoint presentation is a text outline. Each major heading in the outline represents a slide title, and any outline subheadings represent bullet-list items. You can open Word, set the outline mode, and create an outline directly in Word, as shown in the upper-right figure on the following page.

Once you create an outline in Word, you can easily open it within PowerPoint. The basic procedure is shown in the lower-left figure on the following page.

So far I've discussed the PowerPoint-Word interaction from only the Word perspective. You can use PowerPoint's Insert menu to insert objects, including Word tables and documents, into your slides. In addition, you can save PowerPoint objects in other formats. The lower-right figure on the next page shows how to save just the outline portion of a slide show in a format that Word and other programs can read.

TAKE NOTE

▶ USING POWERPOINT OUTLINES

PowerPoint has one limitation when it comes to creating outlines from slides: only text in formatted slide objects such as titles or bullet lists will appear in your PowerPoint outlines. Outlines created in Word will insert properly into a PowerPoint slide, though you may want to change the object type that contains certain text once the translation occurs.

▶ MOVING OTHER OBJECTS BETWEEN PROGRAMS

You have other choices when it comes to exchanging data among Office programs. You can select text inside one application, copy it to the clipboard, and then paste it into another application. For the most part, Office applications are smart enough to retain at least some of the original formatting after data is pasted into its destination program.

CROSS-REFERENCE

Chapter 12 covers in more detail how to insert external objects, such as Word files and other objects, into your PowerPoint slides.

FIND IT ONLINE

ComputerImages offers PowerPoint tips at
http://www.computerimages.com/tip_ppt.html.

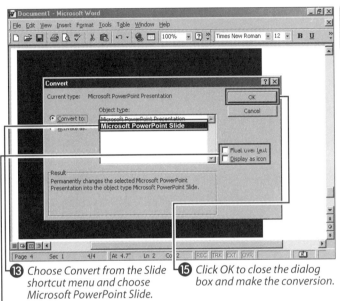

13 *Choose Convert from the Slide shortcut menu and choose Microsoft PowerPoint Slide.*

14 *Click Float over text or Display as icon to change the slide display properties.*

15 *Click OK to close the dialog box and make the conversion.*

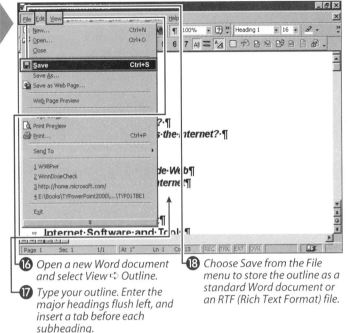

16 *Open a new Word document and select View ➪ Outline.*

17 *Type your outline. Enter the major headings flush left, and insert a tab before each subheading.*

18 *Choose Save from the File menu to store the outline as a standard Word document or an RTF (Rich Text Format) file.*

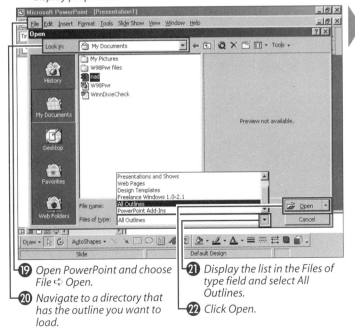

19 *Open PowerPoint and choose File ➪ Open.*

20 *Navigate to a directory that has the outline you want to load.*

21 *Display the list in the Files of type field and select All Outlines.*

22 *Click Open.*

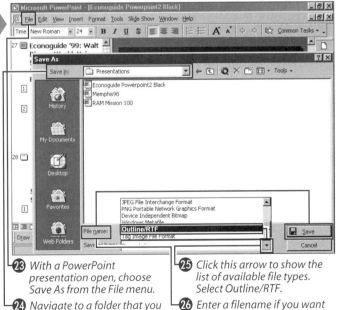

23 *With a PowerPoint presentation open, choose Save As from the File menu.*

24 *Navigate to a folder that you want to use to store the outline or other object.*

25 *Click this arrow to show the list of available file types. Select Outline/RTF.*

26 *Enter a filename if you want something different than the default and click Save.*

PowerPoint and Microsoft Access

For some time, Access was a software pariah. It seemed too difficult to learn for casual users when compared to consumer-level database products, and database professionals rejected it as a lightweight without the power for serious application development. Both the perception and the reality of Access have changed. The interface is easier to use and professionals agree that Access now has enough power for serious work.

Partly due to the nature of database applications, the integration of Access and PowerPoint is not as tight as it is with Word and PowerPoint. Nevertheless, you can use Access to display data fairly easily inside a PowerPoint presentation. The good news about Access is its capability to link to or import data from foreign sources such as dBase III or FoxPro. Therefore, if you use another database product to track sales or do accounting, you probably can still use Access to show this information in PowerPoint.

The easiest way to use Access data in PowerPoint is to create an action button (or any other action object) and hyperlink it to an Access database file. In the upper-left figure on the next page, you can see how to start the process of using an action button. The upper-right figure shows how to create a hyperlink to an action object placed on a current PowerPoint slide.

Once you complete your presentation, use the full power of Access during a slide show by clicking the action object (or button, depending on what you used as the entry point for your action) on a slide (lower-right figure, next page).

Use Access data in PowerPoint to show your audience the latest accounting, marketing, or sales information without reinventing it or risking errors in translating it to PowerPoint. Because you use Access data directly, without importing it into PowerPoint, the information is up-to-date — as long as you have the required Access data files with you at your presentation site.

TAKE NOTE

USING ACCESS DATA IN POWERPOINT

Once you learn your way around Access, you'll discover ways to force Access to load with certain objects onscreen and how to create custom user interfaces. This reduces the amount of Access navigation required during a PowerPoint show. Instead, you can click an action object (or button), show some Access data, and continue with your slides, calling on additional Access data from PowerPoint when desired. You may want to redesign Access data for a PowerPoint presentation, because during a PowerPoint show the audience may have only minimal time to study information.

CROSS-REFERENCE
There are more details on using action buttons and other action objects in Chapter 8. Also see Chapter 15 for more information on hyperlinks.

FIND IT ONLINE
Learn advanced PowerPoint techniques at **http://data.ctn.nrc.ca/ab/content/type14/org246/div918/listings/t7174.htm**.

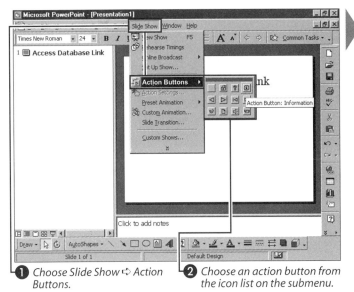

1 Choose Slide Show ⇨ Action Buttons.

2 Choose an action button from the icon list on the submenu.

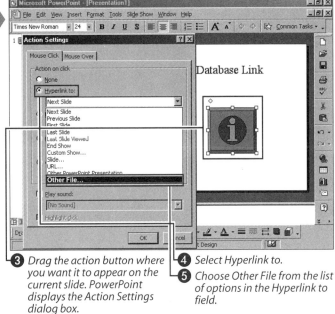

3 Drag the action button where you want it to appear on the current slide. PowerPoint displays the Action Settings dialog box.

4 Select Hyperlink to.

5 Choose Other File from the list of options in the Hyperlink to field.

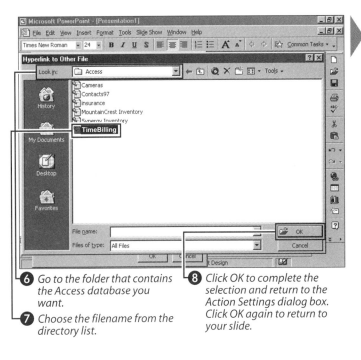

6 Go to the folder that contains the Access database you want.

7 Choose the filename from the directory list.

8 Click OK to complete the selection and return to the Action Settings dialog box. Click OK again to return to your slide.

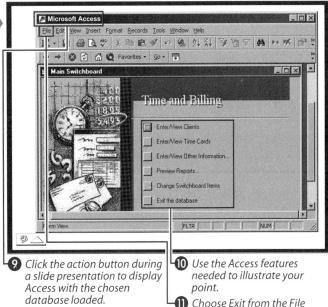

9 Click the action button during a slide presentation to display Access with the chosen database loaded.

10 Use the Access features needed to illustrate your point.

11 Choose Exit from the File menu to close Access and return to your slide show.

PowerPoint and Microsoft Excel

For many computer users, particularly those with backgrounds in accounting or finance, Excel is the Swiss army knife of software applications. Indeed, it is a versatile, intuitive program that supports number crunching, basic database functions, and graphics charting.

Like Access, Excel is well-suited for displaying data in a PowerPoint presentation. You can embed Excel data inside PowerPoint (in essence copying data from the Excel file into PowerPoint), or link an Excel file to make sure the latest data is always available. When you link a file, you create a mirror image of the Excel data inside PowerPoint. If the Excel spreadsheet changes, you see the changes inside PowerPoint as well. You can create an Excel spreadsheet within PowerPoint or insert an existing spreadsheet file into a PowerPoint slide (upper-left figure, next page).

The default settings for Excel fonts don't work well with PowerPoint, which uses relatively large fonts so an audience can see the data. You can easily change the font size, however, as shown in the upper-right and lower-left figures on the next page.

Following the standards of presentation design, include minimal data on each PowerPoint slide. Spreadsheet data, on the other hand, tends to be complex and detailed. Consider breaking Excel data into smaller groupings than you'd normally do in spreadsheet design. Use multiple slides with less data on each one rather than putting everything on a single slide.

Many PowerPoint presenters find that Excel charts are an easier way to use spreadsheet data than trying to present raw figures. Remember, during a presentation you probably won't have time to explain and interpret data for your audience. A chart can summarize data, even relate it to other information, to enhance audience understanding and retention (lower-right figure, next page).

You insert an Excel chart the same way you do any other object: by opening the Insert Object dialog box from the Insert menu. You can create a chart in PowerPoint by entering the data and choosing the chart type. Again, this uses in-place editing, which provides you with a subset of Excel functions while in PowerPoint. You can also use Create from File in the Insert Object dialog box to insert a chart from an existing spreadsheet file. If you do the latter, make sure to create an Excel file that contains only the chart and any discrete data that you want to present with it. The Insert Object facility can't extract portions of Excel files.

> ## TAKE NOTE
>
> ### USING EXCEL DATA WITH POWERPOINT
> If you choose Display as Icon in the Insert Object dialog box, the Excel object you create appears in your slide show as a small icon. You can display its contents by clicking the icon during your presentation. Use this technique for conditional data, which is information you might not use, depending on audience need.

CROSS-REFERENCE
See Chapter 12 for more information on using foreign objects in PowerPoint presentations.

FIND IT ONLINE
Get tips for making effective presentations from the PowerPoint marketing team: **http://www.iup.edu/~halapin/NATALIE/PptWeb/index.htm**.

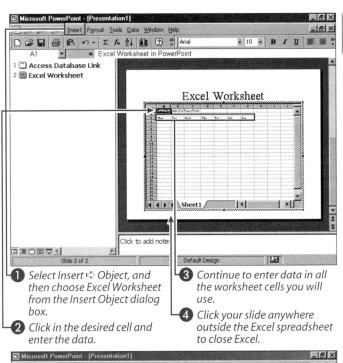

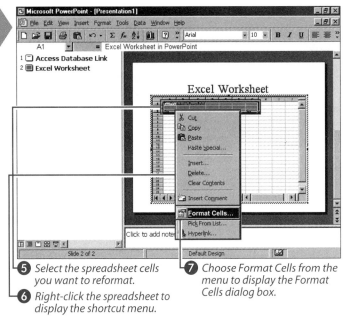

① Select Insert ➪ Object, and then choose Excel Worksheet from the Insert Object dialog box.

② Click in the desired cell and enter the data.

③ Continue to enter data in all the worksheet cells you will use.

④ Click your slide anywhere outside the Excel spreadsheet to close Excel.

⑤ Select the spreadsheet cells you want to reformat.

⑥ Right-click the spreadsheet to display the shortcut menu.

⑦ Choose Format Cells from the menu to display the Format Cells dialog box.

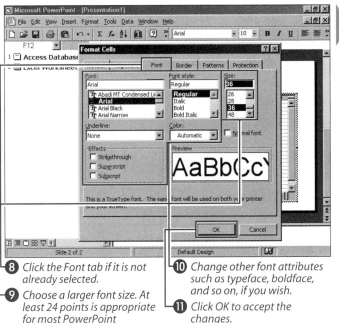

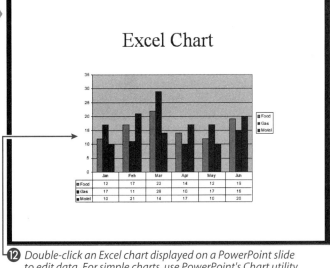

⑧ Click the Font tab if it is not already selected.

⑨ Choose a larger font size. At least 24 points is appropriate for most PowerPoint presentations.

⑩ Change other font attributes such as typeface, boldface, and so on, if you wish.

⑪ Click OK to accept the changes.

⑫ Double-click an Excel chart displayed on a PowerPoint slide to edit data. For simple charts, use PowerPoint's Chart utility instead of Excel.

■ At the main menu, select Insert ➪ Chart to access the Chart utility.

161

PowerPoint and Microsoft Outlook

Outlook, although basically an e-mail program, can also serve as a sort of universal window into your computer and other Office applications. Just as you can use Word or another Microsoft program as your main application, Outlook can serve the same function. You can open Outlook at the beginning of your workday and access other applications through it all day long, providing, in effect, a window into your other applications. I work with people who load Outlook at the start of the day and use it to schedule appointments, communicate via e-mail, launch other applications, track contacts, and more.

For one thing, you can use Outlook to create Office documents and either mail them to someone else or store them in your Outlook Inbox, where you can open and track them. Consider the upper-left figure on the facing page, which shows the start of the creation process for an Office document. Outlook uses a simpler version of the New Office Document dialog box, as you can see in the upper-right figure on the next page.

Once you choose PowerPoint from this dialog box, you are asked if you are creating a document to store inside Outlook or send to someone else. Whichever choice you make, you then see a modified PowerPoint window on top of Outlook. You can use conventional PowerPoint procedures to create one or more slides.

If you elect to store a new presentation or slide within Outlook, you can then exit PowerPoint by choosing Post from the File menu (see the lower-left figure on the following page). This creates an entry in your Inbox that looks like an e-mail message with an attachment, which is the PowerPoint file *Untitled.PPT*.

You can then open the presentation by double-clicking it as you do any other e-mail attachment. You can right-click it to save it to another location or rename it, as shown in the lower-right figure on the facing page.

Continued

TAKE NOTE

MANAGING FILES IN OUTLOOK

You can create multiple folders in Outlook. I use these to store e-mail messages from various sources or about various topics, and to store PowerPoint slides, pieces of Word documents, and other material that I send to other people via e-mail. Use the New command from the Outlook menu to create folders for storing your Outlook materials.

OPENING POWERPOINT FILES IN OUTLOOK

Open PowerPoint files in Outlook by double-clicking the attachment file icon or the message itself. The former opens PowerPoint to display the presentation; the latter opens a subset of PowerPoint, like a viewer, in Outlook so you can view and manage the file.

CROSS-REFERENCE

See Chapter 14 for information on program collaboration, which you can schedule with Outlook's calendar application.

FIND IT ONLINE

Microsoft frequently adds information on Outlook and other Office components. For the latest Outlook add-ins, check **http://www.microsoft.com/outlook**.

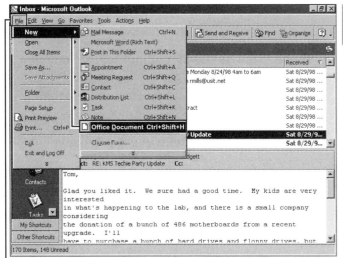

1 Choose File ⇨ New ⇨ Office Document.

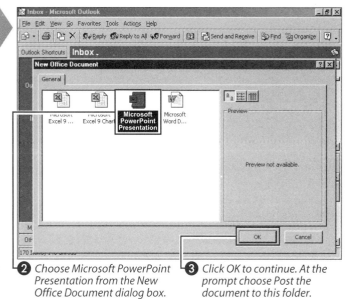

2 Choose Microsoft PowerPoint Presentation from the New Office Document dialog box.

3 Click OK to continue. At the prompt choose Post the document to this folder.

4 In the next dialog box, select Post from the file menu to send the new slide or presentation to your Inbox as Untitled.PPT.

5 Choose File again and select Save As if you also want to store the PowerPoint file under another name elsewhere on your hard drive.

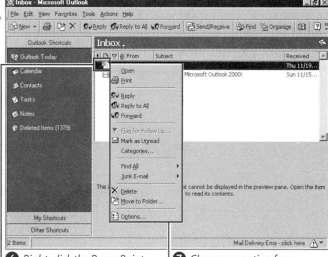

6 Right-click the PowerPoint icon, shown as an attachment in your Inbox, to display a shortcut menu.

7 Choose an option from the shortcut menu, such as Categories to attach category settings to the file, or Options to set priority and other settings.

PowerPoint and
Microsoft Outlook *Continued*

You can also use Outlook to send PowerPoint data directly to another e-mail user without first storing it in the Inbox or other folders. The process is similar to creating a slide or presentation to save on your hard disk, except you see a slightly different dialog box, and the finished file goes directly to your Outbox for delivery via the Internet or another mail system enabled in Outlook.

The first figure on the facing page shows the dialog box you get when you choose New Office Document from the File menu, choose PowerPoint, and then choose Send the document before you create the slide or presentation.

In the upper-right figure on the facing page, you see the PowerPoint create screen inside PowerPoint, along with some instructions for finishing the process and e-mailing the document.

You can also access Outlook within PowerPoint if you want to send an entire presentation or a single slide to another person. The first step is to decide whether you want to send a single slide inside the message or the whole presentation as an attachment (lower-left figure, facing page).

If you choose as Attachment, then the entire presentation file attaches to your e-mail message, which you address with the screen shown in the lower-right figure on the next page. If you choose Single Slide, then the current slide is inserted into the body of your e-mail message. In a graphical e-mail program such as Outlook, it is displayed when the message opens.

Send a presentation to someone to use at another location or to proof during final editing. Send a single slide as a greeting card, a framed photograph, a thank-you certificate, or other single-slide file created in PowerPoint.

TAKE NOTE

▶ SAVING SENT FILES

When you send the PowerPoint file created in Outlook, you can also save the slide or presentation created in Outlook to another disk file for use in another application. Open the Sent Files folder and copy the sent file to another Outlook folder or to a disk file. The file may be in your Outbox if you haven't connected to your mail server since creating the PowerPoint file.

▶ MOVING FILES WITHIN OUTLOOK

Click the Inbox name at the top of your Outlook display and then click the pushpin at the upper right to pin the folder list to your desktop. Now you can drag any files from the current folder — such as the Inbox — onto any visible folder to help with file management.

▶ SENDING FILES ELSEWHERE

You can select Send To from PowerPoint's File menu to send a PowerPoint presentation outline to Word as an RTF file.

CROSS-REFERENCE
See this chapter's first section about Word to learn more about Microsoft's in-place editing, which is also used in Outlook.

FIND IT ONLINE
Use this index of tutorials as a PowerPoint reference:
http://www.commerce.ubc.ca/MBAcore/tutorials/powerpoint.

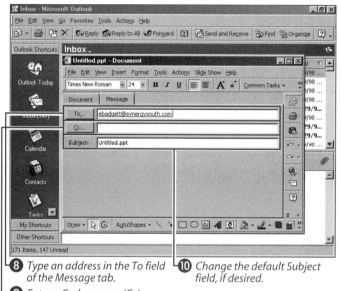

8 Type an address in the To field of the Message tab.

9 Enter a Carbon copy (Cc) address to send the file to another recipient, if you wish.

10 Change the default Subject field, if desired.

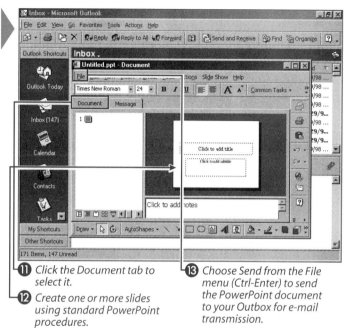

11 Click the Document tab to select it.

12 Create one or more slides using standard PowerPoint procedures.

13 Choose Send from the File menu (Ctrl-Enter) to send the PowerPoint document to your Outbox for e-mail transmission.

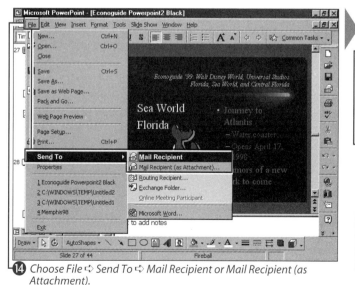

14 Choose File ➪ Send To ➪ Mail Recipient or Mail Recipient (as Attachment).

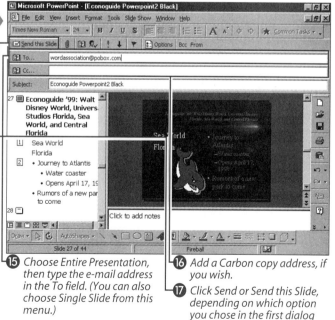

15 Choose Entire Presentation, then type the e-mail address in the To field. (You can also choose Single Slide from this menu.)

16 Add a Carbon copy address, if you wish.

17 Click Send or Send this Slide, depending on which option you chose in the first dialog box.

Personal Workbook

Q&A

1 List the major software components included with Office 2000 and describe what each does.

_____

_____

_____

2 The capability of Word and other products to support PowerPoint commands and menus is called what?

_____

_____

_____

3 What item is most commonly exported from PowerPoint to Word?

_____

_____

_____

4 The Object dialog box is used to insert two general kinds of objects into a PowerPoint slide. What are they?

_____

_____

_____

5 What PowerPoint facility is best for displaying Access data inside a slide show?

_____

_____

_____

6 Why do you need to use the Format Cells dialog box after inserting an Excel spreadsheet into a PowerPoint slide show?

_____

_____

_____

7 What is the best data format for Excel information that you want to include in a PowerPoint presentation?

_____

_____

_____

8 How can you use PowerPoint data inside Outlook?

_____

_____

_____

ANSWERS: PAGE 308

EXTRA PRACTICE

1 Open Outlook and create a PowerPoint slide that you insert into your Inbox for safe storage.

2 Open a PowerPoint presentation and export the show outline into Word.

3 Use the Object dialog box to insert an existing Word document into a PowerPoint slide show.

4 From within PowerPoint, use the Send To command to send a single slide to an e-mail recipient.

5 Open Access and display a table for data entry. Insert a PowerPoint slide into one of the table's fields.

6 Use an action button to hyperlink to an Excel spreadsheet, which you can then display during a PowerPoint slide show.

REAL-WORLD APPLICATIONS

✔ You are working on a PowerPoint presentation that you are giving at a seminar in a distant city. You are almost finished with the presentation and want the program coordinators to view it for compatibility with their hardware and program design. You could easily use the Send To command to transmit the entire file via e-mail for review and editing.

✔ A corporate staff meeting requires that you show recent sales and purchase trends. This information is stored in a standard accounting system, but you want to use PowerPoint to enhance your presentation. After studying the accounting system, you discover that the system can output FoxPro tables. By linking these tables into an Access database you can then create links from within PowerPoint to let you present current, live data during your talk.

Visual Quiz

Describe how to display the screen shown here.

_____

_____

_____

_____

_____

_____

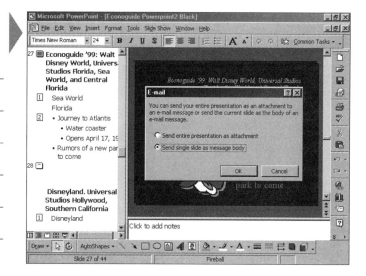

CHAPTER **12**

MASTER
THESE
SKILLS

▶ **Using Rulers and Guides**

▶ **Adding Comments**

▶ **Inserting Slides from Other Presentations**

▶ **Using Text Boxes**

▶ **Using WordArt**

▶ **Using Charts**

▶ **Using Tables**

▶ **Inserting Objects from Other Applications**

Using Other Objects on Your Slides

This chapter is a potpourri of PowerPoint development tools and utilities, plus suggestions on ways to use outside programs and objects in your PowerPoint slides. You can use these additional tools and objects any time you want to do something in a different way.

I've already discussed how you can use other Office 2000 applications to supply objects for your PowerPoint slides and how you can use PowerPoint slides and presentations inside external applications. There are still a few more elements built into PowerPoint that I'd like to discuss, including charts, tables, free-form text boxes, and slide comments.

This chapter also shows you how to take slides you've already created and use them in a new presentation. And you'll learn about text boxes and WordArt, a very useful tool intrinsic to all Office 2000 applications. Plus, I'll show you how to turn on a ruler and grid display to help you place objects on your PowerPoint slides — including text — with great accuracy.

I cover a number of objects and source applications that can be used with PowerPoint, but don't stop with my examples. As a Windows-compliant application, PowerPoint can interface with a variety of external applications to one degree or another. As you work with PowerPoint and external source programs, you'll find that some do a better job than others of integrating with your slide shows. When in doubt, experiment.

One suggestion that I've made in other chapters is to use action objects and hyperlinks. For example, in Windows 98 it's fairly simple to launch multiple programs by clicking Start and choosing programs to run. You could do this as part of a PowerPoint slide show, of course, but it might be more elegant — and certainly easier — to use an action object to load an external program and display its associated file.

Using Rulers and Guides

As long as you're using standard PowerPoint slide designs, you may not have much use for the rulers and guides built into PowerPoint. These are development aids that help you place slide objects precisely. They are particularly useful when you are placing similar objects on a series of slides and you want them to appear in the same place from slide to slide.

The upper-left figure on the next page shows how to turn on the ruler. With the ruler enabled, you have a vertical and horizontal numbered grid. The ruler works somewhat like the grids in Excel or any other spreadsheet program. In PowerPoint, however, the grid numbering starts in the middle of the slide at coordinate 0,0.

You can see from the upper-right figure on the following page how the displayed coordinates can help you place slide objects accurately. As you move the edges of an object, a hairline cursor appears at the cursor position on the vertical and horizontal rulers. Turn on the rulers and experiment with placing a regularly shaped object to see how the ruler display helps you with precise placement.

You can also use an associated tool to help you place objects. PowerPoint guides are a set of intersecting lines that show even more precise cursor placement than the ruler display. Toggle on the guides from the View menu, as shown in the lower-left figure on the facing page. With the guides turned on, you'll see intersecting dotted lines that cross at coordinate 0,0. To help you place an object, grab one of the lines and move it to the location you want to mark, as indicated in the lower-right figure on the following page.

To figure out the exact new intersection of the moved lines, click on one of the lines and note the measurement (shown to two decimal places); then click the second line and note that measurement. Together, the two figures give you a precise intersection shown as inches from center, or 0,0.

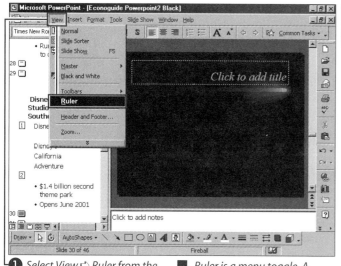

1 Select View ➪ Ruler from the main menu.

■ Ruler is a menu toggle. A check mark beside the entry indicates that rulers are enabled. No check mark means the ruler display has been disabled.

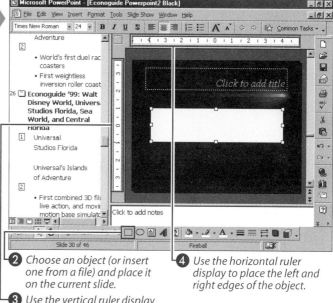

2 Choose an object (or insert one from a file) and place it on the current slide.

3 Use the vertical ruler display to place the top and bottom edges of the object.

4 Use the horizontal ruler display to place the left and right edges of the object.

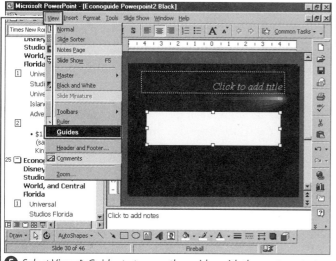

5 Select View ➪ Guides to turn on the guides with the center set at coordinates 0,0.

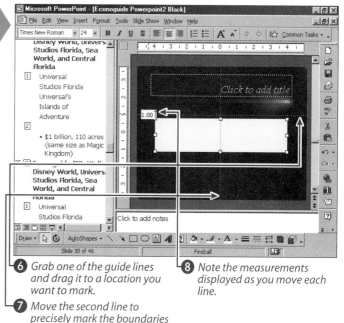

6 Grab one of the guide lines and drag it to a location you want to mark.

7 Move the second line to precisely mark the boundaries of an object you're placing.

8 Note the measurements displayed as you move each line.

171

Adding Comments

As you work with a PowerPoint presentation, you may want to include comments with your slides. Comments are text blocks that you can read but that are not normally intended for the audience (such as sticky notes). I find them helpful to remind me to update a particular image or fact, to help me remember where I secured an individual image, to jog my memory about changes I want to make for future shows, and so on. You can also use comments as additional documentation or instructions for other members of the presentation development team, or for another presenter if you are designing the show for someone else.

The default for comments is hidden. If you pick up a slide show from someone else and there are comments on one or more slides, you won't see them unless the Comment tool is toggled on. When you insert a comment, however, all hidden comments are made visible, along with the new comment you are adding.

The comment process can be started from the Insert menu. The default position for new notes is at the upper-left corner on the current slide. However, after you have entered text for a new note, you can move it anywhere on the slide you wish, as shown in the upper-right figure on the following page.

You can have multiple notes on a slide: just keep using the Insert window each time you are ready to create a new note and then move the notes where you want on the slide. Remember, you will turn off the comments display before presenting the show, so even if a comment box covers a graphic or text, your audience won't see it.

By default, the comment boxes have a yellow sticky-note background, but you have some control over how they appear through the Format Comment dialog box. Open this box from the pop-up shortcut menu associated with the comment box (see the lower-left figure on the facing page).

The Format Comment dialog box is a tabbed display with a number of possible settings, including the background color, the weight and color of the border that surrounds the comment box, and more. Use the formatting tools to differentiate your comments, for example, or to make a comment fit the color scheme of the rest of the slide.

TAKE NOTE

FORMATTING COMMENTS

Use the Text Box tab in the Format Comment dialog box to change margins inside the text box, to specify how text inside the box behaves (e.g., wrap/no wrap), or to turn the text on its side. Click Semitransparent on the Colors and Lines tab to mute the comment display without removing it.

CROSS-REFERENCE

See Chapter 5 for hints on using other intrinsic PowerPoint features for design and presentation.

FIND IT ONLINE

To learn about ungrouping clip art images, visit http://www.memphis-schools.k12.tn.us/admin/tlapages/Ppungroup.

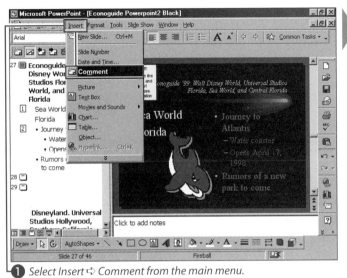

1 Select Insert ➪ Comment from the main menu.

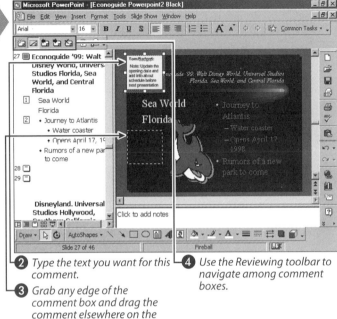

2 Type the text you want for this comment.

3 Grab any edge of the comment box and drag the comment elsewhere on the slide screen.

4 Use the Reviewing toolbar to navigate among comment boxes.

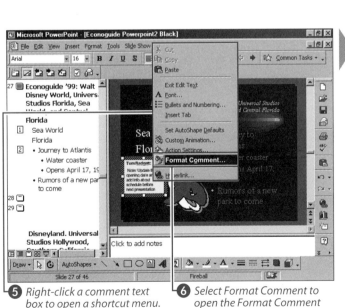

5 Right-click a comment text box to open a shortcut menu.

6 Select Format Comment to open the Format Comment dialog box.

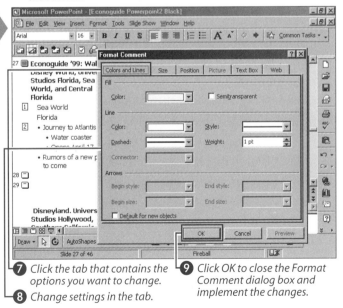

7 Click the tab that contains the options you want to change.

8 Change settings in the tab.

9 Click OK to close the Format Comment dialog box and implement the changes.

Inserting Slides from Other Presentations

One key to developing successful presentations is to design slide shows so that slides can be reused. A program you prepared for the last week's sales-staff meeting, for example, probably contains a lot of material that you can use in this week's executive-staff meeting. Moreover, you can create generic PowerPoint modules that can be inserted into any show. I do many one-time presentations that use basically the same material; thus, I reuse many slides repeatedly, and I create or change only a few slides to customize the show for a particular audience.

A PowerPoint utility that makes this customization process easier is Insert Slides. PowerPoint has a Slide Finder dialog box that lets you browse existing slide files and grab all or some of the slides they contain for use in your current presentation project.

Slide Finder is an excellent tool for adding slides to a new or existing presentation. You can use the scrollbars to view all of the slides in the selected presentation, choose the ones you want to add to your current show, and insert them. To use all of the slides from the selected show, click Insert All without worrying about picking individual slides.

PowerPoint also enables you to archive your favorite and/or most frequently used slides in one place. This useful feature lets you copy selected PowerPoint files into a separate list so you can access them without having to remember — or find — the directory path. You simply tell PowerPoint which file you want to archive and let the program know you want to add the file to the Favorites list. Then, when you want to select a file, you can display the dialog box shown at the lower left of the facing page.

This box works in essentially the same way as the Find Presentation tab. In the case of the Favorites tab, however, you will see only the files you have added to the Favorites list. When you select a file and choose Display, you will see the slides that the file contains.

Finally, you can choose a different view of the slides you want to insert, as shown in the lower-right figure on the next page.

TAKE NOTE

▶ INSERTING SLIDES FROM OUTLINES

Select Insert ⇨ Slides from Outline to insert slides directly from a Microsoft Word outline file — either one you have exported from PowerPoint or one you have designed from scratch in Word.

▶ INSERTED SLIDE FORMATTING

Slides inserted from another presentation acquire the formatting of the new presentation. They lose the color scheme, backgrounds, and other features of the inserted file.

CROSS-REFERENCE

See Chapter 13 for information on using other PowerPoint tools and utilities.

FIND IT ONLINE

Download a sample of Compadre background samples for your presentation slides at **http://www.threed graphics.com/compadre/comp_demos.html**.

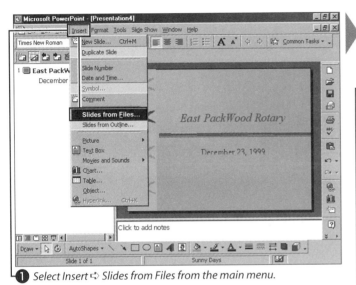

① *Select Insert ⇨ Slides from Files from the main menu.*

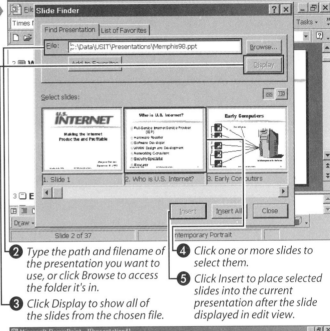

② *Type the path and filename of the presentation you want to use, or click Browse to access the folder it's in.*

③ *Click Display to show all of the slides from the chosen file.*

④ *Click one or more slides to select them.*

⑤ *Click Insert to place selected slides into the current presentation after the slide displayed in edit view.*

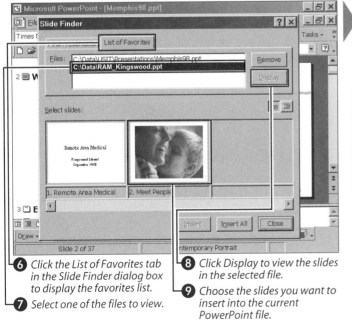

⑥ *Click the List of Favorites tab in the Slide Finder dialog box to display the favorites list.*

⑦ *Select one of the files to view.*

⑧ *Click Display to view the slides in the selected file.*

⑨ *Choose the slides you want to insert into the current PowerPoint file.*

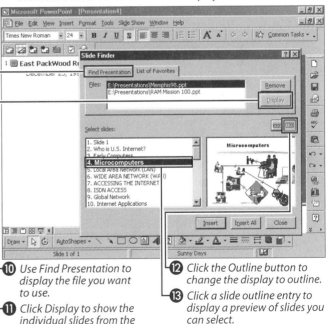

⑩ *Use Find Presentation to display the file you want to use.*

⑪ *Click Display to show the individual slides from the selected file.*

⑫ *Click the Outline button to change the display to outline.*

⑬ *Click a slide outline entry to display a preview of slides you can select.*

Using Text Boxes

I talked earlier in this chapter about using a particular type of text box for comments. You can use other types of text boxes in your slide presentations, however. Predesigned slide layouts in PowerPoint use text boxes for titles and bulleted lists, for example. You can also insert a text-box object from the Drawing toolbar that lets you enter free-form text virtually anywhere on a PowerPoint slide.

The upper-left figure on the facing page shows a new PowerPoint slide text box in the process of being designed. You set the size of the text box by clicking and dragging the mouse. When you release the mouse button, the box you defined is placed on your slide with a wide border around it and with handles you can use to change its shape.

The default settings for new text boxes enable you to place text on a slide without a visible background. In other words, the background for the text is the same as that for the slide. You can change the background and border color of the text box easily using the dialog box shown in the lower-left figure on the following page. This is the same dialog box that you used to edit the comments-box properties. Change colors and other attributes to give your text the desired appearance.

Note that the default font size for a text box is 24 points, which is relatively small by PowerPoint standards. You can change the font size and font attributes at any time, as shown in the lower-right figure on the next page. To apply your changes to all of the text in a box, click the border before applying the attribute changes. When you click inside the text box, the border has a slanted grid appearance; when you click on the border itself to select all text, the border changes to more of a cross-hatch appearance.

TAKE NOTE

DISPLAYING THE DRAWING TOOLBAR

Right-click any displayed toolbar and choose Drawing from the shortcut menu to display the Drawing toolbar if it isn't already visible.

PLACING OTHER OBJECTS ON A SLIDE

The Drawing toolbar contains a number of objects you can use with your slides. The process of creating and using them is basically the same as for text boxes.

PLACING GLOBAL TEXT

Remember that you can force the same text to appear on all slides by creating a text box on the slide master page, which you display from the View menu.

CREATING A BULLET LIST

To turn the text in a text box into a bulleted list, select the text and click on the bullet icon in the Format toolbar.

CROSS-REFERENCE

See Chapter 9 to learn how to format font size, style, and color.

FIND IT ONLINE

For tips and downloadable PowerPoint extras, visit Woody's Workshop at **http://www.zdnet.mcom/pccomp/help/workshop/9811/secrets/secret7.html**.

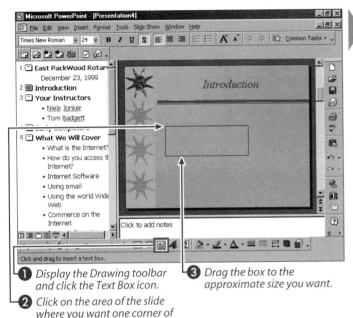

1 Display the Drawing toolbar and click the Text Box icon.

2 Click on the area of the slide where you want one corner of the text box to appear.

3 Drag the box to the approximate size you want.

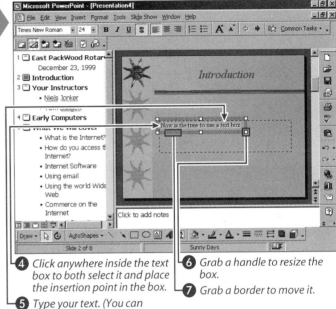

4 Click anywhere inside the text box to both select it and place the insertion point in the box.

5 Type your text. (You can always add more later.)

6 Grab a handle to resize the box.

7 Grab a border to move it.

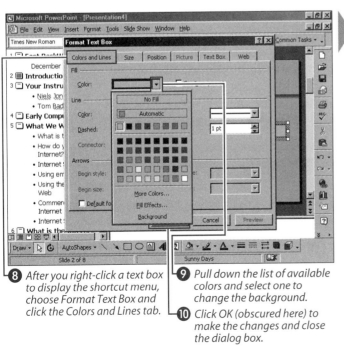

8 After you right-click a text box to display the shortcut menu, choose Format Text Box and click the Colors and Lines tab.

9 Pull down the list of available colors and select one to change the background.

10 Click OK (obscured here) to make the changes and close the dialog box.

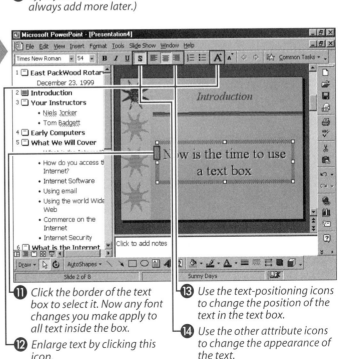

11 Click the border of the text box to select it. Now any font changes you make apply to all text inside the box.

12 Enlarge text by clicking this icon.

13 Use the text-positioning icons to change the position of the text in the text box.

14 Use the other attribute icons to change the appearance of the text.

Using WordArt

The WordArt utility is a relatively simple but quite useful add-in program that you can access from all Office products, including PowerPoint. This program lets you turn a word or short phrase into a graphic image for use as a title or heading. You open the WordArt utility from the Drawing toolbar (see the upper-left figure on the next page). The program includes a number of text color combinations and shapes. After you choose one, you will see the dialog box shown at the upper right of the facing page.

You can type just about anything you want in this box, but WordArt is really intended for titles, company logos, and the like. Long phrases won't fit into the WordArt design, so focus on single words or groups of a few words.

After you enter the text, you will see the formatted text on your PowerPoint slide, accompanied by the WordArt toolbar, as shown in the lower-left figure on the following page. Use the toolbar to add formatting to the WordArt image you just created. You can edit or rotate the text, for example, or change colors. You should be able to find your way around these various options easily with the tool tips (pop-up descriptions of on-screen objects such as toolbar icons that appear when you pause your mouse over them). The Edit Text tool, for example, opens the Edit WordArt Text dialog box (upper-right figure, next page); the

WordArt Gallery icon opens the initial Gallery screen (upper-left figure); you can rotate the text with the rotate tool; and so on.

Additional formatting shapes are available under the WordArt Shape icon, shown in the bottom-right figure on the facing page. You can experiment with these additional shapes as much as you want. As soon as you choose one, you will see the new image on your PowerPoint slide. The text remains selected and the toolbar stays in place, so you can just click on the WordArt Shape icon again and try another shape.

If you choose the Format WordArt icon, you will see a tabbed Format dialog box that you've seen before for text formatting. Some of the items don't work in this context, but you do have a great deal of control over the color of the text. Pull down the color choices in the Color field of this box and you can set the text color, background color, fill, shades, and so on. If you browse these choices, you'll see how WordArt's default formatting options are designed, and you can change them if you like.

TAKE NOTE

MOVING WORDART

Grab the WordArt object with your mouse and move it anywhere on your slide.

CROSS-REFERENCE

See Chapter 9 for more information on setting colors and formatting.

FIND IT ONLINE

Learn to make vertical text with WordArt at
http://www.geocities.com/SiliconValley/Sector/
1809/lesson2.html.

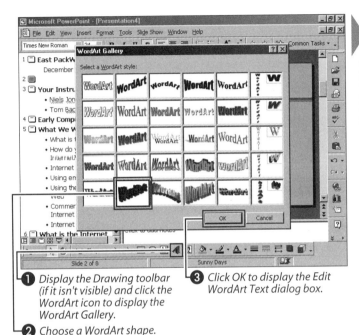

1 Display the Drawing toolbar (if it isn't visible) and click the WordArt icon to display the WordArt Gallery.

2 Choose a WordArt shape.

3 Click OK to display the Edit WordArt Text dialog box.

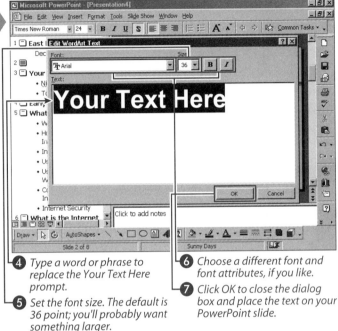

4 Type a word or phrase to replace the Your Text Here prompt.

5 Set the font size. The default is 36 point; you'll probably want something larger.

6 Choose a different font and font attributes, if you like.

7 Click OK to close the dialog box and place the text on your PowerPoint slide.

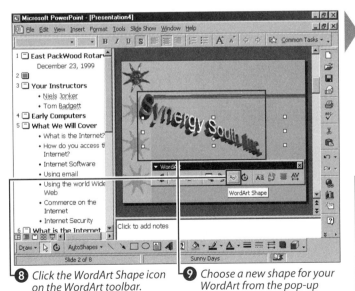

8 Click the WordArt Shape icon on the WordArt toolbar.

9 Choose a new shape for your WordArt from the pop-up display.

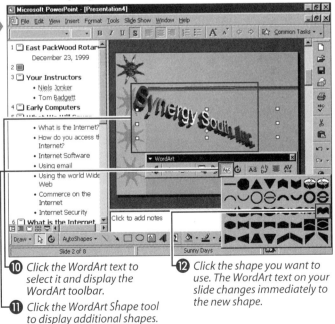

10 Click the WordArt text to select it and display the WordArt toolbar.

11 Click the WordArt Shape tool to display additional shapes.

12 Click the shape you want to use. The WordArt text on your slide changes immediately to the new shape.

Using Charts

As you know, you can use Excel data in your PowerPoint slides (see Chapter 11). This is your best choice if you need to display complex data or if you want to use existing data that is already in a spreadsheet.

Office 2000 includes another shared utility that lets you create charts on the fly. You can access the Chart utility from the Insert menu (see the upper-left figure on the following page). There are two parts to a PowerPoint chart: the data sheet and the chart itself (see the upper-right figure on the facing page).

The sample chart data shows a cross tab or summary data sheet with the corresponding chart in the background. You can use this simple charting utility for a variety of your own data — from sales information to accounting data, employee performance facts to environmental or stock trends. You aren't limited to the three rows and four columns provided in the sample chart. In fact, the Chart utility supports more rows and columns of data than would be practical to show in a single chart on one slide.

As you enter your data into the spreadsheet dialog box, the legend and chart update dynamically, so you can see the results of your changes immediately. You can accept the default Chart formatting and use the completed chart as is with your data in the data sheet. You can also edit the color scheme and other chart features.

There isn't a comprehensive editing screen for your chart. Rather, you right-click a specific Chart object and choose an action from a shortcut menu, as shown in the lower-left figure on the next page. You can use these menus to change the colors of individual chart objects such as the chart walls or columns. You can also change the font used for any text on the chart, edit the 3D view on 3D chart designs, and change the type of chart used to display your data (see the lower-right figure on the next page).

You can step through various chart types and display a sample with the Click and Hold to View Sample button in the Chart Type dialog box. Once you have chosen a new chart type and closed the Chart Type dialog box, the Chart utility uses your custom data to build a new chart with the new type. You can then use the other formatting dialog boxes in the Chart utility to change the color and other attributes of the new chart.

TAKE NOTE

PRINTING CHARTS

Choose the colors of individual chart elements carefully if you intend to print your charts. Some colors are hard to differentiate in black-and-white printouts.

CROSS-REFERENCE

Refer to Chapter 11 for hints on using Excel charts in your PowerPoint slide shows.

FIND IT ONLINE

Here's an interesting tutorial on PowerPoint charts: http://www.cpc.unc.edu/services/admin/design/presentations/ppt_tutorial/sld001.htm.

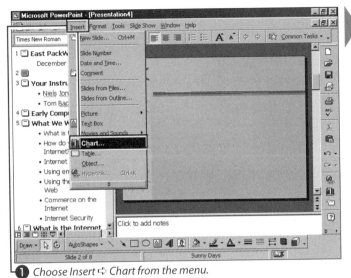

① Choose Insert ➪ Chart from the menu.

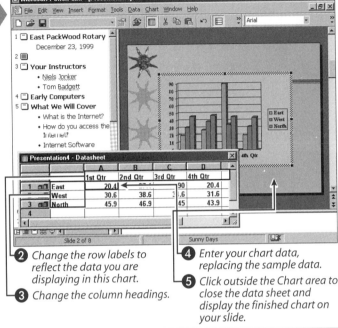

② Change the row labels to reflect the data you are displaying in this chart.

③ Change the column headings.

④ Enter your chart data, replacing the sample data.

⑤ Click outside the Chart area to close the data sheet and display the finished chart on your slide.

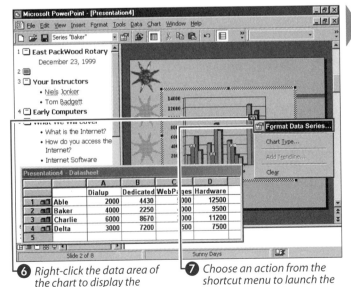

⑥ Right-click the data area of the chart to display the Format Data Series shortcut menu.

⑦ Choose an action from the shortcut menu to launch the editor for the area you selected.

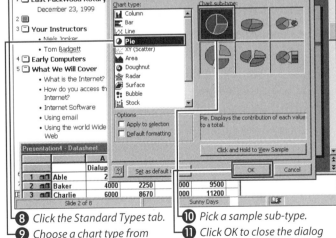

⑧ Click the Standard Types tab.

⑨ Choose a chart type from the list.

⑩ Pick a sample sub-type.

⑪ Click OK to close the dialog box and make the change on your PowerPoint slide.

Using Tables

PowerPoint tables work like charts to help group and summarize data. You should use a table when you want to show numerical relationships instead of graphics comparisons. A chart shows general trends or comparisons: you can see easily that Abel sold about a third more dollar volume of all products than Baker, for example. You can't tell from most charts, however, that Charlie was only 50 units ahead of Delta. For that level of detail, you need a table, which is similar to the data-sheet portion of the Chart utility I discussed earlier.

Start the table process from the Insert menu (see the upper-left figure on the following page). The Insert Table dialog box, shown in the upper right corner of the next page, lets you specify how many rows and columns you want in the table. You don't have to specify the precise number here: you can add and remove cells as you go along. Remember to add one row for column headers and one column for row headers if you need them.

The Tables and Borders toolbar is similar to the WordArt toolbar described earlier in this chapter. It offers several tools that help you format a table. Each tool includes pop-up tool tips, so when you pause your mouse pointer over an icon, a tool tip appears that tells you what utility that icon represents. You can perform a range of tasks from the toolbar, such as splitting a cell if you want to add more information to a single cell without adding a whole new column. You can also control the lines and borders, background colors, and so on.

PowerPoint's extensive shortcut menu, shown in the lower-right figure on the following page, provides further options. (You can access some of these menu items through icons elsewhere on the toolbar.) You can see from this display how easy it is to insert additional rows and columns: simply place the cursor in the row or column next to where you want a new one to appear, and then choose the proper placement from the Table menu.

TAKE NOTE

▶ USING CLIPART WITH TABLES

Although some Office 2000 applications let you place clipart and other images inside table cells, PowerPoint won't. You can, however, select Pictures/ClipArt from the Insert menu to drop an image on top of a table, and then move and size the image so that it appears to be inside a table cell.

▶ RESIZING TABLE CELLS

Table cells don't automatically resize to accommodate new data; instead, the text wraps to the next line. To make long text fit, you can grab a table-cell border and drag a whole column to a different width. Double-click a cell border and the column will automatically resize to hold the widest element in the column.

CROSS-REFERENCE

See Chapter 10 for information on adding clipart and other images to your slides. Images frequently enhance table data.

FIND IT ONLINE

For Microsoft's Hands On PowerPoint tutorial, go to http://microsoft.com/education/curric/office97/pphandon.htm.

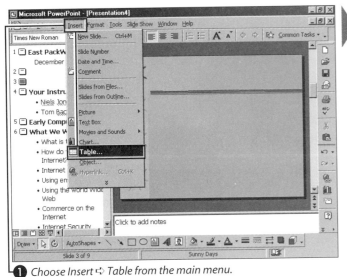

1 Choose Insert ➪ Table from the main menu.

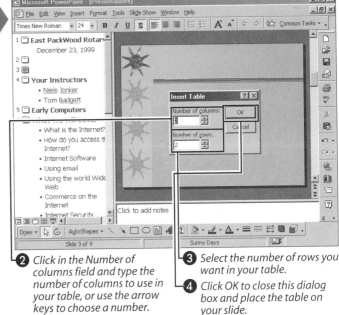

2 Click in the Number of columns field and type the number of columns to use in your table, or use the arrow keys to choose a number.

3 Select the number of rows you want in your table.

4 Click OK to close this dialog box and place the table on your slide.

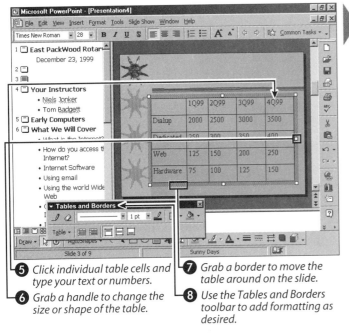

5 Click individual table cells and type your text or numbers.

6 Grab a handle to change the size or shape of the table.

7 Grab a border to move the table around on the slide.

8 Use the Tables and Borders toolbar to add formatting as desired.

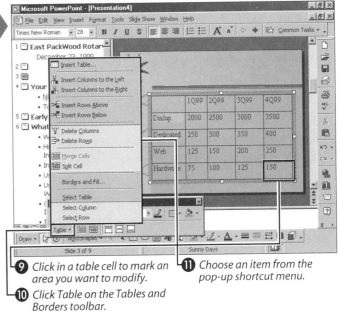

9 Click in a table cell to mark an area you want to modify.

10 Click Table on the Tables and Borders toolbar.

11 Choose an item from the pop-up shortcut menu.

Inserting Objects from Other Applications

You know how to insert objects from other Office applications (see Chapter 11): you simply choose the type of file from the Insert Object dialog box and click OK. Because other Office programs are closely integrated with PowerPoint, this process is easy and intuitive. Other Office programs support what Microsoft calls "in-place editing," which means that PowerPoint takes on attributes of the other Office program that is the source of the object you are creating or editing.

You won't find quite the same level of integration when you use non-Office programs, but it is still easy to integrate objects from other Windows-compliant programs. You use some of the same procedures that you do when working with Office programs. The upper-left figure on the next page shows the beginning of the insert process. The Insert Object dialog box provides a fairly wide range of object types, ranging from Photoshop through a selection of Microsoft products to media clips and more (see the upper-right figure on the next page).

You also have the choice of creating a new object within the application you select, or of inserting an object you have previously created and stored in a file. Remember that when you work with an Office program, you remain in PowerPoint when you work with the external program. If you choose a non-Office program, such as Photoshop, you can still insert a new image, but you will work in the native program itself, as shown in the lower-left figure on the following page.

Even if the application you choose doesn't integrate itself directly into PowerPoint, there are probably some special menu items that link the application back to PowerPoint. These allow you to exit the program and insert the object you created into the current PowerPoint slide.

You can choose any existing object on your hard drive or local-area network, as long as the object is in a file format that PowerPoint supports (lower-right figure, facing page). The list of supported files is too long to cover here, but be sure to check out the Take Note sidebar below for more information about graphics-files support and the need (in some cases) to insert various special filters. PowerPoint should let you insert objects created in most other Windows applications.

TAKE NOTE

CHECKING ASSOCIATED APPLICATIONS

Check which files are associated with what programs with the File Types display from the My Computer Folder Options.

POWERPOINT SUPPORTS MANY GRAPHICS FILES

PowerPoint lets you insert many popular graphics-file formats, but some of them require a separate graphics filter. If you didn't install the filter you need when you installed PowerPoint, you can rerun Setup and add it.

CROSS-REFERENCE

See Chapter 11 for more information on using objects from external applications in your PowerPoint shows.

FIND IT ONLINE

You'll find a workshop on scanning images into PowerPoint presentations at **http://basil.plu.edu/~libr/ workshops/scanning/powerpoint.html**.

USING OTHER OBJECTS ON YOUR SLIDES

Inserting Objects from Other Applications

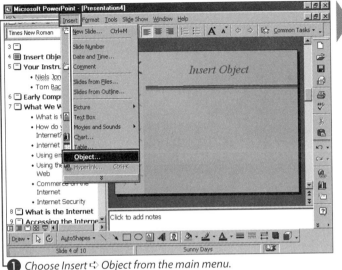

1 Choose Insert ⇨ Object from the main menu.

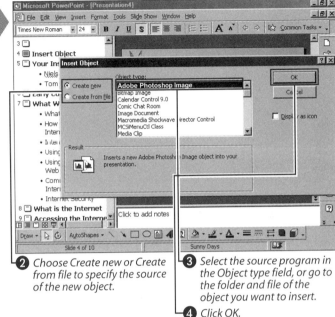

2 Choose Create new or Create from file to specify the source of the new object.

3 Select the source program in the Object type field, or go to the folder and file of the object you want to insert.

4 Click OK.

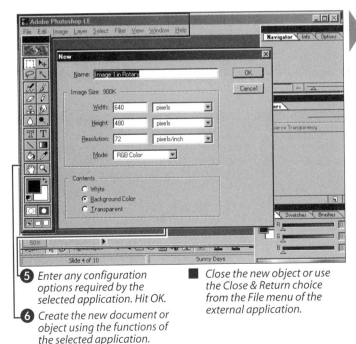

5 Enter any configuration options required by the selected application. Hit OK.

6 Create the new document or object using the functions of the selected application.

■ Close the new object or use the Close & Return choice from the File menu of the external application.

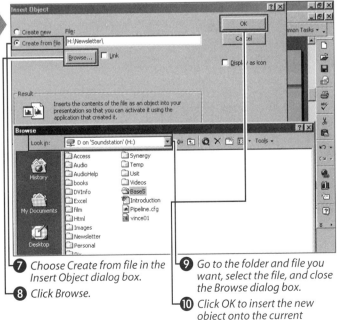

7 Choose Create from file in the Insert Object dialog box.

8 Click Browse.

9 Go to the folder and file you want, select the file, and close the Browse dialog box.

10 Click OK to insert the new object onto the current PowerPoint slide.

Personal Workbook

Q&A

1 PowerPoint supports two on-screen utilities to help you place objects on your slides more accurately. What are they?

_____

_____

2 If you find that you can't launch an application to display an embedded object directly, what PowerPoint utility can you use to make it work?

_____

3 Why would you add "sticky note" comments to your PowerPoint slides?

_____

_____

4 What two programs or methods might you use to place a chart on a PowerPoint slide?

_____

_____

5 Can you insert a graphic into a PowerPoint table? If not, can you think of a way around this limitation?

_____

_____

_____

6 Why would you not want to use a WordArt object for a full paragraph of information?

_____

_____

7 Can you insert objects from any other application into PowerPoint? Why or why not?

_____

_____

8 Describe how to convert text in a text box to a bullet list.

_____

_____

ANSWERS: PAGE 309

EXTRA PRACTICE

① Display gridlines and create an intersection one inch to the left of center and two inches to the bottom of center.

② Display the Slide Finder dialog box, go to an existing presentation file, and add it to the Favorites list.

③ Insert a WordArt object that includes your full name. Change the text to a second format.

④ Create a text box, insert at least two sentences, and then change the background color to make it stand out on the current slide.

⑤ Insert a slide from an outline into an existing presentation file.

⑥ Use an action button or other action object to hyperlink a foreign object to its source application.

REAL-WORLD APPLICATIONS

✔ If you are a regular presenter, you can save development time by creating PowerPoint modules that can serve as slide sources for new presentation designs. Use the Slides from Files option on the Insert menu to view slides in existing files and insert one or all of them into the current presentation.

✔ Suppose you are part of a program-development team. You are putting together the basic graphics for an upcoming PowerPoint show, but someone else will add financial figures and other live data. You could use comments on each slide to tell the other developer about the image you have chosen to help better integrate the additional data into your basic design.

Visual Quiz

Describe how to display the screen shown here.

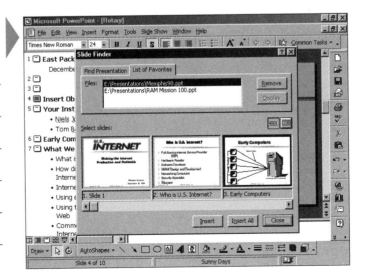

PART

III

CHAPTER **13** **Preparing for the Show**

14 **Presenting the Show**

15 **PowerPoint and the World Wide Web**

Advanced Presentation Skills

Microsoft PowerPoint gives you basic presentation support for small or large groups. It can also help you move beyond the basics to augment your shows with animation, video, sound, and the other features I discussed in the previous chapters.

We're all like PowerPoint: we can prepare and deliver the most basic presentations, or we can stretch beyond the basics to deliver more advanced information in a more advanced manner. PowerPoint's numerous options and open-endedness give you a broad space to play

in. And you can use as many or as few of these advanced features and techniques as you want.

In Chapter 13, I show you how to prepare yourself and your slide show for a presentation. Chapter 14 provides additional information on presenting a PowerPoint show, including using the Meeting Minder, how to broadcast a show, and how to collaborate on a show. Finally, Chapter 15 expands on some of the communications skills introduced in Chapter 14, including how PowerPoint works with the World Wide Web.

CHAPTER **13**

MASTER THESE SKILLS

▶ **Rehearsing the Show**

▶ **Recording Show Narration**

▶ **Creating Summary (Agenda) Slides**

▶ **Using Special Presentation Objects**

Preparing for the Show

At this point, you've designed your slide show, you've double-checked your facts, you have your images in place, and you've created all the slides. Congratulations: You've finished about half the work required to prepare for making your professional PowerPoint presentation. What's left?

Now you must prepare the show. After 15 years on radio and television, five years or so teaching speech and theatre at the college level, and some 20 years of making public presentations for businesses, I've seen it all. And if there is one common thread that ties together these hundreds of talks and slide shows, it is an apparent lack of preparation.

I've watched famous personalities, well-known scientists and architects, poets and writers, educators, politicians, and just plain folk take good ideas, a knowledge of their topic, and a decent slide show, and put an audience into stupor. Worse, some of these presenters made the audience feel uncomfortable — embarrassed, even — through their poor command of their computer and of PowerPoint, and by their approach to the topic.

I can't teach you how to make dynamic, exciting, informative speeches in one short chapter, but let me stress the importance of program preparation. Being prepared includes using as many of the PowerPoint's special features as fits your situation, rehearsing the show, preparing yourself for the unexpected, and focusing on the ideas you want your audience to carry away from your show.

For a number of years before the use of teleprompters, I wrote and anchored a top-50 local television evening newscast twice a day. In those days, film broke and equipment failed with regularity. The only script I had was a 20-second intro; but if the film failed, I could usually provide a one- or two-minute extraneous recap of the field report.

If the computer fails or someone in the audience asks a difficult or antagonistic question, you should be similarly prepared. Don't lose control of the show or lose sight of your objectives for the program, no matter what!

In this chapter, I show you some of the PowerPoint tools that can help you prepare to give your presentation.

Rehearsing the Show

It's trite but true: practice makes perfect. Remember learning to ride a bicycle or to roller skate? Recall what it was like to learn a foreign language or to type? The more you rehearse these activities, the easier they become. One reason that practice works is that a direct connection seems to develop between your body and the underlying mental skills required.

Here's an interesting exercise: Close your eyes and place your hands at your side or in your lap. Now describe to someone else precisely how to walk up to a car, get in, and drive away. Assume this person has never seen a car. In other words, you can't say "open the door" or "insert the key." This inexperienced person you are helping doesn't understand these concepts.

Now imagine that you have 30 minutes to explain to an audience all they need to know to make a buying decision about your new and unusual product or in some other way change their ideas or thought processes about a subject. After all, this is what most presentations are about. You want to educate an audience sufficiently so they change what they feel or believe and so they will take some action now or in the future.

Good show design and rehearsing your presentation are two keys to success here. Consider the top-left figure on the following page, which shows how to open the PowerPoint Rehearse Timings utility. You should use this feature after you've stepped through your show a few times and know what you will say with each slide.

The utility displays your presentation in Slide Show view with a timing toolbar on top (upper-right figure, next page). The timer shows you time for the current slide and total show time. Use this information to balance your presentation, giving the proper weight and importance to each slide.

When you reach the end of the show, you'll see the message box shown at the lower left of the facing page. If you want to start over with the slide timings, choose No in this box.

When you are finished timing your slide show, you'll see the Slide Sorter view with individual slide timings listed under each slide, as in the lower-right figure on the facing page.

TAKE NOTE

▶ JUDGING SLIDE TIMING

According to standard presentation guidelines, you should plan one to two slides a minute for most shows. If you find that one or more slides are taking over two minutes or so, consider splitting these slides in two. Also, animation, progressive text disclosure, and other techniques add interest to a slide so you can safely keep it up longer than the recommended time limit.

CROSS-REFERENCE
See the following section to learn how to record slide-show narration using the timing information you gather in this lesson.

FIND IT ONLINE
You'll find five tips for "killer" presentations at http://www.sandismith.com/powerpt2.html.

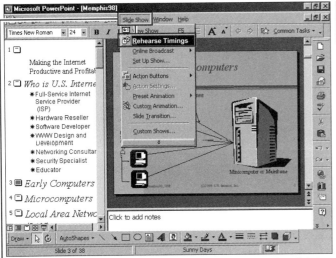

① Choose Slide Show ➪ Rehearse Timings to display the first slide in your presentation and the timing toolbar.

② Begin your presentation and click the Next button on the timing toolbar to present the next slide.

③ Click the Pause button if you need to make notes.

④ Click the Repeat button to repeat the current slide.

■ The center counter shows elapsed time for the current slide; the end counter times the whole show.

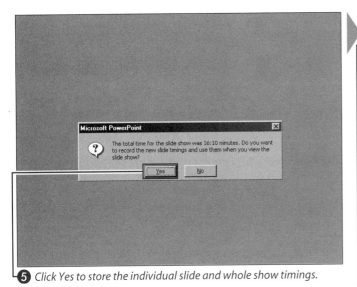

⑤ Click Yes to store the individual slide and whole show timings.

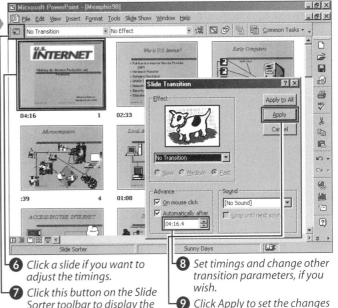

⑥ Click a slide if you want to adjust the timings.

⑦ Click this button on the Slide Sorter toolbar to display the Slide Transition dialog box.

⑧ Set timings and change other transition parameters, if you wish.

⑨ Click Apply to set the changes you have made and to choose another slide.

Recording Show Narration

You'll probably use PowerPoint as a support tool for presentations to a live audience. That's what most people do with this program. However, PowerPoint 2000 is also well-suited to stand-alone, automated shows. You can use this setup for an industry show booth, for example, or as a self-running training platform. To use PowerPoint in this way, you need to record a narration track to accompany your slides.

To do so, you use built-in PowerPoint utilities and the facilities of your PC's sound card. If you have access to professional or near-professional (called "prosumer" in the industry vernacular) audio equipment, you may choose to record narration first on tape, then dub it into PowerPoint. If you own this equipment, you probably are comfortable using external input to your PC, so I'll leave you to handle this process on your own.

If you have a basic sound card and a low-end microphone, you can record narration tracks directly into PowerPoint and associate them with specific slides relatively easily. I've shown the menu sequence for beginning the process of recording narration in the top-left figure on the facing page.

The Narration dialog box has three basic functions: start recording (the OK button), Set Microphone Level, and Change Quality. You may have set the microphone level during PowerPoint installation, in which case you probably don't need to do it again (though you can run this utility at any time). The top-right figure on the facing page shows the dialog box associated with setting the microphone level. To use this utility, you just need to plug a microphone into your sound card and follow the instructions on the screen.

The bottom-left figure on the following page shows your choices for sound quality. You can choose from standard quality settings — telephone, radio, and CD — or you can create your own settings based on a combination of file format and sample rate. The higher the sample rate, the better the quality — and the more storage space required for the audio file. As the tip in this dialog box suggests, you should consider linking large files rather than importing them into PowerPoint. By doing this, you will keep the PowerPoint file smaller and perhaps improve performance.

When the setup is complete, you can begin recording. This process is akin to using Rehearse Timings, except now you can record a script to accompany each slide. At the end of the show, you will see the dialog box I've reproduced in the final figure on the facing page. Choose Yes to set new timings based on your narrations and to save the audio files you created.

TAKE NOTE

SETTING SLIDE TIMINGS
Use Rehearse Timings from the Slide Show menu to set approximate times before you finish your script and record your narration.

CROSS-REFERENCE
See Chapter 10 for more information on using sound in your PowerPoint slides.

FIND IT ONLINE
Syntrillium produces Cool Edit Pro, an incredible sound-editing software package. Get a scaled-down version free at **http://www.mediabuilder.com/5266.html**.

Sound Calibration

If you haven't previously calibrated your sound card (you are asked to do this when you install PowerPoint), you can do it now, before you record narration. Click the Set Microphone Level button on the Record Narration dialog box and follow instructions. You will be asked to speak into your microphone for a few seconds while PowerPoint records the sound and sets the optimum level. The calibration wizard will tell you when the levels have been properly set. You can also change the quality settings to save disk space or to achieve a higher level of sound quality. Click the Change Quality button to do this and follow directions.

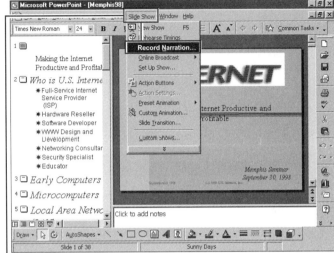

① Select Slide Show ➪ Record Narration to display the Record Narration dialog box.

■ Remember, the position of any menu depends on how often you use this feature and what else you have done recently. PowerPoint menus are dynamic.

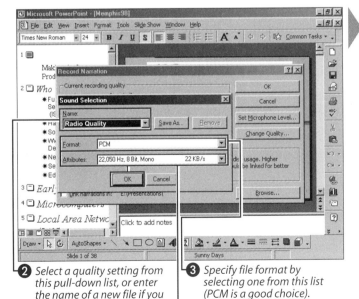

② Select a quality setting from this pull-down list, or enter the name of a new file if you are creating a new one.

③ Specify file format by selecting one from this list (PCM is a good choice).

④ Choose file attributes from this list (or accept the default), and then click OK.

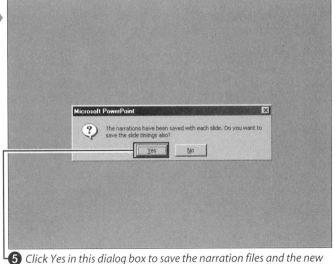

⑤ Click Yes in this dialog box to save the narration files and the new slide timings based on your narration tracks.

Creating Summary (Agenda) Slides

I organize PowerPoint presentations to include several information checkpoints. After the title slide, I include a slide about who I am and summary data about my company. Then comes a bulleted list that shows the major topics I plan to cover. I discuss these high-level topics, and then provide details of each major topic in succession. When I finish a section, I display a review slide — another bulleted list — that lists the major items we just covered. And, after the section review, I use another Summary Slide with the major topics of the next section. You won't spend much time on these summaries, but they help the audience focus on upcoming topics and follow the presentation's organization.

You can make your own bulleted list, of course, but PowerPoint includes a function to help you create these summaries or agenda slides automatically. (Interestingly, PowerPoint menus and help files refer to these slides as both Summary Slides and Agenda Slides.)

To start the summary process, turn on Slide Sorter view and choose Custom Shows from the Slide Show menu. The Custom Show dialog box opens, as shown at the upper-left of the facing page. Create two or more custom shows, using the slides included in the current show (see the upper-right figure on the next page). The idea is to group slides that represent a subtopic within your show.

Once you have two or more subtopics defined with the Custom Shows utility, you are ready to create the Summary Slide, which will contain the titles of the first slides in each of the subtopics. I've shown the start of this process in the lower-left figure on the facing page.

Having made the Summary Slide, you can build hyperlinks to the custom shows listed on this slide, as shown in the bottom-right figure on the facing page.

Now, when you enable Slide Show view and choose a hyperlink in the Summary Slide, the presentation jumps directly to the custom show to which it is linked. Each custom show can have one or multiple slides, because you are using the Custom Show list as hyperlinks, not as separate presentations.

This technique is particularly useful for complex, dynamic shows. You can change the custom shows but the summary information doesn't change.

TAKE NOTE

HIDING SLIDES

Another way to change your slide show is to hide certain slides for a particular presentation. The slides stay in the show, but you won't see them during the presentation. Display the slides you want to hide and choose Hide Slide from the shortcut menu that appears when you right-click them.

CROSS-REFERENCE

See Chapter 4 for more information on custom shows and setting up your show.

FIND IT ONLINE

For a guide to creating multimedia presentations, visit http://www.agocg.ac.uk/AV/reports/durrell/links.html.

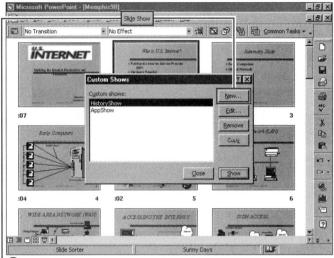

1 *Choose Custom Shows from the Slide Show menu and click New to display the Define Custom Show dialog box.*

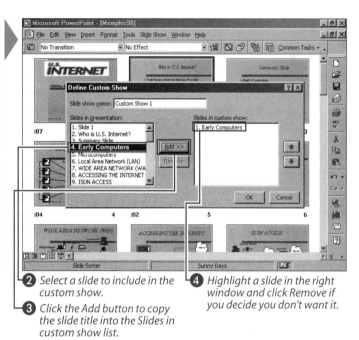

2 *Select a slide to include in the custom show.*

3 *Click the Add button to copy the slide title into the Slides in custom show list.*

4 *Highlight a slide in the right window and click Remove if you decide you don't want it.*

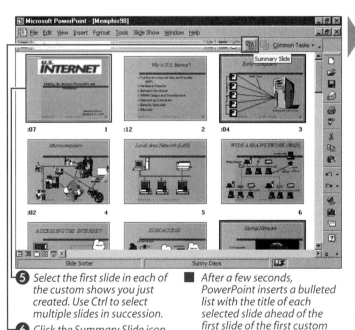

5 *Select the first slide in each of the custom shows you just created. Use Ctrl to select multiple slides in succession.*

6 *Click the Summary Slide icon on the Slide Sorter toolbar.*

■ *After a few seconds, PowerPoint inserts a bulleted list with the title of each selected slide ahead of the first slide of the first custom show.*

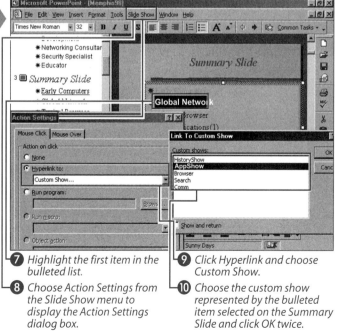

7 *Highlight the first item in the bulleted list.*

8 *Choose Action Settings from the Slide Show menu to display the Action Settings dialog box.*

9 *Click Hyperlink and choose Custom Show.*

10 *Choose the custom show represented by the bulleted item selected on the Summary Slide and click OK twice.*

197

Using Special Presentation Objects

Though you can use PowerPoint as a simple slide projector, you also can use some of its special features to help you during the show and to help refine the presentation for future shows.

The shortcut menu shown at the upper left of the facing page gives you access to several useful presentation tools, including the Slide Navigator. The Navigator is an excellent way to move forward or backward within a presentation in response to audience questions, to return to your Summary Slide, and so on. You can also select a custom show from this facility, so if you have created subtopic groups within your show, you can jump directly to them with the Navigator.

The Meeting Minder can also be useful, particularly if you're using PowerPoint as part of regular, in-company meetings. It is a little difficult to use the Meeting Minder in front of a formal audience, but in the right setting it can be useful (see the upper-right figure on the following page).

The Meeting Minutes tab in this dialog box lets you enter free-form text to document a meeting or make general notes. The Action Items tab, on the other hand, gives you a form to enter specific action items for yourself or other people on your team. You can export the action items into Microsoft Word or Microsoft Outlook for later follow-up or inclusion in another document.

I find the Speaker Notes slide among the more useful presentation utilities (bottom-left figure, next page). This utility gives you a simple text editor dialog box so you can enter text associated with a specific slide. Write yourself notes reminding you to make changes to a slide, to update information, and so on.

You have some control over how the presentation pointer works (bottom-right figure, facing page). Automatic is a good setting because it provides an arrow by default but enables you to use a pen if you want to draw on the slide during the show. Choose a custom pen color to make anything you draw more visible within the slide color scheme you are using.

TAKE NOTE

▶ USING THE PEN

The markings you make on a slide during a show aren't permanent: they go away when you move on to another slide. However, you can use the Erase Pen command from the Screen menu on the Slide Show shortcut menu to erase anything you have drawn on the current slide.

▶ BLANKING THE SCREEN

Use Black Screen from the Screen command on the Slide Show shortcut menu to temporarily blank the slide-show screen. You may want to do this if you get sidetracked by an audience question and want to keep the audience from reading ahead or being distracted by material already on the screen.

CROSS-REFERENCE

See Chapter 4 for more information on presenting your slide show.

FIND IT ONLINE

Get a demo of Itinerary Web Presenter 2.1 at http://www.contigo.com/it21demo.html.

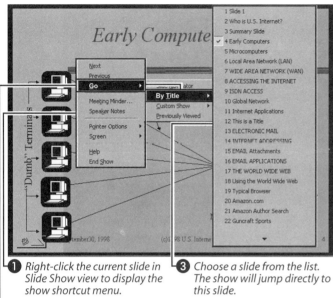

1 Right-click the current slide in Slide Show view to display the show shortcut menu.

2 Select Go ⇨ By Title from the submenu.

3 Choose a slide from the list. The show will jump directly to this slide.

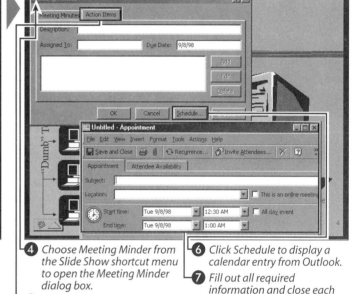

4 Choose Meeting Minder from the Slide Show shortcut menu to open the Meeting Minder dialog box.

5 Click the Action Items tab.

6 Click Schedule to display a calendar entry from Outlook.

7 Fill out all required information and close each dialog box by clicking OK.

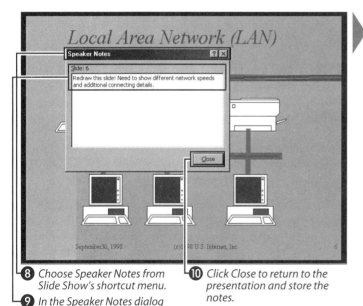

8 Choose Speaker Notes from Slide Show's shortcut menu.

9 In the Speaker Notes dialog box, enter text associated with the current slides. Include reminders, details to add, etc.

10 Click Close to return to the presentation and store the notes.

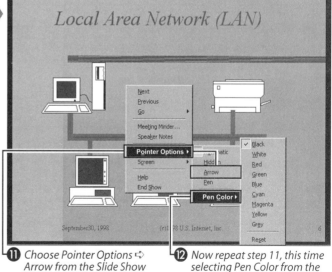

11 Choose Pointer Options ⇨ Arrow from the Slide Show shortcut menu.

12 Now repeat step 11, this time selecting Pen Color from the submenu and choosing a color option.

Personal Workbook

Q&A

1 Discuss why rehearsing a PowerPoint slide show is important.

_____

_____

2 What are the two ways PowerPoint provides for setting slide timings?

_____

_____

3 What is another name for a PowerPoint Summary Slide?

_____

_____

_____

4 What utility is required before you can create a Summary Slide?

_____

_____

_____

5 What menu would you use to change the color of the Slide Show pen?

_____

_____

6 What two utilities are included with the PowerPoint Meeting Minder?

_____

_____

_____

7 How can you hide one or more slides in a show without removing them from the file?

_____

_____

_____

8 What computer hardware is required for recording slide-show narration?

_____

_____

ANSWERS: PAGE 309

EXTRA PRACTICE

1. Display a list of slides that includes the time required for each slide.

2. Open a PowerPoint presentation and create at least two custom shows within it.

3. Enable Slide Show view and temporarily blank the screen.

4. Display the dialog box that is used to specify the quality of the narration audio track for a PowerPoint slide show.

5. Open the dialog box that lets you set microphone levels.

6. Open the Action Items Schedule display.

REAL-WORLD APPLICATIONS

✔ During a formal presentation, a member of the audience points out an error in one of your slides. You can impress the audience and save face by opening the Speaker Notes dialog box and typing a note to yourself to correct the error while the audience watches.

✔ You have an existing PowerPoint slide show that you use for occasional in-house training. Now your schedule is becoming more hectic and it is difficult for you to conduct some of the classes. You can record a narration track and use action settings to create a self-running training module for some of these sessions.

Visual Quiz

Describe how to display the screen shown here.

_____

_____

_____

_____

_____

_____

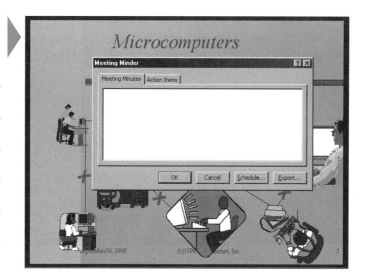

CHAPTER **14**

MASTER
THESE
SKILLS

▶ Using Meeting Minder

▶ Navigating Through Your Show

▶ Using Online Collaboration

▶ Using the Web in Discussions

▶ Broadcasting the Show

▶ Using the Send To Feature

Presenting the Show

You know, getting there really is only half the fun. I don't know about you, but I find something satisfying about researching a PowerPoint presentation, choosing the design template, and selecting what objects to include and how to present them. It is a creative communications endeavor that you can share with your audience, or with someone else who may actually present the show. And, like teaching in a classroom, business, or family setting, this research and preparation frequently helps you develop a level of understanding about your own material that you simply wouldn't have achieved otherwise.

But there's also a great deal of satisfaction in presenting the show, using the tool you have developed to make a point or change attitudes. And PowerPoint presentation tools can help you, including some tools that go beyond the design and development utilities I've discussed already. Moreover, PowerPoint contains additional features that help you share your presentations with other individuals and with a larger community over an intranet or the Internet.

There are actually two important sides to a successful PowerPoint presentation: the slide show itself and what you, as the presenter, do with the design. As I discuss in Chapter 13, you will be more successful in presenting your ideas — whether or not you use PowerPoint — if you are intimately familiar with your material and if you have practiced enough to be really comfortable in front of an audience. With these issues out of the way, you can concentrate on using PowerPoint and its associated utilities to their fullest.

In this chapter I show you how to use live presentation tools such as the Meeting Minder and slide-show navigation utilities. I also discuss ways to collaborate with other PowerPoint users about a show, plus ways to share the slides with a broadcast audience or an individual using the Sent To feature for email and for transferring files across an intranet.

In addition to the skills discussed in this chapter, the Internet and World Wide Web material covered in the next chapter are important for getting the most out of PowerPoint's communication facilities. Study what I cover here, but then move on fairly quickly to the next chapter. Taken together, the two sets of information will help you advance to a new level of PowerPoint use and understanding.

Using Meeting Minder

Introduced PowerPoint's Meeting Minder utility briefly in the last chapter. Here I want to give you more details about its operation and offer some suggestions for using it successfully.

How do you work? Do you still reach for the yellow pad or your pocket notebook when you want to write down a telephone number or address, or do you pick up a Personal Digital Assistant (PDA) to record the information electronically? If you're in the former group, you may need to adjust your thinking a little to make the most of Meeting Minder. If you belong to the latter camp, using this utility will probably seem very comfortable to you.

Here's the concept: You're in front of an audience, PowerPoint is in Slide Show view, and you're making your points. As you discuss the topics you've been asked to cover, and members of the audience ask questions and make points, new ideas come to mind. In fact, you may want to keep formal minutes of the meeting or assign attendees particular tasks or action items. Instead of taking notes on the trusty yellow pad, you can display the Meeting Minder and make these notes inside PowerPoint.

The Meeting Minder concept won't work too well if you're standing in front of a formal audience. I, for one, find it too distracting for me *and* for the audience. However, for in-house presentations, committee meetings, board meetings, and the like, the Meeting Minder is a versatile and useful tool.

Launch this utility from the Slide Show view, as shown in the upper-left figure on the facing page. Once you have the Meeting Minder displayed, you can use it to take notes (upper-right figure, next page).

Meeting Minder is more than just a vehicle for taking notes or minutes during a show. You can also use it to record action items for yourself or other members of the presentation or management team (lower-left figure, next page).

Finally, there's Meeting Minder's schedule, which I have shown in the bottom-right figure on the next page. Use this feature to schedule follow-up meetings or other events associated with the current show.

TAKE NOTE

► USING SCHEDULE FOR THE FIRST TIME

The first time you use Meeting Minder's schedule, you may have to configure Outlook Express if you don't already have it installed and configured. Configuration uses a wizard — it's easy.

► KEEPING MEETING MINDER DATA

After entering Meeting Minutes or Action Items, make sure you save the slide show when you are finished or when you exit Slide Show view. This will store the notes, action items, and schedule information with the PowerPoint slide file.

CROSS-REFERENCE

Consult the show-navigation section later in this chapter for additional hints on presenting your show.

SHORTCUT

Choose Speaker Notes from the Slide Show view shortcut menu to enter notes linked to specific slides.

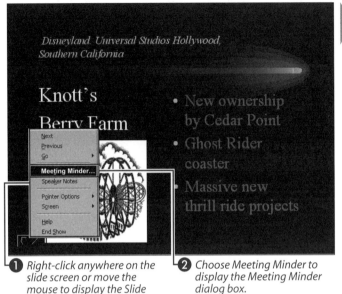

1 Right-click anywhere on the slide screen or move the mouse to display the Slide Show shortcut menu.

2 Choose Meeting Minder to display the Meeting Minder dialog box.

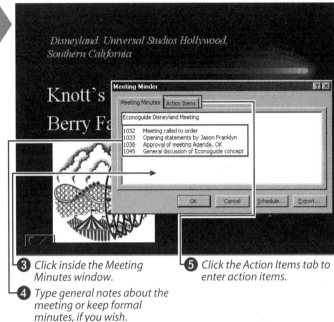

3 Click inside the Meeting Minutes window.

4 Type general notes about the meeting or keep formal minutes, if you wish.

5 Click the Action Items tab to enter action items.

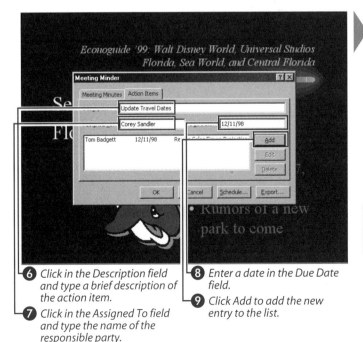

6 Click in the Description field and type a brief description of the action item.

7 Click in the Assigned To field and type the name of the responsible party.

8 Enter a date in the Due Date field.

9 Click Add to add the new entry to the list.

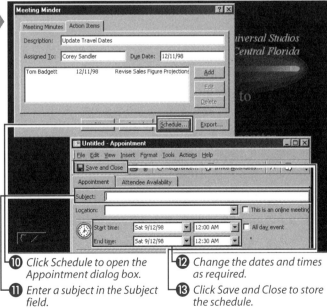

10 Click Schedule to open the Appointment dialog box.

11 Enter a subject in the Subject field.

12 Change the dates and times as required.

13 Click Save and Close to store the schedule.

Navigating Through Your Show

Getting around within a PowerPoint slide show is easy and straightforward. Once you turn on Slide Show view, you press the Spacebar, click the left mouse button, or press the Page Down key to advance to the next slide. You can use the Page Up key to back up one step. Note that I'm talking about one step, not one slide. If you have just viewed a slide with animation or progressive display, the Page Up key reverses the last action. This can be useful for backing up one item on a bullet list to answer a question or to review a point.

Frankly, that's usually the way I do it. I stand up, turn on Slide Show view, and step through the slides, one after the other. And that's just the way it should work, for the most part. But that's not the full PowerPoint story. This program is an excellent tool for staff meetings, seminars, in-house corporate training, classroom training, and more. These settings are generally less formal and probably involve more audience interaction with the speaker. In these situations, you'll find the program's additional navigational features especially useful.

PowerPoint has three additional navigation tools to help you jump directly to a slide without stepping forward or backward through intervening slides. You can access these facilities from the Slide Show shortcut menu, as shown in the upper-left figure on the facing page.

In the upper-right figure, I've shown the Slide Navigator dialog box, which lets you scroll backward and forward within a show so you can choose a specific slide to display. The Last slide viewed section of this dialog box helps you keep your bearings as to where you are and where you've been.

You can also jump directly to a specific slide from the By Title view, as shown in the lower-left figure on the next page. There is a slight difference between this navigation method and the Slide Navigator display. The By Title menu lists all slides in order, enabling you to jump to the one you choose from the list. The Slide Navigator gives you additional information, including the last slide displayed and the current slide on the screen. In the By Title display, the current display has a check mark beside it.

The other way to navigate a slide show is via keyboard shortcut keys. You can learn about these keys with Slide Show Help, shown in the bottom-right figure on the next page.

> **TAKE NOTE**
>
> **VIEWING THE LAST SLIDE DISPLAYED**
> In the Slide Show shortcut menu, select Go ⇨ Previously Viewed to view the last slide displayed.

CROSS-REFERENCE
See Chapter 4 for additional hints on presenting your PowerPoint slide show.

SHORTCUT
If you know which slide you want to display, bypass the Slide Show shortcut menu and type the slide number and press Enter. The slide you specified will be displayed.

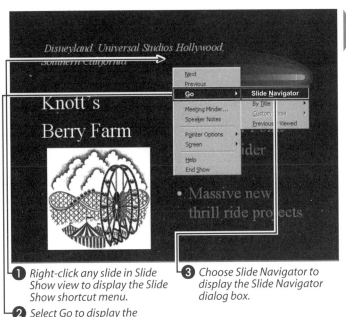

❶ *Right-click any slide in Slide Show view to display the Slide Show shortcut menu.*

❷ *Select Go to display the supplemental Go menu.*

❸ *Choose Slide Navigator to display the Slide Navigator dialog box.*

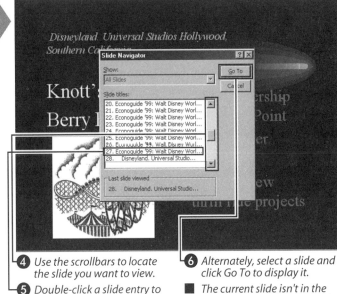

❹ *Use the scrollbars to locate the slide you want to view.*

❺ *Double-click a slide entry to display that slide.*

❻ *Alternately, select a slide and click Go To to display it.*

■ *The current slide isn't in the list. Its position is indicated by a blank box with a dotted-line border.*

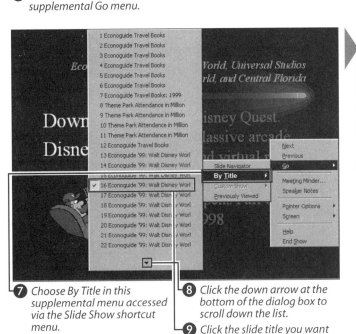

❼ *Choose By Title in this supplemental menu accessed via the Slide Show shortcut menu.*

❽ *Click the down arrow at the bottom of the dialog box to scroll down the list.*

❾ *Click the slide title you want to display.*

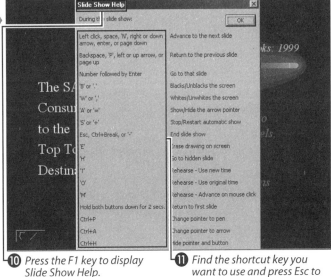

❿ *Press the F1 key to display Slide Show Help.*

⓫ *Find the shortcut key you want to use and press Esc to remove the help screen so you can use the shortcut.*

Using Online Collaboration

Though you can use PowerPoint effectively without an Internet connection, not having Internet access limits the scope of Office 2000. With an Internet connection, you can establish meetings with other users, as shown in the upper-left figure on the facing page.

This facility uses another Office 2000 program, NetMeeting. The version you see from inside PowerPoint has a slightly different user interface (upper-right figure, next page) than you'll see if you launch NetMeeting from the Start menu.

When you establish a connection, the other user sees your PowerPoint show and an Online Meeting toolbar appears on your PowerPoint screen (see the lower-left figure on the facing page). From this toolbar, you can open chat windows, disconnect the session, and allow others in the meeting to edit your slide show.

After you enable editing, you'll see this ominous message: "You have enabled other users to edit this document. You may have a security issue if you leave the document unattended." Click OK in this dialog box to continue, but remember that you have, indeed, opened up PowerPoint to others in this meeting. All they can do is modify your slide show and save it to disk — though, if you were to share the Windows Explorer application, other people in the meeting would have access to your disk drive and could delete files. Just be careful what you share.

With editing enabled, if another participant clicks the PowerPoint screen, the mouse cursor changes to show their initials, indicating that they are in control of the application. They can add slides, edit slides, save the presentation, and so on. You can click the screen to regain control. Use this collaborative connection to work together on finishing a PowerPoint show.

If you enable Chat, you'll see a screen similar to the lower-right figure on the next page. When the Chat window opens, you can type messages in the lower part of this dialog box. This sample shows only two people in the meeting, but you could have several connections active simultaneously. The Send to field lets you send your comments to everyone or only one person at a time.

Continued

TAKE NOTE

USING ONLINE COLLABORATION FOR THE FIRST TIME

The first time you use NetMeeting, you'll have to fill out a short screen with personal information. You only have to do this once.

MANAGING AN ONLINE MEETING

You can pull down a list of meeting participants in the field at the left of the Online Meeting toolbar. The next two icons let you call another user or disconnect a user.

DOING MORE ONLINE

Launching NetMeeting from the Start menu (Start ➪ Programs ➪ Internet Explorer ➪ Microsoft NetMeeting) provides additional options, including two-way voice and video communications.

CROSS-REFERENCE
See Chapter 15 for more information about using PowerPoint in an online environment.

FIND IT ONLINE
For the latest on Microsoft online-collaboration software and to update NetMeeting, go to **www.microsoft.com/netmeeting**.

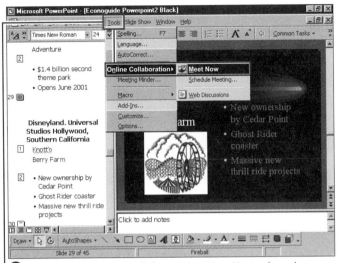

1 Select Tools ⇨ Online Collaboration ⇨ Meet Now to launch NetMeeting and connect to other users.

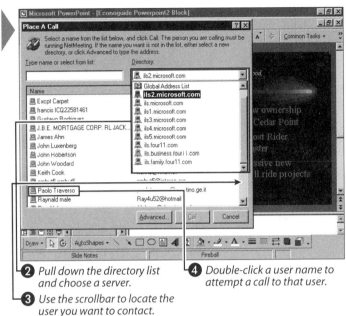

2 Pull down the directory list and choose a server.

3 Use the scrollbar to locate the user you want to contact.

4 Double-click a user name to attempt a call to that user.

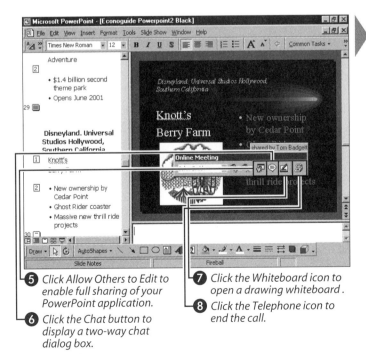

5 Click Allow Others to Edit to enable full sharing of your PowerPoint application.

6 Click the Chat button to display a two-way chat dialog box.

7 Click the Whiteboard icon to open a drawing whiteboard.

8 Click the Telephone icon to end the call.

9 Click in the Message window of this dialog box and type a word or comment.

10 Press Enter to send the message to other people in the session and to copy it into the top window.

Using Online Collaboration

Continued

From inside PowerPoint you can also schedule an online meeting. Just choose Schedule Meeting from the supplemental Online Collaboration menu (see the upper-left figure on the next page). You'll see the tabbed dialog box shown in the upper-right corner of the facing page; the Appointment tab is on top. If you know the email address of the person you want to notify of this meeting schedule, you can type it in the To field. Or you can click the To button to open your address book if the name you want is stored there.

The Schedule Meeting utility sends an email to specified recipients notifying them of your online meeting request. They can accept the invitation by dragging the message from their email inbox onto the calendar in Outlook, Microsoft's email and contact manager client (included in Office 2000).

You can use this same facility to schedule a regular meeting, as shown in the lower-left figure on the facing page. Use these settings to establish a meeting that occurs at the same time on the same day of the week. You can use Appointment Recurrence for daily or weekly meetings of a committee working on an upcoming PowerPoint presentation, for example.

If you're using Outlook on a local-area network that includes a central Exchange Server (check with your LAN administrator), you may have access to the schedules of other people in your organization. This lets you view times when other people with whom you want to meet are available for scheduling an online session before you pick a time (see the lower-right figure on the facing page).

This dialog box is actually a part of Outlook, so study Outlook Help for additional information on using the schedule. You can tell from the figure I've shown that this utility offers considerable flexibility. You can use Attendee Availability to schedule resources, such as meeting rooms and projectors, as well as people. Individual schedules are color-coded (see the "Tentative," "Busy," "Out of Office," and "No Information" buttons at the bottom of this dialog box).

Outlook's scheduler works best on a local-area network on which you can share information through a common calendar. But email with Outlook works almost as well if you keep everyone in the email loop.

TAKE NOTE

USING INTRANET COLLABORATION

You don't have to use Microsoft or another foreign host for online collaboration. Contact your local LAN administrator for information on setting up an intranet discussion or chat server for online meetings within your company.

USING CHAT

Part of Internet Explorer 4 and Windows 98 is a graphical chat program that uses Internet Relay Chat. This, too, is a good way to communicate with distant co-workers about your PowerPoint projects.

CROSS-REFERENCE

There are other means of online communication available with PowerPoint. See the next two tasks for more information.

SHORTCUT

To send a whole file to a NetMeeting participant, use File Transfer in the NetMeeting Tools menu or simply press Ctrl-F.

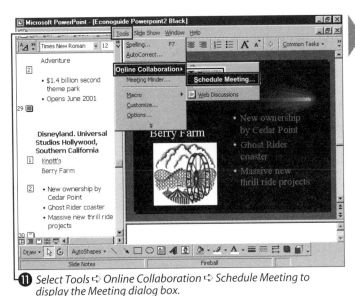

⓫ Select Tools ➪ Online Collaboration ➪ Schedule Meeting to display the Meeting dialog box.

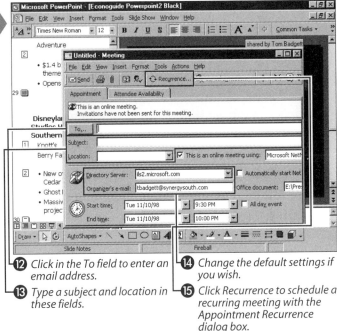

⓬ Click in the To field to enter an email address.

⓭ Type a subject and location in these fields.

⓮ Change the default settings if you wish.

⓯ Click Recurrence to schedule a recurring meeting with the Appointment Recurrence dialog box.

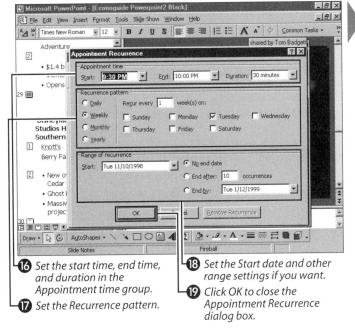

⓰ Set the start time, end time, and duration in the Appointment time group.

⓱ Set the Recurrence pattern.

⓲ Set the Start date and other range settings if you want.

⓳ Click OK to close the Appointment Recurrence dialog box.

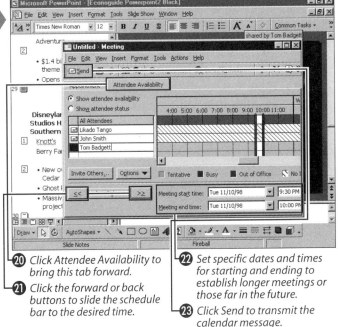

⓴ Click Attendee Availability to bring this tab forward.

㉑ Click the forward or back buttons to slide the schedule bar to the desired time.

㉒ Set specific dates and times for starting and ending to establish longer meetings or those far in the future.

㉓ Click Send to transmit the calendar message.

Using the Web in Discussions

With each new release of Office since Office 95, Microsoft has enhanced the online features and added new communications options. With the industry-wide trend toward Web interfaces for all software, it is natural to use a Web screen for discussions. Part of this system also includes subscriptions, a feature of Windows 98 and of Microsoft Explorer. This lets you enter into a discussion about a document and also subscribe to it, so you know almost immediately when any changes are made to it.

A Web discussion is a lot like an Internet newsgroup: you log into a discussion page to read comments from others and to make comments of your own about a fairly narrow topic or range of topics. This utility can be used for in-house connections or for general, open connections, as you might see with NetMeeting. Your system administrator or webmaster can set up a Web-discussion site. Once that's done, you start a connection with the procedure shown in the upper-left figure on the next page.

The first time you use this utility, you'll need to tell PowerPoint what Web discussion server to use with the dialog box shown at the upper right of the facing page. The discussion Web server has to be configured to host these dialog boxes, so the server address you put here will be supplied by your network administrator or someone else who has asked you to participate in this PowerPoint online discussion. If this server requires a secure connection, check the Secure connection required box in the Discussion Servers dialog box.

Next you'll see a Discussion Options dialog box (lower-left figure, following page), but again, only the first time you launch this utility. You can return to this dialog box later to add servers, but it will not be displayed automatically after your first use of Web discussion.

The next screen you see may vary slightly, depending on how the Web discussion server is set up. You most likely will be asked for a user name and password through a dialog box similar to the one in the bottom-right figure on the facing page. Again, this information will come from a network administrator, webmaster, or someone else who has established this discussion page for you. The user name and password may the same as those used for your online connection, or (more likely) they may be entirely different.

Continued

TAKE NOTE

ACCESSING DISCUSSION OUTSIDE POWERPOINT

You may want to access Web Discussions from outside PowerPoint. From the Internet Explorer 5.0 main screen, you can click on the Discussion button at the far right of the Explorer toolbar. Or you can click View on the main Explorer menu, click the Explorer Bar, and then choose Discussions.

CROSS-REFERENCE
See Chapter 15 for more information on how PowerPoint uses the Internet and the World Wide Web.

FIND IT ONLINE
Here's an interesting reference page that gives additional insight into Web discussions: **http://dowland.dcrt. nih.gov/wid/sessions/9discussion/.**

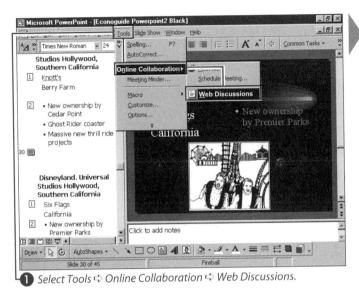

1 Select Tools ➪ Online Collaboration ➪ Web Discussions.

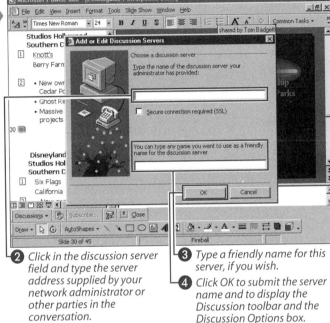

2 Click in the discussion server field and type the server address supplied by your network administrator or other parties in the conversation.

3 Type a friendly name for this server, if you wish.

4 Click OK to submit the server name and to display the Discussion toolbar and the Discussion Options box.

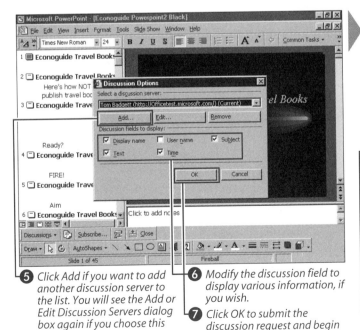

5 Click Add if you want to add another discussion server to the list. You will see the Add or Edit Discussion Servers dialog box again if you choose this option.

6 Modify the discussion field to display various information, if you wish.

7 Click OK to submit the discussion request and begin the online session.

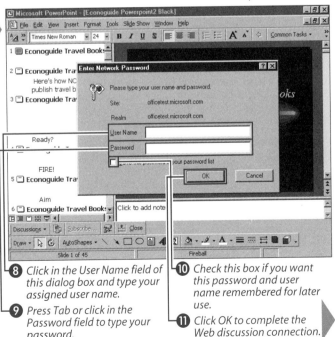

8 Click in the User Name field of this dialog box and type your assigned user name.

9 Press Tab or click in the Password field to type your password.

10 Check this box if you want this password and user name remembered for later use.

11 Click OK to complete the Web discussion connection.

Using the Web in Discussions

Continued

A few seconds after entering a proper user name and password, you'll notice a new toolbar at the bottom of the PowerPoint screen (as shown in the top-left figure on the facing page). This toolbar gives you access to the features of the selected discussion page. The first menu item is duplicated in the icon between the Discussions and Subscribe buttons. When you select this first menu item or the icon, you will see the dialog box shown in the top-right figure on the next page.

Here you can type a topic and text for your own posting about the current presentation file. When you click OK in this dialog box, your topic and text are posted to the discussion page, in the same way you'd post to an online newsgroup. As soon as you submit the posting, you should see it appear at the bottom of your PowerPoint screen, as shown in the lower-left figure on the next page. You can read this post — and others you will receive from other participants in this discussion — and reply to it, too. You can edit and delete posts from your local files as well, using the shortcut menu shown in this figure.

If you've used Internet Explorer very much, you know about Web subscriptions, a feature that notifies you when a specified Web site changes. This system enables you to track product updates, new drivers that have been added, and the like. The subscription function that is part of the PowerPoint Web-discussion feature is similar. It will notify you when changes are made to the page, when new discussion items are uploaded, and so on, as shown in the bottom-right figure on the next page. You can also specify how to be notified of changes, how often you will be notified, and more.

Another utility helps you track only the discussion items you really want to see. Select Filter from the Discussions menu, and you can choose to receive messages only from a certain group or participant, or to receive only those messages that have been posted within a particular time frame. For example, you could specify that you want to see only messages that have been posted in the last 48 hours, or during the last 7 days. This helps you avoid reading old messages that aren't relevant to the current discussion.

TAKE NOTE

CHANGING OPTIONS

Clicking Discussion Options in the Discussions menu displays the Discussion Options dialog box, from which you can add a Web discussion server to your list using the Add Discussion Servers dialog box (shown on the previous page). This lets you maintain multiple discussion servers for work you have in progress.

CROSS-REFERENCE

See Chapter 16 for information on creating custom toolbars and general toolbar management.

FIND IT ONLINE

For a detailed discussion of collaborative issues and Outlook, go to **http://www.microsoft.com/exchange/support/ deployment/inc/collabsolutions_topcontent.txt**.

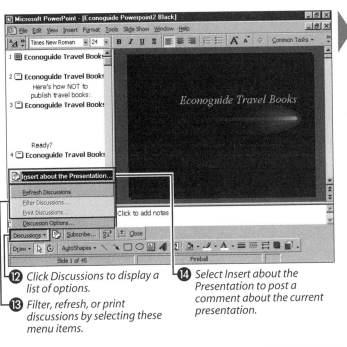

12 Click Discussions to display a list of options.

13 Filter, refresh, or print discussions by selecting these menu items.

14 Select Insert about the Presentation to post a comment about the current presentation.

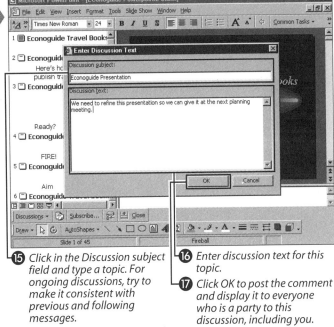

15 Click in the Discussion subject field and type a topic. For ongoing discussions, try to make it consistent with previous and following messages.

16 Enter discussion text for this topic.

17 Click OK to post the comment and display it to everyone who is a party to this discussion, including you.

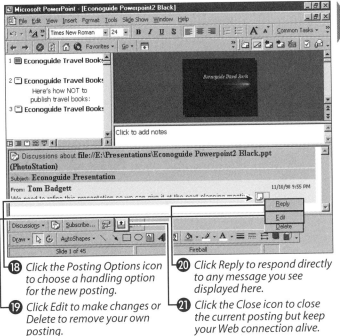

18 Click the Posting Options icon to choose a handling option for the new posting.

19 Click Edit to make changes or Delete to remove your own posting.

20 Click Reply to respond directly to any message you see displayed here.

21 Click the Close icon to close the current posting but keep your Web connection alive.

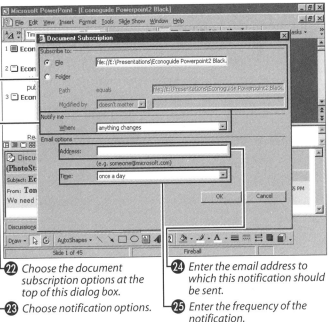

22 Choose the document subscription options at the top of this dialog box.

23 Choose notification options.

24 Enter the email address to which this notification should be sent.

25 Enter the frequency of the notification.

Broadcasting the Show

The collaboration tools included with Office 2000 are two-way utilities. You schedule a meeting with someone on your corporate LAN or on the Internet and connect through a server to talk in real time and to share a PowerPoint presentation so you can work on it together.

The Broadcast facility is different. It is a one-way utility that lets you transmit your PowerPoint slide show to one or hundreds of users over a LAN or the Internet. You might use it to disseminate new budget, sales, or training information to people who work in different locations. The more you use these kinds of online features, the more time and money you save, because your co-workers don't have to travel for a meeting.

As the term implies, broadcasting lets you send the same information to many users at the same time. Like collaboration, broadcasting uses an external program. In this case, it's Microsoft's NetShow utility, which supports a variety of streaming data transmission and reception formats.

Start the broadcasting process with the menu sequence shown in the top-left figure on the facing page. The first dialog box you see after this step simply lets you choose whether to create a new schedule or to update an existing one. Choose New and click OK to see the dialog box shown in the upper-right corner of the facing page. When you've completed the general information you can change the Broadcast settings (lower-left figure, next page) if you wish.

Remember that NetShow, the utility you will use to conduct the PowerPoint broadcast, is a sophisticated streaming-media program. It has two components: the server and the reader (or player). All PCs with Internet Explorer or Windows 98 have the player. Office 2000 includes some server components, which is why you can conduct a NetShow broadcast with up to 15 users without a server. If your audience will be larger than 15, however, you'll need to work with your network administrator to install and configure a NetShow server.

Continued

Continued

TAKE NOTE

► USING THE ADDRESS BOOK

You can see from the lower-left figure on the facing page that the Schedule a New Broadcast dialog box offers a link to the Address Book — yet another example of the tight integration of Office software components. Use the Address Book button to access a list of email addresses if you need help finding the response address, in case it isn't you.

► USING VIDEO

Audio support for a PowerPoint broadcast is enabled by default. If you have a camera and want to use video as part of the NetShow program, you must specify a NetShow server in Server Options (bottom-right figure, next page).

CROSS-REFERENCE

Chapter 15 talks more about using PowerPoint's Web-centric features.

FIND IT ONLINE

For more information about NetShow, the player and encoder, go to **www.microsoft.com/netshow**.

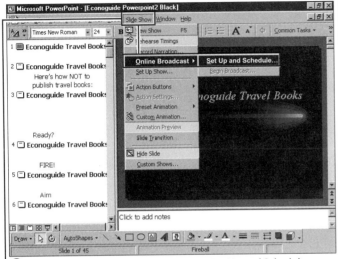

1 Click Slide Show ⇨ Online Broadcast ⇨ Set Up and Schedule to display the Broadcast Schedule dialog box.

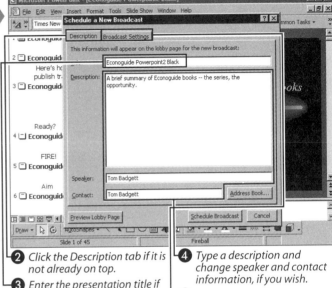

2 Click the Description tab if it is not already on top.

3 Enter the presentation title if it is different from the default, which will be the name of the open PowerPoint file.

4 Type a description and change speaker and contact information, if you wish.

5 Click the Broadcast Settings tab to continue the setup.

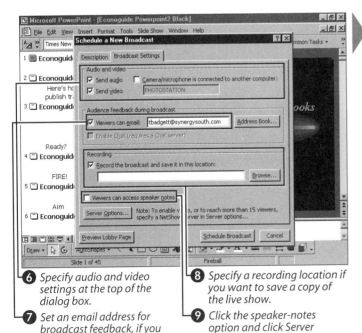

6 Specify audio and video settings at the top of the dialog box.

7 Set an email address for broadcast feedback, if you wish.

8 Specify a recording location if you want to save a copy of the live show.

9 Click the speaker-notes option and click Server Options.

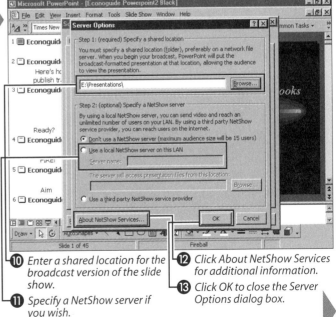

10 Enter a shared location for the broadcast version of the slide show.

11 Specify a NetShow server if you wish.

12 Click About NetShow Services for additional information.

13 Click OK to close the Server Options dialog box.

Broadcasting the Show
Continued

Almost finished. Just a few more settings and you'll be ready to try PowerPoint broadcasting. With the description, broadcast settings, and server options taken care of, you are ready to actually schedule the broadcast. Refer again to the bottom-left image on the previous page. See the Schedule Broadcast button? When you click it, you'll see the dialog box shown at the upper-left of the facing page.

If you haven't specified a NetShow server, you'll see an interim dialog box reminding you that your broadcast is limited to only 15 viewers without the server. If you change your mind and you want to specify a server, click No in this box and go back to the Server Options dialog box. Otherwise, click Yes to see the scheduling dialog box shown in the top-left figure on the next page.

What happens next depends on how your computer is configured. To use the broadcast facilities you have selected, NetShow needs access to Exchange and email. Therefore, if you haven't previously configured your email and Exchange settings, you may see a series of screens that configure this function. Just accept the defaults on each of these screens.

Once the settings are all done, you can start the broadcast from the Slide Show menu, as shown in the upper-right image on the facing page. When you choose to start the broadcast, you'll see the dialog box shown in the lower-left figure on the facing page. This box gives you a chance to make some final adjustments to the show hardware and to set an opening message for the audience.

You can create an audience message using the dialog box shown in the bottom-right figure on the following page.

TAKE NOTE

► USING NETSHOW

You may have to download additional NetShow components before broadcasting works properly. If things don't work as they should, and you get a message saying you need other components, point your browser to **www.microsoft.com/netshow** and download the latest player and server components. Once you've installed these updates, your broadcast facilities should work as advertised.

► CHANGING YOUR MIND

You can reconfigure broadcast settings if you want to change any of the initial settings, including the time of the broadcast. Display the Broadcast Schedule dialog box by selecting Slide Show ➪ Online Broadcast ➪ Set Up and Schedule. Choose Change settings or reschedule a broadcast from this initial dialog box.

► SAVING BROADCAST SETTINGS

The schedule and other broadcast settings you specify in these steps are stored within the PowerPoint file you will be sending. Just remember to save the file after you have set up a broadcast and your broadcast settings will be available the next time you open the file.

CROSS-REFERENCE

See Chapter 14 for additional ideas on presenting PowerPoint slide shows.

FIND IT ONLINE

Microsoft has a new Media Player that is compatible with NetShow and other multimedia files. Get it at **www.microsoft.com/windows/mediaplayer**.

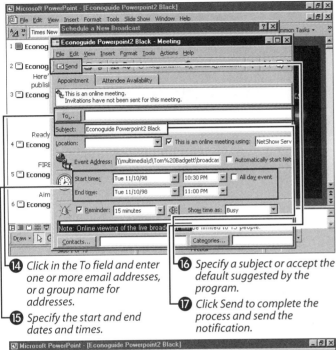

14 Click in the To field and enter one or more email addresses, or a group name for addresses.

15 Specify the start and end dates and times.

16 Specify a subject or accept the default suggested by the program.

17 Click Send to complete the process and send the notification.

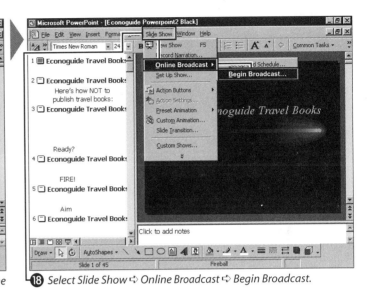

18 Select Slide Show ⇨ Online Broadcast ⇨ Begin Broadcast.

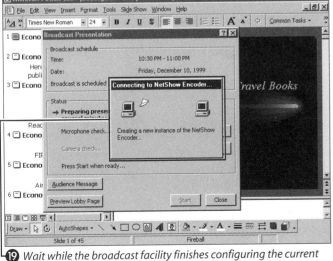

19 Wait while the broadcast facility finishes configuring the current broadcast.

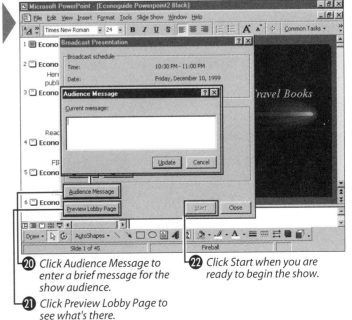

20 Click Audience Message to enter a brief message for the show audience.

21 Click Preview Lobby Page to see what's there.

22 Click Start when you are ready to begin the show.

Using the Send To Feature

Office 2000 applications include a Send To feature on the main File menu that lets you send the current file to a variety of destinations. I introduced Send To when I talked about using PowerPoint with Microsoft Word in Chapter 11. However, there's some additional functionality I didn't talk about there that you may want to use.

Send To acts as an automatic email utility, enabling you to send a single PowerPoint slide in the body of an email message — or send an entire presentation as an email attachment — without having to load a separate email client. You can also use Send To to create a route whereby you send a file sequentially to a series of people until it comes back to you with any edits and changes added along the way.

The top-left figure on the facing page shows you how to start this process; the figure in the upper right shows you the routing dialog box where you set it all up. This box is pretty self-explanatory: All you need to do is add a subject and a message, and then set the routing options before entering the addresses you want to receive the file.

You can create a round-robin list by sending the file to people one at a time. In this scenario, you send the file to recipient one, who makes any changes or suggestions before sending it to recipient two, and so on. If you check the Return when done button, you'll get back a copy of the file after everyone has seen it. Even if you don't expect the other users to make

changes, it's a good idea to have the file loop back to you so you at least know when everyone has seen it.

To enter the recipients' email addresses, click Address (in the routing slip dialog box) to display the Address Book (lower-left figure, facing page). Choose addressees from among existing entries or, if you need to, create new entries. When you have entered all the recipients in the To field, you can click OK to return to the Add Routing Slip dialog box, as shown in the bottom-right figure on the next page.

Now you can rearrange the order of the email recipients if you want before sending the file on to the recipient list.

TAKE NOTE

▶ SEND TO IN REVERSE

You can use Send To from other Office applications to send data to PowerPoint. Choose PowerPoint from the Send To menu within Microsoft Word, for example. Conversely, Microsoft Word is a choice on PowerPoint's Send To menu.

▶ SENDING TO AN ONLINE MEETING PARTICIPANT

Having made an online meeting connection, you can select Send To ⇨ Online Meeting Participant to transmit a file to a person in the meeting.

CROSS-REFERENCE

See Chapter 11 for additional details on using Outlook mail to send PowerPoint files to someone else.

SHORTCUT

Click the E-mail icon on PowerPoint's mail toolbar to open your default email client with the current slide already inserted. This in-place edit allows a quick send.

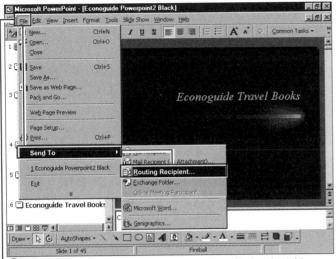

1 Select File ⇨ Send To ⇨ Routing Recipient to display the Add Routing Slip dialog box.

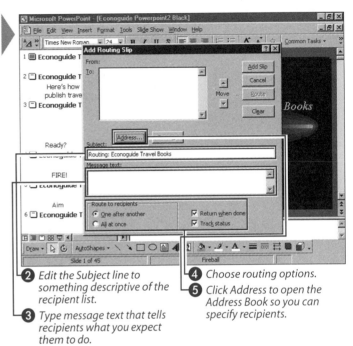

2 Edit the Subject line to something descriptive of the recipient list.

3 Type message text that tells recipients what you expect them to do.

4 Choose routing options.

5 Click Address to open the Address Book so you can specify recipients.

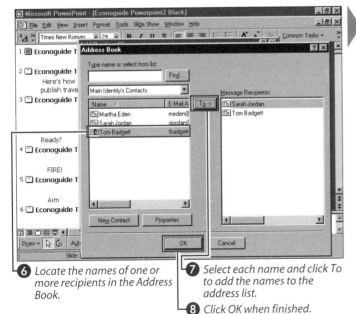

6 Locate the names of one or more recipients in the Address Book.

7 Select each name and click To to add the names to the address list.

8 Click OK when finished.

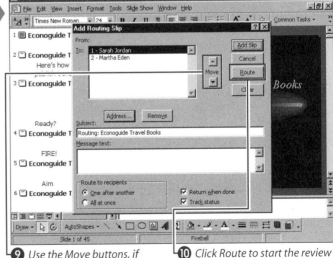

9 Use the Move buttons, if required, to change the order in which you want the recipients to receive the file.

10 Click Route to start the review process by sending the message to the sequential list.

Personal Workbook

Q&A

1 What presentation utility would you use to keep general notes or meeting minutes during a PowerPoint slide show?

_____

_____

_____

2 What two methods can you use to display the Slide Show shortcut menu?

_____

_____

_____

3 What Microsoft utility outside PowerPoint is used for Online Collaboration?

_____

_____

_____

4 What are the main differences between Online Collaboration and Web Discussions?

_____

_____

_____

5 How would you use the Send To feature to get several colleagues to read and edit a PowerPoint show?

_____

_____

_____

6 What PowerPoint facility would you use to send a PowerPoint show to 15 or more users simultaneously?

_____

_____

_____

7 What are the differences between the Slide Navigator and By Title lists in a PowerPoint slide show?

_____

_____

_____

8 Where are the broadcast settings for a PowerPoint show stored?

_____

_____

_____

ANSWERS: PAGE 310

EXTRA PRACTICE

❶ Display the Action Items dialog box from within the Slide Show view of a PowerPoint presentation.

❷ Display a list of slides in the current show, by title, with the Slide Show view active.

❸ Launch the collaboration dialog box and choose an online participant with whom you could communicate and share a PowerPoint presentation.

❹ Display the keyboard-shortcut reference list from a PowerPoint Slide Show view of a presentation.

❺ Display the Set Up and Schedule dialog box for an online broadcast.

❻ Display the Schedule Meeting dialog box for Online Collaboration.

REAL-WORLD APPLICATIONS

✔ You are the chairman of a committee charged with collectively designing a PowerPoint presentation for an upcoming national seminar. Committee members live in various parts of the country, but you want to work closely with them during the design. You can use Online Collaboration to discuss the design and show interim versions, then use Send To in a routing list to have each team member suggest edits in turn before returning the final version to you.

✔ Your company has a number of offices across the country. The firm is launching a new marketing and sales program, including new products and procedures. You want to give each salesperson ample training in the new procedures, regardless of their location. You can use a PowerPoint presentation that you broadcast to all employees to provide the training without the travel.

Visual Quiz

Describe how to display the screen shown here.

_____

_____

_____

_____

_____

_____

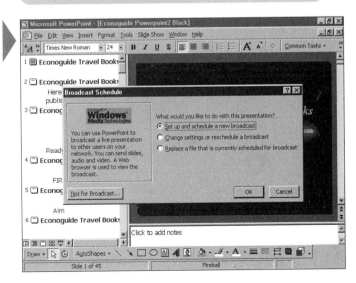

CHAPTER **15**

MASTER
THESE
SKILLS

▶ Using Hyperlinks

▶ Saving a Slide Show as a Web Page

▶ Moving PowerPoint Web Pages to a Server

▶ Accessing PowerPoint Shows on the Web

PowerPoint and the World Wide Web

Whatever you do with your computer today, you can't really escape the Internet and the Web. Windows 98, Explorer 5, Office 2000 — all share a Web-centric design that helps reduce cross-platform differences, makes learning easier, and offers options for presenting and using your data.

PowerPoint 2000 is part of that Web-oriented design. I've already shown you the concept of hyperlinks inside PowerPoint, but you can do much more with it that makes use of the Internet and the Web. You can save your PowerPoint slide shows as HTML (Hypertext Markup Language) files, for example, so you can load them directly into a browser such as Explorer 5. Or you can copy the HTML version of a PowerPoint show to a Web server so you can share your show with the broadest audience of all — the global Internet community.

You can get along very well with PowerPoint without these specific Web features, of course, but you shouldn't ignore this level of functionality. Couple PowerPoint 2000 with Windows 98 and even a 28,800 bps Internet connection, and you have a new level of software. Virtually instant communication with other users around the world, the ability to save information to an Internet address, broadcasting and collaboration (see Chapter 14), and conventional Web-page data sharing are all part of the PowerPoint 2000 experience. Moreover, Office 2000's user interface recognizes the increasing influence of the Internet on how we use our computers and the way we communicate.

In this chapter, I introduce the Web components that are part of Office 2000 and PowerPoint. These features aren't difficult to use, but they may require you to change at least a little bit how you think about computers and computer software. To actually use some of these features, you'll need an account with an Internet Service Provider (ISP) to provide you with Internet access and Web-hosting services. If you don't have Internet access and Web hosting, start working on that now. The Internet is quickly becoming as important and indispensable as the cell phone, copy machine, and fax services. You'll want to be part of this revolutionary development.

Using Hyperlinks

If you use the Web, you use hyperlinks every day. Even if you aren't on the Web right now but you use Windows software, you've probably used hyperlinks as part of online help.

Hyperlinks are a simple but elegant concept. Suppose you are reading an online article about jazz. Within the article, you encounter a reference to trumpets as jazz instruments. By clicking on the reference, you are transferred immediately to another server, in Germany perhaps, that discusses the history of trumpets, displays pictures of trumpets, and offers sample sounds. As you read this article, you see a reference to a famous trumpet player. By clicking on this reference, you jump to yet another server to read a biography of this musician. This article mentions the artist's jazz history and includes a link to an article on jazz...

See? The concept of hyperlinks is changing the way we create educational material and the way we learn and study.

You can use this same concept in your PowerPoint slide shows. You can create a hyperlink from any PowerPoint text or other object. Consider the first figure on the facing page. You can select Hyperlink from the shortcut menu to link a highlighted item — such as a word, phrase, or photograph — to another slide. This command opens the Insert Hyperlink dialog box, which you can see at the upper right of the facing page.

This rich dialog box offers many options for choosing where you go when you click a hyperlink in a PowerPoint presentation. By default, the suggested hyperlinks include recently visited Web pages. If you were to choose one of these, and you have an Internet connection when you present your slide show, a click on the hyperlink would display the specified Web address. Without a show-time Internet connection, you should consider using the hyperlink to jump to another slide (in the same presentation or a different one). If you choose a ScreenTip and enter text for it, you can point to the hyperlink to view the tip text during a slide show (see the lower-left figure on the next page).

Once you have created a hyperlink, the shortcut menu changes slightly to offer additional options when you select Hyperlink, as I have shown in the lower-right figure on the next page. When you select Edit from this shortcut menu, you will see the Edit Hyperlink dialog box, which is really the same dialog box you used to create the hyperlink in the first place. Note that each of these dialog boxes is slightly different depending on your choice in the Link to column.

Continued

TAKE NOTE

▶ REMOVING HYPERLINKS

You can remove a link by choosing that option in the Hyperlink supplemental menu (accessed via the slide-shortcut menu).

CROSS-REFERENCE

See Chapter 8 for some more information on using hyperlinks.

SHORTCUT

Highlight a slide object or text and press Ctrl-K to display the Insert Hyperlink dialog box, bypassing the menus.

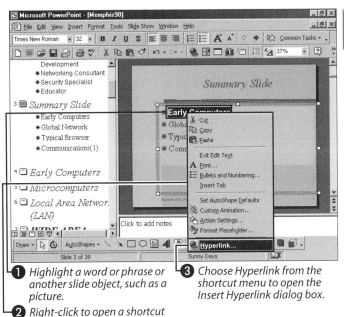

❶ Highlight a word or phrase or another slide object, such as a picture.

❷ Right-click to open a shortcut menu.

❸ Choose Hyperlink from the shortcut menu to open the Insert Hyperlink dialog box.

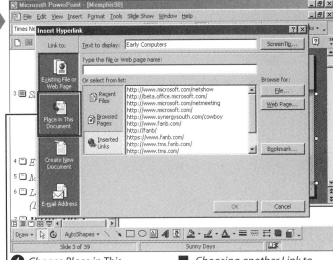

❹ Choose Place in This Document from the Link to list.

■ Choosing another Link to option displays a different options screen.

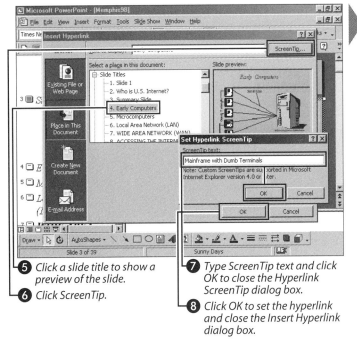

❺ Click a slide title to show a preview of the slide.

❻ Click ScreenTip.

❼ Type ScreenTip text and click OK to close the Hyperlink ScreenTip dialog box.

❽ Click OK to set the hyperlink and close the Insert Hyperlink dialog box.

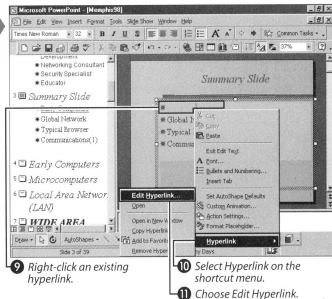

❾ Right-click an existing hyperlink.

❿ Select Hyperlink on the shortcut menu.

⓫ Choose Edit Hyperlink.

Using Hyperlinks
Continued

Hyperlinks to other slides within the same slide show is just one possibility. As I hinted earlier, you can link to a live Web page, to an email address, and to a new document (which you can create from the Insert Hyperlink dialog box). And you can create a bookmark within the current slide show and use that as a connection point for a hyperlink.

As you'll see later in this chapter, you can save your slide show as a Web document and store it on a Web server, which makes hyperlinks to Web pages even more useful. PowerPoint will probably never replace FrontPage, but you can certainly use a PowerPoint slide show to create a set of pages off of a main site. Schools and trainers use this technique frequently because they already have complete PowerPoint presentations that cover topics they want to share or promote over the Web.

The upper-left figure on the facing page shows how to expand the range of possible links. The items in this dialog box include PowerPoint help files that I have viewed recently, Web pages I've visited, and other files and locations. PowerPoint 2000 is closely linked to Internet Explorer 5, which is also closely tied to disk navigation, online help, and the Web. In fact, when you choose some of these hyperlinks inside a PowerPoint show, Internet Explorer launches automatically, so you view the information through the browser even if the link is not to a Web page.

If you click Recent Files, you'll see a list of files you have recently used from your hard drive or network connection. You can link to almost anything, as long as you have the application associated with that file type installed on your computer. You can reference a Word document or accounting information and have Word or MS Money launch to display the data.

In the upper-right figure on the next page, I've shown how to create an email hyperlink. Remember to select Hyperlink from the slide shortcut menu to display the Edit Hyperlink or Insert Hyperlink dialog box. An email link could be quite useful if you are presenting your slide show on the Web.

The lower-left figure on the next page shows how to create a new document, and at the lower right I've shown how to find files on your hard drive that aren't displayed in one of the Hyperlink dialog boxes.

TAKE NOTE

INSERTING HYPERLINKS

Text hyperlinks are attached to a single word unless you highlight a whole phrase before creating the hyperlink. Click inside a word to create a hyperlink to that word; highlight multiple words to create a hyperlink associated with the entire phrase. If you are making presentations for other users, ease them into using hyperlinks: include words such as "click here" when you want to present one. Later, as they become more accustomed to hyperlinks, you can simply highlight words or phrases that contain them.

CROSS-REFERENCE
See the next section in this chapter for information on creating a Web page from a PowerPoint show.

SHORTCUT
Click an Office filename in the Insert Hyperlink dialog box and then click Bookmark to display a list of slides, bookmarks, or other directly accessible locations within that file.

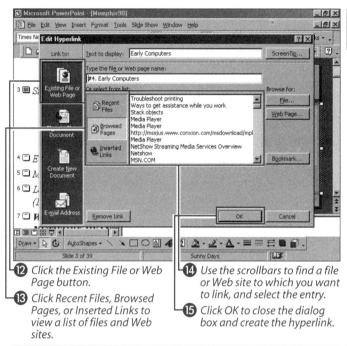

12 Click the Existing File or Web Page button.

13 Click Recent Files, Browsed Pages, or Inserted Links to view a list of files and Web sites.

14 Use the scrollbars to find a file or Web site to which you want to link, and select the entry.

15 Click OK to close the dialog box and create the hyperlink.

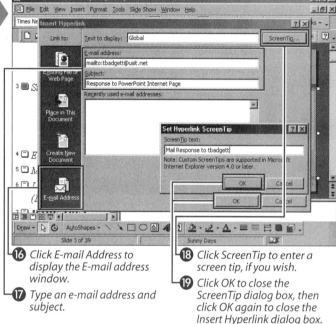

16 Click E-mail Address to display the E-mail address window.

17 Type an e-mail address and subject.

18 Click ScreenTip to enter a screen tip, if you wish.

19 Click OK to close the ScreenTip dialog box, then click OK again to close the Insert Hyperlink dialog box.

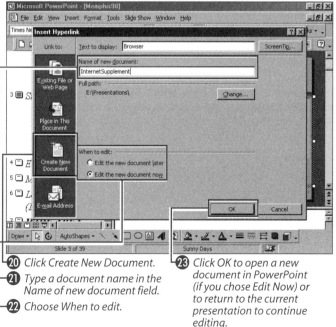

20 Click Create New Document.

21 Type a document name in the Name of new document field.

22 Choose When to edit.

23 Click OK to open a new document in PowerPoint (if you chose Edit Now) or to return to the current presentation to continue editing.

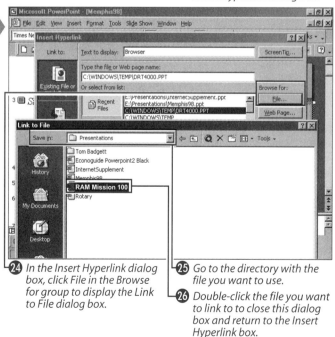

24 In the Insert Hyperlink dialog box, click File in the Browse for group to display the Link to File dialog box.

25 Go to the directory with the file you want to use.

26 Double-click the file you want to link to to close this dialog box and return to the Insert Hyperlink box.

Saving a Slide Show as a Web Page

As a graphical program that includes support for hyperlinks, PowerPoint is a natural for the Web. And, with its intrinsic HTML converter, you can save a slide show as a Web page quickly and easily.

To prepare for a Web-based PowerPoint show, simply create a presentation in the normal way, store it in the normal way — just to make sure you have a safe copy of it — and then use the Save as Web Page menu (shown in the top-left figure on the facing page) to store a Web-page version of the file.

In most cases, the save produces two objects in the chosen directory: an HTML master file and a new subdirectory containing the images from your slide show. This new subdirectory contains more than just individual PowerPoint slides. There are separate images for each slide object, so the number of files in this directory can be fairly large. Just remember, if you move or remove this new Web site, the files inside the Files subdirectory go with the main HTML document.

You now have local Web-page content that you can view with any Web browser. You can use a special toolbar inside PowerPoint to help this navigation. Right-click any PowerPoint toolbar and select Web to display the Web toolbar. This toolbar gives you Web navigation tools such as display home page, pick from favorites, and more. You can use it to open local hard-disk files — HTML or other types — or to launch Internet Explorer and open a Web site.

Now, to open the new Web site, use the Go button on the Web toolbar, as shown in the lower-left figure on the facing page.

The default format for your new PowerPoint Web site is a split screen that shows the slide show outline on the left and the slides on the right (lower-left figure, facing page). If you want, you can expand this default display to fill the screen. Use the Page Down key to move forward in a full-screen PowerPoint slide show displayed in full-screen Web format.

TAKE NOTE

PREVIEWING THE WEB SITE

Use Web Page Preview from the PowerPoint File menu to view the probable results of converting the presentation to a Web format.

DISPLAYING LOCAL POWERPOINT WEB SITES

Use the Open menu selection from the File menu within Internet Explorer to load the new Web site from your hard drive. You can also type the full path to the file in the Address line of Explorer's navigation toolbar, or you can use Go from the PowerPoint Web toolbar.

CROSS-REFERENCE

See the next task, "Moving PowerPoint Web Pages to a Server," for information on getting your PowerPoint presentation from your hard drive to a Web server.

SHORTCUT

Click the Expand/Collapse outline button on the browser window just below the outline section to change the outline view of your PowerPoint Web site.

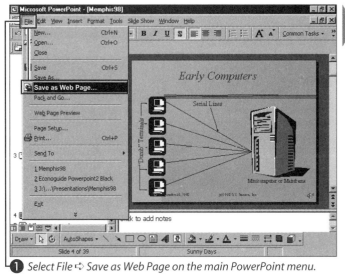

1 Select File ➪ Save as Web Page on the main PowerPoint menu.

2 Go to the directory you want to hold the HTML file.

3 Click the arrow to display the Save as type list.

4 Choose Web Page from this file-type list.

5 Click Save to store the presentation as a Web page.

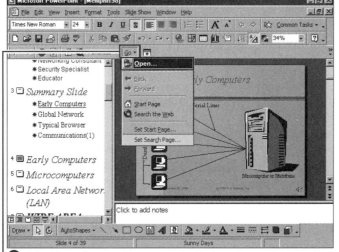

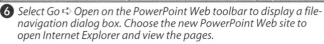

6 Select Go ➪ Open on the PowerPoint Web toolbar to display a file-navigation dialog box. Choose the new PowerPoint Web site to open Internet Explorer and view the pages.

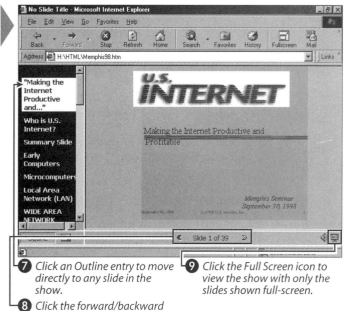

7 Click an Outline entry to move directly to any slide in the show.

8 Click the forward/backward buttons to step sequentially through the slides.

9 Click the Full Screen icon to view the show with only the slides shown full-screen.

Moving PowerPoint Web Pages to a Server

Y ou can access a Web-format version of your PowerPoint slide show directly from your hard drive or over a local-area network (a direct connection among computers that lets them share hardware and software resources). You might want to share the presentation with other people who don't have PowerPoint. By converting the slide show to Web format, you open up your presentation to Macintosh users, people with UNIX machines — essentially, anyone with a Web browser — whether they access the file over the Internet or from a local file over a LAN.

For LAN access, you only need to store the PowerPoint Web site at a location on the network that is accessible by the people you want to use it. Loading the file from a network drive is virtually the same as loading it from your local hard drive, so any number of users can access it. Because it is a Web-format file, multiple users can open it simultaneously.

On the other hand, if you want to share the file with co-workers at remote offices, or as part of a broadly distributed Web site, you'll need to copy the HTML file and all associated graphics and slides to a Web server somewhere. I can't tell you precisely where to store your file on a Web server because I don't know where your Web server is. You'll have to consult your Internet Service Provider (ISP) or your local network administrator for that information. I can show you how the process generally works, however.

You may use standard FTP (File Transfer Protocol) to upload your Web files, or, if your ISP supports it,

you can use FrontPage Extended Web format. If your Web server is part of your local-area network, you might simply save or copy the files in the conventional Windows manner.

However, using the Web Publishing Wizard, a general-purpose utility included with Office 2000 and Explorer 5, you can use several different upload procedures. In the upper-left figure on the facing page, I've shown you how to launch the Web Publishing Wizard from the Start menu.

The next three images on the following page show you how to use the wizard to copy your Web-page files to a Web server. Again, I've shown typical directories and procedures. Check with your ISP or LAN administrator for details.

Continued

TAKE NOTE

INSTALLING THE WEB PUBLISHING WIZARD

If the Web Publishing Wizard isn't available on your Start menu, it may not be installed. Insert the Office 2000 software distribution disc, choose Add/Remove Programs from the opening screen, and click on Office Tools. Choose Web Publishing from the Office Tools list and click Run from My Computer in the pop-up menu. Finally, click Update now in the Update dialog box to add the wizard to your computer.

CROSS-REFERENCE
See Chapter 14 for additional hints on using the Internet with PowerPoint.

FIND IT ONLINE
For more information on using the Web Publishing Wizard, try this Microsoft site: **http://www.microsoft.com/windows/software/webpost/wp2.htm**.

PowerPoint and the World Wide Web

Moving PowerPoint Web Pages to a Server

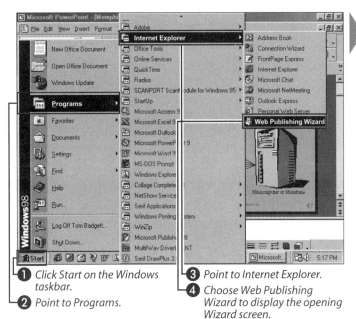

❶ Click Start on the Windows taskbar.

❷ Point to Programs.

❸ Point to Internet Explorer.

❹ Choose Web Publishing Wizard to display the opening Wizard screen.

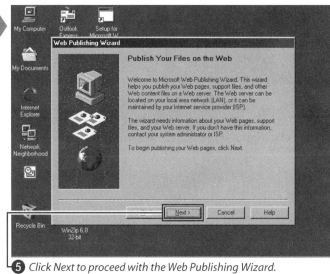

❺ Click Next to proceed with the Web Publishing Wizard.

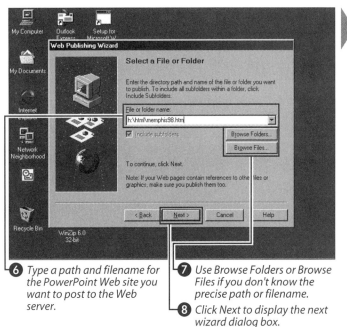

❻ Type a path and filename for the PowerPoint Web site you want to post to the Web server.

❼ Use Browse Folders or Browse Files if you don't know the precise path or filename.

❽ Click Next to display the next wizard dialog box.

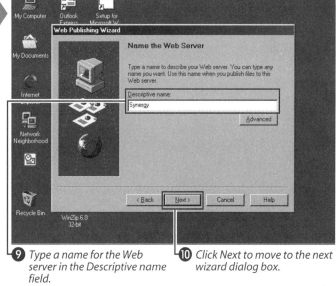

❾ Type a name for the Web server in the Descriptive name field.

❿ Click Next to move to the next wizard dialog box.

Moving PowerPoint Web Pages to a Server *Continued*

The Web Publishing Wizard process described here is representative of the Internet connection I use. Your specific process will be different, but generally the same.

In the top-left figure on the facing page, I've shown a continuation of the Web Publishing Wizard process. This screen asks for the Internet address (the Uniform Resource Locator, or URL) at which to publish the PowerPoint Web slide show. If you don't know what this means or if you're not sure of the correct address, ask your ISP or LAN administrator. The Local directory field at the bottom of this dialog box is the location where you stored the PowerPoint presentation as an HTML file. This directory is on your local hard drive or somewhere on your local-area network.

The top-right figure on the facing page is a password dialog box. Most likely, you'll have to supply a specific user name and a password to gain access to the Web server where you want to store your files. You may not be the administrator of this Web site, so your normal Internet access user name and password may not work. You'll have to find out what the administrator user name and password are to be able to access the directory that holds your files.

The Web Publishing Wizard may be able to determine from your Windows Internet setup how to route the files to the Web site. If not, you'll see the dialog box shown at the lower left of the facing page. This is where you choose the type of file transport you want the wizard to use. FTP is almost always a good choice, but some ISPs disable FTP if you have FrontPage extensions enabled. And with some ISPs you'll have to specifically request FrontPage extensions for FTP to work.

The bottom-right image on the next page shows how to enter the specifics of an FTP upload. If you chose HTML or FrontPage earlier in the wizard, your screen may now appear a little different from my example. After this final setup screen you may also see another dialog box that simply tells you that the wizard is ready to complete the upload, or you may be asked for a little more information. Simply answer the questions and follow the wizard to the end.

TAKE NOTE

USING GENERIC FTP

Windows 98 includes an FTP client that you can access from the Run button on the Start menu. A DOS window will open with an ftp> prompt: Type Help at this prompt for a list of commands. You can also use a shareware FTP client such as WS_FTP, which is graphics-oriented and a lot easier to use (see "Find It Online," below, for the location). I like raw FTP — it gives you a lot of control over how your files are uploaded.

CROSS-REFERENCE

See the next section in this chapter to learn about accessing your PowerPoint Web pages once they are on an Internet Web server.

FIND IT ONLINE

To download a wonderful shareware FTP client, go to the Ipswitch Web site at **www.wsftp.com**.

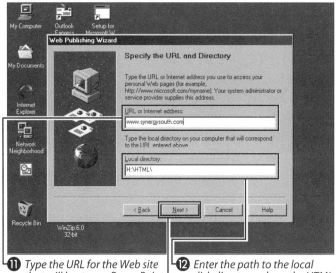

🔵**11** Type the URL for the Web site that will host your PowerPoint show. You may need help from your ISP or LAN administrator for this information.

🔵**12** Enter the path to the local disk directory where the HTML document and associated files are stored.

🔵**13** Click Next.

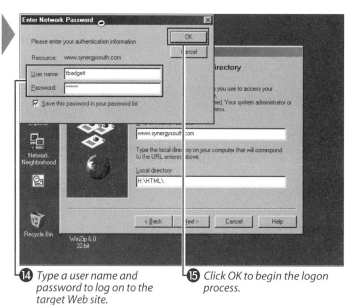

🔵**14** Type a user name and password to log on to the target Web site.

🔵**15** Click OK to begin the logon process.

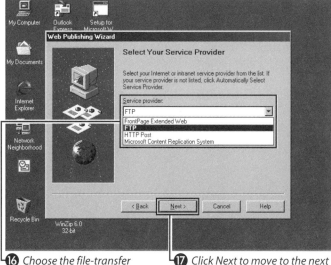

🔵**16** Choose the file-transfer method you wish to use. FTP is generally a good choice, but consult your ISP or LAN administrator for the correct option.

🔵**17** Click Next to move to the next wizard screen.

◼ Read the Service Provider declaration, if you see it, and click Next to display the Select Your Service Provider box.

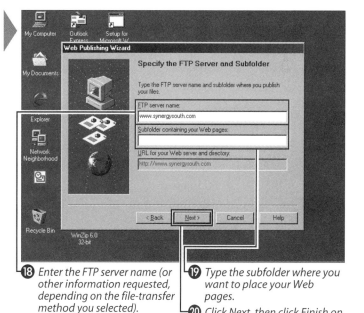

🔵**18** Enter the FTP server name (or other information requested, depending on the file-transfer method you selected).

🔵**19** Type the subfolder where you want to place your Web pages.

🔵**20** Click Next, then click Finish on the final wizard screen to complete the process.

Accessing PowerPoint Shows on the Web

You've created a PowerPoint slide show, saved it to your hard drive as a Web page, and copied the Web version to an Internet or intranet Web server. Now I'll show you how to access the file and help other Web users access your information.

I introduced Web-browser access of the Web version of a PowerPoint slide show earlier in this chapter when I showed you how to use the PowerPoint Web toolbar to access the file on your local or network drive. Let's look at some additional issues for using a Web browser to view a PowerPoint slide show. Consider the upper-left figure on the next page. It shows a fairly typical Windows 98 desktop screen with a couple of options for launching Internet Explorer 5. (These options apply to other Explorer versions and other browsers as well.)

When you open your browser, the default home page is displayed. It won't be the PowerPoint page you just uploaded, unless you've reset the default home page inside your browser. To access your PowerPoint page, enter the address in your browser, as I've shown in the upper-right figure on the facing page.

What you see when you press Enter depends on whether you have entered a full path to the actual file or renamed the default PowerPoint file with the Web default *index.html* (see "Take Note," this page). The lower-left figure on the next page shows a directory list and not the expected PowerPoint Web file. That's

because the name of the file that contains the PowerPoint HTML code is Memphis98.htm. By default, Internet Explorer, Netscape, and other browsers expect the name of the main file within a Web-site subdirectory to be index.htm.

In the lower-right figure on the facing page you can see the PowerPoint Web page, which is displayed when I click the name of the file in the previous directory listing, or if I change the name of the file to index.htm or index.html.

With Web-based PowerPoint, you can share information around the world, or use the very latest version of a PowerPoint presentation no matter where you are.

TAKE NOTE

▶ CREATING AN INDEX.HTM FILE

A URL has three components: the Web domain (www.synergysouth.com), the subdirectory where the Web site is located (Internet), and the name of the file you want to display (Memphis98.htm). Index.htm is the default, but PowerPoint won't create an index.htm file automatically. The main HTML file will be named the same as your PowerPoint file. After the HTML file is created, use Windows Explorer to rename it Index.htm. This makes your Web address simpler.

CROSS-REFERENCE
You can even use the features discussed in Chapter 10 on the Web version of your PowerPoint presentations.

SHORTCUT
Click Favorites on your Explorer toolbar to add your PowerPoint presentation to the list of Web sites you can access directly.

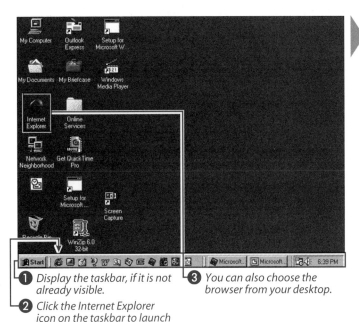

1 Display the taskbar, if it is not already visible.

2 Click the Internet Explorer icon on the taskbar to launch the browser.

3 You can also choose the browser from your desktop.

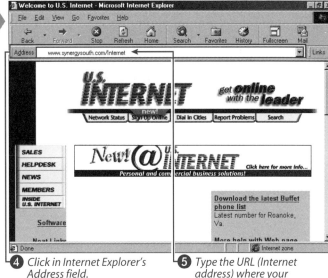

4 Click in Internet Explorer's Address field.

5 Type the URL (Internet address) where your PowerPoint Web page is stored and press Enter.

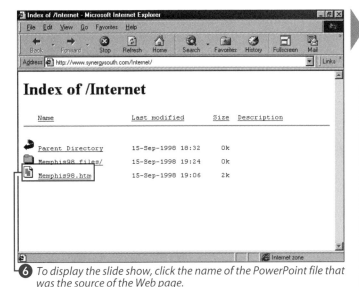

6 To display the slide show, click the name of the PowerPoint file that was the source of the Web page.

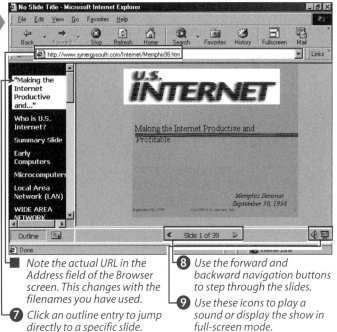

■ Note the actual URL in the Address field of the Browser screen. This changes with the filenames you have used.

7 Click an outline entry to jump directly to a specific slide.

8 Use the forward and backward navigation buttons to step through the slides.

9 Use these icons to play a sound or display the show in full-screen mode.

Personal Workbook

Q&A

1 I believe that the Web-based hyperlink document design will change the way we think about learning and reading. Do you agree? Why or why not?

_____

_____

2 Once you've created a hyperlink, how can you remove it easily?

_____

_____

3 What is the main difference between a Web hyperlink and a hyperlink within the same slide show?

_____

_____

_____

4 What is the menu sequence for saving the current PowerPoint slide show as a Web page?

_____

_____

_____

5 What intrinsic Office 2000 utility can you use to save the HTML version of a PowerPoint slide show to a Web server?

_____

_____

6 What is the default filename for the Web version of a PowerPoint slide show? Why might this present a problem in accessing this file on the Web?

_____

_____

7 What file transfer protocol is commonly used for saving Web files to a Web server?

_____

_____

_____

8 What does _URL_ stand for? How is it used?

_____

_____

_____

_____

ANSWERS: PAGE 311

EXTRA PRACTICE

1 Open the Hyperlink dialog box using a shortcut menu and a keyboard shortcut.

2 Open the dialog box that lets you save the current PowerPoint presentation as a Web page.

3 Launch the Web Publishing Wizard to upload your Web version of a PowerPoint slide show to a server.

4 Launch Internet Explorer and enter the URL for a PowerPoint Web site you have created.

5 Launch Internet Explorer and load a PowerPoint Web file from your local hard drive or local-area network.

6 Turn on Full Screen display for a PowerPoint slide show displayed in Internet Explorer from a Web page or your local drive.

REAL-WORLD APPLICATIONS

✔ Suppose you travel considerably and use PowerPoint to present sales and other corporate information to a varied audience. You want to use the latest data at all times, so you have someone at the home office regularly update your PowerPoint show. You can convert this show to HTML (Web) so you can always access the latest figures and statistics while you are on the road.

✔ Companies today are increasingly cross-platform operations. Although PowerPoint is available for PCs and Macs, you should consider using HTML as a universal file format. Microsoft has declared that its ultimate goal is for HTML to be the universal file format for all users and all applications: it'll likely be the wave of our computer future.

Visual Quiz

Describe how to display the screen shown here.

_____

_____

_____

_____

_____

_____

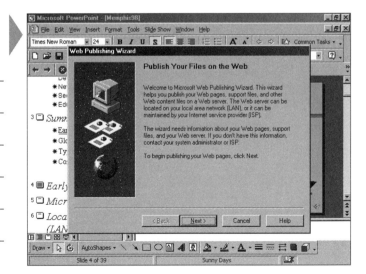

PART

IV

CHAPTER **16** **Customizing PowerPoint**

17 **Using Macros**

18 **Compatibility Issues**

19 **PowerPoint Design Tips**

Programming and Customization

Among the powers of PowerPoint is its chameleonlike ability to become what you want it to be. You can add and remove items from toolbars, for example, or even design your own toolbars and menus. Suppose you want to create a truly custom version of PowerPoint for a group of users who need to use only a small portion of its features. You can do this with PowerPoint's customize options. In this section, I also show you how to move toolbars around the PowerPoint screen so you can have them appear where they're most convenient for you.

You can also preprogram some features, such as printing a custom set of audience handouts, using PowerPoint's macro options. Macros are simple, easy-to-write computer programs that can save you a lot of time and keystrokes by doing away with redundant keyboard and mouse activities. I use these macro features to prepare teaching materials for several classes so that all the printouts look the same and I don't have to remember from time to time what I've done before.

In this part we also consider compatibility issues, which may arise as you work with different versions of PowerPoint or when you want to incorporate data from other programs in your presentations. And we explore design tips that can help you customize your presentation while sticking to the golden rules of design.

CHAPTER **16**

MASTER
THESE
SKILLS

▶ **Using Customize Features**

▶ **Reviewing and Setting Options**

▶ **Using the Common Tasks Toolbar**

▶ **Creating Custom Toolbars**

Customizing PowerPoint

When I first started using computers in the mid-1970s, hardly anything was standard. The larger machines from the same manufacturer ran the same set of operating systems, and there were programming languages that were mostly standard; but for the end user — the person who actually used the machine to accomplish tasks — there was very little continuity from computer to computer. Virtually every application was custom.

In the early 1980s, the Visicalc spreadsheet changed the way we used our computers. It marked the beginning of standard applications with a reasonably common user interface that enabled users to move from computer to computer to do their work. As the Windows operating system has matured and with the advent of the HTML (Web) interface, using computers has become easier than ever.

Though PowerPoint's user interface isn't quite as universal as that of a spreadsheet or word-processing program, it does share the command set and the overall look and feel of the Microsoft Office software suite. Consequently, if you are familiar with another Office program, such as Word or Excel, you will find it relatively easy to pick up the additional skills required to produce presentations with PowerPoint.

Nevertheless, there are times when you want a presentation design that is uniquely yours. Moreover, there is a trend in corporate computing to customize software to the point that users see only the menus and commands the company wants them to use to achieve a set of required tasks.

Built into PowerPoint is a structure for customizing toolbars and menus — essentially, how the program works — so you can streamline or adjust its operation to more nearly fit your particular needs or the needs of your corporate users.

This chapter shows you the major areas in which you can customize PowerPoint — enough so that you should have a pretty good idea about how to make it your own program. You'll also have a good starting point for going beyond this discussion if you choose.

Using Customize Features

I've talked about customization throughout this book, showing you such things as setting custom headers and footers for slides, notes pages, and handouts. I mentioned moving menus and toolbars in Chapter 1. And I've discussed creating custom PowerPoint presentations from basic building blocks of slides.

In this section, I provide more detail on customizing the look and feel of PowerPoint by changing menus and toolbars. One change I make in PowerPoint (and in any program I can, really) is to add the close-file command to the toolbar. By doing so, I can close an open document with a single click on a toolbar. The upper-left figure on the facing page shows you how to start this process, while the upper-right figure shows the steps involved in adding a command to one of the visible toolbars. You can be as creative as you like in placing commands on toolbars. Add new toolbars to the display and add new commands to them.

The Categories list in the Customize dialog box groups PowerPoint commands by the type of operation associated with each command. At the bottom of this list is Built-in Menus. Choose this category to add an entire PowerPoint menu to a toolbar. When you click a menu icon on a toolbar, you'll see the entire list of commands associated with that standard PowerPoint menu.

Also at the bottom of the Categories list is a New Menu category (lower-left figure, next page). This

selection lets you create your own menu and place it wherever you like. Once you have placed the new menu item, repeat the process shown in the upper-left figure on the next page. Simply drag the commands you want on this new menu onto it from the Customize dialog box.

Once you have modified or added menus and toolbars, you can customize them in other ways. For example, with the Customize dialog box still on the screen, you can right-click a toolbar icon (even if you've added it to a menu) to access a shortcut menu with a list of options, including changing the button image (lower-left figure, facing page).

Continued

Continued

TAKE NOTE

▶ REMOVING TOOLBAR ICONS

You can remove a toolbar icon as easily as adding a new one. Open the Customize dialog box as described above, and then drag an unwanted toolbar icon off of the toolbar and drop it anywhere. Replace it later using the Customize procedure described in this section.

▶ QUICK CUSTOMIZING

One quick way to customize PowerPoint is by adding and removing toolbars. Right-click any toolbar and check those you want to see and uncheck those you don't. Without doing anything special, you can definitely achieve a custom look and feel.

CROSS-REFERENCE
See Chapter 9 for customizing hints at the slide-design level.

FIND IT ONLINE
For a tutorial on customizing your toolbars, visit http://www.commerce.ubc.ca/MBAcore/tutorials/powerpoint/ppt3.html.

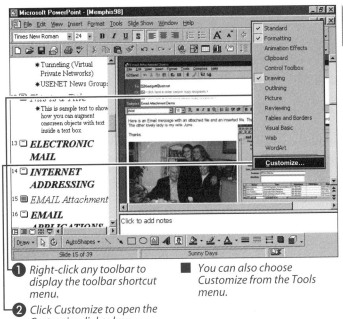

1 Right-click any toolbar to display the toolbar shortcut menu.

2 Click Customize to open the Customize dialog box.

■ You can also choose Customize from the Tools menu.

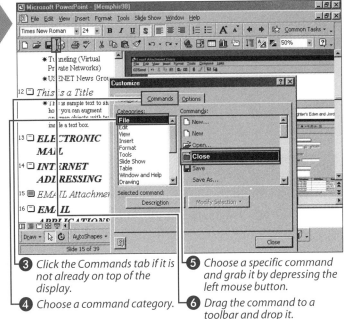

3 Click the Commands tab if it is not already on top of the display.

4 Choose a command category.

5 Choose a specific command and grab it by depressing the left mouse button.

6 Drag the command to a toolbar and drop it.

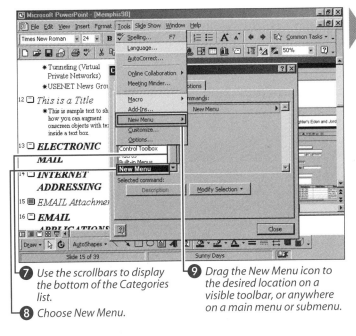

7 Use the scrollbars to display the bottom of the Categories list.

8 Choose New Menu.

9 Drag the New Menu icon to the desired location on a visible toolbar, or anywhere on a main menu or submenu.

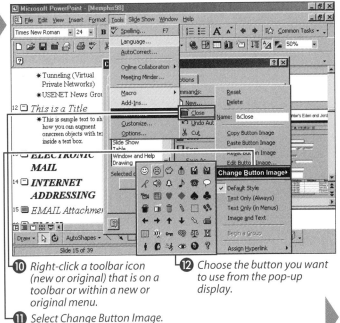

10 Right-click a toolbar icon (new or original) that is on a toolbar or within a new or original menu.

11 Select Change Button Image.

12 Choose the button you want to use from the pop-up display.

245

Using Customize Features
Continued

You can explore the shortcut menu associated with customizing toolbar items on your own, of course, but I want to highlight some of the issues with it.

The Reset and Delete items at the top of the display (see the top-left figure on the following page) restore an icon to the PowerPoint default and remove the selected icon, respectively. You can use Copy and Paste as you are accustomed to doing from any Windows Edit menu to copy an existing icon to a new position. And the Edit Button Image option presents a simple editor for changing an existing icon or even designing a new one from scratch (top-right figure, facing page).

The group of options beginning with Default Style and ending with Image and Text (again, top-left figure, next page) lets you set the style for displaying icons and text. Experiment with these commands as you modify your menus. Generally, when your toolbars are full, you don't have room for a lot of text. If you have customized toolbars so that they include only a minimum set of icons for a specific set of users, such as beginners, then you probably want to include text prompts with the buttons.

You can also assign a hyperlink to a toolbar button. You can create a hyperlink to open a directory, run a program, launch a Web page, insert a picture, and so on.

Returning to the Customize dialog box, you'll notice that it contains three tabs. I haven't mentioned the Toolbar tab yet because it is mostly a duplication of the pop-up shortcut menu you see when you right-click any toolbar (see "Creating Custom Toolbars," later in this chapter). You can turn toolbar displays on or off using either route.

If you click the Options tab, you see some settings that should be fairly self-explanatory. These choices enable you to set the appearance of menu and toolbar options. I like to turn off the second option (Menus show recently used commands first), which tries to guess what menu items you use most and then presents only the most common ones. This sounds like a good idea, but it means that menu items are constantly jumping around as your menu preferences change. At my age, I like to keep things simple.

Finally, check out the bottom-right image on the facing page. I've shown the Menu animations pop-up menu, which lets you decide how PowerPoint menus are displayed.

CROSS-REFERENCE

Refer to Chapter 15 for more information on using hyperlinks.

FIND IT ONLINE

Want to do more with icon editing? Here's a top-rated editor you may want to try: **www6.zdnet.com/cgi-bin/texis/swlib/hotfiles/info.html?fcode=000chj**.

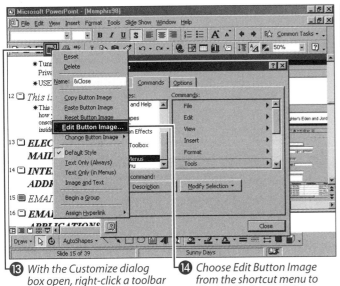

13 With the Customize dialog box open, right-click a toolbar icon.

14 Choose Edit Button Image from the shortcut menu to display the Button Editor dialog box.

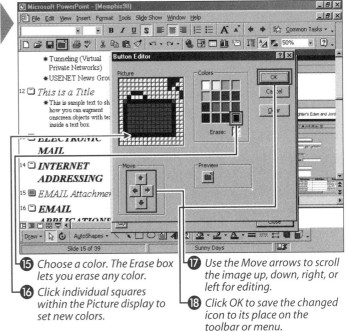

15 Choose a color. The Erase box lets you erase any color.

16 Click individual squares within the Picture display to set new colors.

17 Use the Move arrows to scroll the image up, down, right, or left for editing.

18 Click OK to save the changed icon to its place on the toolbar or menu.

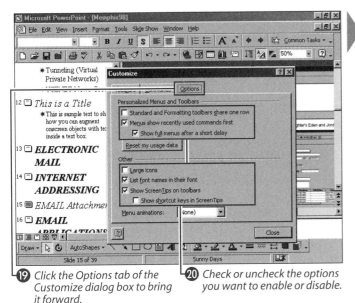

19 Click the Options tab of the Customize dialog box to bring it forward.

20 Check or uncheck the options you want to enable or disable.

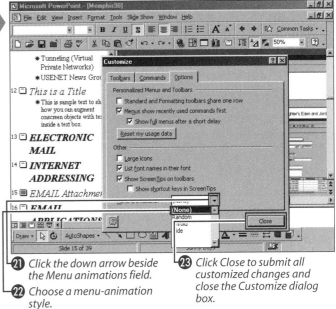

21 Click the down arrow beside the Menu animations field.

22 Choose a menu-animation style.

23 Click Close to submit all customized changes and close the Customize dialog box.

Reviewing and Setting Options

This section covers a group of PowerPoint options that you can set to control program operation. The top-left figure on the next page shows the opening Options dialog box display. This six-tab box lets you configure such PowerPoint features as what operations are available during a slide show, printing and saving defaults, and how the spell checker works.

The two groups on the View tab are default options for your working screen and Slide Show screen. The Startup dialog box selection at the top of this list is the screen displayed when you launch PowerPoint; it lets you create a new file, load an existing file, and so on. If you uncheck this option, PowerPoint opens with a blank presentation and the New Slide dialog box displayed.

The bottom group on the View tab is for configuring how menus can be displayed, whether you see a pop-up menu button during a slide show, and whether you want PowerPoint to automatically insert a black slide at the end of your show. (By default, PowerPoint 2000 includes a black slide at the end of all shows unless you change that option here.)

The General tab (top-right figure, next page) controls some operational tasks. The option I change most often is the number of previously viewed presentations (the Recently used file list), which is the list that appears on the opening PowerPoint dialog box and at the bottom of the File menu.

If you click the Web Options button on the General tab, you get a five-tab Web Options dialog box, shown in the lower left figure on the facing page. These options control settings used when you save a PowerPoint presentation as a Web page (i.e., as an HTML document). The best way to learn about these settings is to change one or two at a time, then save a presentation as a Web page and note the changes.

The Edit tab in the Options dialog box (bottom-right figure, facing page) controls a number of operational settings that you should recognize easily. I don't change these unless a particular application requires it.

The Print, Save, and Spelling and Style tabs give you some other settings to adjust, but for the most part, you can leave them alone. These settings control such aspects as whether PowerPoint uses background printing, how often AutoRecover saves a mirror of your active presentation, and whether spelling will be checked as you type. Click each of these tabs to review the possible settings available to you.

TAKE NOTE

CHANGING THE DEFAULT SAVE LOCATION

You may want to change one setting on the Save tab — the default file-save location. Set this to the top of the tree where you save most of your PowerPoint files to reduce typing or navigation during a file-save.

CROSS-REFERENCE

See the previous section of this chapter for additional customizing hints.

FIND IT ONLINE

Download a copy of PowerPoint Animation Player at http://www.download.com/PC/Result/TitleDetail/0,4,164-17088-g,501000.html.

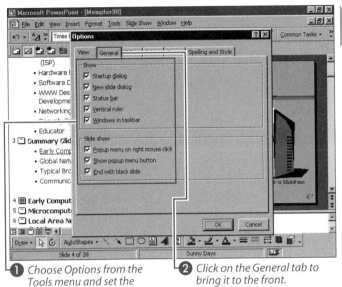

❶ Choose Options from the Tools menu and set the desired options.

❷ Click on the General tab to bring it to the front.

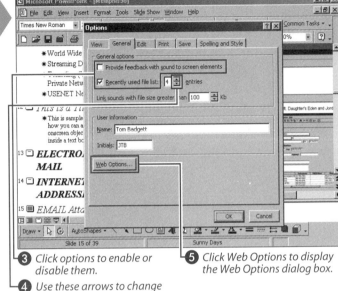

❸ Click options to enable or disable them.

❹ Use these arrows to change the number of recently used files that will be displayed on the File menu.

❺ Click Web Options to display the Web Options dialog box.

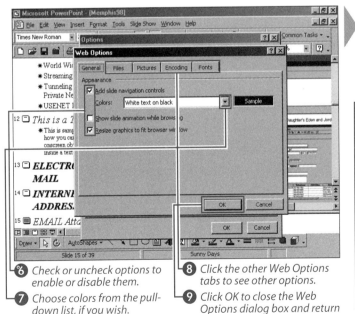

❻ Check or uncheck options to enable or disable them.

❼ Choose colors from the pull-down list, if you wish.

❽ Click the other Web Options tabs to see other options.

❾ Click OK to close the Web Options dialog box and return to the Options dialog box.

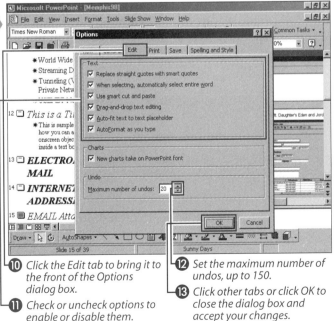

❿ Click the Edit tab to bring it to the front of the Options dialog box.

⓫ Check or uncheck options to enable or disable them.

⓬ Set the maximum number of undos, up to 150.

⓭ Click other tabs or click OK to close the dialog box and accept your changes.

Using the Common Tasks Toolbar

The Common Tasks toolbar, which you can open by clicking the Common Tasks button on the standard toolbar, holds three tasks you will use quite a lot as you work with PowerPoint: New Slide, Slide Layout, and Apply Design Template. When you click the Common Tasks button, this separate toolbar drops down so you can access these commands, as shown in the top-left figure on the facing page.

There is one obvious difference between this pop-up toolbar and other toolbars. Do you see the bar at the top? It's a title bar, but because the toolbar is docked with another toolbar, you cannot see the title. To help make this toolbar more useful and more individualized, you can drag it away from the docked location and position it anywhere on the PowerPoint screen, as shown in the top-right figure on the next page. Notice that the title bar now takes on a new personality, showing the title of the toolbar and including a close icon in the upper-right corner of the toolbar. Once the toolbar is undocked, you can change its shape and place it anywhere you find convenient on the PowerPoint screen.

Can you think of something else—an obvious something else—you might want to do with this toolbar? How about adding the commands that you use most often, thereby transforming this toolbar into your own, personal common tasks toolbar?

Review the Customize section earlier in this chapter for information on how to add commands to this menu. Hint: Use the Customize selection from the toolbar shortcut menu, shown in the lower-left figure on the next page.

There's another little customize trick you can use with this toolbar: dock it somewhere else. This toolbar is embedded in the Common Tasks button on the standard toolbar by default. I've shown it as a floating toolbar in the top-right figure; a floating toolbar rides on top of other things on your PowerPoint screen, and you can move it around as required. A docked toolbar is attached to a screen edge, as shown in the bottom-right figure on the facing page.

As you can see, I added some buttons to the Common Tasks toolbar via the Customize dialog box before docking it on the left side of the PowerPoint screen.

TAKE NOTE

RESTORING COMMON TASKS

Right-click any toolbar to display the toolbar shortcuts menu. Then you can uncheck the Common Tasks toolbar from the toolbar list on this shortcut. When you do, you'll have to drag it off the standard toolbar and redock it where you want it.

CROSS-REFERENCE

See the following section for information on creating a new, custom toolbar from scratch.

FIND IT ONLINE

For a Quickstart guide to Office toolbars, go to http://www.dt.uh.edu/~jose/docs/MSoffice.htm.

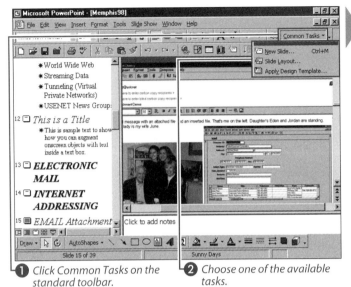

1 Click Common Tasks on the standard toolbar.

2 Choose one of the available tasks.

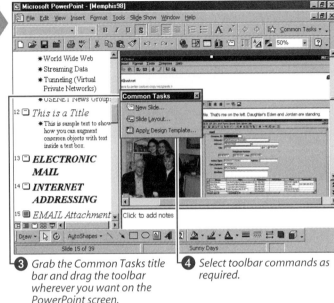

3 Grab the Common Tasks title bar and drag the toolbar wherever you want on the PowerPoint screen.

4 Select toolbar commands as required.

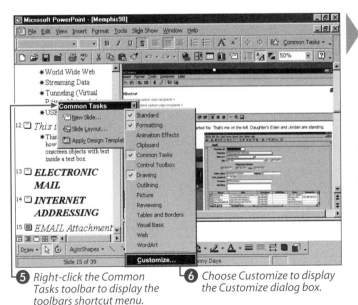

5 Right-click the Common Tasks toolbar to display the toolbars shortcut menu.

6 Choose Customize to display the Customize dialog box.

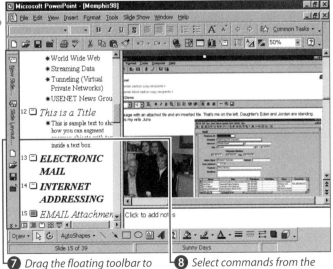

7 Drag the floating toolbar to an edge of the PowerPoint screen, where it will dock automatically.

8 Select commands from the docked toolbar as required.

Creating Custom Toolbars

I've shown you how to customize existing toolbars and menus, and how to move toolbars so they appear where you want them as you work with PowerPoint slide design. This section explains how to create your own toolbars by mixing and matching existing commands into your own custom grouping.

To do this, you'll use the Toolbars tab of the Customize dialog box, shown in the top-left figure on the facing page. Add a toolbar with the New Toolbar dialog box (top-right figure, next page). You can use any name you want for your custom toolbar, but shorter is better. When you first create a toolbar, it is empty. To add commands to it, you'll use the procedure detailed in the bottom-left figure on the next page. You've seen this before: you simply drag commands from the Commands window of the Customize dialog box onto the new, custom toolbar.

When you drag these command icons onto a toolbar, all you see are the icons, which include tooltips. (Tooltips, or pop-up descriptions of what toolbar icons do, appear when you pause your mouse over an icon.) You won't see any text to describe the new commands.

You can add text to the commands with the tool icon shortcut menu, shown in the bottom-right figure on the facing page. You may not want to display full text with each icon — you certainly won't if the number of commands on your custom toolbar is fairly large. If you have only a few commands on this new toolbar, however, adding text can help you, and others, make the most of its commands.

Of course, because this custom toolbar is like any other (except you can delete it from the Customize dialog box, something you can't do with standard toolbars), you can drag it anywhere on the screen. You can dock it to an existing toolbar, for example, or to an edge of the PowerPoint screen.

TAKE NOTE

▶ USING HYPERLINKS

A custom toolbar is an ideal place to use hyperlinks. Create a custom toolbar, add some command buttons, use the Button Editor or Change Button dialog box if you want to customize the look of the toolbar, and then create hyperlinks for each toolbar icon. Using hyperlinks lets you create custom functions for use in PowerPoint without having to do any programming.

▶ DELETING A CUSTOM TOOLBAR

You can't delete standard toolbars, but you can completely remove a custom toolbar. Open the Customize dialog box, click the custom toolbar on the Toolbars tab, and then click the Delete button.

▶ MOVING TOOLBAR ICONS

Change the order of toolbar icons by opening the Customize dialog box and dragging the icons to new positions on the toolbar. You can also drag icons from one toolbar to another in this manner.

CROSS-REFERENCE

See Chapter 17 for more customizing tips.

FIND IT ONLINE

For more on toolbars, visit **http://islab.asu.edu/ islab/alcp/help/bottom.html**.

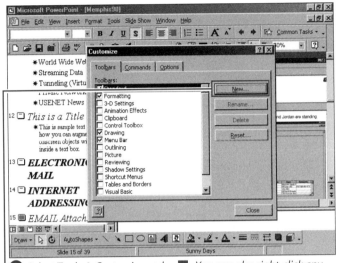

1 Select Tools ➪ Customize and click New to display the New Toolbar dialog box.

■ You can also right-click any toolbar and choose Customize from the shortcut menu.

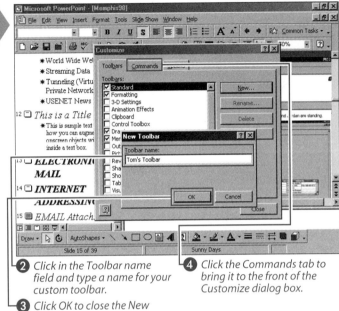

2 Click in the Toolbar name field and type a name for your custom toolbar.

3 Click OK to close the New Toolbar dialog box and return to the Customize dialog box.

4 Click the Commands tab to bring it to the front of the Customize dialog box.

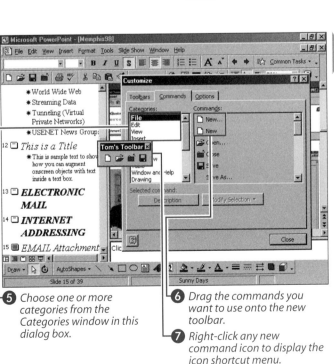

5 Choose one or more categories from the Categories window in this dialog box.

6 Drag the commands you want to use onto the new toolbar.

7 Right-click any new command icon to display the icon shortcut menu.

8 Choose Image and Text to display a text description of the toolbar commands beside the icon. Repeat for each icon you want to label.

9 Click Close to close the Customize dialog box.

Personal Workbook

Q&A

1 What general type of software could be considered responsible for standardized software? Can you recall the name of the first commercial product in this genre?

_____

_____

2 There are two ways to display the Customize dialog box. What are they?

_____

_____

3 What is the command sequence for creating a custom toolbar?

_____

_____

_____

4 Describe how to change the default directory where PowerPoint loads and saves files.

_____

_____

_____

5 How can you use hyperlinks with toolbars?

_____

_____

6 What is the purpose of the _Reset my usage data_ button on the Options tab of the Customize dialog box?

_____

_____

_____

7 How do you change the number of files shown in the opening PowerPoint dialog box and on the File menu? What is the maximum number of files you can show in this list?

_____

_____

_____

8 Can you delete a custom toolbar? How? What about standard PowerPoint toolbars?

_____

_____

_____

ANSWERS: PAGE 312

EXTRA PRACTICE

1 Display the Customize dialog box and show the Tools command list.

2 Display the main Options dialog box.

3 Display the Style Options dialog box.

4 Display the Web Options dialog box.

5 Display the dialog box that lets you set the maximum number of fonts within a presentation.

6 Display the dialog box that lets you set the spelling and style options.

REAL-WORLD APPLICATIONS

✔ Customizing features can be very useful in a corporate environment. Suppose you have a team charged with developing a series of PowerPoint presentations for a major corporate event. You can remove standard toolbars and create custom toolbars to guide the team through using PowerPoint features to develop the slide shows.

✔ The nice thing about PowerPoint is, you can use the Customize features to make the program work more your way. Remove toolbar and menu items you simply never use, for example. Once you try customizing, you'll start creating your own menus and toolbars. Group functions you use most frequently into custom toolbars that float in a convenient location on the editing screen. There's more than one place you can have it your way!

Visual Quiz

Describe how to display the screen shown here.

_____

_____

_____

_____

_____

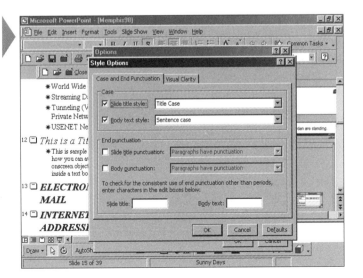

CHAPTER **17**

MASTER
THESE
SKILLS

▶ **Recording New Macros**

▶ **Playing and Editing Macros**

▶ **Setting Macro Security Options**

Using Macros

Software macros are another of those features that relatively few people use. Like many other software concepts, macros have a reputation for being difficult to learn and to use. This was once true: Early applications that supported macros required the user to learn a programming language and to write programming code to harness the power of macros.

Today, most macro facilities let you simply record the steps you want to use and play them back when you want. For advanced users, Microsoft Office 2000 includes Visual Basic so you can write truly sophisticated programs to customize your Office applications—and it also lets you write macros. If you simply want to avoid doing the same task over and over again, you can use a macro to store the steps involved and repeat them for you, saving you the trouble. A macro, then, is a computer program designed to conduct a single task or a series of closely related tasks.

Macros help you avoid repetitive work. Should you use a macro for a given procedure? I use this rule of thumb: If you perform an application task more than once and if the number of keystrokes and other operations required to program a macro is fewer than the number required to perform the task by hand, then a macro is a logical choice.

Besides reducing time and keystrokes for repetitive tasks, macros reduce the chance of errors by automating regular tasks. Suppose you use PowerPoint as a teaching tool and you print Notes Pages as a student study and reference manual. With each class you modify the presentation, then print a fresh version for copying and distribution. You can automate the printer setup and the actual printing process with a macro so that your manuals turn out the same every time.

Similarly, you could automate the process of configuring a show, creating other output, inserting graphics, choosing templates, and so on. As you work with PowerPoint, think about tasks you conduct more than once, and then consider whether it is worth the time to learn about macro programming to automate any of the steps.

This chapter introduces you to the basics of PowerPoint macro programming. It provides enough information to get you started writing (recording) your own useful computer programs, if you wish.

Recording New Macros

I'm not going to delve into complex macro programming in this book; that's a topic for another venue. But I do want to provide some examples of macro programming so you get the idea of how it works. Macros provide a powerful tool and can save you time if the work you do with PowerPoint is regular and sometimes repetitive. You should see from this chapter that macro programming isn't particularly difficult, and this knowledge can open up a new world of presentation possibilities for you.

Consider the example I mentioned at the beginning of this chapter: you want to print Notes pages in a particular format as part of a regular class or other PowerPoint presentation. A macro lends itself well to this type of repetitive, multistep operation.

The upper-left figure on the facing page shows you how to start recording a new macro. The dialog box in the upper-right figure lets you name the macro and enter some other parameters. When you have finished the recording setup, you're ready to record the program. Close the initial Record Macro dialog box, and a small Stop Recording dialog box appears on the screen, telling you that recording is in process and allowing you to stop it.

As I have mentioned, recording a macro is as simple as conducting the steps you want to store in the macro. For this example, I'll open the Print dialog box and set some parameters, as I've shown in the bottom two figures on the facing page. As you can see, the procedure for printing does not change because you are recording a macro. The macro recorder simply captures your mouse movements and keystrokes and stores them in a special format inside your presentation so it's easy to play back the steps.

When you have finished the series of steps you want to record for this macro, click the Stop button on the main PowerPoint screen, or choose Stop Recording from the Macro menu.

That's just one example of how macros can be useful. You might also use a macro from inside a slide show. Record the macro first, and then use an action button linked to the macro. When you enable Slide Show view and click the action button, the macro executes. Remember that unless you specify differently, macros are recorded and stored inside the current presentation, so they'll be available any time that presentation file is open.

TAKE NOTE

STOP BUTTON

The Stop button displayed on your screen while a macro is being recorded is actually a toolbar. If you don't see it when you record a macro, right-click any toolbar and choose Stop Recording from the list of available toolbars.

CROSS-REFERENCE

Review the use of Action buttons in Chapter 8 so you can set up macros to run during a slide show.

FIND IT ONLINE

To learn more about recording macros, visit **http://discovery.mc.duke.edu/ arhtml/win/ cmacros1.htm**

1 Choose Tools ⇨ Macro ⇨ Record New Macro to open the Record Macro dialog box.

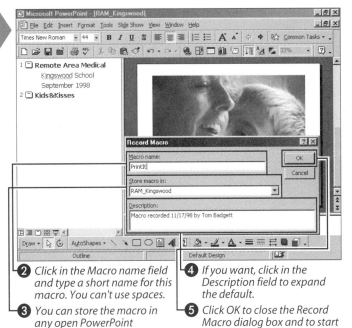

2 Click in the Macro name field and type a short name for this macro. You can't use spaces.

3 You can store the macro in any open PowerPoint presentation.

4 If you want, click in the Description field to expand the default.

5 Click OK to close the Record Macro dialog box and to start recording the macro.

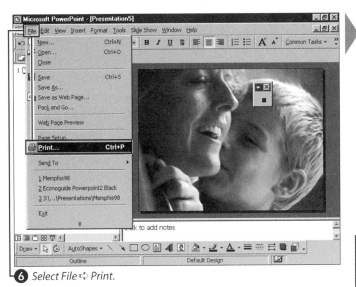

6 Select File ⇨ Print.

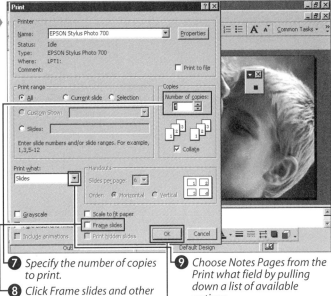

7 Specify the number of copies to print.

8 Click Frame slides and other parameters you want to repeat.

9 Choose Notes Pages from the Print what field by pulling down a list of available options.

10 Click OK to start printing.

Playing and Editing Macros

The real object of recording a macro in the first place is to play it back so it can work for you. I'll show you how to do that in this section.

Before you can successfully play back a macro, you must understand what you need to do before starting the macro. If the macro depends on a certain text block, menu, or dialog box being selected, then you have to conduct this preliminary step before you can run the macro.

With the prerequisite established, you're ready to run the macro using the menu sequence shown in the upper-left figure on the following page. When you choose the Macros menu option, you'll see the Macro dialog box shown in the upper-right figure on the facing page. Once you click the Run button, the instructions you recorded will be performed.

Whether you see anything on the screen while the macro runs depends on what steps you have recorded. If you recorded systems-type tasks, such as printing the current presentation (as I did in the recording example in the previous section), you may see an hourglass, but you won't see the printer dialog box and other information as the macro plays. On the other hand, if your macro changes the look of the screen or conducts other visual tasks, you'll see the results on your screen. In either case, you may not see the menus and other controls that you used to create the macro.

If you want to make minor changes to an existing macro, or just get a better understanding of the technology behind macros, you can reach the macro editor in two ways: by clicking Edit in the Macro dialog box, or by choosing Visual Basic Editor from the macro supplemental menu (lower-left figure, facing page). When you launch the editor, you'll see the somewhat cluttered screen shown in the lower right on the next page. If no macro is loaded, click the Run button on the editor toolbar and choose the macro you want to edit. Then, in the Macro dialog box, click Edit instead of Run.

TAKE NOTE

SAVING MACRO EDITS

You can edit macro instructions (such as the number of copies to print) for a one-time change. Just don't save the presentation that stores the macro after you make the change. To make a permanent change, make sure you save the presentation file after you edit the macro instructions.

CROSS-REFERENCE

See the previous section of this chapter for information on recording macros.

FIND IT ONLINE

Get PowerPoint add-ons at **http://softseek. mdonline.net/Business_and_Productivity/ Microsoft_Office/PowerPoint_Add_Ons/**.

① *Choose Tools* ⟿ *Macro* ⟿ *Macros.*

■ *You can press Alt-F8 to display the Macro menu, bypassing the menu sequence.*

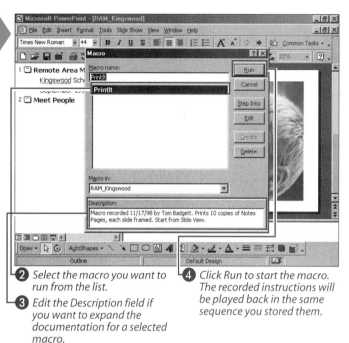

② *Select the macro you want to run from the list.*

③ *Edit the Description field if you want to expand the documentation for a selected macro.*

④ *Click Run to start the macro. The recorded instructions will be played back in the same sequence you stored them.*

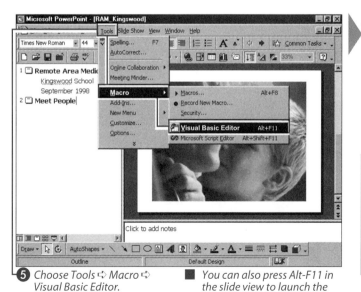

⑤ *Choose Tools* ⟿ *Macro* ⟿ *Visual Basic Editor.*

■ *You can also press Alt-F11 in the slide view to launch the editor.*

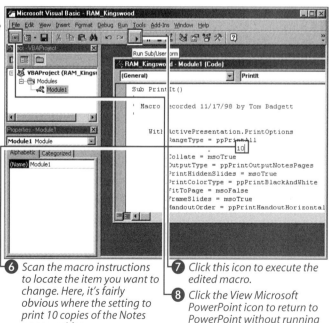

⑥ *Scan the macro instructions to locate the item you want to change. Here, it's fairly obvious where the setting to print 10 copies of the Notes pages resides.*

⑦ *Click this icon to execute the edited macro.*

⑧ *Click the View Microsoft PowerPoint icon to return to PowerPoint without running the macro.*

Setting Macro Security Options

Once you have installed one or more macros, you'll see the warning message shown at the upper left of the facing page when you load any presentation file with a macro (assuming you're using the default PowerPoint configuration).

This warning is displayed because PowerPoint's default security settings tell the program to warn you about macros. Why? Because of the rise in macro viruses. Just a few years ago, computer experts were telling users not to worry about loading data files from programs. These spreadsheets, word-processor documents, presentations, and the like were harmless because they weren't executable files; they weren't programs. Only programs could process instructions that might damage your computer or computer data.

Now, with the growing number of macros in end-user documents, the possibility of a virus being introduced through a macro is very real. Macros are programs, after all, and while you and I are probably interested in only the most basic macro instructions, the Visual Basic programming language included with PowerPoint makes possible some very sophisticated programs.

So this warning is a good thing. If you're working with sensitive material — say, presentation files with proprietary financial or technical data — and your files may be shared among various users, you may want to adjust PowerPoint's default security settings.

The upper-right figure on the next page shows you how to launch PowerPoint's security features. The lower-left figure shows the Security Level tab in the Security dialog box. Read the information associated with each level. The Medium setting is chosen for a good reason: it enables you to run macros developed by you and by people you know, but it also warns you when you load a file containing macros.

To use the highest level of security, you must be using macros that contain a digital signature. A complete discussion of digital signatures is beyond the scope of this book; however, developers who work with Visual Basic can secure a digital certificate that uniquely identifies the developer and the associated macro. (For more information, point your browser to **http://digitalid.verisign.com** or to **http://www. microsoft.com/ie/ie40/oe/certpage.htm**.)

If you select the High security level and load a presentation containing unsigned macros, the macros will be disabled. If your presentation contains signed macros, you'll see a warning message similar to the one in the lower-right corner of the facing page.

TAKE NOTE

▶ USING SIGNED MACROS

You must have Internet Explorer 4.0 or later installed to use digital signatures.

CROSS-REFERENCE
See Chapter 16 for additional information on custom additions to PowerPoint.

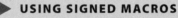

FIND IT ONLINE
Here's a good resource for more macro-virus info and ways to counter these bugs: **www.microsoft/ office/antivirus**.

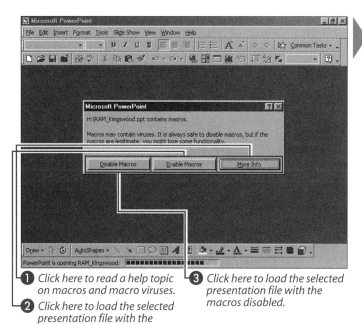

① *Click here to read a help topic on macros and macro viruses.*

② *Click here to load the selected presentation file with the macros enabled.*

③ *Click here to load the selected presentation file with the macros disabled.*

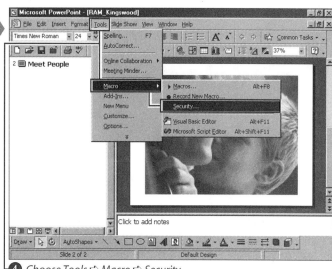

④ *Choose Tools ⇨ Macro ⇨ Security.*

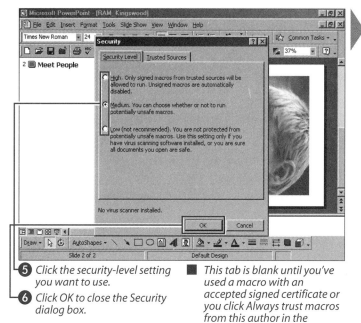

⑤ *Click the security-level setting you want to use.*

⑥ *Click OK to close the Security dialog box.*

■ *This tab is blank until you've used a macro with an accepted signed certificate or you click Always trust macros from this author in the Security Warning dialog box.*

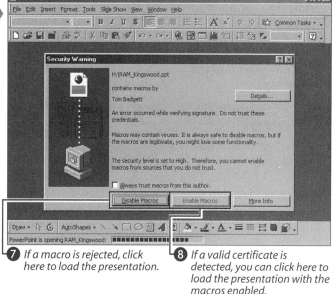

⑦ *If a macro is rejected, click here to load the presentation.*

⑧ *If a valid certificate is detected, you can click here to load the presentation with the macros enabled.*

Personal Workbook

Q&A

1 Macros in PowerPoint 2000 are written in what computer programming language?

_____

_____

_____

2 How can you remove the Stop Recording toolbar from the screen while you are recording a macro? How can you restore it?

_____

_____

3 What is the keyboard shortcut for displaying the Macro dialog box that enables you to choose and run recorded macros?

_____

_____

_____

4 There are two ways to display the Visual Basic Editor for macros. What are they?

_____

_____

5 Describe how you would edit an existing macro. Why would you edit a macro?

_____

_____

_____

6 What will you see on the PowerPoint screen while a macro is running?

_____

_____

_____

7 If the Stop Recording toolbar is not visible, how do you turn off macro recording?

_____

_____

_____

8 If you open the Macro dialog box with macro names visible but the Run button is not accessible, what has probably happened?

_____

_____

ANSWERS: PAGE 313

EXTRA PRACTICE

1 Display the Record Macro dialog box and enter a macro name.

2 Use the Tools menu to display the Macro dialog box so you can play a recorded macro.

3 Disp lay the Security dialog box and change the default security setting to High. Close the box.

4 Choose Edit from the Macro dialog box and run the macro from inside the Visual Basic Editor.

5 Change the Description associated with an existing macro.

6 Use a keyboard shortcut to display the Visual Basic Editor.

REAL-WORLD APPLICATIONS

✔ You have created macros to carry out repetitive tasks in PowerPoint, but because the presentation contains sensitive information and may be circulated among a number of users, you want to verify that the macros have not been changed. You log into the Verisign Web site, secure a digital signature, and install it in PowerPoint, using instructions provided by the PowerPoint Help file.

✔ As a corporate trainer, you use PowerPoint for regular employee training. Your training presentations are updated regularly. To make it easier to supply all students with PowerPoint printouts, you can create a macro that sets up the print job and prints the desired number of copies.

Visual Quiz

Describe how to display the screen shown here.

_____

_____

_____

_____

_____

_____

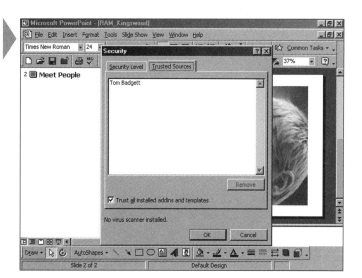

CHAPTER **18**

MASTER
THESE
SKILLS

▶ **Saving a Slide Show to Another Format**

▶ **Saving Files Online**

▶ **Opening Other File Formats**

▶ **Saving PowerPoint Slides as Graphics**

Compatibility Issues

There's always good news and bad news when companies such as Microsoft release new software. I'm always interested in the new release of operating systems, word-processing programs, spreadsheet software, database programming—almost anything. As a result, I always seem to be on the bleeding edge of technology. I'm one of those people with the earliest release of new hardware and software, but also the same person who suffers with early software problems and system incompatibility when I have to work with other people.

This can be a major issue in a corporate environment. In my company, for example, a few people always upgrade to the latest software release as soon as it is available. Some of us have to because we work in customer support; others want to because they are technically oriented and are interested in the newest products.

But we don't upgrade everybody at once. For one thing, we prefer for software to go through at least one revision after public release before we deploy it systemwide. Also, buying 100 or more copies of each new software package is expensive. So at any given time we have some

people running the very latest software release, another group with the penultimate release, a few with an older version, and a handful running Macintosh software. But we all have to work together.

Thankfully, Office 2000 is better at backward compatibility than other releases have been, and there are options for saving Office 2000 files to an older format. For the most part, you should be able to share your PowerPoint 2000 files with users of PowerPoint all the way back to version 4.0, including older Macintosh versions. (Until Office 98 was released for the Mac, PowerPoint 4.0 was the only Mac format.)

This chapter discusses these kinds of compatibility issues, and shows you how to access PowerPoint's solutions for storing information in other file formats and for loading information from external sources, including older versions of PowerPoint. You'll find additional information on working with data from external sources in chapters 11 and 15. Note that before you depend on older-format files, you should conduct some tests to make sure the features you have used to build your show translate to the other version of the program.

Saving a Slide Show to Another Format

The good news about the PowerPoint 2000 release is that even with increased functionality, the file format—the way information in your PowerPoint presentations is stored on disk—is the same (or at least compatible with) PowerPoint 97, the previous version of the program. That means if you are upgrading to Office 2000 from Office 97, you shouldn't have any file-format issues with existing files. Likewise, other users who still have Office 97 should be able to load and use your PowerPoint 2000 files without any glitches.

You can't load PowerPoint 2000 files in PowerPoint 95 or earlier, but you can save PowerPoint 97/2000 files in PowerPoint 95 format. The figure at the upper left of the facing page shows you the start of the process; the upper-right figure shows you how to choose the file format for Windows 95. The Presentation format at the top of this list is the PowerPoint 2000 format.

After you select the file format, you will see a warning message similar to the one at the lower left on the facing page. If your show is a basic one, this won't concern you. If you're using complex features, such as animation, then read the Help file.

Again, conduct some tests when you save files in different formats, but you may not want to use the PowerPoint 95 format. With PowerPoint 97 and later, Microsoft did a much better job of compressing files to reasonable sizes. You won't notice the difference (or it will be insignificant) on small presentations or those with no pictures or screen shots. On larger shows, however, the difference can be shocking.

For example, the Memphis98 presentation used as a sample earlier in this book requires 3,584K storage (about 3.5 megabytes) in PowerPoint 2000. It contains a number of screen shots and other graphics images in 39 slides. When I save that file in PowerPoint 95 format, the size jumps to 74,662K (more than 74 megabytes!). Want to maintain compatibility with PowerPoint 2000 and PowerPoint 95 (by selecting the PowerPoint 97-2000 & 95 Presentation choice in the Save as type list)? That takes nearly 78 megabytes.

The best alternative for cross-application and even cross-platform compatibility is HTML. In fact, Microsoft claims, "At the heart of Office 2000's Web support is the vision that users can choose HTML as their only file format." When I use HTML format (lower-right figure, next page), the storage requirement for my sample file is 5.25 megabytes, which is a really good compromise between the PowerPoint 2000 and PowerPoint 95 format options.

TAKE NOTE

SETTING FILENAMES

If you want to use the same directory for both versions of the file, enter a new name in the File name field of the Save As dialog box.

CROSS-REFERENCE
See Chapter 15 for more information on using the Web Page file format.

FIND IT ONLINE
For a PowerPoint presentation on how to save your slides, check out http://www.ed.uiuc.edu/ed-online/cter/SVASWP/sld003.htm.

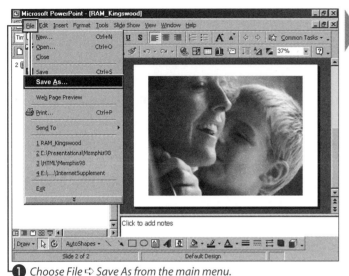

1 Choose File ⇨ Save As from the main menu.

2 Click on the down arrow in the Save as type field to view a list of available file types.

3 Choose PowerPoint 95.

4 Navigate to the folder you want to hold the PowerPoint 95 format file.

5 Click Save.

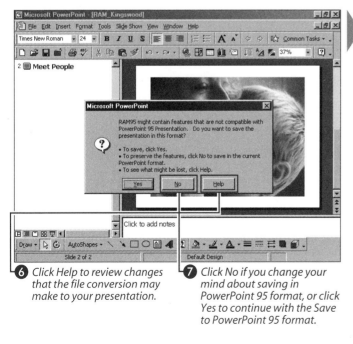

6 Click Help to review changes that the file conversion may make to your presentation.

7 Click No if you change your mind about saving in PowerPoint 95 format, or click Yes to continue with the Save to PowerPoint 95 format.

8 Choose Save As from the File menu, then open the Save as type list and select Web Page.

9 Go to a directory you want to use.

■ Remember that a subdirectory will be created under the selected directory to store your slides and graphics.

10 Click Save to complete the Web Page save process.

Saving Files Online

When you get used to the cross-platform compatibility offered by the Web Page format, you may long for ways to share files other than using Save As from the File menu. In Chapter 15 I showed you how to publish your Web-format PowerPoint shows to a Web server. From there, other users, who can be anywhere in the world so long as they have Web access, can view your presentation.

However, if you work for a company with multiple offices, or you want to work jointly on a presentation with someone else, you should consider using PowerPoint's built-in FTP (File Transfer Protocol) facility. With FTP, if you have access to a public or private server, you can save PowerPoint files across the Internet almost as if you were saving to your local hard drive. This technique gives other, remote users direct access to all aspects of your presentation, in whatever format you want to use.

To use FTP as a file storage path, you'll have to work with your system administrator, Internet Service Provider, or some third party to gain read/write access to an FTP site somewhere on the Internet. Once this step is complete, you can use Save As to configure the path and use this remote location like a local drive. See the upper-left figure on the next page to see how to start the process.

The Add/Modify FTP Locations dialog box (upper-right figure, next page) enables you to specify the parameters for connecting to an FTP server. You access FTP locations in two ways: either as Anonymous or as a user with a username and password. If you are accessing a public site, you probably will do so anonymously. However, as an anonymous user, you typically can download files but not upload them. To save a file to an FTP site (upload it, actually), you'll need a site to which you have user rights.

After you have added one or more FTP locations, you'll see that the Save As dialog box has these new locations visible. When you choose one, you will see the directory structure of the remote FTP host.

This server could be a UNIX box, Windows NT Server, or something else, but you don't care. You should be able to navigate the directory structure as you do your local hard drive. If you've connected as an anonymous user, the pub directory is a likely choice. Otherwise, your ISP or the other party responsible for this site will tell you which directory to use.

TAKE NOTE

CONNECTING TO FTP SITES

To connect to a remote FTP site, you'll need some kind of connection to the server. Whether you use the Internet or a direct connection, you will have to configure Windows dialup networking or another type of remote connection, such as a network or ISDN link. Your LAN administrator or ISP can help.

CROSS-REFERENCE
See the next section on opening files for more information. You may also find useful information in Chapter 15.

FIND IT ONLINE
Want to know how to create HTML presentations in PowerPoint? Visit **http://www.tunet.net/train/train11.htm**.

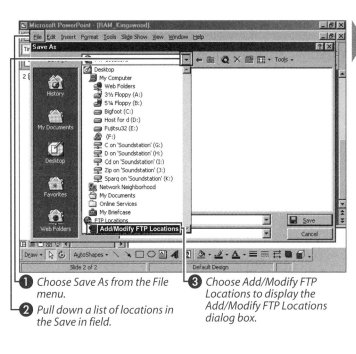

1 Choose Save As from the File menu.

2 Pull down a list of locations in the Save in field.

3 Choose Add/Modify FTP Locations to display the Add/Modify FTP Locations dialog box.

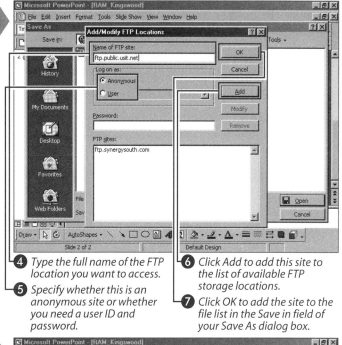

4 Type the full name of the FTP location you want to access.

5 Specify whether this is an anonymous site or whether you need a user ID and password.

6 Click Add to add this site to the list of available FTP storage locations.

7 Click OK to add the site to the file list in the Save in field of your Save As dialog box.

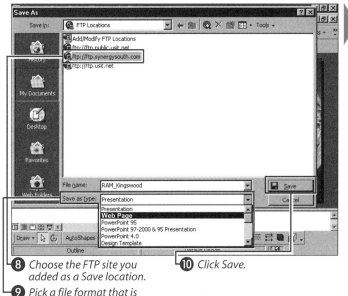

8 Choose the FTP site you added as a Save location.

9 Pick a file format that is different from the native PowerPoint 2000 presentation format, if you like.

10 Click Save.

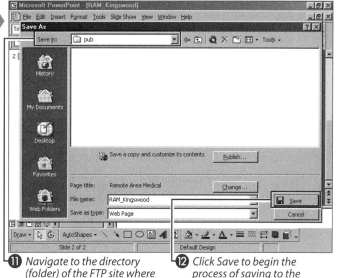

11 Navigate to the directory (folder) of the FTP site where you want to store your file.

12 Click Save to begin the process of saving to the remote directory.

271

Opening Other File Formats

You may have saved a PowerPoint 2000 file in another format or you may be using someone else's files that are in another format. If these files are PowerPoint-compatible, opening them is as simple as making a selection in the Open dialog box, shown in the upper-left figure on the facing page. Notice the icon beside the selected file in this figure: It shows both PowerPoint and Internet Explorer (Web page) icons, indicating that the file is compatible with both formats. You can also tell from these icons what type of Web page the file is.

You can load Web files that didn't originate in PowerPoint as well, but the results in the slide-show environment are variable — maybe good, maybe bad — depending on how the file is formatted. (You can try it — you may be pleasantly surprised or disappointed.) The same is true of other external files, including Excel spreadsheets, Word documents, and so on. And, of course, you can open older PowerPoint files in the same way. PowerPoint 2000 will recognize them and convert them during the open process.

Suppose you are using an FTP site for exchanging PowerPoint files, as described in the previous section. Loading these files over an FTP link is similar to saving them in the first place and not much different from opening a PowerPoint presentation from a local hard drive.

The upper-right figure on the next page shows you the Open dialog box with the FTP locations already entered. You don't have to use the Add/Modify FTP Locations dialog box unless you want to use a location different from those already created.

In the lower-left figure on the facing page, you can see the HTML file I saved earlier. Notice the subdirectory associated with this file. Remember that in Web Page format, PowerPoint separates the HTML code and the file elements. When you open the file in PowerPoint, the conversion is made and everything works in PowerPoint as if it were a native PowerPoint file. If you change the file and save it on your local drive, all of the elements should come with the new file.

If the directory structure of the FTP host (or your LAN) is complex, you can save time by specifying the final directory in the File name field of the Open dialog box (bottom-right figure, next page). On the server I use, some of the interim subdirectories have hundreds of subdirectories of their own. Navigating in the usual way can be time-consuming.

TAKE NOTE

LOADING FOREIGN FILES

You will notice a difference in loading "foreign" files and loading native PowerPoint 2000 files. The process will take longer — sometimes a lot longer — and you may see progress reports on the status bar at the bottom of the screen that tell you what PowerPoint is converting or loading.

CROSS-REFERENCE

See Chapter 12 for more ideas on using foreign information within PowerPoint 2000.

FIND IT ONLINE

For an example of PowerPoint online, and some tips on creating presentations, try **www.coe.ou.edu/ ecn/ multi/mm2/do_don't.ppt**.

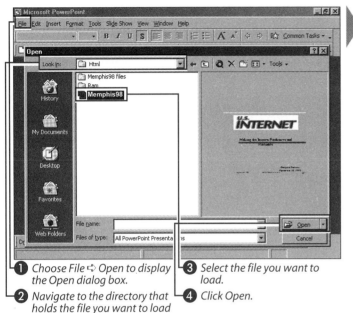

① *Choose File ⇨ Open to display the Open dialog box.*

② *Navigate to the directory that holds the file you want to load (HTML, PowerPoint 95, etc.).*

③ *Select the file you want to load.*

④ *Click Open.*

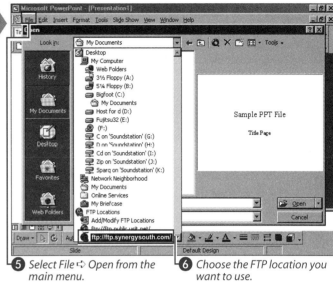

⑤ *Select File ⇨ Open from the main menu.*

⑥ *Choose the FTP location you want to use.*

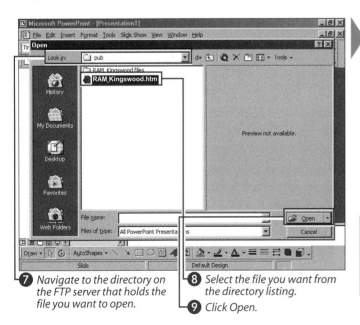

⑦ *Navigate to the directory on the FTP server that holds the file you want to open.*

⑧ *Select the file you want from the directory listing.*

⑨ *Click Open.*

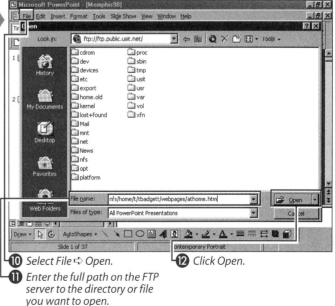

⑩ *Select File ⇨ Open.*

⑪ *Enter the full path on the FTP server to the directory or file you want to open.*

⑫ *Click Open.*

Saving PowerPoint Slides as Graphics

PowerPoint 2000 is versatile in that it allows you to open presentation files saved in previous versions of the program and save a presentation to an older format. You can save a presentation as a Rich Text Format (RTF) outline, which you can read in virtually any word-processing program. You can use the Save as Web Page option to create an HTML file, which can be stored on a Web server or local-area network, where it can be displayed by almost any Web browser. Together, these save options provide tremendous flexibility to enable you to share PowerPoint presentations with just about anybody who has a computer.

There may still be times, however, when you want to share your PowerPoint work with someone who doesn't have any of these options available. In such cases, you can store your presentation using a graphics file format — a format that almost certainly can be read by some program on virtually any platform. When you choose Save As from the File menu (top-left figure, facing page), you have a number of format options, including popular graphics file formats that will let you save a single PowerPoint slide or an entire presentation in a graphics format. I've shown some of the graphics format options in the lower-left figure on the facing page.

Which format you choose depends on what you want to do with the finished files. If you're sharing the images with someone using a different computer platform than you, make sure they can read the format you choose. Also consider the quality of the resulting images. Although a JPEG format, for example, provides excellent compression that results in relatively small file sizes, you won't get as good quality if you're saving slides that include screen shots or photographs as you will with a TIFF (Tagged Image File Format) file. In one test I ran, a slide that included one small screen shot and some text required 34K of storage in JPEG format and over 94K in TIFF format. However, the TIFF file was decidedly better quality overall.

If you choose to save a single slide, PowerPoint creates one file for the current slide. If you want to save all slides in a graphics format, PowerPoint creates a subdirectory within the directory currently chosen and creates a separate graphics file for each slide. The files are named Slide1, Slide2, Slide3, and so on, with the appropriate file extension for the save format you've selected.

TAKE NOTE

VIEWING GRAPHICS SLIDES

Once your PowerPoint slide show is saved in a graphics format, you won't use PowerPoint to view the slides. You can do that with any program capable of displaying the file format you used.

CROSS-REFERENCE

See the previous task for more information on file formats.

FIND IT ONLINE

Here's one of many file-format references you can find online: **www.program.com/resources/graphics_format.html**.

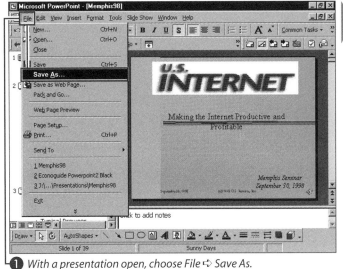

1 With a presentation open, choose File ⇨ Save As.

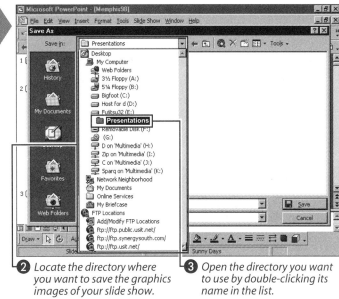

2 Locate the directory where you want to save the graphics images of your slide show.

3 Open the directory you want to use by double-clicking its name in the list.

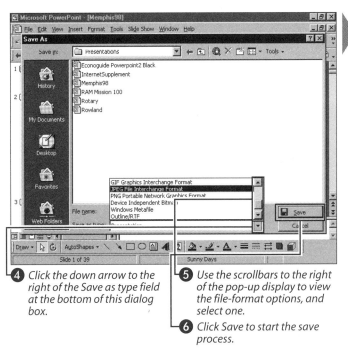

4 Click the down arrow to the right of the Save as type field at the bottom of this dialog box.

5 Use the scrollbars to the right of the pop-up display to view the file-format options, and select one.

6 Click Save to start the save process.

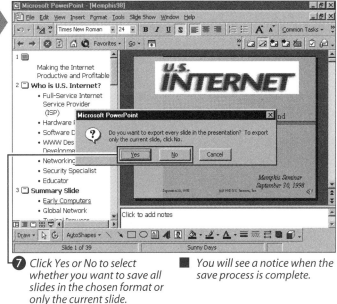

7 Click Yes or No to select whether you want to save all slides in the chosen format or only the current slide.

■ You will see a notice when the save process is complete.

Personal Workbook

Q&A

1. File formats determine how PowerPoint data is stored. What is the most important overall consideration for PowerPoint 2000 users working with files created with previous versions of the software?

_____

_____

2. How can you ensure that users of earlier versions of PowerPoint will be able to load the files you create in PowerPoint 2000?

_____

_____

_____

3. Microsoft is recommending a common, universal file format for PowerPoint and other Office programs. What is this format? How can it be called universal?

_____

_____

4. What is the meaning of the abbreviation *FTP*? How is it important to PowerPoint 2000 users?

_____

_____

5. What does the term *anonymous FTP* mean?

_____

_____

6. Describe the size differences between PowerPoint 95 files and PowerPoint 2000 files.

_____

_____

7. Why do you think loading files in Web Page or other formats takes longer than loading native PowerPoint 2000 files?

_____

_____

_____

8. Who should you contact about securing an FTP site that you can use to share PowerPoint files with remote users?

_____

_____

_____

_____

ANSWERS: PAGE 314

EXTRA PRACTICE

❶ Use the Save As dialog box to save a PowerPoint 2000 file in PowerPoint 4.0 format.

❷ Display the Add/Modify FTP Locations dialog box and enter **ftp.usit.net** as an anonymous FTP location.

❸ Use the Open command from the PowerPoint File menu and display the directory of the FTP site.

❹ Continue the previous example by navigating to the pub/ram director to display a list of all available files in this directory (remember the Files of type field!).

REAL-WORLD APPLICATIONS

✔ As a training director for a company with multiple locations, you want to regularly share PowerPoint training files you produce with your counterparts in other locations. You arrange with a local Internet Service Provider to obtain an FTP site where you can store files in Web Page format. This enables remote users to download the files and have full control over changes and presentation.

✔ You are responsible for chairing a short-term committee charged with planning an upcoming national conference. You use PowerPoint to display the major issues and to provide a format for individual committee members to share data with others in their companies. By saving the presentation in Web Page format and publishing it on the Web, you provide cross-platform and cross-application compatibility.

Visual Quiz

Describe how to display the screen shown here. Careful! There's a trick to providing full information on this one.

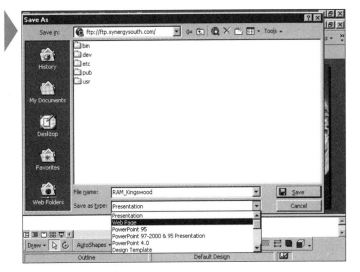

CHAPTER 19

MASTER THESE SKILLS

▶ Design Effective Slides

▶ Design for Proper Mood or Effect

▶ Design for Random Control

▶ Use Brainstorming

▶ Use Outlining

▶ Use a Storyboard

▶ Write a Script

▶ Use Text Effectively

▶ Use Photographs

PowerPoint Design Tips

PowerPoint makes the job of designing and producing professional, meaningful presentations a lot easier than in the old days of colored pens and flip charts. The computer tools, coupled with the drawings, text tools, and forms packaged with the software, can help virtually anyone look like a professional presentation designer.

However, the presentation business has reached the same stage that desktop publishing achieved several years ago. The tools are more powerful, are easy to use, and are widely available, but those of us who have little or no experience in producing presentations can't always use these tools effectively.

A detailed treatise on professional presentation design is beyond the scope of this book — and beyond my expertise. However, there are some design considerations that are easily learned and that, when considered during the making of your show and its individual slides, can make your work more effective.

That's the topic of this chapter: I'll share some experience that can help you do a better job with the tools PowerPoint offers. As you study these hints, keep in mind that PowerPoint is not designed as a standalone presentation tool. The slides and screens you create with it are intended to be accompanied by a human presenter. Even if you have used music and narration as part of a high-end presentation design with PowerPoint, you may well stand up to control the presentation, to answer questions, or to add personal comments during the show.

With that in mind, part of the planning and design of a PowerPoint presentation should focus on how the human presenter and the material you design can work together to achieve the ultimate goal. I'll discuss general considerations in using PowerPoint presentation material, show you ways to help plan a presentation, and talk about some of the issues involved with designing individual slides. The processes and examples in this chapter are slightly different from what you've seen in the rest of the book because I'm dealing with more general concepts.

Design Effective Slides

The key to successful presentations is twofold. As you design any presentation, be aware of the power of the visual part of it, but don't forget that the audience also expects to hear something. What they see should supplement what is being said.

You've probably noticed that it can be distracting or even irritating to try to read a lot of material while someone is talking. You tune out the words to concentrate on the visual, or you skim the visual to listen to what is being said. Therefore, the visual component of a presentation should be brief. You can shorten on-screen presentations by breaking some of the normal rules of language. A bulleted list, for example, doesn't always require a subject and verb, and you can use creative symbols in place of standard bullets to enhance the visual. That way, the bullets themselves become part of the message (see the top two figures on the facing page).

The goal is to help the audience grasp the information as quickly as possible and to help them retain it. Whatever you can do to make the experience a visual one will enhance the process. However, a parallel goal is to keep slides simple while emphasizing visual content to improve information retention.

Consider the figure in the lower-left corner on the facing page. This sample slide is relatively simple and should be easy for the viewer to understand, interpret, and remember. At the same time, the visual image adds subtle meaning to the text, which you will amplify during your presentation.

The sample slide in the lower-right figure, on the other hand, is too complex. It has too much information on the screen, and would not be easy for most viewers to understand. Remember that presentation slides are designed to augment what a speaker says, not to carry all of the information.

Some of the same design rules and guidelines you would use for desktop publishing or photographic composition also apply to presentations. After all, the components of a presentation are slides or pages — individual units that are linked together to form the whole. The difference between PowerPoint slides and a printed page or a photograph, of course, is that you can use sound and motion in addition to layout, color, shape, and shading to get your message across. Successful presentations use the available tools in a creative way that is appropriate to the audience you hope to reach and to the message you hope to convey.

TAKE NOTE

CREATING SLIDES

Follow these steps to simplify your slide design process:
▶ Create titles (perhaps from your outline)
▶ Add text
▶ Insert graphic elements where appropriate
▶ Set the duration or control (how the slide will change)
▶ Add sound, music, or narration as required
▶ Test the presentation for length and effectiveness

CROSS-REFERENCE

For more tips on designing and creating PowerPoint presentations, see Chapters 3 and 5, plus this chapter's sections on brainstorming and script writing.

FIND IT ONLINE

If you can't find an appropriate clipart image for custom bullets, open the ClipArt Gallery and click on Clips Online to download more clips.

Simple Bullet List

- Use Short Sentences
- Keep Structure Parallel
- Enhance With ClipArt
- Limit Six Lines Per Slide

■ *Format the slide as a bullet list.*

■ *Create three to six items.*

■ *Accept PowerPoint standard bullets.*

Custom Bullet List

- Use Short Sentences
- Keep Structure Parallel
- Enhance With ClipArt
- Limit Six Lines Per Slide

■ *Turn off bullets by clicking the bullet icon on the Format toolbar.*

■ *Select Insert ➪ Picture ➪ ClipArt.*

■ *Choose a ClipArt category and then an image to use.*

■ *Resize the image and position it for use as bullets.*

MyCompany Advantages

- Downtown
- Experienced
- Competitive
- Reputation

■ *You don't necessarily need verbs for bullet lists.*

■ *Use lists as a speaker outline.*

■ *For more details, add material to notes.*

MyCompany Advantages

- Convenient Downtown Location Provides Easy Access With No Parking Problems
- Experienced Staff Helps You Get the Best Service Among All Similar Companies
- Competitive Pricing Helps Your Company's Budget Every Time
- Our Reputation Is Among the Best of Any Similar Company in Town

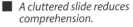

■ *A common mistake is too much detail.*

■ *Full sentences are hard to read on screen.*

■ *A cluttered slide reduces comprehension.*

Design for Proper Mood or Effect

In designing a presentation, keep this general guideline in mind: Do you want the audience to remember specifics, or is a general idea the more important consideration? In a sales presentation, for example, is it more important for the audience to remember technical specifications and statistics, or do you want to convey a concept or an overview of what the product can do for them or for their business?

There is no "correct" answer to these general questions. The correct response depends on the type of selling you are doing—and *any* presentation is selling, whether you are promoting a concept, a product, or yourself—and what you want the viewer to do, think, or feel at the end of the presentation. But I can make some observations on how to accomplish either of those goals.

To leave the viewer with a concept, feeling, or idea: reduce the amount of text on-screen, use motion video and photographs, show people doing something with the product, show people who appear pleased or satisfied, and emphasize what is being done over how it is being done. The top two figures on the following page illustrate this concept.

Remember, we retain visual information such as pictures better than text. So whenever you can, impart ideas visually. You'll have a better chance of keeping the audience interested, and the audience will have a better chance of retaining the information.

To emphasize factual details over concept: use text and charts, use no more than six lines per slide, state and restate ideas (using different methods and terms), and simplify your screens. You can also use photographs or art to help viewers link raw data to the real world, but do this within the context of keeping the slides relatively simple. I've tried to illustrate this concept in the bottom two figures on the facing page.

TAKE NOTE

GRAPHIC FILE FORMATS

Photographs and motion video can cause PowerPoint presentation files to become quite large. Remember that with computer presentation the maximum resolution is 72 dots per inch — using greater resolution just makes larger files. And you may want to restrict your images to 640 by 480 pixels to reduce file size. Experiment, too, with file formats to achieve the best quality with the highest possible compression (in other words, the smallest file size).

CROSS-REFERENCE
See Chapter 10 for more information on using these objects in your slide designs.

FIND IT ONLINE
The Stock Market (www.stockmarketphoto.com) is one of many stock-photo agencies that offer high-quality photographs for use in your presentations.

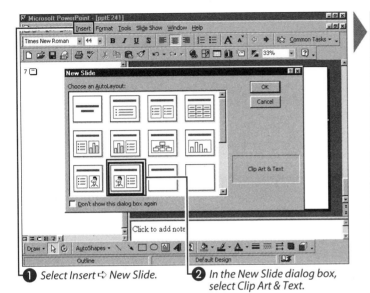

1 Select Insert ➪ New Slide.

2 In the New Slide dialog box, select Clip Art & Text.

■ Double-click the placeholder clipart to open the ClipArt Gallery.

■ Select a picture from the Gallery.

■ Add text to the bullet-list template beside the clipart.

■ Notice the nature of the text and clipart: Use general or conceptual ideas instead of factual data.

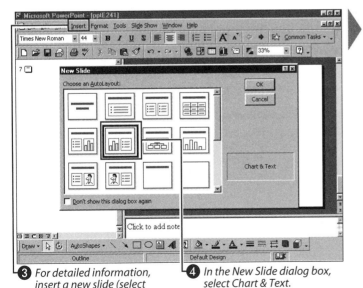

3 For detailed information, insert a new slide (select Insert ➪ New Slide).

4 In the New Slide dialog box, select Chart & Text.

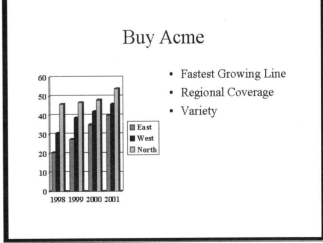

■ Double-click the placeholder chart and enter numerical data in the spreadsheet.

■ Notice the bullet list beside the chart on this slide.

Design for Random Control

One design concept I sometimes find useful is to include random control on some or all slides. During a presentation you should be aware of the level of audience understanding. If it becomes obvious that the audience is confused (or worse, bored), you should be able to back up the show or branch to an entirely different segment that presents the data in a different way, adds more detail, reduces detail, and so on.

You exercise this control by having hyperlinks on presentation screens, by including hidden slides, and by assuming manual control of the slides. A presentation that is under the control of the presenter is more flexible than one that proceeds automatically.

The top-left figure on the facing page shows you how to hide one or more slides. The top-right figure reviews setting up a hyperlink to one of these hidden slides or to any other slide within your presentation.

Don't forget the Web. Although you can create PowerPoint hyperlinks within a single presentation, or to another presentation on your machine, PowerPoint supports hyperlinks that go beyond your local PC to display Web pages or local HTML files.

You can anticipate your audience and include hyperlinks on slides featuring technical information or on slides that usually generate viewer questions. This gives you someplace to go if one or more members of your audience request more detail. You can also include an object on every screen that jumps to a screen with a complete list of screens and interactive buttons. By including links on a summary slide to another slide with more detail, you have the ability to compress or expand the information you present depending on audience needs. I've illustrated this concept in the lower-left figure on the facing page.

Another way to use branching is to maintain two presentations, one behind the other. One presentation is a summary and can be used for audiences who need only cursory information. The other offers more detail and can be used for different audiences or to expand on an idea if the audience wants it. You can hyperlink to the secondary presentation, or you can simply load both presentations before you start your show and switch to the secondary program at will (see the sidebar in the lower-right corner, facing page).

The basic advice is to be creative. Look at the message you want to convey, consider the audience, and be aware of the broad range of presentation tools available in PowerPoint. Then don't hesitate to listen to feedback from users and viewers of your finished product and make changes as necessary.

TAKE NOTE

JUMPING DIRECTLY TO A SLIDE

Hyperlinks on individual slides give you complete control over show navigation. However, don't neglect PowerPoint's built-in features. Right-click anywhere on a slide while in Slide Show mode, click Slide Navigator, and select a slide to view.

CROSS-REFERENCE

See Chapter 15 for more information on using hyperlinks to enhance your slide shows.

FIND IT ONLINE

You'll find plenty of PowerPoint add-ins, templates, and other support material at www.microsoft.com/powerpoint.

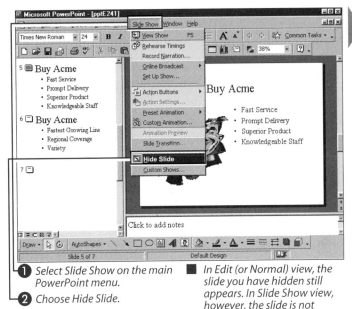

1 Select Slide Show on the main PowerPoint menu.

2 Choose Hide Slide.

■ In Edit (or Normal) view, the slide you have hidden still appears. In Slide Show view, however, the slide is not visible.

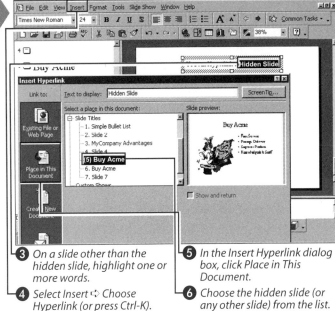

3 On a slide other than the hidden slide, highlight one or more words.

4 Select Insert ➪ Choose Hyperlink (or press Ctrl-K).

5 In the Insert Hyperlink dialog box, click Place in This Document.

6 Choose the hidden slide (or any other slide) from the list.

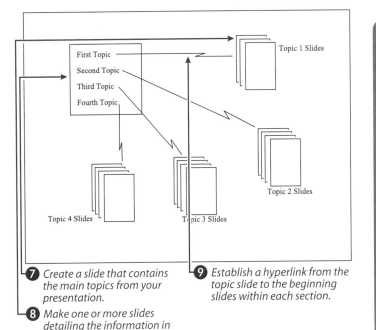

7 Create a slide that contains the main topics from your presentation.

8 Make one or more slides detailing the information in each of the topics.

9 Establish a hyperlink from the topic slide to the beginning slides within each section.

Switching Between Presentations

Hyperlinks provide an elegant way of accessing information in a second PowerPoint presentation: simply choose a filename from the Hyperlink dialog box. On the other hand, you can also just load two instances of PowerPoint and switch between them at will. To do this, launch the program and open the first presentation. Launch PowerPoint a second time and launch the secondary presentation. Switch one version of PowerPoint into Slide view. Point to the task bar and locate the second instance of PowerPoint and bring it to the forefront. Switch this program so it is also in Slide view. Now switch between versions of PowerPoint by selecting them from the taskbar.

Use Brainstorming

Brainstorming can be a complex or a fairly simple process. We've all used the term casually, I suspect. If you take brainstorming to a more formal level, you can accomplish surprising things.

The first step is to ask yourself basic questions that include who, what, when, where, why and how. These general questions can take more specific forms: Who is the audience? What does the audience know or believe about the subject? What does the audience expect to learn or achieve? What do I want to accomplish? What should the audience feel, know, or do differently after the presentation?

Some of the answers may be obvious. Your supervisor may tell you to prepare a show on a specific topic, for example, and provide you with a general message and what should be accomplished.

Other answers may not be so obvious, but brainstorming can help. I've summarized the process in the sidebar on the facing page. This part of the process can take from hours to weeks, depending on what you are trying to uncover. Notice that I said "uncover." Brainstorming can actually help you discover concepts, ideas, even concrete facts that you didn't know you knew or needed to know.

Be prepared to write down new ideas at any time. Relax and be creative. Don't worry about order, but leave room under each item for subtopics. The top-right figure on the next page shows the result of one brainstorming session for a presentation about the Internet.

When you reach this stage of thinking, you should have a fairly long list of ideas. They may seem unrelated at this point: That's okay. Now use a separate piece of paper for each of these topics. If you wrote 75 topics, then you should have 75 pages with one idea at the top of each one. Now repeat the previous process for each idea.

Next, sort the topics. Arrange them in order of importance, highlight the important ideas under each main topic, and extract the important subtopics into a list organized by order of importance.

At this point you may want to bring other people into the process, or you may want to use more formal tools such as PowerPoint's brainstorming template, which I have shown in the bottom two figures on the next page.

CROSS-REFERENCE
For more information on designing PowerPoint presentations, see Chapters 3 and 13.

FIND IT ONLINE
Certain software (including PowerPoint's brainstorming template) can help you brainstorm. Check out Paramind Software (**www.paramind.net**).

How to Brainstorm

1. Write a topic word or phrase at the top of a page.
2. Spend 10 to 20 minutes writing down every idea. Don't edit, judge, or qualify.
3. Take an 8- to 24-hour break.
4. Start another session by reviewing your previous work quickly.
5. Repeat steps 1 through 3 several times. You are through with this first phase of brainstorming when it becomes difficult to come up with new topics.

Internet	Business Applications?
Global	Personal Applications?
Real Applications Arriving	Dedicated Hardware/Software?
Marketing/Selling Products	Cost?
Searching still difficult	Directories—How can I find people?
Need better software	Cost? Cost + Benefit?
Universal access?	The Future

■ *Use a yellow pad, word processor, or text editor to make a list.*

■ *Put the main topic at the top of the page.*

■ *Write down everything that comes to mind for 10 minutes or so.*

■ *Repeat the process several times to create a complete list.*

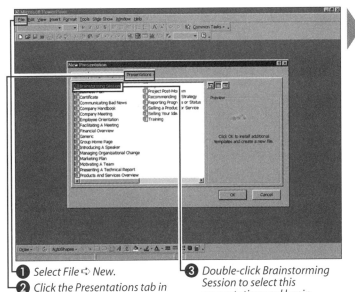

❶ *Select File ⇨ New.*

❷ *Click the Presentations tab in the New Presentation dialog box.*

❸ *Double-click Brainstorming Session to select this presentation and begin creating your new presentation.*

❹ *Click the vertical scrollbar at the right of the slide window to step through the slides.*

■ *Familiarize yourself with the topics suggested by the template.*

■ *Fill in the bullet lists with your own information.*

■ *Expand the template to meet your personal goals and objectives.*

Use Outlining

I've worked with a lot of writers and presentation designers, all of them creative individuals. With a few exceptions, their general attitude about outlining is fairly negative — it's considered unnecessary baggage in the creative process. That's far from true. Whatever preconceived notions about outlining you bring to the presentation table, try to set them aside. Outlining is a useful tool that augments the creative process.

An outline can help you organize material, identify major topics and the subtopics that support them, and weed out irrelevant or ineffective ideas. In addition, an outline can help others see your vision for the presentation, making it easier for them to help you identify strengths and weaknesses before you have progressed too far to make changes easily.

The outline is an organizational tool, so the more organized it is, the better it can do its job. The formality of your outline style should vary according to the number of people you expect to read it. If your outline is simply for your own reference, then adhering to strict outline format is less important. If, on the other hand, you expect to distribute the outline to several other people, a more formal approach is desirable.

I've listed some outlining guidelines in the top two figures on the facing page. I've organized the first sample into a fairly classic outline format as well. Obviously, this isn't the only format, but this basic design should serve your personal needs and the needs of others in your organization who may review it with you. Again, it's fairly simple — a desirable trait for PowerPoint slide design.

If you conduct the brainstorming and outlining steps properly, the hard work should already be done when it comes time to build the storyboard (see the next task). All you will need to do is use the main outline headings as slide titles and fill in the description from the subheadings on each slide.

Once you have created the detailed outline and reviewed it, you can import the outline into a PowerPoint presentation, as shown in the bottom two figures on the facing page. If you have made a detailed outline, you may find that there is too much information in your slide show. Editing in the outline view is a simple way to create a basic presentation that you can then expand with graphics and other objects.

TAKE NOTE

POWERPOINT AND OUTLINES

PowerPoint has a useful outline view of each presentation — another way to see the slide show. You can use this view to help you visualize the organization of your presentation. Keep in mind, though, that the outline process I am talking about here is more formal and is designed to help you understand the overall presentation — both slides and narration. This outline should be created in Word or another quality word processor.

CROSS-REFERENCE
See Chapter 12 for hints on using PowerPoint outlines.

FIND IT ONLINE
Want a different kind of creative and outlining software tool? Try www.inspiration.com.

A Standard Outline

I. Use a consistent numbering system
  A. Roman numerals at the highest level
  B. Capital alphabetic characters at second level
  C. Numbers followed by periods at the third level
II. Provide at least two entries at each level
  A. No A. without a corresponding B.
  B. no 1. without an accompanying 2.
III. Use consistent style
  A. Single words and phrases (topical outline)
  B. Sentences (sentence outline)
IV. Use parallel headings and subheadings
V. Main headings that represent slide topics make
   storyboard development easier

Importing Your Outline

When you outline outside PowerPoint for slides you will create inside PowerPoint, be ready to edit the outline when you import it into PowerPoint. The outlining process will help organize your work, but the outline is probably wordier than PowerPoint slides should be. Simply open PowerPoint and use File Open to open the Word outline or import a .TXT file from another application. Use the Outline beside each slide or work on the slides themselves to tighten slide material. Finally, add a PowerPoint color scheme and graphics or clip art to complete the presentation.

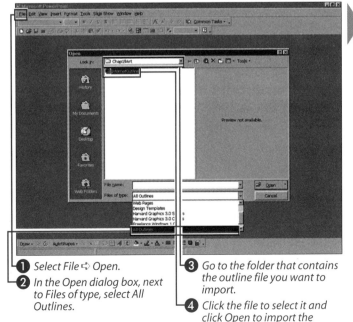

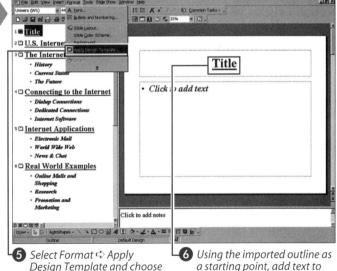

① Select File ➪ Open.

② In the Open dialog box, next to Files of type, select All Outlines.

③ Go to the folder that contains the outline file you want to import.

④ Click the file to select it and click Open to import the outline.

⑤ Select Format ➪ Apply Design Template and choose a template from the next dialog box.

⑥ Using the imported outline as a starting point, add text to the basic title and subtitle information already there.

■ Add graphics, animation or other objects as required.

Use a Storyboard

Think of a storyboard as a graphical representation of the outline. It can be a simple hand drawing or a complex, well-drawn creation. Whether you draw a storyboard by hand or use a computer drawing tool, it may be an important part of the creative process. As a presentation grows more complex, you'll ultimately save time by drawing a storyboard before you begin building the presentation in PowerPoint.

I'll acknowledge an exception to this storyboard rule. PowerPoint's Slide Sorter view can also help you visualize your presentation. You can use it to build a storyboard while you build the presentation. In this case, you are using PowerPoint to make a storyboard that is really part of the presentation itself.

For all but the simplest shows, however, the best approach is to rough out the story on paper. The idea is to use the outline as a basis for drawing a simple representation of each slide in your program.

Think of a PowerPoint presentation as a series of slides, modules, or events — some of them placed sequentially and some of them lying parallel. One of these lines contains the slides you will use during the presentation. Associated with each slide is another unit that represents music, sound, or narration. In addition, you can specify a special effect (fade, wipe, dissolve) as the transition between slides.

I've shown a basic storyboard fragment in the top-left figure on the facing page. You should include any art such as drawings or photographs, plus placement of text, windows, and other special effects. You can note on the drawing what sound, if any, will be associated with each slide (top-right figure, facing page).

The first storyboard after the outline can serve as a doodling session — part of the initial planning. This is a chance for you to put in a primitive visual form the outline you have developed during brainstorming. As with other steps in the design process, you may have to go through this procedure several times to refine the design, locate problems, add new ideas, and get input from other members of the design team or other experts in your organization.

If all of this seems overly complicated, don't let it be. You won't spend very long on any of these steps for a simple presentation, and for a longer presentation, focusing on an organized procedure can make the whole process relatively easy. I've shown some benefits of storyboarding in the lower-left corner on the following page. In the lower right are various ways you might organize the information you are presenting in a PowerPoint show.

TAKE NOTE

USING STORYBOARDS

A storyboard is like an outline — it's a guide. Don't fall into the trap of blindly following a storyboard. It is easy to do, given that it may take several hours and the work of several people to prepare. For the most effective presentation, update the storyboard as you proceed with production of the actual show.

CROSS-REFERENCE
See Appendix B for additional hints on designing presentations in PowerPoint.

FIND IT ONLINE
For information on storyboard software, go to www.powerproduction.com.

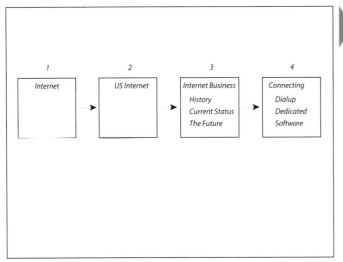

- *Use paper or a drawing program to sketch slideshow flow and titles.*
- *A basic storyboard includes only slide flow, main titles, and subtitles.*
- *Add whatever information you need to help program development.*

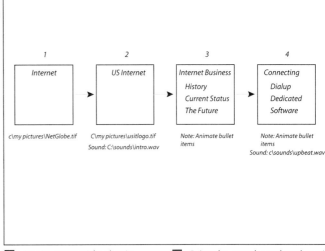

- *Again, start with a basic storyboard.*
- *Expand basic information to help you visualize the finished show.*
- *Print the storyboard and use it as a guideline for final presentation development.*

Benefits of Storyboarding

A storyboard can accomplish a number of important goals:

- ▶ Establishing the order of the slides
- ▶ Determining the number of slides
- ▶ Creating the general design of each slide
- ▶ Identifying special effects (sound, video, wipes, and so on.)
- ▶ Determining what resources are needed to produce the slides
- ▶ Giving other team members a vehicle for reviewing the presentation and making changes
- ▶ Providing an archival copy of the information

Informational Schemes

Consider these ways of organizing story information:

- ▶ Deductive Organization — moves from the general to the specific
- ▶ Inductive Organization — moves from the specific to the general
- ▶ Chronological Organization — describes a sequence of events in chronological order
- ▶ Process Organization — presents the steps involved in a process or procedure where each step must occur in a given order
- ▶ Agenda Organization — presents information in a "random" order, although a successful agenda organization must tell the audience what the order is

Write a Script

Like a movie script, the presentation script provides a textual representation of all of the elements of the final show. Whereas the storyboard is a visual representation of all or part of the show elements, everything that will be part of the presentation should appear in a script, including slide descriptions, text and how it will be presented, slide number, duration of each module, narration (if any), sound effects, music, graphics elements, and video.

As with some of the other creative elements I've discussed in this chapter, scripts aren't something you'll use with PowerPoint if your presentations are basic and relatively short. If you're using PowerPoint as a formal training tool, for interactive education, or to aggressively sell a product or idea, then a script — even a simple one — might help you create a more successful presentation.

If you've ever read a play script, then you have a fair idea of how a script is structured. The top-left figure on the facing page shows a basic script fragment. For your own use, something with a similar design is all you really need. The script is really just a tool to help you formalize the more general concepts you created during outlining and storyboarding.

Like storyboarding, scripting is a personal activity. You can design your own script format and style, but you should always consider the concepts I've listed in the second figure on the following page.

The answers to questions such as these will help you determine how serious you need to be about designing a complete and consistent script style. As you can see in the lower-left figure on the next page, a more formal script may contain additional elements.

Remember that while you want to include a lot of detail in a working script, you also want to strive for clarity and an uncluttered appearance. This helps those who may be unfamiliar with the show to help you during production or during the proofing and testing process. Just as you want to give each of your slides an open, uncluttered feel, the script used to produce the presentation should also feel open and accessible.

The process of moving from a script to a finished PowerPoint presentation should be fairly familiar to you by now. In general, I suggest you start with the basic PowerPoint elements, then add any additional features such as sound or animation. One technique I sometimes find helpful is to place elements of the script within the Notes pages section of the slide show (see the bottom-right figure, next page).

TAKE NOTE

RECORDING SCRIPT AUDIO

A script is essential if you will use a formal narration track with your PowerPoint show. Use a projector to display the finished PowerPoint presentation and give a copy of the script to the computer operator, the audio technician, and the announcer. The script thereby becomes a blueprint for all to follow as production progresses.

CROSS-REFERENCE

As you work with PowerPoint scripts for the first time, review the earlier sections in this chapter on outlining and storyboarding before writing a script.

FIND IT ONLINE

If you're serious about scriptwriting — for PowerPoint or other endeavors — check this Web site for related software: www.writerscomputer.com.

Introduction to Internet
Working/Design Script – Preliminary
Version 1.3

SLIDE #2
MUSIC: Intro.wav
NARRATOR: U.S. Internet is one of the oldest Internet Service Providers in the nation. We were the 100th commercial ISP. Today we are among the top 20 providers in terms of services, experience, and leadership.

MUSIC OUT

SLIDE #3
NARRATOR: The Internet is one of the newest business and personal fads to hit the country. Whether or not you know what the Internet is, it is only a matter of time before it directly affects your life.

One problem with understanding the Internet is the physical design. The Internet is more than a network of computers – it is a network of networks . . .

■ *Type slide numbers and titles.*
■ *Include narration and other information.*
■ *Scripts for your own use can be very basic.*

Scriptwriting Hints

As you write a script, keep these points in mind:
▶ Who will use the script?
▶ Are several people working on the production?
▶ How complex is the production?
▶ How will the presentation be produced?
For more formal scripting, remember these points as well:
▶ Split the page, placing audio information on the left and visual information on the right.
▶ Number the scenes or slides in each module.
▶ Include filenames or other information where possible.
▶ Write instructions in all caps and narration in upper- and lowercase.

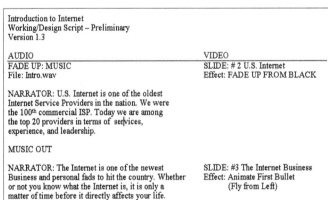

Introduction to Internet
Working/Design Script – Preliminary
Version 1.3

AUDIO	VIDEO
FADE UP: MUSIC	SLIDE: # 2 U.S. Internet
File: Intro.wav	Effect: FADE UP FROM BLACK
NARRATOR: U.S. Internet is one of the oldest Internet Service Providers in the nation. We were the 100th commercial ISP. Today we are among the top 20 providers in terms of services, experience, and leadership.	
MUSIC OUT	
NARRATOR: The Internet is one of the newest Business and personal fads to hit the country. Whether or not you know what the Internet is, it is only a matter of time before it directly affects your life.	SLIDE: #3 The Internet Business Effect: Animate First Bullet (Fly from Left)
One problem with understanding the Internet is the physical design. The Internet is more than a network of computers – it is a network of networks . . .	Effect: Animate Second Bullet (Fly from Left)

■ *Use a word processor or scripting program.*
■ *Separate the page into audio and video segments.*
■ *Describe visual, effects, and audio components for each slide.*

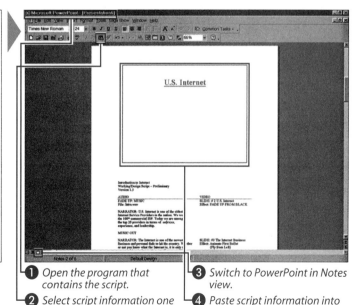

1 *Open the program that contains the script.*
2 *Select script information one slide at a time and copy to clipboard.*
3 *Switch to PowerPoint in Notes view.*
4 *Paste script information into the notes area of each slide.*

Use Text Effectively

Although PowerPoint uses color and graphics well, you shouldn't ignore the importance of text in designing effective presentations. At least half of business-oriented presentation material is still text-based. In PowerPoint and other presentation programs, text displays are sometimes called text charts.

Text charts are used for tables of organization, flow charts, timetables, sales presentations, and summaries. The name notwithstanding, text charts may incorporate a variety of graphic elements — scanned images, graphs, and art — as well as grids, boxes, lines, and shading, along with basic text.

At its simplest level, a text chart may be nothing more than a bullet list. Language, properly applied, is still a good way to present information.

But you may also expand the use of text in these ways and more: to present information that includes too many data types or too much information for a graph; to list exact values instead of graphic approximations; to show information that varies widely between the highest and lowest numbers; to show any data where the exact amount is critical.

You can see how text can work to your advantage by studying the top two figures on the facing page. In the left is a graph that includes data too widely separated for meaningful interpretation. In the right is the same information displayed as a text chart, where the precise data is easily interpreted.

The guidelines for designing a text chart slide are generally the same as for any other slide: Choose typefaces and type sizes carefully, use small amounts of data on each slide, keep information on each slide closely related, be as specific as possible, use short phrases, use upper- and lowercase characters, and avoid using hyphens.

As a general rule, sans serif fonts are a better choice than serif fonts. Serifs tend to disappear or blur, particularly if you are projecting the image. I've shown a font comparison in the lower-left figure on the facing page.

Type size is also important. In general, the maximum viewing distance from a presentation screen is six times the screen diameter. For a 30-inch by 40-inch screen, the maximum viewing distance should be about 20 feet away (40 inches × 6 = 240 in./12 = 20 feet). If you are using a standard 14-inch PC screen, no one should sit than about 7 feet away (14 inches × 6 = 84 in./12 = 7 feet). The final figure on the facing page shows some type size comparisons in a text-chart format.

TAKE NOTE

WHEN NOT TO USE A TEXT CHART

Text can show precise data, but it's not the best choice for conveying trends or concepts instead of factual data. Use a spreadsheet fragment in a text chart for direct numerical interpretation; use a graph to show rising or falling sales trends and the like.

CROSS-REFERENCE
Refer to Chapter 11 for more information on using charts and spreadsheets within your PowerPoint presentations.

FIND IT ONLINE
Try an online search for "text charts" to find some interesting samples and software. One slide tip page I uncovered was **www.graphicsland.com/slidetip.htm**.

Graph—Too Complex

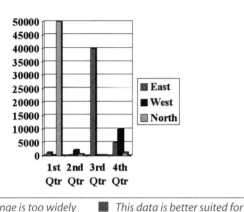

- The data range is too widely dispersed.
- The highest and lowest figures are difficult to interpret.
- This data is better suited for a text chart.

Text Chart Comparison

	Q1	Q2	Q3	Q4
East	1000	10	40000	5000
West	5	2000	10	10000
North	50000	500	100	1000

- A text chart provides precise data.
- It's easier to interpret widely dispersed data.

Font Usage

Use different font styles for different applications:
- ▶ Times is a popular Serif type
- ▶ Arial is a popular Sans Serif type
- ▶ COPPERPLATE IS A BOLD TITLE TYPE
- ▶ *Allegro is a specialty type (Use sparingly!)*

Different Font Sizes

You can use font size to convey importance or emphasis. With PowerPoint, just be sure you have used fonts large enough to be seen by everyone in the audience. The font-size comparisons below help you see relationships among different font sizes. All samples are shown in Arial type.

8 Points
10 Points
12 Points
14 Points
18 Points
24 Points

Use Photographs

Photographs in PowerPoint can help viewers relate the information on the slide to the real world.

Consider the examples in the top two figures on the facing page. The first illustration shows a bulleted list against a plain background. The second sample shows the same list against a photograph. The text information appears the same way in both cases, but the photographic background helps the viewer relate the text to something real.

Also, a photograph can improve data retention. A list that deals with automobiles could be placed over a picture of a car, for example. General sales information could be presented over a picture that suggests selling, such as a cash register. If you don't have or can't get a photograph, use a graphic image as the next best choice. You can use something you have drawn from scratch or a clipart image.

Where do you get photographs and other images for your presentations? There are many sources, including company brochures, letterhead, business cards, or catalogs; annual reports, user manuals, sales aids, engineering reports; art used by fellow employees in previous presentations; product samples, intracompany reports, letters; and videotape still frames.

You can scan many of these images into the computer in a format that PowerPoint can use directly. The "Capturing Video" sidebar on the next page shows you how to scan an image directly into PowerPoint, assuming you have a Twain-compliant scanner installed in your computer.

If you don't have access to a scanner, find a company that offers scanning services. They'll take your image, scan it, and return a computer .TIF, .PCX, or other file format compatible with PowerPoint.

One good source of still color images for your presentations is videotape or a video camera fed directly into a video-capture board. Most video hardware includes some form of software driver to let you capture a still-frame image. Simply set up your camera on a tripod, light it to show what you want, and take a few seconds of tape. Then hook up your VCR to the video-capture board and take a snapshot.

This technique lets you capture shots from physical images such as computer keyboards or hardware, parts of your company, equipment used by your company, or scenes of your town or area. Once the image is captured and stored in a graphics file format, you can use it just as you would any other graphics image from your computer.

TAKE NOTE

USING SOMEONE ELSE'S PHOTOGRAPHS

Though it might be tempting to do so, you can't legally scan an image from a magazine or a book and then use it in your presentation without obtaining permission from the publisher. Likewise, you can't use a Web-page photograph you don't own unless you get permission.

CROSS-REFERENCE

See Chapter 10 for more information on using photographs in PowerPoint.

FIND IT ONLINE

If you're interested in using video images, consider Radius, Inc.'s Photo DV, available at **www.radius.com**.

Western Tours

- Cactus Trails
- Cattle Drives
- Western Towns
- Horseback Riding
- Custom Tours

- ■ *A conventional bullet list can provide technical detail.*
- ■ *Without color or images, the list is bland.*

- ■ *A plain list doesn't include supplemental information.*

- ■ *Select Insert ⇨ Picture from File.*
- ■ *Go to the folder and file you want to use and click Insert.*

- ■ *Right-click the image, choose Order from the shortcut menu, and then Select Send to Back.*
- ■ *Change text color to make words visible on the picture.*

Capturing Video

You'll need a special port to capture video for use in your PowerPoint slides. Many new laptop and desktop machines designed for multimedia include special video ports that let you plug in a video camera or VCR. If your computer doesn't include a video port, you can add one. Many third-party companies, including Matrox and 3Com (U.S. Robotics), offer video cards that can capture standard video data. If you have a digital video camera, you may need an IEEE-1394 direct-digital card. These are available from such companies as Radius and Adaptec. Associated software lets you capture motion video or a series of frames as individual pictures.

The Ease of PhotoCDs

Most photofinishers can give you Kodak PhotoCD images. To use PhotoCD images in PowerPoint, just make sure the PhotoCD filter is installed. Select Insert ⇨ Picture from File and then point to a PhotoCD image. If the PhotoCD filter isn't installed, you will be prompted to insert the PowerPoint distribution CD to complete the process. PhotoCD images are extremely high-quality — better than you can get with most digital cameras — so this is a good way to obtain high-resolution images. Besides, you can use existing slides or film by having a photofinisher convert them to PhotoCD format.

Personal Workbook

Q&A

1 Describe how effective PowerPoint slide design is different from the rules you learned in high school or college English class.

_____

_____

2 How would you change your slide design if you want the audience to remember general ideas or trends instead of specific factual data?

_____

_____

3 PowerPoint's built-in hyperlink feature lets you jump directly to another slide or even a location on the Web. Can you think of at least three ways that this feature would be useful?

_____

_____

4 How might you use brainstorming to help you design a PowerPoint presentation? Can you describe a formal brainstorming technique?

_____

_____

5 How would you create a PowerPoint outline without using PowerPoint? How can you use this outline directly to produce PowerPoint slides?

_____

_____

6 What is a _storyboard_? How might it help you in designing PowerPoint slides? Why would you not want to use a storyboard?

_____

_____

7 Consider your current applications for PowerPoint shows. Do you think a script would help you create a better show? Why or why not?

_____

_____

8 Which is more useful in PowerPoint presentations: text or graphics? Why?

_____

_____

_____

ANSWERS: PAGE 315

EXTRA PRACTICE

① Create a new presentation in PowerPoint using the brainstorming template. Study the slides this presentation contains. Note how Microsoft has implemented brainstorming techniques in this template.

② Open any existing PowerPoint presentation. Choose any slide and select a word or a small graphic. Create a hyperlink from this text or object to another slide within the same presentation.

③ Open any PowerPoint file and select Insert ⇨ Picture ⇨ Clip Art to display the Clip Gallery. Click the Photographs icon on the Pictures tab and choose a photograph to insert.

REAL-WORLD APPLICATIONS

✔ As MIS Director for Internet-is-Us, you have been asked to prepare a technical description of your company's network structure for a prospective connectivity supplier. You know that some of the people at the meeting will be salesfolk, but you suspect there might also be one or more technical people who would want more detail than the sales staff. You design your PowerPoint show so that it is effective regardless of the viewer.

✔ You are the marketing director of Acme Airline and Storm Door Company. The executive staff says that sales are down in the western region and they want a presentation in one week that outlines your new ideas for improving sales there. You use brainstorming to discover new ways to market your products, and translate these ideas into an effective PowerPoint presentation.

Visual Quiz

Describe how to display the screen shown here. Careful! There's a trick to providing full information on this one.

_____

_____

_____

_____

_____

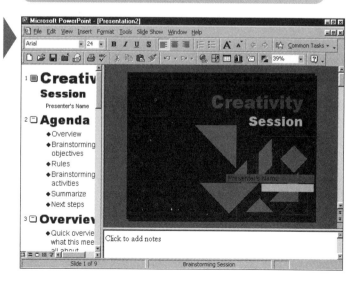

Appendix A: Personal Workbook
Answers

Chapter 1

see page 4

1 What are three ways to open the PowerPoint 2000 program?

A: You can open PowerPoint by (a) selecting Open Office Document or New Office Document from the Start menu or the Office shortcut bar; (b) choosing PowerPoint from Programs (on the Start menu), from the Office Shortcut bar, or from My Computer; or (c) choosing a PowerPoint file from any folder.

2 How do you discover the keyboard shortcuts for menu items?

A: Keyboard shortcuts appear to the right of menu entries. Not all menu items are accessible through shortcuts, but if a shortcut is available, you'll see it on the menu.

3 Describe two ways to make PowerPoint display all available choices under a specific menu.

A: You can either pause the mouse cursor over a menu until all items are displayed, or click the down-facing chevron (arrows) at the bottom of the collapsed menu to display the whole thing.

4 Describe how to change which toolbars are shown on the PowerPoint screen.

A: It's easy! Just right-click any toolbar to display a shortcut menu that lists all toolbars. Uncheck the toolbars you don't want to see and check the ones you do.

5 The Normal PowerPoint view shows three program elements. What are they?

A: You see an outline of the current slide show at the left of the screen, the current slide on the right, and slide notes at the bottom of the display, beneath the slide.

6 How can you tell which PowerPoint menu items open a dialog box?

A: Menu items that open a dialog box include three dots (an ellipsis) at the end of the menu name.

7 **What is the procedure for displaying a shortcut menu?**

A: Right-click the on-screen object for which you want to display a shortcut menu. Not all objects have a shortcut menu, but most do.

8 **How can you exit a shortcut menu without choosing any of the menu choices?**

A: Press Esc or click the screen anywhere outside the menu display.

Visual Quiz

Q: Describe how to display the opening wizard screen shown here.

A: Choose Set Up Show from the Slide Show menu, and then click Projector Wizard.

Chapter 2

see page 20

1 **Describe the three basic types of online help available in PowerPoint 2000.**

A: You can get help from the Office Assistant, through conventional hypertext help (the help Windows programs have always had), and via the World Wide Web (the newest, most current help you can find).

2 **How do you turn on the What's This? mouse cursor?**

A: Select What's This? from the Help menu or press Shift-F1. When the cursor changes to a question mark, click any PowerPoint object to view a pop-up description of it. Press Esc to cancel the What's This? function.

3 **What is the single keystroke you can use to display the Office Assistant character?**

A: Press the F1 function key. If the assistant doesn't appear, you have him hidden. Choose View the Office Assistant from the Help menu.

4 **How can you turn off the Office Assistant to use standard text-based help?**

A: Choose Hide the Office Assistant from the Help menu.

5 **What menu sequence displays information about your version of PowerPoint and shows you technical data about your computer system?**

A: Select About Microsoft PowerPoint from the Help menu.

6 **How do you give your Office Assistant a new personality?**

A: Choose Office on the Web from the Help menu and navigate to the new Assistant site.

7 **When you see the What would you like to do? prompt, what PowerPoint help object is on the screen?**

A: The Office Assistant.

8 **When do you use the PowerPoint Detect and Repair feature?**

A: Any time PowerPoint seems to be operating incorrectly — though, if you use PowerPoint frequently, it's a good idea to use this feature regularly as a preventive measure. This utility will reinstall required components and conduct other cleanup operations that will help PowerPoint run faster and better.

Visual Quiz

Q: How do you display this screen?

A: Press F1 to display the Office Assistant, then click Options to open the Options dialog box.

PERSONAL WORKBOOK ANSWERS

Chapter 3

see page 30

1 **You can start a new PowerPoint presentation in four basic ways. What are they?**

A: (a) Choose New Office Document from the Start menu or Office shortcut bar; (b) Click New on the standard toolbar; (c) Select New from the File menu; or (d) Choose AutoContent Wizard, Design Template, or Blank Presentation from the PowerPoint startup dialog box.

2 **How do you change text on an existing text slide?**

A: Click inside the text box to select it, then use standard editing keys (Backspace, Del, the arrow keys, and so on) to make changes.

3 **Describe the difference between a design template and a presentation design.**

A: A design template offers basic color, font, and other designs but does not include any real data. When you choose a design template, you get a single slide. A presentation design, on the other hand, uses design templates as the basis for a complete slide show that addresses a theme, such as a corporate financial report. Presentation designs include dummy text that you can replace with your own text to produce a complete slide show.

4 **What is the AutoContent Wizard and how do you start it?**

A: The AutoContent Wizard is a series of PowerPoint dialog boxes that help you choose a template, presentation design, and other features to form the basis of a complete slide show. Launch the AutoContent Wizard from the startup dialog box or by selecting File ➪ New.

5 **PowerPoint supports presentation types in addition to a conventional slide show with a stand-up presenter. What are they?**

A: You can use PowerPoint to create Web presentations, overheads in black-and-white or color, 35mm slides, and automated kiosk shows. PowerPoint also includes design templates for award certificates and signs, and you can use PowerPoint features for booklet covers and other single-sheet designs.

6 **The AutoLayout section of the New Slide dialog box enables you to choose how individual slides appear. How do you open this dialog box?**

A: Select Format ➪ Slide Layout (the dialog box will have a different name) or Insert ➪ New Slide. You will also see this dialog box when you create a new PowerPoint presentation.

7 **How can you edit the font characteristics of existing text on a PowerPoint slide?**

A: Select the text you want to change and choose Font from the Format menu or from the text object's shortcut menu.

8 **When might you want to create a PowerPoint presentation with only one slide?**

A: If you're making a certificate, report cover, For Sale sign, or other single-sheet product.

Visual Quiz

Q: Describe how to open the dialog box shown here.

A: Select File ➪ New, and then click the Presentations tab in the New Presentation dialog box. Next, click the Preview button at the upper right of this tab, and then click Corporate Home Page to display a preview of this template.

Chapter 4

see page 42

1 **How much time can you expect to spend preparing a 20-minute PowerPoint presentation?**

A: If you know your topic, you should be able to produce a credible, though basic, PowerPoint presentation in about an hour. Some people say they spend as much as an hour on each minute of PowerPoint work, but it shouldn't take this long if you know the program and your topic.

2 **What dialog box do you use to specify how your PowerPoint presentation will be displayed?**

A: Use the Set Up Show dialog box, which you select from the Slide Show menu.

3 **Describe how to create a show that uses only a specified range of slides from a PowerPoint presentation.**

A: Select Slide Show ⇨ Custom Shows and follow the instructions in the Custom Shows dialog box.

4 **How can you turn off animation and narration in a PowerPoint slide show that has these features incorporated into its design?**

A: In the Set Up Show dialog box (which you can access via the Slide Show menu), click Show without animation.

5 **What is the purpose of the Projector Wizard?**

A: The Projector Wizard helps ensure that your computer's video card is properly configured for the projector you are using. It also tests to make sure the projector is plugged in and is functioning properly.

6 **What two general types of projector technology are commonly used with PowerPoint presentations?**

A: Integrated LCD projectors that work like self-contained slide projectors and LCD panels that sit on top of a conventional overhead projector to project your PowerPoint show.

Visual Quiz

Q: **Describe how to display the dialog box shown here.**

A: Load a PowerPoint presentation for which you want to create a custom show. Select Slide Show ⇨ Custom Shows, and then click New in the Custom Shows dialog box. You will see a display of all slides in the current presentation. Use this list to create one or more custom shows.

Chapter 5

see page 54

1 **Can you think of two different applications for PowerPoint's Notes pages?**

A: Sure. They make excellent audience handouts if you want to provide additional details not on the regular slide printouts. Notes pages also make good reference notes for speakers: You outline the major topics you want to cover with each slide and use the Notes pages as your notes while you talk.

2 **What PowerPoint utility corrects common typing mistakes as you make them?**

A: AutoCorrect. This feature is available automatically, but you can add new terms and make other edits to it by selecting Tools ⇨ AutoCorrect.

PERSONAL WORKBOOK ANSWERS

③ **What PowerPoint feature lets you place recurring text at the bottom of each slide?**

A: Footers. Choose Header and Footer from the View menu.

④ **What PowerPoint facility would you use to change the location of header and footer information on slides, handouts, and Notes pages?**

A: View Master Pages by selecting View ⇨ Master.

⑤ **What menu sequence would you use to find a word or phrase somewhere within the current slide show?**

A: Select Edit ⇨ Find or press Ctrl-F.

⑥ **How can you add custom words to the spell-checker dictionary?**

A: Easy! Click the Add button in the dialog box that appears when the spell checker finds a word it doesn't recognize.

Visual Quiz

Q: **Describe how to display the screen shown here.**

A: Select Tools ⇨ AutoCorrect, and then click Exceptions in the AutoCorrect dialog box.

Chapter 6

see page 72

❶ **What dialog box is used to install a new printer for use by PowerPoint?**

A: Actually, you use the Add Printer Wizard, a series of dialog boxes. Launch this wizard by clicking the Start button, selecting Settings ⇨ Printers, and then double-clicking the Add Printer icon in the Printers dialog box.

② **What file extension does PowerPoint automatically add to a printer output file?**

A: .PRN.

③ **Describe how to change the default on-screen slide format to 35mm slides.**

A: Select File ⇨ Page Setup to display the Page Setup dialog box. In this box, pull down a list of available options in the Slides sized for field, and choose 35mm Slides.

④ **How can you print the current slide show without using the Print dialog box?**

A: Use Ctrl-P or click the Print icon on the standard toolbar.

⑤ **What keyboard shortcut opens the Print dialog box?**

A: Ctrl-P.

⑥ **Why would you want to install a printer definition and drivers for a printer you don't own?**

A: So you can create .PRN files in the proper format to print on a remote printer.

Visual Quiz

Q: **Describe how to open the dialog box shown here.**

A: Select File ⇨ Print, and in the Print dialog box, click Properties. Now click the Graphics tab in the Print Properties dialog box. Note: Different printers have different properties displays. Yours may not have a graphics tab, but it will have other configuration/setup tabs that you can explore.

Chapter 7

see page 88

1 **How does the use of color influence the effectiveness of your PowerPoint presentation?**

A: Color sets mood. Different colors can help you emphasize to an audience the mood or topic you are presenting with PowerPoint.

2 **With the exception of a full-color photograph or other image, what is the suggested maximum number of colors you should use in a PowerPoint presentation?**

A: About five colors is the recommended maximum.

3 **What point size would you use to create a text block with characters approximately one inch tall?**

A: Text size is measured in points, with each point equal to 1/72 of an inch. Therefore, text about one inch tall would be sized at 72 points.

4 **A collection of all the characters available for a particular typeface and style is the definition of what PowerPoint screen object?**

A: Font.

5 **What keyboard combination do you use to move a PowerPoint object by small increments?**

A: Use the Ctrl key in combination with the keyboard arrow (cursor) keys.

6 **What Office 2000 resource can you use in PowerPoint to store, view, and select clipart, sound, photographs, or video clips?**

A: The ClipArt Gallery.

7 **What PowerPoint feature would you use to change the default number of slides on handout pages to nine?**

A: Make the change in the Handouts group of the Print dialog box, accessible from the File menu.

8 **Once you've removed a Slide Master object, such as a footer element, how would you replace it?**

A: Select Format ⇨ Apply Presentation Design and then choose the design you originally used to format your show.

Visual Quiz

Q: **Describe how to display the screen shown here.**

A: Select View ⇨ Master, and then choose Handout Master from the Master supplemental menu.

Chapter 8

see page 104

1 **PowerPoint includes two types of slide animation. What are they?**

A: Preset animation and custom animation.

2 **What is meant by Laser Text animation?**

A: This preset animation style enables you to display slide text one character at a time, accompanied by a laserlike sound. (Come on! Lasers don't really make any noise — unless, of course, they're powerful enough to cut through something.)

3 **How are slide animations and slide transitions similar? How are they different?**

A: Slide transitions use special effects to display slides — you can have a slide fly in from the left or appear through a set of blinds, for example. Slide animation also causes slide objects to move, but it deals with individual slide objects instead of the entire slide.

Personal Workbook Answers

4 **Describe two ways to display the PowerPoint custom animation dialog box.**

A: Choose Custom Animation from the object's shortcut menu or from the main Slide Show menu.

5 **What technical consideration might force you to change the color of an animated object in a PowerPoint slide show?**

A: An animated object might be hard to see if its color is too close to the color of the slide background or other objects over which it passes during the animation process.

6 **What two methods can you use to advance slides with transitions?**

A: You can specify that slide advances and transitions occur when you manually press the Spacebar or the left mouse button during a slide show. You can also choose automatic or timed advance from the Transitions dialog box.

7 **How do you display the Action Button submenu?**

A: Choose Action Settings from the Slide Show menu or from the slide's shortcut menu.

8 **What menu sequence do you use to animate slide objects that aren't action buttons?**

A: Select Slide Show ⇨ Custom Animation.

Visual Quiz

Q: Describe how to display the screen shown here.

A: On the Slide Show menu, point to Action Buttons. Grab the Action Buttons title bar and drag the supplemental dialog box to the middle of the PowerPoint screen. You can reposition many similar objects simply by dragging them to the new location.

Chapter 9

see page 116

1 **Describe when you use the PowerPoint AutoLayout dialog box.**

A: This dialog box appears when you insert a new slide into an existing presentation or when you create a new presentation from scratch. Use the AutoLayout box to set the default objects that appear on new slides.

2 **How do you display the Common Tasks toolbar?**

A: Click Common Tasks on the Format toolbar.

3 **What main-menu entry would you use to place a company logo on a PowerPoint slide?**

A: Select View ⇨ Master.

4 **Describe two ways to change the font within a selected block of text.**

A: Select Format ⇨ Font or right-click the selected text and choose Font from the shortcut menu. You can also pull down a list of available fonts from the list on the Format toolbar.

5 **Besides dragging the cursor, how can you select a single word? A sentence?**

A: Double-click anywhere inside a word to select it. A triple-click inside a sentence will select the entire sentence.

6 **What PowerPoint dialog box would you use to add texture or patterns to a slide background?**

A: Select Format ⇨ Background, pull down the color-selection list at the bottom of the Background fill group, and choose Fill Effects to display the Fill Effects dialog box.

7 Describe what happens to your custom slide background when you apply a different design template.

A: Nothing! A custom slide background overrides template settings.

8 What color may denote excitement or danger to an audience?

A: Red.

Visual Quiz

Q: Describe how to display the screen shown here.

A: Select Format ⇨ Slide Layout, and in the Layout dialog box, choose Bulleted List. Click inside the bulleted list to select it, and then click the border of the list to select all items. Now, from the Format menu, select Bullets and Numbers and click the Character button to display the Bullet dialog box.

Chapter 10

see page 132

1 What is the main purpose of the ClipArt Gallery?

A: The ClipArt Gallery helps you organize clipart images, photographs, sounds, and motion-video clips for use in Office software, including PowerPoint.

2 Describe how to add a new category to the ClipArt Gallery.

A: Select Insert ⇨ Picture ⇨ Clip Art to display the ClipArt Gallery. From the main ClipArt Gallery dialog box, choose Import Clips, and then navigate to a folder containing a graphic image you want to insert into the gallery. In the Properties dialog box (which appeared when you selected an image), click the Categories tab and choose New Category.

3 What is the difference in displaying the Gallery for pictures and for sounds and movies?

A: When you select Insert ⇨ Pictures, the Gallery contains tabs for Pictures (clipart), Sounds, and Movies. If you choose Movies or Sounds from the Insert menu, then the ClipArt Gallery contains only a single tab: Motion Clips if you chose Movies or Sounds if you chose Sounds.

4 How can you play a sound file that you have already inserted into a PowerPoint slide?

A: It depends on how you inserted the sound. When you add a sound, PowerPoint asks if you want it to play automatically when you display the slide during a show. If you choose yes, the sound plays when you present the slide; otherwise, you can click the sound icon during a show to play the sound. You can also play a sound inserted into a slide by right-clicking the sound icon in Slide Show view and selecting Play Sound from the shortcut menu.

5 How do you size a sound or movie clip to fit the current slide design?

A: Click the sound icon and drag one or more object handles to the display size you want.

6 If you cover the entire slide with a picture or other image, why is it important to include a slide title?

A: So this slide appears in the show outline.

7 What is the maximum image resolution you should use for PowerPoint images? Why?

A: You can use any resolution you want, but 144 dots per inch — twice the computer-screen display resolution — is plenty. Higher-resolution images simply take up more space and cause the slides to load slower.

Personal Workbook Answers

8 **What movie format is compatible with the ClipArt Gallery and PowerPoint slides?**

A: PowerPoint is compatible only with the Windows .AVI format.

Visual Quiz

Q: **Describe how to display the screen shown here.**

A: With a PowerPoint presentation loaded, point to Movies and Sounds on the Insert menu, then choose Movies from Gallery to display the Insert Movie dialog box. Click a category to display a list of available motion clips. Right-click a clip to select it and to display a shortcut menu. Choose Clip Properties from the shortcut menu to display the Clip Properties dialog box.

Chapter 11

see page 152

1 **List the major software components included with Office 2000 and describe what each does.**

A: PowerPoint is supplied in several configurations to address the needs of a variety of users. Standard Office 2000 includes Microsoft Word for word processing, Excel for spreadsheet design, PowerPoint for presentations, and Office tools to help with several operations, including the ClipArt Gallery. Other versions of Office 2000 include Access for database design and FrontPage for Web-site design. Point your browser to **www.microsoft.com/office** to learn about the latest versions of Office 2000.

2 **The capability of Word and other products to support PowerPoint commands and menus is called what?**

A: In-place editing or, sometimes, interoperability.

3 **What item is most commonly exported from PowerPoint to Word?**

A: The PowerPoint show outline.

4 **The Object dialog box is used to insert two general kinds of objects into a PowerPoint slide. What are they?**

A: New objects created specifically for your presentation in native applications such as Word or Excel, and objects that exist in a stored file.

5 **What PowerPoint facility is best for displaying Access data inside a slide show?**

A: An Action button that links to the Access database you want to use.

6 **Why do you need to use the Format Cells dialog box after inserting an Excel spreadsheet into a PowerPoint slide show?**

A: Cells inserted into PowerPoint from Excel lose their formatting and may appear too small to view properly inside PowerPoint.

7 **What is the best data format for Excel information that you want to include in a PowerPoint presentation?**

A: Data presented as an Excel Chart is generally easier for a PowerPoint audience to interpret than raw spreadsheet data.

8 **How can you use PowerPoint data inside Outlook?**

A: Outlook can serve as a universal window into Office applications, including PowerPoint. You can create new presentations or access existing presentations from within Outlook. Of course, you can also use the program to email PowerPoint slides or presentations to other people.

Personal Workbook Answers

Visual Quiz

Q: Describe how to display the screen shown here.

A: Click the e-mail icon on the PowerPoint toolbar.

Chapter 12

see page 168

❶ **PowerPoint supports two on-screen utilities to help you place objects on your slides more accurately. What are they?**

A: The ruler and the guides. Enable these facilities with the View menu.

❷ **If you find that you can't launch an application to display an embedded object directly, what PowerPoint utility can you use to make it work?**

A: Use an Action object hyperlinked to the application you want to use.

❸ **Why would you add "sticky note" comments to your PowerPoint slides?**

A: These on-slide notes can help you remember things you need to tweak in your presentation. They can also provide additional information about your show to anyone else who may be presenting it.

❹ **What two programs or methods might you use to place a chart on a PowerPoint slide?**

A: Office includes a basic charting facility that you can use for fairly simple numerical comparisons. For more complex data, or data that already exists somewhere else, use Excel.

❺ **Can you insert a graphic into a PowerPoint table? If not, can you think of a way around this limitation?**

A: You can't insert a graphic into a table directly, but you can create a text box and insert an image into that.

When you move the text box on top of a table, it can appear as if the image is actually part of the table.

❻ **Why would you not want to use a WordArt object for a full paragraph of information?**

A: WordArt is designed for titles or single-word objects. A full paragraph in WordArt would be too complex for easy viewing during a slide show.

❼ **Can you insert objects from any other application into PowerPoint? Why or why not?**

A: Yes, for the most part. Microsoft applications generally work well together, enabling you to insert objects directly in most cases. You can usually insert objects from any other Windows application by copying the object to the Clipboard and then copying it from the Clipboard onto your PowerPoint slide.

❽ **Describe how to convert text in a text box to a bullet list.**

A: Select the text, and then click the bullet-list icon on the Format toolbar.

Visual Quiz

Q: Describe how to display the screen shown here.

A: Select Insert ⇨ Slides from Files and then click the List of Favorites tab. Note: If you have not previously entered one or more PowerPoint files into the List of Favorites, this display will be blank.

Chapter 13

see page 190

❶ **Discuss why rehearsing a PowerPoint slide show is important.**

A: Practice with anything does, indeed, make perfect. You want your presentation to appear as professional as possible, to impart the information you need to share

PERSONAL WORKBOOK ANSWERS

with the audience, and to meet the timing target for the show.

② **What are the two ways PowerPoint provides for setting slide timings?**

A: You can use Rehearse Timings from the Slide Show menu, or use Record Narration (also on the Slide Show menu), which will automatically set slide timings for you.

③ **What is another name for a PowerPoint Summary Slide?**

A: Summary Slides are also called Agenda Slides.

④ **What utility is required before you can create a Summary Slide?**

A: You must first use Custom Shows from the Slide Show menu to create one or more custom shows.

⑤ **What menu would you use to change the color of the Slide Show pen?**

A: Use the Slide Show shortcut menu. Select Pointer Options ⇨ Pen Color to display a list of possible colors.

⑥ **What two utilities are included with the PowerPoint Meeting Minder?**

A: Meeting Minutes and Action Items. You can also use the Schedule utility to display a calendar for setting future events from within the Meeting Minder.

⑦ **How can you hide one or more slides in a show without removing them from the file?**

A: Choose Hide Slide from the Slide Show menu.

⑧ **What computer hardware is required for recording slide-show narration?**

A: You need a sound card with a microphone input.

Visual Quiz

Q: **Describe how to display the screen shown here.**

A: Open a PowerPoint presentation and switch to the Slide Show view by selecting View ⇨ Slide Show. Right-click anywhere on the current slide to display a shortcut menu, then choose Meeting Minder from the shortcut menu.

Chapter 14

see page 202

① **What presentation utility would you use to keep general notes or meeting minutes during a PowerPoint slide show?**

A: The Meeting Minder, accessible from the Tools menu and from the Slide Show shortcut menu.

② **What two methods can you use to display the Slide Show shortcut menu?**

A: You can right-click anywhere on a slide displayed in Slide Show view, or you can click the Slide Show pop-up menu button at the lower left of the slide display. You won't see this button in Slide Show view until you have moved the mouse when each slide is displayed.

③ **What Microsoft utility outside PowerPoint is used for Online Collaboration?**

A: NetMeeting.

④ **What are the main differences between Online Collaboration and Web Discussions?**

A: Online Collaboration uses NetMeeting for live, real-time contact with a remote user over the Internet or on a corporate intranet. Web Discussion, on the other hand, is more like a newsgroup in that you sign on to a discussion page, read comments from other users left at various times, and then add your comments to the existing ones.

⑤ How would you use the Send To feature to get several colleagues to read and edit a PowerPoint show?

A: Open the slide show you want to share and select File ⇨ Send To. From the Send To menu, choose Routing Recipient to display the Profile dialog box. Click OK to accept the suggested profile and then fill out the Internet Email dialog box. Finally, fill out the Add Routing Slip information to specify who will receive the file and whether you will send it simultaneously to all recipients or to each recipient sequentially.

⑥ What PowerPoint facility would you use to send a PowerPoint show to 15 or more users simultaneously?

A: You could use the Mail Recipient selection from the Send To menu on the PowerPoint File menu. When you see the email header dialog box, enter as many email addresses as you want or choose a mailing list from your address book. You can also use the Routing Recipient choice as described in the previous question. In addition, you can use the NetShow feature to broadcast a show to multiple recipients. Up to 15 users can view the show simultaneously without your having to set up a special NetShow server.

⑦ What are the differences between the Slide Navigator and By Title lists in a PowerPoint slide show?

A: The By Title menu lists all slides in order and enables you to jump to the one you choose from the list. The Slide Navigator gives you additional information, including the last slide displayed and the current slide on the screen. The current slide in the By Title display has a check mark beside it.

⑧ Where are the broadcast settings for a PowerPoint show stored?

A: Inside the PowerPoint file you send. However, for this information to be retained, you must remember to save the file after you have specified the broadcast settings.

Visual Quiz

Q: Describe how to display the screen shown here.

A: From the Slide Show menu, point to Online Broadcast and click Schedule a Broadcast.

Chapter 15

see page 224

① I believe that the Web-based hyperlink document design will change the way we think about learning and reading. Do you agree? Why or why not?

A: My opinion is that electronic books linked via wireless networking to a local host and thence to the Internet, where data storage is unlimited, are the future of learning and research. Hyperlinks to data stored in remote locations with unlimited depth is a far cry from library research and books in the conventional manner.

② Once you've created a hyperlink, how can you remove it easily?

A: Highlight the link, choose Hyperlink from the Insert menu, and click Remove Link in the Edit Hyperlink dialog box.

③ What is the main difference between a Web hyperlink and a hyperlink within the same slide show?

A: A Web hyperlink requires an Internet connection, which may or may not be possible during a live slide show. On the other hand, you can hyperlink to any slide within a current slide show at any time, whether or not you have a link to the Internet.

④ What is the menu sequence for saving the current PowerPoint slide show as a Web page?

A: Select File ⇨ Save as Web Page and specify a folder and filename for the HTML version of the slide show.

Personal Workbook Answers

5 What intrinsic Office 2000 utility can you use to save the HTML version of a PowerPoint slide show to a Web server?

A: Use the Web Publishing Wizard, accessible from inside the Internet Explorer group by clicking Start on the Windows taskbar and selecting the Programs list.

6 What is the default filename for the Web version of a PowerPoint slide show? Why might this present a problem in accessing this file on the Web?

A: Microsoft products default HTML filenames to the extension .HTM. With modern browsers, this likely isn't a problem, but with Web products that expect to see a full .HTML extension — as is the practice in the UNIX environment — files using only .HTM might not be recognized.

7 What file transfer protocol is commonly used for saving Web files to a Web server?

A: FTP (File Transfer Protocol).

8 What does URL stand for? How is it used?

A: URL stands for Uniform Resource Locator. It is used to specify the location of a file, Web page, or other online object. URLs use various codes to specify the type of object and, thus, its location within a server.

Visual Quiz

Q: Describe how to display the screen shown here.

A: Click Start on the Windows taskbar and select Programs ⇨ Internet Explorer. Choose Web Publishing Wizard to display the opening wizard screen.

Chapter 16

see page 242

1 What general type of software could be considered responsible for standardized software? Can you recall the name of the first commercial product in this genre?

A: Spreadsheets were the first general-purpose software that permitted end users to control their computing environment without difficult programming. The first commercial program in this genre was VisiCalc.

2 There are two ways to display the Customize dialog box. What are they?

A: Right-click any PowerPoint toolbar or choose Customize from the Tools menu.

3 What is the command sequence for creating a custom toolbar?

A: Display the Customize dialog box using one of the methods listed in the previous answer. In the Customize box, click the Toolbars tab and click New. Fill out the New Toolbar dialog box and then add commands to your toolbar with the Commands tab on the Customize toolbar.

4 Describe how to change the default directory where PowerPoint loads and saves files.

A: Select Tools ⇨ Options and then click the Save tab in the Options dialog box. Enter a new default path for saving PowerPoint files in the tab's Default file location field.

5 How can you use hyperlinks with toolbars?

A: Create a custom toolbar, add some command buttons, use the Button Editor or Change Button dialog box if you want to customize the look of the toolbar, and then create hyperlinks for each toolbar icon.

6 What is the purpose of the Reset my usage data button on the Options tab of the Customize dialog box?

A: This button causes PowerPoint to forget your menu-usage patterns so that menu displays are reset to PowerPoint factory defaults.

7 How do you change the number of files shown in the opening PowerPoint dialog box and in the File menu? What is the maximum number of files you can show in this list?

A: Display the Options dialog box by selecting Tools ⇨ Options. Click the General tab and change the number of entries in the Recently used file list. The maximum number of files you can specify here is 9.

8 Can you delete a custom toolbar? How? What about standard PowerPoint toolbars?

A: Yes. Any toolbar you have created can be removed easily by (1) displaying the Customize dialog box (right-click any toolbar and choose Customize), (2) clicking the Toolbar tab, and then (3) selecting the custom toolbar you want to remove and clicking Delete. You cannot remove standard PowerPoint toolbars, but you can choose not to display them by unchecking the name of the toolbar(s) you want to remove in the toolbar shortcut menu.

Visual Quiz

Q: Describe how to display the screen shown here.

A: Select Tools ⇨ Options and click the Spelling and Style tab in the Options dialog box. Click the Style Options button on this tab.

Chapter 17

see page 256

1 Macros in PowerPoint 2000 are written in what computer programming language?

A: Visual Basic for Applications.

2 How can you remove the Stop Recording toolbar from the screen while you are recording a macro? How can you restore it?

A: As with other toolbars, you can add and remove the Stop Recording toolbar from your PowerPoint screen at will. Click the close button (the small X in the upper-right corner of the dialog box) to close it. If you want it back, display the toolbar's shortcut menu and select Stop Recording from the list of toolbars.

3 What is the keyboard shortcut for displaying the Macro dialog box that enables you to choose and run recorded macros?

A: Press Alt-F8 to display the Macros dialog box.

4 There are two ways to display the Visual Basic Editor for macros. What are they?

A: You can select Tools ⇨ Macro ⇨ Visual Basic Editor or press Alt-F11 and choose Edit from the Macro dialog box.

5 Describe how you would edit an existing macro. Why would you edit a macro?

A: To edit an existing macro, you'd select Edit from the Macro menu. You might want to simply change a constant value or menu item you previously recorded. You could change the number of copies you print with a printing macro, for example.

Personal Workbook Answers

6 **What will you see on the PowerPoint screen while a macro is running?**

A: Normally, nothing. Although running a macro steps through menu items or issues mouse-clicks, the menu-selecting and most interim steps conducted during the course of a macro usually do not appear on the screen as each command is executed.

7 **If the Stop Recording toolbar is not visible, how do you turn off macro recording?**

A: Choose Stop Recording from the Macro menu, which is accessible from the Tools menu.

8 **If you open the Macro dialog box with macro names visible but the Run button is not accessible, what has probably happened?**

A: A security setting may have turned off macro execution.

Visual Quiz

Q: Describe how to display the screen shown here.

A: Select Tools ⇨ Macro ⇨ Security and click the Trusted Sources tab. Note: If you have not established trusted sources using PowerPoint's security features, this dialog box will be blank.

Chapter 18

see page 266

1 **File formats determine how PowerPoint data is stored. What is the most important overall consideration for file formats between PowerPoint 2000 and previous versions of the program?**

A: Some formats are compatible with other versions of the program and some aren't. Although PowerPoint 2000 can load all previous PowerPoint formats, only PowerPoint 97 can load PowerPoint 2000 files. If you are sharing files with users of earlier versions of PowerPoint, save your files in HTML (Web) format or use File ⇨ Save As to them in an older PowerPoint format.

2 **How can you ensure that users of earlier versions of PowerPoint will be able to load the files you create in PowerPoint 2000?**

A: Again, save the files in HTML format.

3 **Microsoft is recommending a common, universal file format for PowerPoint and other Office programs. What is this format? How can it be called universal?**

A: HTML is Microsoft's file format of choice for future programs. It is universal in the sense that HTML browsers are available for PC, Macintosh, UNIX, and other computer platforms. If you have a current browser, you don't need PowerPoint or some other source program to view file contents.

4 **What is the meaning of the abbreviation FTP? How is it important to PowerPoint 2000 users?**

A: FTP stands for File Transfer Protocol. Many people find FTP useful for transferring PowerPoint files (and other files) to a Web site or to a common location on a corporate intranet.

5 **What does the term anonymous FTP mean?**

A: Normally, when you log into a host computer, you must have a previously assigned user name and password to access any facilities on that host. Many host computers establish an anonymous account to allow all users to download information via FTP. This option is useful if you want to share a PowerPoint presentation with a broad audience, even people you don't know, via a Web site or other public online location.

6 **Describe the size differences between PowerPoint 95 files and PowerPoint 2000 files.**

A: PowerPoint 95 used minimal compression, so if you created a moderately complex slide show in this version of the software, you could end up with file sizes of 10MB, 20MB, or more. PowerPoint 97 and PowerPoint 2000 use fairly efficient compression schemes that can shrink a 10MB file containing graphics to 1MB or less.

7 **Why do you think loading files in Web Page or other formats takes longer than loading native PowerPoint 2000 files?**

A: File conversion is the answer. Although PowerPoint can read HTML file formats, the program must convert the file into PowerPoint to permit you to edit it and use other PowerPoint program facilities.

8 **Who should you contact about securing an FTP site that you can use to share PowerPoint files with remote users?**

A: The administrator of your FTP site. This person may be a LAN manager or ISP webmaster.

Visual Quiz

Q: Describe how to display the screen shown here. Careful! There's a trick to providing full information on this one.

A: Select File ⇨ Save As and, in the Save As dialog box, pull down a list of available locations in the Save in field. Now choose an FTP site. Note: You must first choose Add/Modify FTP Locations and create a valid FTP address to be able to save files via FTP from inside PowerPoint.

Chapter 19

see page 278

1 **Explain how effective PowerPoint slides don't always obey the rules you learned in high school or college English class.**

A: PowerPoint slides don't necessarily require complete sentences or correct punctuation. In general, keep your PowerPoint material short and to the point, even if you violate standard rules or conventions of English composition.

2 **How should you change your slide design if you want the audience to remember general ideas or trends instead of specific factual data?**

A: When you present specific data, you typically use precise numbers, step-by-step instructions, and so on. To convey general concepts, reduce the amount of text on the screen, use motion video and photographs, and show people doing something with the product (and appearing pleased or satisfied). Emphasize *what* is being done over how it is being done.

3 **PowerPoint's built-in hyperlink feature lets you jump directly to another slide or even a location on the World Wide Web. Can you think of at least three ways that this feature might be useful?**

A: You might use hyperlinks to jump to a slide providing additional details about a concept you're presenting (say, if the audience requests more information). Or you can use a hyperlink to open a corporate Web site — your own or someone else's — to provide background information about a company, product or service. You could also use a hyperlink to launch a secondary presentation that branches off to another topic or provides more detail on the current topic.

Personal Workbook Answers

④ How might you use brainstorming to help you design a PowerPoint presentation? Can you describe a formal brainstorming technique?

A: Brainstorming can help you uncover ideas or concepts that should be included in a presentation. A rather formal brainstorming session might go like this: Write the main topic at the top of a piece of paper. Spend 10 minutes or so jotting down every aspect or idea you can think of that relates to this topic. Don't edit these ideas at this point: wait a few hours and repeat the process. Do this several times until you can no longer think of new topics fairly quickly. Now write each of your subtopics at the top of a new piece of paper and repeat the process.

Finally, organize the topics, rejecting those that have no bearing on the current topic, until you have a rough outline of the material you think you should cover. Refine the outline and create slides from this material.

⑤ How would you create a PowerPoint outline without using PowerPoint? How can you use this outline directly to produce PowerPoint slides?

A: You could use the outlining feature in Microsoft Word. When your Word outline is complete, open PowerPoint and load the outline file. PowerPoint creates a separate slide for each main outline topic and adds subtopics as bullet items.

⑥ What is a storyboard? How might it help you in designing PowerPoint slides? Why would you not want to use a storyboard?

A: A storyboard is a graphic representation of your PowerPoint presentation. It can help you design a complex presentation by showing the precise slide sequence and listing the graphics and text elements you want to include. A storyboard is particularly useful if you are creating a presentation in a team with different individuals assigned to different tasks. You proba-

bly wouldn't want to use a storyboard for a simple presentation — in such cases, it can be more trouble than it's worth.

⑦ Think about your current applications for PowerPoint shows. Do you think a script would help you create a better show? Why or why not?

A: To help you decide whether to use a script, consider these questions: Will you use narration? Will you use animation or other special objects in your show? Is the show a one-time event, or will you use it repeatedly? As with storyboards, scripts are extremely useful for complex programs and for ones you will use repeatedly. A one-time, fairly simple show might best be produced "on the fly," without going to the effort of using a formal script.

⑧ Which is more useful in PowerPoint presentations: text or graphics? Why?

A: You can't have one without the other, obviously. However, we tend to remember graphics (visual) elements better than plain words. When you can supplement words with appropriate pictures and other graphics, you will have a more effective presentation.

Visual Quiz

Q: Describe how to display the screen shown here.

A: Select File ➪ New, then click the Presentations tab in the New Presentation dialog box. Double-click Brainstorming Session to select this presentation and begin creating a new presentation.

Appendix B:
Designing Slides

In some ways, a slide or a computer screen is like a printed page. Taken together, all of the elements in either medium create a *layout*. A layout is the arrangement of the elements that make up the page or screen. Some of the possible elements of a PowerPoint screen are

- Text
- Graphics
- Photographs
- Boxes and other static objects
- Motion video
- Color space

No single element of a layout is intended to stand on its own: Every slide element should relate in some way to every other element and, in some cases, to one or more elements on previous or subsequent slides.

If you change the typeface or typestyle used for a heading, for example, it may change how much information will fit on the page, necessitating a change in the type used for the rest of the screen. (See Chapter 19 for additional information on fonts and using text in your slide designs.) If you give your slide more colored space, you may no longer be able to fit all of the elements you had on the screen. And if you change the font or background on one slide, you should consider making the same changes to other slides in the presentation for consistency.

Here are some general guidelines to remember as you work on slide design:

- Each slide should address a single concept or idea
- Slides should follow a logical progression, each building on the other
- In general, a simple design is best
- The viewer must be able to digest each slide quickly and easily
- Use no more than six lines of text on a slide
- Mix uppercase and lowercase text (i.e, initial caps); *don't use ALL CAPS*
- Choose a color appropriate to the mood you want to convey
- Avoid using too many colors (five colors per slide maximum)
- Use photographs and video wherever possible

Also, be aware of how most of us view a page, screen, or photograph. The scanning pattern usually is a backward "S" that starts at the upper-left corner, moves through the middle toward the right side, zooms to the left about three-fourths of the way down, and exits on the lower right. Obviously, items you want to emphasize should be placed at points on the "S" that reinforce the natural scanning pattern.

Consider using motion to focus the viewer's eye on the desired area of the slide. You can insert short video clips, for example, or animated objects. You could also insert a brief sound element to encourage the audience to focus on a particular slide.

Appendix B: Designing Slides

As you design each screen, remember this general rule: Visual material augments a presentation. It adds information to what the speaker is saying and helps the audience to retain or interpret the speaker's message. Don't use motion video, animation, or any other technique simply because you can; use it because it is the proper thing to do in a given situation.

One way to think about adding this material is to ask what questions a visual may answer. If it provides information about where something is, how something works, how much is involved (cost, quantity, and so on), who is involved or affected, when you do something or use something, or why this information is important, then that visual is doing its job.

Here are some general guidelines about creating audience interest with your slides:

High Interest Value	Low Interest Value
Photos	Words
Color	Black-and-white
White (blank) space	Solid (filled) space
Bold type	Italic type
ALL CAPS	Lowercase
Large type	Small type
Wide lines	Thin lines
Large area	Small area
3D	2D

The list demonstrates that ALL CAPS gets more attention than initial-capped text. However, you don't want a chart with all uppercase text because it is too difficult to read. We are used to reading text that is both upper- and lowercase. Use all caps for headings, titles, and other text you want to emphasize, and then revert to normal initial caps for the rest of the text.

Index

2D, 319
35mm slide presentation type, 34
35mm slides, 302, 304
   Slides sized, 76
3D, 126, 319
©, 68
(Cc) address, 165
.AVI format, 308
.PRN extension, 304

A

About Microsoft PowerPoint, 301
Access, 158–159, 308
   documents, using in
      presentations, 36
Access data, 308
action button, 306
   Access data, 158–159
   motion video clip, 133
action buttons, 112–113, 115
Action Items, 198, 199, 204, 205, 310
Action object, 309
Action Settings, 197
Add button, 12, 45
Add Printer Wizard, 304
Add Routing Slip, 220–221
Address Book, 216, 220–221
Adobe, 146–147
agenda slides, 196–197, 310
amplifiers, 142
animated objects, 306
animation, 206, 247, 303, 305
   action buttons, 112–113, 115
   adding , 106–107, 108–109

reasons to use, 105
slide transitions, 110–111
sounds, 110–111
time required, 43
turn off, 44
announcements, 38
anonymous FTP, 314
anonymous site, 270, 271
Answer Wizard, 24, 25
application tasks, when to use
      macros, 257
applications
   file associations, 184
   running with Help, 29
Apply Design Template, 250
Appointment, 210
Appointment dialog box, 205
Artsy template, 36
aspect ratio, 100
attachments, 163, 164–165
Attendee Availability, 210
audience
   design considerations, 38
   distance from screen, 92
audience handouts, 303
Audience Message, 219
audience size, delivery medium, 48
audio, PowerPoint broadcast, 216
audio equipment, 194
audio system preamp, 142
AutoContent Wizard, 6–7, 34–35,
      41, 302
AutoCorrect, 62
   configuration, 68–69
AutoCorrect utility, 303
AutoLayout, 32, 36, 302, 306
AutoLayout designs, presentation
      designs, 38

AutoLayout dialog box, 118–119
   bullet or numbered list, 128
AutoRecover, 248
AVI file, 146, 148
Azure design template, 122
Azure template, 36

B

Back button, 24
Background, 32, 306
   changing slide, 94–95, 96–97
   dialog box, 96
   samples, 174
   slide, 122–123, 124–125
   templates and, 126
Banner layout, 76
black, 90
Black Screen, 198
Black-and-white, 319
blinds, 110
blue, 90, 120
Blue Diagonal design template, 90,
      91, 94–95, 122
Blueprint template, 36
BMP format, 134
bold, 64
Bold type, 319
booklet covers, 38
Bookmark, 228
border, printing, 80
Borders and Frames, 94–95
boxes, 110, 318
brainstorming, 316
Brainstorming design template, 106

Index

broadcast, show, 216–217, 218–219
broadcast settings, 311
browsers, 312
Built-in Menus, 244
bullet lists, 176–177, 206, 307
    default fonts and font size, 38
    type size, 92
bullets, format, 128–129
bundled software, 153
Button Editor, 247, 312
button image, 244, 246
buttons. *See also* action buttons
    Add, 12, 45
    Back, 24
    Clips Online, 138
    Forward , 24
    Frame Slides, 56
    interactive with presentation, 112–113
    Minimize, 137
    Options, 24
    Preview, 122
    Properties, 79
    Remove, 12
    Slides, 81
    toolbar, appearance of, 12
buttons, toolbar, hyperlink assignment, 246
By Title lists, 311
By Title view, 206–207

C

cables, projection, 48
calendar. *See* Outlook
calendar entry, 199
Camera animation, 106
Canon BJC–620, 78–79
capital letters, 318, 319
Carnegie Coach, 41
Categories list, 244
CD player, 142
CD-ROM, images, 136
CD-ROM drive, 142
cells, resizing, 182
Century Schoolbook, 92

certificate, 302
certificate, anti-virus protection, 263
certificates, 38
Change Button dialog box, 312
characters, changing individual, 126
chart, 309
Chart utility, 161, 180–181
charts, 118, 160–161, 180–181
    color, 120
Chat, 208, 210
checkerboards, 110
chevron, 128
Choose By Title, 207
classroom training, 206
Clemson University, 122
clipart, 172
    as background, 94
    in footer, 99
    in tables, 182
ClipArt Gallery, 94, 133, 134–135, 305, 307, 308
    adding images, 138–139, 140–141
Clipboard, 309
Clipit, 22–23
Clips Online, 134, 138
close-file command, 244
collaboration, online, 208–209, 210–211, 220, 223
collated output, 81
color, 32, 305, 307, 318, 319
    background, 96, 122
    changing master, 90–91
    comments, 172
    erase, 247
    experiment , 71
    overall scheme, 120–121
    presentation designs, 38
    printing, 74
    templates, 36
    Word Art, 178
color theory, 120, 131
commands, close–file, 244
comments, 172–173, 309
Common Tasks, 12
Common Tasks toolbar, 118, 250–251, 306
Compadre background samples, 174
company logo, 178, 306
    add to footer, 98

compatability, 314–315
    background, 267
    open other file formats, 272–273
    saving files online, 270–271
    saving slide show to different format, 268–269
    saving slides as graphics, 274–275
compression, 82, 274
computer, projecting images, 76
computer internal clock, matching presentation date tot, 60
computer projection, direct, 48–49
computer screen, 38, 48
ComputerImages, 156
computers, historical perspective, 243
confidential report, 103
contact management. *See* Outlook
Contents, help, 24
context menus. *See* shortcut menus
Control Panel, Printers dialog box, 74–75
Cool Edit Pro, 194
Copies & Methods tab, 78
Copy and Paste, 246
copyright, 98
copyright notice, 60
copyright symbol, 68, 128
corporate colors, 131
corporate procedures, 151
corporate symbols, 131
corporate theme, 131
corporate trainer, 265
corporate training, 277
custom, 312
Custom Animation dialog box, 108–109
Custom setting, slide size, 76
Custom Settings, page layout, 77
Custom Shows, 303, 310
Custom Shows dialog box, 44–45
Custom Toolbars, 252–253, 312
Customize dialog box, 14–15, 312
customizing
    Common Tasks Toolbar, 250–251
    Custom Toolbars, 252–253
    features, 244–245, 246–247
    Options, 248–249
    usefulness of, 243

D

data storage size, 50
database programming. *See* compatibility
databases. *See* Access
date, 60
  adding to footer, 60
  footer, 98
Date and Slide number boxes, 35
dBase III, 158
default directory, 312
delete, custom toolbar, 252
Delete items, 246
design
  bullet format, 128–129
  changing master colors, 90–91
  changing slide background, 94–95, 96–97
  color scheme, 120–121
  fonts, 126–127
  number format, 128–129
  presentation, 38–39
  slide background, 122–123, 124–125
  slides, 318–320
  templates, 36–37, 122, 126–127
Design Template, 33, 65, 302
design templates, 90, 91
designs, rulers and guides, 170
desktop, temporary storage area, 100
Detect and Repair feature, 26–27, 301
dialog boxes, 300
  basics, 14–15
dialup networking, 270
dictionary, 62, 304
digital cameras, 124, 134, 138, 140
digital signatures, 262, 265
digital video camera, 133
digital video editors, 146, 148
directory structure, 272
discussions, Web use, 212–213, 214–215
disk space, graphics, 134
Display as Icon, 160
Dissolve, 106

dissolves, 110
dollar signs, 131
DOS, 234
drag and drop, slide objects, 98
drawing toolbar, 12–13, 170, 176, 178
drawings, background, 124
Drive-In animation, 106
drivers, printer, 82
Drop-In animation, 106
Due Date, 205
duplication, discouraging, 103

E

edit
  font characteristics, 302
  macro, 313
  macros, 260–261
Edit Button Image, 246
Edit Picture, 10
Edit tab, 248
editing
  by email, 167
  Excel data, 161
  footer data, 98–99
  Handouts, 100–101
  master text, 92–93
  Notes, 100–101
  online meetings, 208
  Word, 154
  WordArt, 178
em dash, 68
email, 210, 228, 229, 309. *See also* Outlook
  NetShow access, 218
  Send To, 220–221
  transfer files, 50
email addresses, 216
Embed TrueType fonts option, 50, 51
emboss text attribute, 126
employee introductions, 151
Employee Orientation presentation type, 34
employees, photographs, 133
Erase Pen command, 198

error, 201
  printer output files, 82
errors, Detect and Repair utility, 26–27
Excel, 160–161, 243, 308, 309
  charts, 180
  copy spreadsheet cells, 136
  documents, using in presentations, 36
Excel spreadsheets, 272
Exceptions dialog box, 68
Exchange, NetShow access, 218
Exchange Server, schedules, 210
Expand/Collapse outline button, 230
Explorer 5, 225

F

F1 function key, 301
fades, 110
Favorites list, 174
features, customize, 244–245, 246–247
file compression, 268, 274, 315
file conversion, 315
file extensions, 304
file formats, 314–315
file formats, pictures, 134
file management
filename, 236, 268, 312
files
  opening non-PowerPoint, 272–273
  printing to, 82–83
  save online, 270–271
Fill Effects, 306
Fill Effects dialog box, 122–123, 124–125
financial figure, 187
Find and Replace, 64–65
Firewire. *See* IEEE 1394
floppy disks, transfer a large presentation file to another computer, 50

INDEX

Fly From Top animation, 106
folders
    email, 162
    Outlook, 162
fonts, 126–127, 302, 305, 306
    bullets, 129
    change, 38, 92–93
    defined, 92
    Embed TrueType option, 50, 51
    Excel data, 161
    Find and Replace to locate, 64, 65, 66
    printers, 78
    point size, 92
Footers, 35, 60–61, 71, 304
    modifying data, 98–99
For Sale sign, 302
format, 314–315
    bullets, 128–129
    comments, 172
    handouts, 59
    numbers, 128–129
    slides with Word, 154
    WordArt, 178
Format AutoShape, 96–97
Format Comment dialog box, 172–173
Format Data Series shortcut menu, 181
formats, non-PowerPoint
    opening files, 272–273
    saving Slide Shows, 268–269
formatting, text, 38–39
Forward button, 24
FoxPro, 158
Frame Slides button, 56
FrontPage, 234, 308
FTP, 232, 234–235, 270–271, 272–273, 312, 314
FTP site, 277, 315
FTP sites, remote connection, 270

G

General tab, 248, 249
GIF format, 134
gradient settings, 122
graphics, 309, 318
    as action button, 112
    add to footer, 98
    animation settings, 106–107
    background, 124–125
    bullets, 128
    file formats, 184
    open a shortcut menu, 11
    presentation designs, 38
    printers, 78
    resizing, 94
    save PowerPoint slides as, 274–275
    templates, 36
    time required, 43
    Undo, 66
    when not to use, 182
graphics filter, 184
gray, 90
Grayscale, 80
green, 120
grid, invisible, 170
Grouping menu item, 10
guest speakers, introducing, 41
guides, 170–171, 309

H

handles, 94
Handout Master, 100–101
Handouts, 58–59, 305
    editing, 100–101
    Page Setup, 76
    printing, 85
Headers, 60–61
headings, 318
    type size, 92
headphones, 142

Help, 301
    Detect and Repair, 26–27
    Help System, 24–25
    Office Assistant, 22–23, 301
    online, 21
    Outlook, 210
    running with applications, 29
    text–based, 301
    tooltips, 252
    What's This?, 301
Helvetica, 92
Hewlett-Packard 5MP PostScript printer, 78
Hewlett-Packard printer, 82
Hide Picture menu item, 10
Highlight click, 112
homonym errors, 62
HP LaserJet III, 74
HTM extension, 312
HTML, 225, 230–231, 243, 268, 272, 273, 312, 314
hyperlink, 112, 311, 315
    toolbar button, 246
hyperlinks, 226–227, 228–229, 309, 312
    custom toolbar, 252
    Help system, 24
hypertext help, 301
Hypertext Markup Language. *See* HTML

I

I-Link. *See* IEEE 1394
icon editing, 246
icons
    default sound, 144
    Excel object, 160
    toolbar, change order, 252
    toolbar, removal, 244
IEEE 1394 high-speed serial interface cards, 146
image resolution, 307
Inbox, 162, 164

Index, help, 24
in-house corporate training, 206
in-house training, 201
initial caps, 319
ink jet printers
    paper, 78
in-place editing, 154
install, Web Publishing Wizard, 232
installation
    printer, 74–75
    templates, 36
instructions, macro, 260
Internet, 310. *See also* Web
    broadcasting shows, 216–217
    hyperlinks during show, 112
    loading and saving files, 14
    sending presentations, 50–51
Internet Explorer, 272, 312
    local PowerPoint web sites, 230
    NetShow utility, 216
    Web subscriptions, 214
Internet Explorer 4
    chat program, 210
    digital signatures, 262
Internet Explorer 5, 153, 228, 236
    Web Discussions, 212
Internet Service Provider, 277
Iomega Corporation, 146
ISDN link, 270
ISP, 232, 234, 270
Italic type, 319
Itinerary Web Presenter, 198

J

JPEG, 274

K

key management personnel., 133
keyboard, object placement, 98
keyboard shortcut keys, 206–207
keyboard shortcuts
    display, 301
    exit, 301
    Macro dialog box, 313
    menu items, 300
keywords, 140
kiosk shows, 302
Kodak Photo CD, 124, 151

L

LAN, 272, 315
    Broadcast, 216–217
    directory structure, 272
    online collaboration, 210
LAN access, 232–233
LAN administrator, 232, 234
landscape formatting, 58
Landscape orientation, 76
language setting, spelling checker, 62
laptop, 53
Large area, 319
Large type, 319
laser printers, 74
    paper , 78
Laser Text animation, 106, 305
layout, 318
    changing slide layout, 118–119
    design templates, 126–127
    text boxes, 176
LCD projectors, 303
LCD screens, 48
lists, 176–177
    bulleted, 206
    color, 120
    format, 128–129

Local directory field, 234
local disk directory, 235
lowercase, 318, 319

M

Macintosh, 232, 267, 314
macros, 313–314
    background, 257
    editing, 260–261
    playing, 260–261
    recording new, 258–259
    security, 262–263
Mail Recipient, 165
marketing and sales program, 223
Master Pages, 304
masters
    color change, 90–91
    defined, 89
    editing Handouts, 100–101
    editing Notes, 100–101
    modifiying footers, 98–99
    Slide Background changes, 94–95,
        96–97
    text changes, 92–93
Media Player, 218
Meeting Minder, 46, 199, 204–205,
    310
Meeting Minutes, 198, 310
meeting participants, 208, 220
Memphis98, 268
menu
    dialog box, 300
    display choices, 300
menu bar, 19
menu items, keyboard shortcuts, 300
menus
    basics, 8–9
    customization, 244–245, 246
    Macro, 260
    shortcut, 10–11
microphone, 142, 194, 310
Microsoft, application help, 21
Microsoft Access. *See* Access

Microsoft Excel. *See* Excel
Microsoft Outlook. *See also* Outlook
    action items, 198, 199
    Schedule Meeting utility, 210
    Speaker Notes, 199
Microsoft Photo Editor, 136
Microsoft Word, 243, 308. *See also*
    Word
    action items, 198
    outlining, 316
    Send To feature, 220
Microsoft's Hands On PowerPoint
    tutorial, 182
Minimize button, 137
modules, 187
    use in multiple presentations, 43
monitor screens
    history, 105
    history , 133
monochrome printer, 16, 80
mood, 305, 318
motion, 318
MotoDV, 146
Mountain design template, 122
mouse-click, action buttons, 112
movies, 307. *See also* video
Movies and Sound, 308
My Computer, launch program, 6

N

narration, 303
    recording, 194–195, 310
    turn off, 44
Nature template, 36
navigation, 248
    keys, 46
    slide show, 206–207
NetMeeting, 208–209, 310
NetShow, 311
    server specification, 218
    utility, 216
New Office Document dialog box, 32

New Presentation dialog box,
    Certificate, 38
New Slide, 250
New Slide AutoLayout, animation,
    106
New Slide dialog box, 32, 36
Normal PowerPoint view, 300
Normal view, notes, 56, 59
Notes
    editing, 100–101
    Page Setup, 76
    printing, 80
    view, 56–57
Notes and Handouts tab, 60
Notes Master, 100–101
Notes Pages, 56–57, 259, 261, 303
numbers
    format, 128–129
    tables, 182–183

O

objects
    change, 118
    charts, 180–181
    guides, 170–171
    from other applications, 184–185
    presentation, 198–199
    resize, 100
    rulers, 170–171
    select, 6
    tables, 182–183
    WordArt utility , 178–179
Office 2000, 6, 225. *See also*
    compatibility, Clip Art
    Gallery
    backward-compatibility, 267
    Clipboard, 136–137
    dictionary sharing, 62
    insert objects from, 184–185
    installation diskettes, 36
    PowerPoint interaction, 153–167
Office 97, 21, 268

Office Assistant, 22–23, 105, 301
    clipart images, 140
    dialog box, 14, 22
    Pack and Go Wizard, 50
    shortcut menu, 10–11
Office Resource Kit, 38
Office Tools, 232
online, saving files, 270–271
Online Broadcast, 311
online collaboration, 208–209,
    210–211, 220, 223, 310
online help, 21, 301
Online Meeting toolbar, 208–209
On-screen presentation style, 34
open
    blank presesentation, 32–33
    non-PowerPoint files, 272–273
    PowerPoint, 6–7
    PowerPoint 2000, 300
Open dialog box, 14
opening wizard, 301
operating systems. *See* compatibility
Options, reviewing and setting,
    248–249
Options button, 24
Order, 10
Order & Timing, 108–109
Orientation group, 76
outline, 156, 308, 316
Outline file, 174
Outline view, 46
outlines, expand/collapse button, 230
Outlook, 162–163, 164–165, 308
Outlook Express
    collaborative issues, 214
    Meeting Minder, 204
overhead foils, 74
    use of color, 90
    presentation type, 34
overhead projectors, 48
overheads, 302

P

Pack and Go Wizard, 50–51
Page Setup, 76–77
Palatino, 92
paper, 78
Password, 213, 214, 234, 270, 271, 314
Pattern background, 124–125
patterns, 306
PC World Today, 118
PCL (Printer Control Language) codes, 82
PC's sound card, 194
PCX format, 134
Pen, 46, 47, 310
pen color, 198
permission
    for sounds, 142
    use images, 134
Personal Digital Assistant (PDA), 204
photographs, 90, 94, 115, 274, 305, 307, 318, 319
    adding to slides, 134–135, 136–137
    ClipArt Gallery, 138–139, 140–141
    obtaining, 151
Photoshop, 184
Picture background, 124–125
Picture Bullet dialog box, 128–129
pictures
    adding to slides, 134–135, 136–137
    ClipArt Gallery, 138–139, 140–141
    reasons to use, 133
    in tables, 182
    undo changes, 67
Pinnacle Data Systems, Inc., 146
PKZIP, 82
placeholders, 118–119
play, macros, 260–261
play options, sound, 144
Plug and Play, printer installation, 74
point size, 92, 305
pointer, 198, 199
pointer devices, 46, 47
Pointer Options, 310
Portrait orientation, 76
Posting Options icon, 215
PostScript printer, 82–83

PowerPoint
    compatibility issues, 267–277
    customizing, 243–255
    editing masters, 89–103
    macros, 257–265
    pictures, sound and movies, 133–151
    presentation, 203–223
    show preparation, 191–201
    slide design, 318–320
    Web uses, 225–239
PowerPoint 2000
    Access, 158–159
    animation, 105–115
    AutoCorrect configuration, 68–69
    basics, 5–19
    creating presentations, 31–41
    delivering presentations, 43–53
    dialog boxes, 14–15
    Excel, 160–161
    Find and Replace, 64–65
    Handouts, 58–59
    headers and footers, 60–61
    Help, 21–29
    installation diskettes, 36
    layout and design changes, 117–131
    Menus, 8–9
    Notes Pages, 56–57
    Office 2000, 153–167
    open, 300
    opening, 6–7
    other objects, 169–187
    Outlook, 162–163, 164–165
    printing, 73–85
    Shortcut Menus, 10–11
    Spell Checker, 62–63
    Toolbars, 12–13
    Undo, 66–67
    views, 16–17
    Word, 154–155, 156–157
PowerPoint 95, 268, 269, 273, 315
PowerPoint 97, 268, 314, 315
PowerPoint Animation Player, 248
PowerPoint text, hyperlink, 226
PowerPoint Viewer, with Pack and Go presentations, 53
Premier 5.0, 146–147
preparation time, estimated, 43
presentation design, 302
    background designs, 94
Presentation Objects, 198–199

Presentation Type Wizard dialog box, 34
presentation types, 302
presentations, 203–223
    animation, 105–115
    AutoCorrect configuration, 68–69
    broadcasting, 216–217, 218–219
    charts, 180–181
    comments, 172–173
    creating, 31
        AutoContent Wizard, 34–35
        design templates, 36–37
        opening a blank, 32–33
        presentation designs, 38–39
    customizing, 196
    delivery, 43–53
        pack and go, 50–51
        projecting, 48–49
        set up, 44–45
        view, 46–47
    editing masters, 89–103
    Find and Replace, 64–65
    Handouts, 58–59
    headers and footers, 60–61
    headings, 178–179
    Meeting Minder, 204–205
    mood , 117, 124
    movies, 133
    navigation, 206–207
    Notes Pages, 56–57
    objects, 170–171, 184–185
    online collaboration, 208–209, 210–211
    photographs, 133
    printing, 73–85
    reusing, 117
    Send To feature, 220–221
    sharing by email, 164–165, 167
    slides from other presentations, 174–175
    sound, 133
    Spell Checker, 62–63
    start new, 302
    tables, 182–183
    text boxes, 176–177
    themes, 131
    titles, 178–179
    Undo, 66–67
    Web discussions, 212–213, 214–215
    Web links , 112
    Web promotion, 228

preview
sound, 144
Web Page, 230
Preview button, 122
Preview Lobby Page, 219
Preview window, 60
print, 38, 258, 259, 304
Print tab, 248
printer
drivers, 304
installation, 74–75
monochrome, 16, 80
selecting, 78–79
using one you don't have, 74
printing
choice what to print, 80–81
to a file, 82–83
handouts, 58–59
installing a printer, 74–75
Notes pages, 56
objectives, 73
Page Setup, 76–77
selecting a printer and properties,
78–79
slides, 58
printouts, 265
PRN extension, 304
product introductions, 151
program-development team, 187
programming, macros. *See* macros
progressive display, 206
Project Overview presentation type, 34
projector, 38
Projector Wizard, 14, 301, 303
projector-setup wizard, 48–49
projectors, 48–49, 303
proofreading presentations, 73
Properties button, 79
Properties, selecting, 78–79
proprietary financial data,
protecting, 262
prosumer, 194
Publisher, 153

Q

question-mark icon, 50
Quicktime format, 146
quotes, changing straight to smart, 68

R

radio quality, 142
Radius, Inc, 135, 146
Record Narration, 310
recording
macros, 258–259
narration, 194–195
slide-show narration, 310
red, 90, 120, 307
Redo, 66–67, 71
rehearsal, 192–193, 309
Rehearse Timings utility, 44, 192–193,
310
Relay Chat, 210
Remove button, 12
Repair. *See* Detect and Repair
Replace Font utility, 64, 65, 66
report cover, 302
Reset items, 246
Reset my usage, 246, 313
resolution, computer screen, 48
review, by email, 167
RGB projector, 49
Rich Text Format. *See* RTF
road shows, 50–51, 167
sending handouts ahead, 85
Rocky, 22–23
round-robin list, 220
Routing Recipient, 311
RTF, 164, 274
ruler, 170–171, 309
Run button, 260

S

sales presentation, 48
save
files online, 270–271
slide show as Web page, 230–231
slide shows in non-PowerPoint
format, 268–269
slides as graphics, 274–275
Save tab, 248
scanned art, 50
scanners, 124, 134, 138, 140
scanning pattern, 318
ScanPort color scanner, 140–141
Schedule Meeting, 210–211
screen captures, 50
screen shots, 115, 274
screen size, design and, 19
ScreenTip, 226, 229
script, 316
search phrases, 64
Search the Web, 14
Secure connection, 212
security, macros, 262–263
security setting, 314
Select Filter utility, 214
Selling a Product or Service
presentation type, 34
seminars, 206
Send To feature, 80, 220–221, 311
Send to field, 208
Sent Files folder, 164
server, uploading PowerPoint Web
pages, 232–233, 234–235
servers, 270
address, 213
Discussion, 213
NetShow specification, 218
secure connection, 212
set up, 44–45
Set Up Show, 301
Set Up Show dialog box, 14, 303
shadow text attribute, 126
shortcut menu, 10–11, 46
customizing toolbar items,
246–247
Hyperlink, 226
presentation tools, 198–199
ruler or guide display, 170

shortcuts
Format Data Series, 181
menu, 182–183
toolbar, 250
Show type group, 44–45
shows
pack and go, 50–51
projecting, 48–49
set up, 44–45
view, 46–47
signs, 38
single-sheet product, 302
size field, 56
slide
animations, 305
changing background, 94–95,
96–97
display individual, 206
Slide Background, 96
Slide Color Scheme, 32, 96
**Slide Color Scheme dialog box,
120–121**
Slide Finder dialog box, 174–175
slide layout, 76, 96, 250
Slide Layout dialog box, 118–119
Slide Master
background, 122–123
changing background, 94–95
changing master text, 92–93
design template, 126–127
global text, 176
modifying footer data, 98–99
object, 305
view, 91
Slide Meter, 46
Slide Navigator, 198, 311
Slide Navigator display, 206–207
slide number, 60, 98
slide object
hyperlinks, 226
ScreenTip, 227
Slide Show, 8–9, 248
accessing on Web, 236–237
change presentation style, 34
preparation, 191–201
saving as Web page, 230–231
shortcuts to navigate, 10
transitions, 110–111
Slide Show Help, 206–207
Slide Show menu, 14
generic slide list, 53
Rehearse Timings, 194
start broadcast, 218–219

Slide Show shortcut menu, 206–207
Slide Show view, 44, 310
add action buttons, 112–113
animation, 106
macro execution, 258
Meeting Minder, 204
navigating, 206–207
Rehearse Timings utility, 192
shortcut menu, 199
viewing presentations, 46–47
**Slide Shows, saving in non-
PowerPoint format, 268–269**
slide sorter view, 16, 46
editing presentations, 38, 39
summary process, 196–197
timings, 192, 193
slide timings, 310
slide transitions, 305
action buttons with, 112
animated, 110–111
reasons to use, 105
Slide view, 46
slides
adding, 36
adding movies, 148–149
adding pictures, 134–135, 136–137
adding sounds, 144–145
agenda, 196–197
automatic advance with transition,
110
background, 122–123, 124–125
changing order of handout, 58
charts, 180–181
comments, 172–173
design, 318–320
guides, 170–171
hiding, 196
layout, 118–119
miniature versions, 16
objects, 169
from other applications, 184–185
from other presentations, 174–175
printing, 58–59
rulers, 170–171
save as graphics, 274–275
skipping, 46, 112
summary, 196–197
tables, 182–183
text boxes, 176–177
timing, 192, 194
WordArt utility, 178–179
Slides button, 81
Slides from Files option, 187

Small area, 319
Small type, 319
smiley face, 128
Snap to Object utility, 170
software, printer. *See* drivers, printer
software upgrades, compatibility
issue, 267
Solid (filled) space, 319
sound, 50, 94, 307
action buttons, 112
adding to slides, 144–145
with animation, 108, 110–111
card, 142, 310
quality, 194
reasons to use, 133
recording, 142–143
without a sound card, 44
time required, 43
Sound Calibration, 195
speaker, add not detract, 117
speaker icon, 144
Speaker Notes, 198, 201, 204, 258, 303
speakers, 142, 303
Spell Checker, 62–63
add word sequences to
AutoCorrect, 68
dictionary, 304
Spelling, 62
Find and Replace, 64–65
tab, 248
spreadsheet software. *See*
compatibility
spreadsheets, 243, 308, 312. *See also*
Excel
staff meetings, 206
Standard Office 2000, 308
Start menu, launch program , 6
sticky note, 309
Stop button, macro, 258
Stop Recording toolbar, 313
storyboard, 316
Strategic template, 36
Style tab, 248
subdirectory, 236
submenus, 8
subscriptions, 212, 214
subtopics, bridge with transitions, 110
Suggest, 62
Summary Slide, 198, 310
summary slides, 196–197
Symbol dialog box, 128
Syntrillium, 194

INDEX

T

tables, 182–183, 309
Tables and Borders toolbar, 182–183
Tagged Image Format File. *See* TIFF
tape deck, 142
task bar shortcuts, creation, 6
technical data, protecting, 262
technical speeches, increasing
    understanding, 115
Tektronix printer manufacturing
    company, 90
television, large-screen, 48–49
templates, 6–7, 307
    background design, 94
    Brainstorming design, 106
    design, 36–37, 65, 91, 122, 126–127
    missing, 36
text, 316, 318
    attributes, 64
    bulleted lists, 128
    change, 302
    changing footer data, 98–99
    changing master, 92–93
    color against backgrounds, 124
    editing Handouts, 100–101
    editing Notes, 100–101
    emboss and shadow attribute, 126
    fonts, 126–127
    fonts and font sizes, 38
    hyperlinks, 228
    insertion point, 118
    to suit background, 97
    undoing entries, 66
text boxes, 176–177
    comments, 172
text outline, 156
texture, 306
Texture background, 124–125
themes, presentation, 131
Thin lines, 319
TIFF, 134, 274
time, footer, 98
time, needed to prepare show, 43
    checking show length, 44
Times New Roman, 38

Times Roman, 92
timing, transition, 110
timings
    bypass preset, 44
    slides, 192, 194
Title Master slide, 92–93, 99
title slide, 60, 89
titles, 60, 176–177, 178
    color, 120
    movie slide, 148
    type size, 92
    typeface or style, 117
toolbars
    basics, 12–13
    Common Tasks, 118, 250–251
    custom, 244, 252–253
    dialog box customization, 16
    display, 300
    drawing, 12–13
    hyperlinks, 312
    macro, 258, 260
    PowerPoint menus, 112
    shortcut menu, 10
    Stop Recording, 313
    Web discussions, 214
Tools menu, Customize menu
    display, 8
tooltips, 252
training, 48
transitions
    action buttons with, 112
    reasons to use, 105
travel, 239
Twain-compliant scanner, 138
type, 319
Type size, 92
typeface, 92, 318
    change, 117
typestyle, 318
Typewriter animation, 106
typing
    AutoCorrect, 68
    undo, 66
typos, automatic correction of, 62, 68

U

underline, 64
Undo, 71
Universal Resource Locator. *See* URL
universal style definition, 89
University of Georgia, 56
UNIX, 232, 270, 314
uppercase, 318
URL, 234, 235, 236, 312
U.S. Internet, 133
usage, reset, 246
user ID, 270, 271, 314
user interfaces, Access, 158
User Name, 213, 214

V

Verisign Web site, 265
VGA projector, 49
video, 94, 307, 318
    adding to slides, 148–149
    capturing, 146–147
    PowerPoint broadcast, 216
    reasons to use, 133
    time required, 43
Video Director 200, 146
video recorder, 124
view, 46–47
    scanning pattern, 318
    slides saved as graphics, 274
View menu, 309
View tab, 248
views, basics, 16–17
viruses, macro, 262
Visicalc, 243, 312
Visual Basic, 257, 262
Visual Basic Editor, 260–261, 313

W

Wagner Institute for Color Research, 90
warning messages
  file format, 268, 269
  macros, 262, 263
Web
  accessing PowerPoint shows on, 236–237
  background, 225
  discussion use, 212–213, 214–215
  help, 21
  hyperlinks, 226–227, 228–229
  images, 134
  presentations, 34
  saving slide shows as web pages, 230–231
  search phrases, 64
  uploading web pages, 232–233, 234–235
Web Discussions, 310
Web domain, 236
Web Options button, 248
Web Options tab, 249
Web Page, 269, 315
  format, 270–271
  loading files from, 272–273
  save as, 311
  saving slides as graphics, 274
Web presentations, 302
Web Publishing Wizard, 232–233, 234–235, 312
Web sites, 22
  advanced PowerPoint techniques, 158
  AutoCorrect, 68
  changing background, 96–97
  charts tutorial, 180
  Clemson University, 122
  clip art, 128
  color theory, 90
  Compadre background samples, 174
  Computer Services tutorial site, 76
  ComputerImages, 156

creating a master, 100
design and color schemes, 120
downloadable .AVI files, 148
effective presentations, 160
fonts, 92
graphics in PowerPoint, 94
hints on improving meeting and presentation skills, as well as hardware and design tips, 44
Iomega Corporation, 146
limitations on use, 48
Media Service tutorial, 10
Microsoft, 22, 26
Microsoft PowerPoint Animation Player, 106
Microsoft's Hands On PowerPoint tutorial, 182
newer printer software, 74
Office 2000 updates, 26–27
Office Resource Kit, 38
Outlook, 162
Pack and Go, 50
PC World Today, 118
Pinnacle Data Systems, Inc., 146
PowerPoint background, 96
PowerPoint Basics tutorial, 8
PowerPoint enhancements and add-ins, 36
PowerPoint Help menu, 6
PowerPoint lessons, 60
PowerPoint presentation, 98
PowerPoint tips, 46
PowerPoint tutorial, 14
Presentation Recommendations page, 82
presentation resources, 48
print setting, 78
printing your slide presentation, 80
Radius, Inc., 146
scanning images, 184
sound cards, 142
sounds, 108, 110
stock-photo agencies, 124
template archive, 126
toolbar, text enhancement, and view button functions, 12
tutorials index, 164
Undo and other PowerPoint features, 66

ungrouping clip art images, 172
University of Georgia, 56
using handouts, 58
video information, 146
view options, 16
Woody's Workshop, 176
WordArt vertical text, 178
WWW.Computer-Tips.com:, 154
Web sites, listed by address
  Cool Edit Pro, 194
  file-format references, 274
  HTML presentations, 270
  icon editing, 246
  Itinerary Web Presenter, 198
  macro-virus info, 262
  Media Player, 218
  multimedia presentations, 196
  NetShow, 216, 218–219
  online collaboration software, 208
  Outlook collaborative issues, 214
  PowerPoint add-ons, 260
  PowerPoint Animation Player, 248
  PowerPoint online, 272
  presentation tips, 192
  Quickstart guide to Office toolbars, 250
  recording macros, 258
  shareware FTP client, 234
  slide saving, 268
  toolbar customization, 244
  toolbars, 252
  Web discussions, 212
  Web Publishing Wizard, 232
Web support, 268
What's This?, 22, 301
White (blank) space, 319
white space, 120
Wide lines, 319
Windows, 243
Windows 95, 5
  printer installation, 74
Windows 98, 5, 225, 236
  chat program, 210
  launch multiple programs, 169
  NetShow utility, 216
  object selection, 6
  printer installation, 74
  subscriptions, 212
  Windows Sound recorder, 142–143

INDEX

Windows CD-ROM, 26
Windows Clipboard, screen copy,
    136–137
Windows disk-defragmenting
    utility, 26
Windows Explorer, 208, 236
    launch program, 6
    opening compressed files, 82
    subscriptions, 212
Windows NT Server, 270
Windows Sound recorder, 142–143
wipe, 110
Wipe Right animation, 106
wizards
    Add Printer, 304
    Answer, 24, 25
    AutoContent, 34–35, 302

basics, 14–15, 19
Detect and Repair, 26–27
Pack and Go, 50–51
Projector, 303
projector setup, 48–49
Woody's Workshop, 176
Word, 154–155, 156–157, 164, 308
    copying text, 136
    dictionary sharing, 62
    documents, using in presentations,
        36
    Find and Replace, 64
    outline file, 174
    printing Notes pages, 56, 57
Word documents, 272
word processing, 308. *See* Word
WordArt utility, 178–179, 309

WordPad, view the printer file
    output, 83
word-processing programs. *See*
    compatibility
World Wide Web, 301
WS_FTP, 234

yellow, 90